DAILY GRACE

DAILY GRACE

The Mockingbird Devotional, Vol. 2

A Mockingbird Publication

Charlottesville, VA

A NOTE OF GRATITUDE

Many thanks to the writers who contributed to this publication. Even more thanks to the readers. Whether you read our first devotional and asked for another, or have picked up *Daily Grace* on its own, thank you for turning these pages. Thanks to CJ Green, head editor of this collection, for overseeing the project, coordinating with writers, and laying out the manuscript. Thanks also to Kendall Gunter for your meticulous proofing and invaluable input; Margaret Pope for editorial assistance and impeccable organization; and Benjamin Self for your sharp eye on the book's final draft. To churches, ministries, and the countless individuals who make up our Mockingbird community—your support made this endeavor endeavor-able.

INTRODUCTION

Fifty-two years old, and he was dying. Afflicted by a brutal case of COVID-19, Jason Denney lay alone in a hospital room in Orlando, Florida, struggling to breathe. It was March, 2020, and widespread fear of contagion prevented his family from sitting at his bedside. Through FaceTime, he had already said goodbye to them. A priest had administered his last rites. This was it—not only was Denney's life ending, but so, too, it seemed, was the world.

Then the door opened. A woman, Rosaura Quinteros, entered the room. She had visited before, every morning for six days. Originally from Guatemala, she now worked in the hospital as a housekeeper—a line of work often considered "invisible." Her job was to mop the floors, pull trash, and disinfect surfaces. As she worked, she and Denney made small talk, first chatting about the weather, then discussing more meaningful topics: their children, their faith. He confessed that he had likely infected his 16-year-old son, and on top of his physical suffering, he was also afflicted by guilt.

Even so, Quinteros assured him that all would be well. She promised that both God and the doctors were caring for him. Most importantly, as Denney reported to CNN's Daniel Burke, "She was not scared to be close to me."

And slowly, he began to recover. Quinteros' very presence offered relief, took his mind off his suffering, and brought him hope. English was not her first language, but "When a patient is treated with compassion and love," she said, "language is not a barrier."

Denney's suffering was acute and, in many ways, unique. Even so, all of us can relate to some part of this story. Whether we've experienced a

1

suffocating pain, loneliness, or guilt, we have all found ourselves in a place we never thought we'd be. We do not need to be living through a pandemic to feel as if we're in the midst of the apocalypse. Today's headlines—*any day's headlines*—certainly stoke a state of panic. Life is hard, you may have noticed.

But maybe, unlike Denney, you suffer from a sickness of your own making. Maybe you can't stop blurting out careless remarks in front of your in-laws. Or maybe you're taken aback by how quickly your convictions go out the window when money is on the table. Maybe you've gotten into trouble and stiff-armed help when it's come your way. It may seem that your illness is not a virus but *your very self*. Know, then, that you're not alone—far from it! Actually, the company is good. As St. Paul wrote in his letter to the Romans, "Wretched man that I am! Who will deliver me from this body of death?" (7:24).

We search for deliverance everywhere: in relationships, in work, in the escapism of a good book or TV show. We may find ourselves scanning the Self-Help section at the bookstore where we can find tips for getting healthy and tricks for cultivating purpose, meaning, or passion. But unfortunately these listicles so often amount to mere demands—advice and endless suggestions that are powerless to bring about the help we need. It's a lot like the classic *New Yorker* cartoon that takes place on a crowded beach: Just off the shore, sharks encircle a flailing swimmer while a lifeguard looks on disinterestedly. The caption reads, "Visualize yourself not dying, and then be that reality."

But as the 1928 Book of Common Prayer boldly put it, "We have no power in ourselves to help ourselves." If you have ever felt like that flailing swimmer—or if you *currently* feel like that flailing swimmer—then this devotional is for you.

Our prayer is that you will be able to open this book, to any page, and find relief. That you'll find real hope in something beyond yourself. That you'll be reminded of news so good, in fact, that you might be suspicious it's *too* good. But what we've put together is not a fine fancy. Theologically speaking, it's robust and carefully considered. With contributions from over sixty writers, this devotional represents a diversity of experiences and voices: women and men, young and old, from a variety of denominations. We have students, parents, teachers, writers, and pastors who have spent lifetimes ministering to people across demographics.

What do we all have in common? A belief in the surpassing grace of God—*and* the forgetfulness of human beings. We believe that the gospel often goes in one ear and out the other, and that we need to be reminded of it constantly. Which is why our organization is, after all, called Mock-ingbird. We sing the same gospel song repeatedly, whether through online essays, podcasts, conferences, or books like the very one in your hands. As is typical, *Daily Grace* (like daily grace!) makes no demands; you do not need to read this book every day. But you can if you want to.

The entries have been arranged in a vaguely seasonal order. Easter-related devotions can be found in the spring, Christmas in December. We have also provided a thematic index, which can be found at the end of the book. Con-sider this a resource for when you want to read about a specific element of spiritual life—ranging from "faith" to "doubt," and everything in between. There is a scriptural index, too, if you are looking for commentary on a spe-cific passage.

Our team liked the idea that even in its earliest phases, this project would be led by the Holy Spirit, so we forewent any major design plan; for most entries, the writers selected whichever verses they were most drawn to. Amazingly, what came back to us was a wide range of beautiful, grace-filled, and occasionally obscure scriptures, along with heartfelt, colorful commentary.

Now we pray that you, too, will be led by the Spirit as you proceed. We pray that through the words printed here, the grace of God will make itself known to you in a fresh way. We pray that you will encounter God—our invisible caregiver—who is "not afraid to be near us." Who is with us, and loves us, and has mercy on us. Even now.

— The Editors
Charlottesville, VA, 2020

DAILY GRACE

January 1

> So if anyone is in Christ, there is a new creation: everything old has passed away; see, everything has become new! (2 Corinthians 5:17)*

The Italian novelist Cesare Pavese once said, "The only joy in the world is to begin." A newborn baby is a fitting example. So is the clean-slate feeling that comes on New Year's Day.

Experience goes to show, however, that any sense of newness usually lasts as long as it takes to drive a new car off the lot. Babies grow older. January turns to February in the blink of an eye. In this sense, Christian joy is unlike any other kind of joy. It is the only thing that lets us truly say the old is gone forever; the new has come, and it's come to stay. How can this be?

The Bible makes perfectly clear that God is not in the business of self-betterment, but of death and resurrection. Christianity is not a life-long program to make you a better person, but the proclamation that Jesus entered into the ultimate ending, death, in order to give you the ultimate beginning, eternal life. Through Jesus, your fresh start—your "new you"—began in a manger. It was established on a cross and fulfilled in the resurrection of Jesus Christ. Now and forever.

Of course, we experience this truth in a constant cycle. Life is full of beginnings and endings. Every joy that "comes in the morning," however, is an echo of that blessed Easter morning, when Jesus began his reign that will last forevermore.

— *Sam Bush*

---

* Unless otherwise indicated, scripture quotations are from the New Revised Standard Version.

January 2

And [Jesus] cured many who were sick with various dis-
eases, and cast out many demons...

In the morning, while it was still very dark, he got up
and went out to a deserted place, and there he prayed. And
Simon and his companions hunted for him. When they
found him, they said to him, "Everyone is searching for
you." He answered, "Let us go on to the neighboring towns,
so that I may proclaim the message there also; for that is
what I came out to do." (Mark 1:34-38)

The pattern of the spiritual life, if we take Christ as our model, seems to
be one of engagement and retreat. Hardly anything has occurred in Mark's
account before Jesus withdraws to a deserted place to pray. He takes a deliberate pause from healing the sick and casting out demons.

The pattern of modern life, on the other hand, is nonstop engagement.
We cannot even enjoy the little breaks given to us at stoplights or in waiting
rooms. We go from one moment to the next, never fully engaged or disen-
gaged. Call it a culture of distraction.

Not surprisingly, distraction has become a major source of contemporary guilt—just ask any parent of young children about the last time their
child asked them to put down their phone.

What do you seek distraction from? Could be grief, or loneliness, or
doubt, or mortality, or hunger, or guilt itself! Could be the voice of internal criticism, or anything really.

The disciples do not follow the same pattern as Christ. Their need leads
them to seek out their teacher the moment he goes missing. "Everyone is
searching for you," they say with unintended irony.

And so they interrupt Jesus' prayers—they get in the way of his time
with God. Note that he does not meet them with a rebuke or with a rejection. Nor does he give them a lesson about retreat and engagement. He
responds with kindness and renewed focus.

Jesus, it turns out, doesn't want to be distracted from preaching the gospel. That's where his energy lies: in spreading the news that, with mercy and
love, God has interrupted—and will continue to interrupt—the panicked

pattern of human history. That he brings rest to the weary and hope to the guilty.

> *Lord, please interrupt our distractions today with your peace,*
> *and open our ears afresh to hear your gospel of grace. Amen.*

— David Zahl

January 3

Another said, "I will follow you, Lord; but let me first say farewell to those at my home." Jesus said to him, "No one who puts a hand to the plow and looks back is fit for the kingdom of God." (Luke 9:61-62)

Whenever you hear a "Yes, but…" run for your life. Because wherever a Yesbutter is, the party is not: "Yes, but first change out of those clothes." "Yes, but not too loudly, please." "Yes, but only in moderation."

Yesbutters, or *control freaks* as they are better known, are always effectively saying, "Yes, but on my terms." They want their cake both ways. They have been dealt the cards, and have decided they want a new deal. Ultimately, they cannot accept reality. And in order to deal with the reality that they cannot accept, they build contingency plans to resurrect some false modicum of control. How do I know? I am a Yesbutter. If I am surprised by an invitation I wasn't expecting, I balk. I hedge. I equivocate. I am not good at going with the flow.

Throughout the New Testament, Jesus is offering a new direction. And while we are to assume that his fork in the road leads travelers to greener pastures, Jesus encounters several people who have *plans*, thank you very much—jobs to do, families to feed, duties to fulfill—and can't just drop everything. *Blessed are the flexible*, yeah, sure, but tell that to my kid's violin instructor…

Jesus is the Great Interrupter. He interrupts our regularly scheduled programming to bring us Yesbutters an invitation to reality. Sometimes it is a welcome invitation to let loose and enjoy the party. Other times, the reality we're being asked to face looks more like a funeral. Jesus doesn't ask that we *like* what's on offer, but he warns us about the perils of a life spent denying it. This is what the invitation to faith looks like on a daily basis: to accept what's real over what we'd prefer to be real.

And so, a proper prayer for a Yesbutter like myself:

> Lord, grant me the courage to yield. Help me to say yes to the world you've given me today, with no buts about it.

— *Ethan Richardson*

The LORD your God is in your midst,
  a mighty one who will save;
he will rejoice over you with gladness;
  he will quiet you by his love;
he will exult over you with loud singing. (Zephaniah 3:17 ESV)

In *The Magician's Nephew*, C. S. Lewis tells the story of Polly and Digory, two children who use magical rings to travel between worlds. Eventually they end up in a world of complete darkness. As they sit in the dark, a voice begins to sing. Lewis narrates the scene: "There were no words. There was hardly even a tune. But it was, beyond comparison, the most beautiful noise [Digory] had ever heard. It was so beautiful he could hardly bear it." The powerful voice belongs to Aslan, and it brings the land of Narnia to life.

Aslan's singing causes the stars to appear in the sky and the sun to rise, revealing vibrant colors and valleys and rivers. Lewis comments that such developments were exciting for the bystanders; that is, "until you saw the Singer himself, and then you forgot everything else."

The chaos of today, and the lies of the Enemy, can be deafening; our whole world can feel dark and empty. And yet, we have the promise of God's presence, a roaring Lion whose singing brings light into our lives. And when that light reveals his face, allowing us to bask in his glory and might, everything else fades away. We see a loving Father who owes us nothing, and yet *chooses* to sing and rejoice over his children—not because of anything we've done but because of the immense love he has for us.

— *Margaret Pope*

January 5

Two others also, who were criminals, were led away to be
put to death with him. When they came to the place that is
called The Skull, they crucified Jesus there with the criminals, one on his right and one on his left. Then Jesus said,
"Father, forgive them; for they do not know what they are
doing." (Luke 23:32-34)

When we consider the death of Jesus, the self-sacrifice, we must never forget that he is dying for the sake of the very people who are putting him to
death. Even as he is being tortured and executed, he returns nothing but
love, prayers and forgiveness in the face of unspeakable anger and cruelty;
the injustice is unfathomable.

The death of Jesus is quite unlike the death of other historic figures
whom we might deem "heroic." Very often, men and women of virtue have
been willing to be killed by their enemies for the sake of their friends, or
have fallen victim to a lone, deranged perpetrator and were mourned by
many devotees. Even more often, men and women have been killed as they
themselves sought to kill those whom they deemed evil. But the death of
Jesus is extraordinary in its solitude, pacifism, and unanimity. Jesus dies
alone, willingly, peaceably, and almost everyone agrees that it's a great idea.

When we reflect on the death of Jesus, we must always remember that
we are in the crowd, condoning or demanding his death with our words,
actions, or silence, and that we can never possibly grasp the meaning of
God's death at our hands—the tear it rends in creation, and yet the redemption it somehow births, in spite of us. Each and every day, we speak and act
in such a way that repudiates and rejects Jesus, and yet he died for us, and
did so forgivingly. If Jesus dies for and forgives even those who execute
him, our hope is assured, not because of anything we have done or might
do, but only on account of his unflinching mercy.

— R-J Heijmen

January 6

"The LORD will fight for you, and you have only to keep
still." (Exodus 14:14)

At the climactic moment of the Old Testament's Exodus drama, when
God's beloved Israel teeters on the brink of destruction, when the next few
moments will determine whether the nation perishes by an Egyptian blade
or a Red Sea wave—at this critical juncture, what does God tell Israel to do?

Fight? Swim? Surrender? No, through Moses he tells them, literally,
to shut up. That's the basic meaning of the Hebrew verb *charash*, translated more politely here as "keep still." Eugene Peterson paraphrased it well:
"GOD will fight the battle for you. And you? You keep your mouths shut!"

Of course, that's relatively good advice about 99% of the time. But when
it comes time to watch the Warrior Lord flex his salvific muscles to save us,
it's *always* good advice. Open your ears and listen as Christ speaks life into
you in the face of the ancient Egyptians of death and sin. Open your eyes to
see how he leads you into the Red Sea of the baptismal waters, and casts all
your sins into the depths of that sea (Mic 7:19). Open your hands to receive
the sweet, honeyed manna that falls from him who is the Bread of Life.

Cherish the *charash*. The Lord fights for us. He needs no encouragement, no pleading, no confessing, certainly no vain promises of I'll-make-it-
worth-it. It's already worth it for our Savior, because he delights in nothing
more than doing for us what we could never do for ourselves. He endured
the cross, fought those Egyptians, buried hell in a muddy grave at the bottom of the Red Sea, and carried us all across and out the other side onto
the shore of life everlasting.

— *Chad Bird*

January 7

The stone that the builders rejected
   has become the chief cornerstone.
This is the LORD's doing;
   it is marvelous in our eyes. (Psalm 118:22-23)

This passage is referred to many times in scripture: Jesus quotes it as an explanation of the parable of the unfaithful tenants, the ones who went to the extreme of killing the son of an absentee vineyard owner (Mt 21, Mk 12, Lk 20). It is also used by Peter in his great sermon recorded in Acts 4, as well as by Paul in Ephesians, and by Peter again in his first letter, to explain that the rejected and murdered Jesus had, in fact, become the cornerstone of the new church.

Is this not a principle that we praise in our worship, but resist in our lives? Is it possible that the parts of us which we reject, because they expose our weaknesses, are the very parts of us that Christ knows can become the foundation of our relationship with him?

This might be true about our family, about our past, about our psychology; what we see as a weakness—something of which we are guilty and ashamed—is in fact the very foundation of our relationship with Christ. Is this not what caused us to turn to Him in the first place, and probably causes us to return to Him again and again?

> *O Lord, help me not to be ashamed of the parts of me that I naturally reject. Help me to present to you my "dirty feet" for your cleansing. And help me to be grateful for these weaknesses that cause me to turn to you.*

— Mary Zahl

January 8

Beloved, we are God's children now; what we will be has
not yet been revealed. What we do know is this: when he
is revealed, we will be like him, for we will see him as he
is. (1 John 3:2)

I still procrastinate...all the time. I'm still out of shape and non-athletic.
I still scorn people who aren't like me. I still fear confrontation. I'm still
passive-aggressive in relationships. At the heart level, I haven't changed
much since I was a kid, nor have I changed drastically since I got saved 20
years ago. I'm still the center of my perceived universe; I let others in, from
time to time, but often on a conditional basis.

After all this time, I'm still me, but that's supposed to be good news,
right? In our culture, aren't we encouraged to know ourselves, be ourselves,
find ourselves? But like the first sinners, the only thing I increasingly know
is that I'm naked, that I lack righteousness, that ultimately I'm not actually
enough according to the demands of the day.

In forty years, I haven't fundamentally changed, but neither has God's
love for me in Jesus Christ. The writer of Hebrews affirms that "Jesus
Christ is the same yesterday and today and forever" (13:8). He's still alive,
still interceding as my righteousness before God. Still forgiving my sins
before I can commit them, still absolving me of my refusal and inability to
change.

In this age, ironically, we are hindered from changing by the very demand
that we change. We hear the demand from our culture, our parents, our
spouses, the Sermon on the Mount, or the internal voice accusing us (since
the law is written on our hearts). Change is difficult because the law is still
present, and where the law practically reigns, change is impossible, or at
least tenuous at best. Nope, in 40 years, I haven't changed, but one day, I
will be changed. In Christ, the law is fulfilled. When he returns, we will
be changed because we will be freed from the unbearable burden of having
to look to ourselves for justification. Instead, we will finally be set free to
"see him as he is."

— Jason Thompson

January 9

[B]ut those who wait for the LORD shall renew their
strength,
they shall mount up with wings like eagles,
they shall run and not be weary,
they shall walk and not faint. (Isaiah 40:31)

I love running. I also hate running. Running and I have been frenemies for over two decades now, since my college days when I would set goals on the treadmill at the school fitness center. Since then, I've struggled through every run—even the good ones aren't easy!—and have managed to finish three half-marathons and a few smaller races along the way. I'm quite proud of this, you see, because my accomplishments in this arena have resulted from training, sacrifice, determination, and effort.

Not so in the spiritual arena. The most I can bring to the finished work of Christ is...absolutely nothing. I've sat through countless sermons that have said otherwise, paying lip service to grace while adding a *but* to the end, followed by a list of things we can do to "help" God with his work. Isaiah, however, tells us to do nothing but *sit there!* We are enlisted to *wait*, and it is in this waiting—not self-imposed effort or struggle—that God shows up and does, well, everything.

And what an *everything* it is. Flying like a bird? Can't relate personally, but sounds cool. Run and not be weary? SIGN ME UP. In a sport that has been fueled by my effort and contained by my limitations, what would it feel like to run tirelessly? I will never know on this side of heaven, but the promise is here. What does it mean, though?

A few verses before this, Isaiah describes God as one who "does not faint or grow weary." I don't think it's a coincidence that this is the same language used in verse 31. What that means to me is that rather than making us into champion athletes, he is making us more like *himself*. God does not create a training regimen for us, but works *in us* and, over time, transforms us so that we resemble him. What would it feel like to trust God for this process? To know that, as we wait—expectantly, trustingly—he is accomplishing the mightiest and unlikeliest of works? I think it may just feel like freedom—that of a flying bird, or a runner who never slows.

— *Stephanie Phillips*

January 10

> Then the LORD spoke to the fish, and it spewed Jonah out
> upon the dry land. (Jonah 2:10)

Of all the Bible's "minor" prophets, Jonah's story is the best known. This renegade prophet fled from God's orders, catching a boat to the west when he had been told to travel east. God frustrates Jonah's flight with a massive storm on the sea, a storm that threatens the lives of both Jonah and the ship's crew. Once the crew realizes the storm is God's judgment on Jonah, Jonah himself volunteers to be thrown overboard to save the rest of the crew. Floating in the middle of the Mediterranean, destined to drown and die as God's AWOL prophet, Jonah is famously saved by a large fish that swallows him up and carries him to dry land.

Let's observe the fact that Jonah's three days in the belly of a fish were not part of God's punishment but of God's rescue. How odd is it that God would choose such a vessel for saving his wayward prophet! Of all the prayers recorded in the Bible, the prayer from Jonah 2 comes from the most bizarre place: the inside of a fish's belly. God delights in saving his people through the strangest of circumstances. The thing that feels like a judgment (three days in a fish's stomach doesn't sound like any sort of heavenly blessing!) is actually the saving work of God. Who would have guessed?

When it comes to the "strange ways that God saves," perhaps the only other Bible story that could rival Jonah's pescatarian salvation is the gospel itself. It's no surprise that Jesus describes his death and resurrection as "the sign of Jonah" (Mt 12:39). God saves Jonah with the gulp of a large fish, and God saves the world by having Jesus Christ swallowed up by death itself. The NRSV translation graphically says Jonah was "spewed" upon the dry land. We could equally say that hell spewed up the risen Christ as unfit for its domain, the first of many to be rejected from the confines of Sheol.

Be on the lookout for the strange and unexpected. Perhaps the thing that looks like the judgment of God may actually be the vehicle by which God is saving you. It may not be a fish or a crucifixion, but don't write off the career troubles, family strife, or financial hardship as mere inconveniences. God has saved with much stranger things.

— *Bryan Jarrell*

17

January 11

[A] man was there with a withered hand, and [the Phar-
isees] asked [Jesus], "Is it lawful to cure on the sabbath?"
so that they might accuse him. He said to them, "Suppose
one of you has only one sheep and it falls into a pit on the
sabbath; will you not lay hold of it and lift it out? How
much more valuable is a human being than a sheep! So it
is lawful to do good on the sabbath." Then he said to the
man, "Stretch out your hand." He stretched it out, and it
was restored, as sound as the other. (Matthew 12:10-13)

A few weeks ago we were having one of those Saturdays when kids had
basketball games scheduled on top of one another. My hair was made out
of basically just dry shampoo. And we had only eaten donuts. So I ordered
my usual at a Starbucks that is not my usual.

And I used the app which lets you order on a phone and never have to
deal with an actual person. But this was not a Glory Story Starbucks. This
was a Starbucks of the Gospel.

It was a train-wreck. And not because there were a lot of customers.
There were three people in line. They were moving slowly because of the
employees. One of them was an old guy. Really old. Like, too old to be
doing that kind of intense work. And the other guy was this young guy,
who wore a beanie hat, and had a severe speech impediment. There was
one middle-aged woman back there. And she seemed utterly exasperated.
And I was like, *Damn these people.*

And then, spoken over me, which is literally the only way God gets
through to me, I heard this voice: *Damn* these people? *These are the people
Jesus would have loved.*

Honestly, the thought, or the Holy Ghost, or whatever it was, knocked
the breath out of me.

And then it occurred to me that I am one of those people too. I may be
younger, with better taste in hats, and a clearer sense of speech, but I too
am wounded and in need of healing. I too am a slow worker with a withered hand. I too am one of those damned people that Jesus loves and takes
the time to heal.

— *Sarah Condon*

January 12

> Now before faith came, we were imprisoned and guarded
> under the law until faith would be revealed. Therefore the
> law was our disciplinarian until Christ came, so that we
> might be justified by faith. But now that faith has come, we
> are no longer subject to a disciplinarian, for in Christ Jesus
> you are all children of God through faith. (Galatians 3:23-26)

When you ask most people, "What is faith?" the response typically involves something we generate.

For some, faith is an acceptable form of superstition, or it is a substance that can be moved and swayed based on our experiences and the experiences of those around us. I will often hear people say, when things are going great in life, "Well, you know, I just have a lot of faith. I feel really close to God right now." But when things go terribly wrong, that same person will say, "I just don't know if I believe in God anymore. Why is he testing my faith?" This definition—and sadly it is very common—roots the meaning of faith in our subjective experience and what we are doing. However, this definition of faith is not what St. Paul is talking about in the Epistle to the Galatians.

For St. Paul, faith does not hinge upon what we see and experience. Rather, faith hinges upon what we have heard that God has done for us, through his Son Jesus Christ. Replace "Jesus" with "faith" in the above text, and it begins to make profound sense.

According to St. Paul, faith for the Christian finds its roots in the incarnation and in the saving work of Christ's life, death, and resurrection *for you*. As St. Paul writes: "But when the fullness of time had come, God sent his Son, born of a woman, born under the law, in order to redeem those who were under the law, so that we might receive adoption as children" (Gal 4:4-5). As Christians, the gospel of Jesus is not some dispensable narrative that simply encourages us to have more faith. Rather, the content and context of the Christian faith is Christ alone.

— *Jacob Smith*

January 13

"Have I not commanded you? Be strong and of good courage; be not frightened, neither be dismayed; for the LORD your God is with you wherever you go." (Joshua 1:9 RSV)

Jürgen Moltmann often used to state that God is both with us and for us. Mary and I liked it when he said that, for it seemed to cover the two main things about God, at least in relation to pain.

First, God never leaves us alone. *We are in fact never alone!* You are never in a dark room with no one to listen and hear.

Second, God is an advocate *for* us, because we simply cannot testify in our own defense. What a person says in his own defense is typically self-protective and biased. We need a defender. God, in the Person of His Son, is our Defender.

These are not just fine words and hopeful suppositions. The Lord said to His in-over-his-head servant Joshua that He would never leave Joshua, no matter what trouble he got into and no matter where he found himself as a result of it.

My Mary has a strong dread of being alone. I don't have quite the same dread, but ultimately, no, I do not wish to be alone. Nobody really wants to be alone, and especially when they are in pain, let alone when they are dying. If you are in distress tonight, "be not frightened, neither be dismayed; for the LORD your God is with you wherever you [are]."

— *Paul Zahl*

January 14

You have kept count of my tossings;
  put my tears in your bottle.
  Are they not in your record? (Psalm 56:8)

I have a friend who has made use of a "God box" in her prayer life. Every time something comes up that gives her trouble—a disappointing string of dates, an unfair reprimand at work, even a bad case of allergies—she writes it down on a piece of paper, folds it up, and puts it in her God box.

It sounds like something a kid would do, but it's brilliant. My friend says it helps her to see what's within her control and, most importantly, what isn't. For the things that aren't, the act of putting them in the God box helps her detach from it, to literally put it away, trusting that if it's going to change at all, God will have to do something.

One of the perks of this activity is that, every month or two, when her box has reached full capacity, she sifts through the pieces of paper. If the prayer remains a prayer, she keeps it in the box; but if not, she pulls it out. She's told me that it is amazing to see how many prayers have been addressed, without her doing a thing.

This is just a small taste of the real "God box" the psalmist alludes to here. With God, every "tossing" has been counted, every tear bottled up. This is commiseration at its most intimate. God is not simply the record-keeper of all sins, the old Naughty-List Maker. He is the recordkeeper of tears. He is the one who knows, with microscopic precision, the weight you're carrying around with you today. The psalmist sings that, not only has God kept track of all your sufferings, but that he has done so to eventually mend every last one of them (v. 9).

I asked my friend: What about the pieces of paper that she can't pull out, the ones that go on, year after year, unaddressed? Do they grate on her?

Yes, she said. Of course they do. But so many have been answered that it seems foolish to think of God as absent. They give her hope that one day, even the oldest, most yellowed prayers will be pulled out and happily discarded. Until then, you keep depositing them back into the box. You weep and you pray and you try to remember that someone's listening—someone's counting all your tears in a bottle.

— *Ethan Richardson*

January 15

But this I call to mind,
    and therefore I have hope:
The steadfast love of the LORD never ceases,
    his mercies never come to an end;
they are new every morning;
    great is your faithfulness.
"The LORD is my portion," says my soul,
    "therefore I will hope in him." (Lamentations 3:21-24)

The book of Lamentations chronicles the Israelites' grief over the violent destruction of Jerusalem and the exile of its inhabitants. Metaphorically speaking, each of us have or will at some point encounter our own exiles, the destruction of our own Jerusalems. Whether it's the loss of a loved one, the loss of a job, or the loss of a marriage, we are bound to be afflicted in this brutally fallen world.

The above passage calls to mind a single word for me: *surrender*. On the surface of things, surrender is primarily an act of giving up. The result: a vacancy. But if you think about it, when we truly surrender—when we surrender our sense of control, our sense of wellbeing, our expectations, the hope we have in our abilities and our own strength—we usually do so in unspoken anticipation that something else, something greater will take its place.

Even in war, the losing side waves a white flag in exchange for *life*. Similarly, as Christians, what follows our surrender has nothing at all to do with lack. Rather, when we surrender our grief, our losses, our failures, our control, our addictions, we are animated with a new strength, a new hope, a new life that is far beyond the hollow shell of our actual selves. In a sense, this is exactly what the author of Lamentations is saying here.

When our love has limitations, "the steadfast love of the LORD never ceases."

When we (and everyone around us) have fallen short, "his mercies never come to an end."

When we (and everyone around us) are unfaithful, "great is His faithfulness."

When we are empty, thirsty, longing, "The LORD is our portion."

Dear one, there is an improbable abundance in surrender, even—*especially*—at your direst point of need. What small or large detail of your life is God calling you to surrender to him today? May your hands be open to let go, and to receive instead his grace.

— *Charlotte Getz*

January 16

Humble yourselves therefore under the mighty hand of
God, so that he may exalt you in due time. Cast all your
anxiety on him, because he cares for you. Discipline yourselves, keep alert. Like a roaring lion your adversary the
devil prowls around, looking for someone to devour. Resist
him, steadfast in your faith, for you know that your brothers and sisters in all the world are undergoing the same
kinds of suffering. (1 Peter 5:6-9)

When I got sober, my first sponsor happened to be an Episcopal priest. In
one of our first meetings, he pointed to the verses above as an accurate, biblical description of the addiction that had caused my unraveling. He told
me to imagine that my "adversary" was alcohol. Therefore, in the language
from the Book of Common Prayer, my task in recovery was to "Be sober, be
watchful. Your adversary [the addiction] prowls around like a roaring lion,
seeking someone to devour. Resist him, firm in your faith."

The First Step in Alcoholics Anonymous is, "We admitted we were
powerless over alcohol—that our lives had become unmanageable." The
truth is that all of our lives are unmanageable. We are powerless over our
addictions, vices, temptations, and the manifold sins that beset us on every
side. Like alcohol for an addict, the devil seeks nothing but human destruction. What then are we to do?

The power of AA's First Step comes in recognizing our powerlessness.
You could translate the First Step as "humble yourselves therefore under
the mighty hand of God." Only then can we truly accept the help of God,
which is always available.

Likewise, the author of 1 Peter tells us the truth and the solution to the
problem of human sin. First, we must recognize that we are not alone. All
of humanity struggles and falls short. We are not "terminally unique" as we
may believe. Second, we must trust that the God of all grace has called us
and will restore, support, strengthen, and establish us. The God of Jesus
Christ cares for us. To him be the power for ever and ever. Amen.

— *Connor Gwin*

January 17

So out of the ground the LORD God formed every animal of the field and every bird of the air, and brought them to the man to see what he would call them; and whatever the man called every living creature, that was its name. (Genesis 2:19)

When it's time to name creation, God gets the ball rolling by calling the light "day," the darkness "night," and the upward expanse "heaven." But when it's time to christen the animals, he delegates that task to the man. Adam gets to be the mouth of God. "Whatever the man called every living creature, that was its name." It's a funny scene: the Almighty whipping up long-necked giraffes, masked raccoons, and naked mole rats, holding them before Adam, waiting to see what name will pop into his head.

What's not so funny, however, is that as time goes on, the tables are turned: the animals that Adam names become the animals that name Adam's descendants. Thick-headed Israel is a "stubborn heifer" (Hos 4:16). Unfaithful leaders are "all silent dogs that cannot bark" (Is 56:10). And Ezekiel, in a sermon highly unsafe for Sunday School, says idolatrous Israel lusted after false gods with donkey-sized junk (23:20).

When the animals name us, things get ugly real fast. And that's the point, isn't it? Rebellion, betrayal, getting in bed with faux deities—nothing's pretty about that.

But in the Almighty's gracious sense of humor, he ends up with the last laugh. He becomes like an animal himself to save us: "Behold, the Lamb of God, who takes away the sin of the world," John says of Jesus (Jn 1:29 ESV). The Father's Son is "the Lion of the tribe of Judah" (Rev 5:5). For us, who became like animals, God becomes the Lamb, the Lion, the crucified victim surrounded by dogs (Ps 22:16), so that he might recreate us in himself to be stewards of creation once more.

That is God's way, to become all that we are, so that, in Christ, we might become all that God desires us to be.

— *Chad Bird*

January 18

For my thoughts are not your thoughts,
nor are your ways my ways, says the LORD. (Isaiah 55:8)

When we're working with children (and humans in general), our instinct is to take charge and assert our authority. We do this in one of two ways: First, we get louder. Second, we make ourselves bigger to make sure our authority is visible. This always backfires. Anyone who has spent time with children knows that being bigger, louder, and more in-charge may appear to work for a moment but will actually get you nowhere fast.

My thoughts are not your thoughts, nor are your ways my ways. In this profound declaration, God reminds us that our natural approach to life, and specifically to others, is not how God deals with us.

Eighteen years ago, I worked as a behavior therapist in Pittsburgh with children and adults with mental illnesses. I was hired to "fix" people, under the expectation that I would come in and assert an authority that could iron out social-emotional power dynamics. However, after a few weeks in the field, I realized that getting louder, bigger, and more assertive never worked. You cannot "fix" humanity by taking the bull by the horns. Getting louder only builds walls, causes alienation, and ultimately fosters compartmentalization.

To redeem his creation, God did not get louder, bigger, and more assertive. Instead, he became a quiet Word who took on flesh, and emptied himself of all authority, so that—by his death and resurrection—he might tear down the walls that separate us from him and each other. This is good news: that we have a God who, to reach us, releases the reins, despite our bound desire to take the reins and hold onto everything but him. God's love and mercy gently put us in our place. We don't have to be bigger than we are, for he does not handle us as the world does. His "ways are not our ways."

Lord, enable us to stop, consider, and act in mercy when we find
ourselves getting louder, bigger, and grasping for control. For
your ways are not our ways. Your ways are far better. In your
mercy, hear our prayer.

— *Melina Smith*

January 19

So Naaman came with his horses and chariots, and halted at the entrance of Elisha's house. Elisha sent a messenger to him, saying, "Go, wash in the Jordan seven times, and your flesh shall be restored and you shall be clean." (2 Kings 5:9-10)

"Maybe the most grueling path seems the most likely to lead to divinity." The woman who penned that line, Heather Havrilesky, wasn't talking about Old Testament prophets; she was writing about the explosive popularity of extreme fitness. Marathons, Ironmans, and militaristic exercise regimens like CrossFit—these things are big business for a reason. Nothing good ever came easy, right?

When the Syrian general Naaman approached the Israelite prophet Elisha to be cured of his leprosy, Elisha did not counsel a grueling path. Instead, he instructed Naaman to do the opposite of spiritual burpees: Go wash yourself in the Jordan River seven times and your flesh will be restored. That's it.

Naaman was outraged at the suggestion, no doubt because it furthered his humiliation. In modern medical parlance, this great man had good money to pay the top specialists, yet was now reduced, for all intents and purposes, to standing in line at the free clinic. If he was going to be dipped in any river, it should be a mighty one like those in his country, not a muddy stream like the Jordan. Yet such is his desperation that he swallows his pride and obeys.

In his search for healing, Naaman suffers an assault on his ego as well as his default assumptions about pain and gain. He had to be unburdened of his expectations about what a cure looks like—and how much it might cost. He had to learn that God is a God of grace, and that healing can't be earned, only received.

Likewise with all of us. Hard as it may be, we prefer the grueling path because it flatters our efforts. It allows us to take credit for what only God can do. Where is your ego under assault today? Where are you trying to pay for what you've already received for free? Are you desperate enough yet to accept the lighter burden? God does not require your sweat or your pedigree, just your need. That goes for both friends and enemies. He took the grueling path, so that ours might be easy. No burpees necessary!

— *David Zahl*

January 20

Give ear to my words, O LORD;
   give heed to my sighing.
Listen to the sound of my cry,
   my King and my God,
   for to you I pray.
O LORD, in the morning you hear my voice;
   in the morning I plead my case to you, and watch. (Psalm
   5:1-3)

Psalm 5 is often called a morning psalm. The earnest requests that open this psalm focus on daybreak prayers: "O LORD, in the morning you hear my voice; in the morning I plead my case to you, and watch." I've long been a fan of the way *The Message* paraphrases this verse: "Every morning you'll hear me at it again. Every morning I lay out the pieces of my life on your altar and watch for fire to descend."

One January, some friends of mine and I decided to go hiking in the mountains of Arkansas on what turned out to be one of the coldest nights of the year. We did our best to gather kindling and logs for a fire, but most of it was wet. My companions used all their expertise and fanned like crazy, but ultimately the fire never really took off, and we trudged back to our tents cold and defeated.

Thinking back on that failed fire, I find something so honest and also comforting in the grace of this morning psalm. I like this thought of pleading my case, such as it is, before the Lord each morning. I like the thought of laying out every random piece of my desire before God, and waiting for fire from heaven.

So today, I'll be back at it again—piling up hopes and dreams and fears and concerns, praying that heaven's fire truly descends.

— *Larry Parsley*

January 21

He has told you, O mortal, what is good;
    and what does the LORD require of you
but to do justice, and to love kindness,
    and to walk humbly with your God? (Micah 6:8)

Too often we make the life of faith complex. We build up rules and practices and "insights" to adhere to, and feel guilty when we fail to meet our own standards. We agonize over where to give in to the culture around us and where to draw the line, over who is "in" and who is "out." We conflate our faith with some grand plan we have become attached to, or some vision of the ideal Christian life. We assemble a semi-conscious checklist of the "right" theological positions, and confuse theological sophistication with spiritual progress. Like snails whose shells have grown too big, the baggage of the life of faith can become a burden that slows us down as we try to follow Jesus.

The vision of Christian life in this passage from Micah is not like that. It is so simple. What is the good that the Lord requires of us?

Do justice. Attend to the suffering around you today and try to do something, anything, to rectify it, knowing that the Author of all justice is with you, and that the healing of the nations is in His hands, not yours.

Love kindness. Judgment and moral superiority are exhausting and alienating; see them for what they are, and let them go. Wherever you can, choose mercy, choose compassion, choose kindness, and trust God with the consequences.

Walk humbly with your God. Just keep going, one day at a time, on this pilgrimage. See what He brings to you today. Trust that He is with you and knows the way, and that that is all you need to know.

As for everything else? Let it go. You are free today to begin again. The grand plans, the superiority over others, the feeling that it all depends on you—these are not what the Lord requires of you. He wants to do something new. His future awaits.

— *Simeon Zahl*

January 22

The light shines in the darkness, and the darkness did not
overcome it. (John 1:5)

Everyone is a little afraid of the dark. It's okay to admit it. We all know
the way the scant light casts shadows that may or may not be either a suit
hanging in the corner of the room or a monster with evil intentions waiting
to strike as soon as our eyes close. No matter how old we get, the thought
runs through our mind, even as we quickly push it away.

But with darkness, it's not about what is actually there, but what is
not there. Darkness is not dark—it is not a thing in and of itself—but the
absence of a thing, the absence of light. And that absence is spooky. It feels
off. German has a word for this: *unheimlich*, or "un-homey."

In the above verse, John delineates between a world created by God and
the world that God—in the mystery of the incarnation of Jesus Christ—
came into. A world not created for darkness, but that finds itself in darkness.
A world meant for so much more, and yet stuck where it is. The *unheimlich*
feeling of a world as it should be but isn't. The irony should not be lost on
us that the Greek word translated as "overcome" (κατέλαβεν) can also mean
"comprehend." The dark was so deep, and so all encompassing, we couldn't
even see the light when it came. We tend to assume darkness is all there is.

But we are oh so wrong.

Into those uncomfortable shadows and un-homey spaces, the light of
God enters the world. Jesus Christ, fully God and fully man, the creator
of that great light, walks into the dark and finds each of us hidden under
the covers, toes tucked in to keep us safe from the monsters we know are
surely waiting to attack.

Now the darkness is not prepared for its scattering—the monsters still
long for a human snack. But they are in for a surprise at exactly the moment
they believe they have extinguished that light. And in that moment, we
find that night has been banished forever.

— *Ben Maddison*

Then he said to me, "These are they who have come out of the great ordeal; they have washed their robes and made them white in the blood of the Lamb.

For this reason they are before the throne of God,
and worship him day and night within his temple,
and the one who is seated on the throne will shelter
them.
They will hunger no more, and thirst no more;
the sun will not strike them,
nor any scorching heat;
for the Lamb at the center of the throne will be their
shepherd,
and he will guide them to springs of the water of life,
and God will wipe away every tear from their eyes."
(Revelation 7:14-17)

Early seasons of the TV show *Grey's Anatomy* were full of quotable, epic speeches. In Season Three, George's dad tragically dies during surgery. Cristina shares this speech with him: "There's a club. The dead dads club. And you can't be in it until you're in it. You can try to understand. You can sympathize. But until you feel that loss... My dad died when I was nine. George, I'm really sorry you had to join the club."

A decade after first hearing this speech, it came back to me when I learned of a new club: the dead siblings club. My sister died unexpectedly. Much like the dead dads club, you're not in it until you're in it. Even though I had walked with my husband and his family as he had joined the club, nothing could have fully prepared me for it.

Revelation 7 gives us a picture of a new club. It is one that is defined by death and suffering, too. When John sees the great multitude from every nation, from all tribes and peoples, we learn that they are the ones who have come out of "the great ordeal." We are tempted to sort these people into specific clubs, like the dead siblings club or the club for those who acutely suffered in life. But no such distinction is made. Those who have come out of the great ordeal could be any of us, for we have all faced our own challenges and ordeals in life.

But this club isn't just defined by our suffering and mortality. It is also defined by what Jesus has done for us. It is the blood of the Lamb, given and shed for all people through his death on the cross, that defines us. It is the blood of the Lamb that calls us together and offers the promise of a place at God's throne where we are comforted and provided for. It is the blood of the Lamb that guides us to springs of the waters of life and wipes every tear from our eyes.

As I found myself an unceremonious inductee to the dead siblings club, the club of Revelation 7 was my peace. Through the blood of the Lamb, we are God's forever. Welcome to the club.

— *Tasha Genck Morton*

January 24

> He said to them, "Listen to this dream that I dreamed. There we were, binding sheaves in the field. Suddenly my sheaf rose and stood upright; then your sheaves gathered around it, and bowed down to my sheaf." (Genesis 37:6-7)

Joseph's story of redemption is often viewed as the story of a pretty good guy who has some awful things happen to him. And that's true, as far as it goes. "[Y]ou meant evil against me, but God meant it for good" (Gen 50:20 ESV) *is* a powerful motif of the Christian life. There is all sorts of evil meant against us by the devil, and God can bring good out of every bit of it. However, looking back into Joseph's early life, a new theme emerges: God saves even the most obnoxious kid on the playground.

Joseph is a goody two-shoes who announces his ACT score without a hint of actual curiosity on the part of his audience. When I read the story of Joseph's early life in context, I am almost ready to throw him in the pit to be eaten by wild animals myself. He interrupts everyone's breakfast and explains why his father's favoritism toward him is exactly merited. He has a dream where all of them will bow down to him. And he tells them about it. They didn't even ask. We can almost imagine him flipping up the lapel of his prized multi-colored coat as he speaks. Joseph is *that kid.*

As we look at our own lives, what comfort it is to know that our most self-righteous moments do not disqualify us from the kingdom of heaven. In fact, what Joseph himself meant for evil—the one-upmanship of sibling rivalry in the extreme—God meant for good. God can use our own self-aggrandizing for our good. God saves miserable sinners—whether that sinner is the prodigal in the pig pen or the braggart who simply cannot resist saying, "Listen to this..."

May we rest in the reality that we do not need dreams or coats to impress our Lord and Savior. And even when we do not resist the (very 21st-century) temptation of "Look at me! Look at what I've done!" God will pull us out of that pit, too.

— *Ann Lowrey Forster*

January 25

"Zacchaeus, hurry and come down; for I must stay at your
house today." (Luke 19:5)

The internet is full of "life hacks," clever little shortcuts that promise to
get us around life's obstacles. "Use a clothespin to hold a nail when you're
hammering." "Use Doritos for kindling when building a fire." "Turn on your
seat warmer to keep your pizza hot while driving home." When applying
one of these, I feel like I have beaten life at its own game.

At a deeper level, we all create defense mechanisms to compensate for
the ways that life is stacked against us. Some people make everything a
joke. Some learn to function unseen and unheard. Some hone the skill of
controlling others. Just to get by, to defend ourselves, we develop these
patterns early. The problem is that these behaviors often distance us from
other people and from God.

Luke tells us how Jesus encounters a man adept at the life hack. Zacchaeus is a short man. He is also clever. He wants to see Jesus. His hack is
to run ahead of the crowd and climb a tree to get a prime view. I expect
he created similar tricks to defend himself against the hatred of those from
whom he extorted taxes. Zacchaeus positioned himself above the crowd.
But in doing so, he distanced himself from God.

But Jesus assaults the defenses we unwittingly construct against him.
Jesus stops, looks up, and says, "Zacchaeus, hurry and come down; for I
must stay at your house today." This "friend of sinners" breaches Zacchaeus'
defenses and invites himself over for dinner. John Donne wrote:

> Batter my heart, three-person'd God, for you
> As yet but knock, breathe, shine, and seek to mend;
> That I may rise and stand, o'erthrow me, and bend
> Your force to break, blow, burn, and make me new.

Thankfully, God does overthrow, bend, break, blow, and burn in order to
get through to us. God closes the gaps we create and assaults our defenses.
This is terrifying. We build those defenses early in life and trust them to
protect us. But God loves us enough to blast His way through our life hacks,
emotional tricks, and defense mechanisms to get to us.

— *Drew Rollins*

January 26

Let us therefore approach the throne of grace with boldness,
so that we may receive mercy and find grace to help in time
of need. (Hebrews 4:16)

There are so many things that I wish I could do with confidence: talk about classic literature, read and converse in French, comfort my friends whose loved ones are dying. But in reality, I do a lot of things tentatively, unsure of the right next step, afraid to offend or get it wrong. Fear of doing or saying the wrong thing is a common malady, especially in our current age of social media call-out culture. And this fear is understandable, because it is an absolute given that we will do or say something wrong at some point. This is the reality of living in a world full of people infected by sin: we are very capable of hurting one another.

When our sin becomes apparent, judgment tends to follow—from ourselves, from loved ones, from strangers on the Internet. We may then find ourselves afraid once more of doing or saying the wrong thing, being careful to hide our true selves and appear always completely put together (the opposite of approaching with confidence). This denial of our true and imperfect selves is exhausting. The dishonesty of it all weighs us down.

But the throne of grace is different. On this throne sits our God, holy and all-knowing, who resolves righteous judgment once and for all by way of a cross. On this throne sits the One who knows exactly who we are: the good, the bad, the ugly. On the throne of grace, God does not shy away from our sin or turn a blind eye. God sees it all as it is and responds with the words, "Father, forgive them; for they do not know what they are doing."

In this world, the one and only thing we can truly do with confidence is fall to our knees and admit our need for help. Let us do so boldly, knowing that as our fearful, brokenhearted, honest selves, we will be met with open arms.

— *Amanda McMillen*

January 27

"If the LORD delight in us, then he will bring us into this land, and give it us; a land which floweth with milk and honey." (Numbers 14:8 KJV)

I love the fact that the word "delight" is used to describe so many enticing foods. There's "Turkish Delight," Edmund Pevensie's favorite sweet in the Narnia stories. Also "Buddha's Delight," which is made up of mushrooms, tofu, vermicelli, broccoli, carrots, snap peas, scallions, peanuts, soy sauce, rice vinegar, bok choy, garlic, cloves, and Shaoxing wine. Or "Chocolate Delight," made up of pecans, cream cheese, instant chocolate pudding, cool whip, milk, butter, sugar. And "International Delight," hazelnut coffee creamer singles. In Genesis, "Eve saw that the tree was good for food...a *delight* to the eyes" (3:6). Sigh...

When the Hebrew people escaped from slavery in Egypt and were wandering in the wilderness, Moses sent scouts into the Promised Land. They reported that it was a wonderful land, but it was occupied by enemies. However, two of the scouts filed a minority report: "If the LORD delight in us, then he will bring us into this land, and give it us."

Here's the question: Does the Lord delight in us? The dictionary defines "delight" as "a high degree of gratification or pleasure." Does the Lord have a high degree of gratification or pleasure in us?

My honest response? "God would take a whole lot more pleasure in me if I got my act together. God would delight in me if I stopped doing that one thing. God would take delight in me if I was more charitable, if I studied the Bible, if I prayed, if I forgave..." *If, if, if.*

But then, the minority report is transformed into the majority report. Jesus says to the disciples and to us, "Don't be afraid, little flock, because your Father *delights* to give you the kingdom." (Lk 12:32 CSB). No *if.*

No if!

So here's the invitation of the majority report: Insert your own name in this promise from Jesus: "Don't be afraid, _____, because your Father delights to give you the kingdom."

— *Jim Munroe*

January 28

"Do not press me to leave you
   or to turn back from following you!
Where you go, I will go;
   where you lodge, I will lodge;
your people shall be my people,
   and your God my God." (Ruth 1:16)

These are the words of Ruth to her grieving mother-in-law, and they are almost 3000 years old. And yet who wouldn't want to hear them today?

My family has a poodle named Birthday. He follows us wherever we go. Birthday is always easy to find, because he positions himself between you and wherever it is that you are trying to get to. We're constantly having to push him aside. All he wants, it seems, is to be close.

For years, I thought it was annoying, codependent even. Birthday has been a constant impeding and intermediary presence ever since he joined our family.

But recently he was diagnosed with lymphoma. He has maybe a month to live as I write this. And he's sitting right next to me, which is the only place he's ever wanted to be really. It turns out that I'm going to miss his presence very much.

Birthday is like Ruth. His whole life has been committed to staying close. And Ruth, of course, is always close, like God, in whom "we live and move and have our being" (Acts 17:28). As the psalmist says, "Whither shall I go from thy spirit? or whither shall I flee from thy presence? If I ascend up into heaven, thou art there: if I make my bed in hell, behold, thou art there" (139:7-8 KJV). And when Birthday is gone, the truth of Ruth's sentiment will mean even more: *Where you go, I will go.* "[F]or thou art with me" (Ps 23:4 KJV). In spite of all the evidence to the contrary, the truth is that you will never be alone.

— *John Zahl*

January 29

"For those who want to save their life will lose it, and those who lose their life for my sake will find it." (Matthew 16:25)

I love Michael Jordan. I was fortunate enough to see him play a college home game when I visited my older brother at UNC back in the 80s. Even though I'm not a big NBA fan, I watched the Bulls' dynastic run through the 90s with glee and amazement. And when it was first released, I binge-watched ESPN's *The Last Dance*—the documentary about the Bulls' quest for a sixth NBA title.

Michael's self-proclaimed motto, "Win at all costs," is apparently a very good way to achieve success on the basketball court. I don't know if this is how Michael lives the rest of his life, but I hope not, because that would be a terrible way to live. Winning at all costs not only alienates those around you, but also alienates your very being from fulfillment and purpose.

At one point in my career, I tried to save my own life with a job change. This new job seemed like the answer. I was one of the final candidates. When I got the call and learned that I was not chosen, I was crushed. In retrospect, losing that job prospect ended up saving my life and my career!

Closer to a Christian *modus operandi* for life would be something like "Lose at all costs." Enigmatically, but truthfully, Jesus says, "For those who want to save their life will lose it, and those who lose their life for my sake will find it." You can plumb the depths of Jesus' meaning as well as I can, but his cruciform wisdom sure hits home for me. Not only is it true in relation to God, but it is true in relation to those around us.

> Almighty God, your Son went not up to joy but first he suffered pain, and entered not into glory before he was crucified. Mercifully grant that we, walking in the way of the cross, may find it none other than the way of life and peace; through Jesus Christ our Lord. Amen.

— Paul Walker

January 30

This is my comfort in my distress,
    that your promise gives me life. (Psalm 119:50)

Believe it or not, the legacy of infomercials is not restricted only to the mag-nanimous personality of the late Billy Mays, whose buoyant panache made every product a "must-have"—products like Kaboom!, Mighty Putty, the Awesome Auger, and OxiClean. His over-exuberant style became so iconic that every salesperson who followed him was forced to do their best imi-tation. Nevertheless, what endures throughout every infomercial, copycat or not, is the hedged guarantee. There is always a caveat. There is always fine print.

It's almost as if the marketers themselves are owning up to the not-always-effective effectiveness of the widget that is being hyped for making your life better and easier. *If you aren't satisfied, they say, or if you don't achieve the results you were expecting, we're including a 30-day money-back guarantee.* The promises that might sound too good to be true might be— *but for only $19.99, you can try our game-changing gadget risk-free!*

Wouldn't it be gratifying, though, to live your life according to some-thing more certain than "risk-free trials" and "money-back guarantees"?

Enter: the good news of Jesus Christ. News that pronounces even the worst of the worst as the prime targets of God's sin-canceling, shame-de-feating, guilt-erasing love. News that promises life because of Another's death. News that comes with promises unaccompanied by stipulations or qualifications or protective fine print.

That might sound too good to be true. But Jesus himself has guaranteed it by offering his own flesh and blood—by putting down all the money required in this transaction. The gospel is no divine commercial for righ-teousness on sale. It's the announcement of righteousness for free—no fur-ther payment required and no hints of reciprocity.

This is light-years better than any hedged guarantee. That's because it's grace. And as the theologian Robert Capon writes in *The Romance of the Word*, "Grace works without requiring *anything* on our part. It's not expensive. It's not even cheap. It's *free*."

— *Brad Gray*

January 31

[T]he fruit of the Spirit is love, joy, peace, patience, kindness, generosity, faithfulness, gentleness, and self-control.
There is no law against such things. (Galatians 5:22-23)

When we read this list, we may feel as if we are being told who we should
be or what we ought to do: *As a Christian, you should be generous. As a
faithful follower of Jesus Christ, you ought to be patient and kind. You must
become more gentle and joy-filled!* But this list is *descriptive*, not *prescriptive*.
It is proclamation, not exhortation.

Paul does not say, "Become more patient." Paul says, "The fruit of the
Spirit is…patience." To turn the fruit of the Spirit into aspirations is to
stumble back into the law, just like the Galatians. As Paul said earlier in
the epistle, if our righteousness were to come through the law, then Jesus
Christ died for absolutely no reason (2:21).

As law, this list just reinforces the message you hear 3,000 times a day:
You're not good enough. There's always more money you could've left in
the plate; there's always someone for whom you have neither patience nor
kindness; there's always days—if you're like me, whole weeks even—when
you have no joy. But your lack of joy or gentleness or self-control does not
make you an incomplete or inauthentic Christian.

Because notice: After Paul describes the works of the flesh, his voice
changes completely. He shifts from the active voice to *a passive image*: fruit.
He says "fruit of the Spirit," not "works of faith." The opposite of vice isn't
our virtue. The opposite of vice is the Vine of which we are but branches.

What you do not hear in any vineyard is the sound of anyone's effort.
Except the Gardener's. Fruit does not force itself to grow; fruit is the
byproduct of a plant made healthy. To think that you're responsible for
cultivating joy and kindness in your life is to miss Paul's entire point—his
point that, apart from the grace of God in Jesus Christ, you are a dead plant,
but in Him, you have been made alive. Now, in and through you, the Holy
Spirit can grow joy, gentleness, peace, and patience. These are not the attri-
butes by which you work your way to heaven. This is the work heaven is
doing in you on earth.

— *Jason Micheli*

February 1

[The LORD God] drove out the man; and at the east of
the garden of Eden he placed the cherubim, and a sword
flaming and turning to guard the way to the tree of life.
(Genesis 3:24)

When Adam is booted out of paradise, it becomes obvious that God is not
one to shrug at evildoing. He doesn't request that the man vacate the premises; he drives him out. Nor does the Lord hammer a "No Trespassing" sign
on one of the trees; he stations angelic bouncers there with blazing blades.
Adam has zero chance of getting back in. Period. End of story.

Or so it certainly seems.

And we find parallel stories—and griefs—in our own lives. When,
Adam-like, we're entwined in the tangled mazes of our own sordid stories,
we often think, "This is it. I'm done. My life is over." We slouch east of
divorce, east of good health, east of hope, and glance back at all we've lost.
There is no going back. But going forward? That too seems an impossibility. The ink for writing the next chapter of our lives is all dried up. We feel
trapped in the vortex of our own catastrophic narratives.

If our God is anything, however, he is an unstoppable narrator. His ink
keeps flowing. He keeps the story rolling. He is the Storyteller who transforms a catastrophe into (what Tolkien calls) a eucatastrophe—a sudden,
unexpected happy turn of events in which light is born out of darkness.

That divine light dawns in a moment of strange déjà vu. Another man, a
second Adam, is "driven out" from God's chosen land, east of Israel, into the
wilderness (Mk 1:12). Jesus has come to re-humanize humanity, to re-Eden
us, and his first stop is overcoming the very Tempter who duped the first
couple. If you want a job done right, do it yourself, so God becomes man
to do the work himself of saving us and repatriating us to the Eden of his
kingdom. In Jesus, our life is indeed over, but in the best possible way: for
we receive new, abundant life in him.

With the God of grace, the end of the story is always Christ.

— Chad Bird

February 2

Since my people are crushed, I am crushed;
  I mourn, and horror grips me.
Is there no balm in Gilead?
  Is there no physician there?
Why then is there no healing
  for the wound of my people? (Jeremiah 8:21-22 NIV)

I feel at home in this passage because it asks an unaskable question: "Is there no balm in Gilead?" I have a skeptical orientation to anything too sure of itself and anything too happy. This question feels like a much safer place than its better-known and hymnable answer. Yet, suspiciously, just before this verse, Jeremiah makes his own declarations: "The harvest is past, the summer has ended, and we are not saved."

Looking back on this now, we can pity Jeremiah for his too-human, shortsighted outlook. We know that even as Jeremiah spoke, God had plans to redeem Israel through Jesus. But the Bible still holds space for Jeremiah's mourning, which to me, is saying something. Jeremiah and the Israelites suffered, and their mourning was important. And in his own time, Jeremiah was right. There doesn't seem to have been much of a balm in any kind of human sense of a near future.

Perhaps Jeremiah's question feels at home to me because it reminds me of grief, and the weird math we do to justify our broken world in grieving spaces. After my dad died, I felt a strong pull to have a baby. I felt like that would somehow undo the damage done in the breaking of his body, as if -1 + 1 = 0. But this kind of human math is small dice. To me, Jeremiah models here that we don't have to try to know God's wholeness all the time. The way in which brokenness will be made whole is still unknown to us. In spaces of grief, especially, we can ask unaskable questions; once we receive no practical, actionable answer, we can pray for God to open our hearts again—or at least think about praying for God to help us think about maybe opening our hearts. And at some point, we may start to notice the tiniest signs of God's goodness again.

— *Sarah Gates*

February 3

"I am the true vine, and my Father is the vinegrower. He removes every branch in me that bears no fruit. Every branch that bears fruit he prunes to make it bear more fruit. You have already been cleansed by the word that I have spoken to you. Abide in me as I abide in you... I am the vine, you are the branches. Those who abide in me and I in them bear much fruit, because apart from me you can do nothing." (John 15:1-5)

At the end of this parable, the credits roll: *Vinegrower*: God. *Vine*: Jesus. *Branches*: Disciples and All Believers. In our assigned role, we don't have any lines or even stage direction. Branches are more or less inanimate and completely at the mercy of external forces as to whether they produce any fruit at all. This passivity can be especially trying during times of "pruning."

At first glance, the concept of pruning seems cruel. Sometimes a branch in your life looks perfectly strong and healthy, and when that branch is severed, it can feel like a part of you is severed. And yet, the vinegrower is at work. In fact, it would be crueler for the vinegrower to wait for the branch to improve on its own.

What does this mean for you? Well, it means you are not in control of your life. It also means that God is working on you right now, whether you know it or not. He knows what you need, and he is giving you that now. His very Word is what makes you whole. And as he speaks into your life, and as he works out his plan for you, all the while, you are connected to a vine, which is bringing you life and nourishment because the vine is Jesus Christ, apart from whom you can do nothing.

Being a branch connected to the vine might ironically look like you're bound, but abiding in the vine is experiencing freedom like never before—freedom from striving, freedom from wanting to be the vinegrower, freedom from Satan and sin, freedom from yourself, freedom from death.

Whenever you find yourself unable to feel this freedom, simply know that the vine was not merely pruned, but cut down, his fruit poured out and made into wine at the foot of the cross. Three days later, he was raised back up, raising the branches along with him. And he remains in you today.

— Sam Bush

43

February 4

> For I am convinced that neither death, nor life, nor angels, nor rulers, nor things present, nor things to come, nor powers, nor height, nor depth, nor anything else in all creation, will be able to separate us from the love of God in Christ Jesus our Lord. (Romans 8:38-39)

So often, the unshakable truth of Paul's words here gets roadblocked in our heads, instead of making its way into the bedrock of our hearts. After all, we've been separated from God once before, right? (See: *Genesis*.) I look around at the state of the world and wonder how it could be true that God is near, that God is for us. But, like Paul, by the grace of God I remain convinced by his promise.

The promise we have, fulfilled on the cross, is that nothing—*nothing*—can ever separate us from him. This means that your most egregious sin does nothing to change God's love for you. This means that during your most cutting losses, your most crippling grief, when you feel God has fled the burning building and left you there to fry, his love remains and remains and remains. When we hold loosely, barely able to keep our grip, he holds fast. Height nor depth can cause his steadfast love to waver or slip. Neither can doubt nor apathy. He came to be with you and he died to be with you. His love for you is fixed, dear one. It is fixed.

And it is helpful for me to remember that this same truth holds for my fellow brothers and sisters in Christ—even (maybe especially) the ones who seem furthest from reach, perpetrators of the very wrong that continues to saturate our world. As we feel wronged, victimized, or ignored, as we feel left out or villainized, misunderstood or underappreciated even by our fellow Christians, may we remember God's unwavering love for *them* in Christ Jesus our Lord, who came to redeem the whole world.

> *God, give us the grace to see our neighbors—every last one of them—with the fixed and loving eyes of Jesus.*

— *Charlotte Getz*

February 5

You shall love the LORD your God with all your heart, and with all your soul, and with all your might. (Deuteronomy 6:5)

Sometimes it is easy to love the Lord. Sometimes we are still living in the wake of some great blessing (a job, a child, an answer to prayer), and we have seen the hand of Providence in our lives, and it is easy to love the Lord. Sometimes we are with certain people—perhaps those who walked with us in the heady early days of faith, or those who cared for us during a trial—and His reality and His goodness feel near. In such times, we read these words from Deuteronomy, and our heart leaps and we say, "Yes, I do love the Lord, and all the days of my life I will love the Lord. With my heart and soul and strength, I will love the Lord."

But sometimes it is not so easy. Sometimes God feels far away, like a friend we haven't seen in a long time, and loving Him feels abstract. Other times, He seems *all-too near*, and we are not so sure that we like this God of ours who demands so much. Sometimes we aren't sure how to love Him, and sometimes we simply forget about Him, caught up in the urgencies and distractions of the day-to-day.

To love the Lord your God, the theologians tell us, is to move with the deepest grain of the universe. It is to vibrate in tune with the universal melody, and to follow the blueprint of creation. What this means, perhaps unexpectedly, is that God's love is always near to us, and He is not so hard to love as we might think. It means that when you love the person in front of you today, when you delight in them and seek their good, you are in that very moment loving the God who has known them from eternity, who has declared them precious beyond all human understanding (Mt 25:40). *Les Mis* was right: "To love another person is to see the face of God." This is no sentimental piety. God is love, and all the universe was made from love and for love, and it is love alone that called you into existence out of the black.

— *Simeon Zahl*

February 6

Though the fig tree does not bud
and there are no grapes on the vines,
though the olive crop fails
and the fields produce no food...
yet I will rejoice in the LORD,
I will be joyful in God my Savior. (Habakkuk 3:17-18 NIV)

There are times in life when you have to throw your hands up at the sky and say, "Really?" Some circumstances are too absurd to see a divine plan in them. A weird stint at a so-so job. A relationship that never got off the ground. A long, miserable battle with cancer. Or, in the prophet Habakkuk's experience, "the fig tree does not bud...the olive crop fails."

But faith is not a rational decision we make after studying all the evidence. Faith is staked on things unseen. Martin Luther once warned against looking at "the invisible things of God as though they were clearly perceptible in those things that have actually happened." He means that just because the olive crop fails, that does not mean that God has abandoned us. Conversely, a flourishing crop does not necessarily say something about God's favor—contrary to the promises of many "Christian" preachers of prosperity. Note that some of the most unsavory characters in the world seem pretty well-off.

Habakkuk made a similar observation: Israel's enemies were mobilizing. Not good, he thought. Around him were barren crops, desolate fields. Even so, he made a decision: *I will rejoice in the Lord anyway*. There is something bald-faced about this, something audacious, defiant, and frankly insane. When our very sustenance fails, what in the world is there to rejoice about?

God, Habakkuk knows, is our Savior. Though the earth may tremble, and the fields may burn, and the forests may fall, God is our ultimate safety. This is the obstinate voice of hope. As Christians, we find our hope in our literal resurrection from death, which, in the words of Esau McCaulley, "empties...the fear of death—of its power." The barren fields are not the full story.

We may not be able to see a "divine plan," but right now, it's not for us to worry about. One day, the fig tree will bud, without any help from us. In the meantime, we can take a cue from Drake: "These days, I'm lettin' God handle all things above me" ("Jungle," 2015).

— *CJ Green*

February 7

He answered, "I was sent only to the lost sheep of the house of Israel." But she came and knelt before him, saying, "Lord, help me." He answered, "It is not fair to take the children's food and throw it to the dogs." She said, "Yes, Lord, yet even the dogs eat the crumbs that fall from their masters' table." Then Jesus answered her, "Woman, great is your faith! Let it be done for you as you wish." And her daughter was healed instantly. (Matthew 15:24-28)

We're born accountants, and fairness is our currency.

It begins in childhood, when we monitor every glance, every hug, every piece of candy for a sign that our siblings are getting more than we are. *Mom, it's not fair*, we cry, whenever we perceive the slightest imbalance in the ledger. We carry the scales with us throughout our lives, through friendships, into the workplace.

Even in our marriages. *With all my worldly goods I thee endow.* But not my services. It's *your* turn to cook dinner, to do the dishes, to clean the bathroom, to change the diapers.

When it comes to fairness, though, Jesus is a terrible accountant. In this passage from Matthew, he says he was sent *only* to the lost sheep of the house of Israel; in that sense, it is *not fair* to take the children's food and throw it to the dogs. But Jesus is simply unable to stick to the script. He is unable to carefully measure out his love and give it to those who deserve it, in the exact amount that they have earned. He is constantly bringing too much food to the table and letting heaping portions of leftovers fall to those who have earned nothing at all.

And thank God for that.

— *Michael Sansbury*

February 8

Blessed be the God and Father of our Lord Jesus Christ,
who has blessed us in Christ with every spiritual blessing
in the heavenly places, just as he chose us in Christ before
the foundation of the world to be holy and blameless before
him in love. (Ephesians 1:3-4)

Red Auerbach was one of the greatest basketball coaches of all time. When he coached the Boston Celtics in the 1960s, he won nine championships in ten seasons. His teams, led by players like Bill Russell and Sam Jones, were also vital in breaking down racial barriers in the NBA. All in all, he won the title sixteen times in his 29 years with the Celtics.

Auerbach famously loved cigars. Whenever a win seemed assured, he would fire up a cigar right there on the bench and smoke it for the rest of the game. For the Boston faithful, Auerbach's lit cigar became the ultimate symbol of victory. Restaurants in Bean Town would often post a sign reading, "No cigar or pipe smoking, except for Red Auerbach."

There's no evidence that God smokes cigars. But in the above passage, St. Paul declares, "God chose us in Christ before the foundation of the world to be holy and blameless before him in love." Paul declares that our victory—the victory of our being forgiven, of our being loved unconditionally, of our being made new, of Christ's love as the last word—has been assured since "before the foundation of the world."

I'm picturing Jesus sitting on the bench during the game of life, watching us play. He's watching us dribble down the court and trip over our own feet. He's watching us occasionally pass the ball to teammates while mostly hogging it. He's watching us throw some elbows under the basket. He's watching us make a few baskets while often missing the backboard completely.

And all the while, he's smoking that cigar. As St. Paul put it, "This grace was given to us in Christ Jesus before the ages began" (2 Tim 1:9).

I can almost smell the cigar smoke.

— Jim Munroe

The LORD spoke to Moses, saying: Speak to Aaron and his sons, saying, Thus you shall bless the Israelites: You shall say to them,

> The LORD bless you and keep you;
> the LORD make his face to shine upon you, and be gracious
>   to you;
> the LORD lift up his countenance upon you, and give you
>   peace.

So they shall put my name on the Israelites, and I will bless them. (Numbers 6:22-27)

"Let me give you a blessing," my grandfather says as we hug goodbye. I step back, and he makes the sign of the cross on my forehead, praying over me these words from Numbers 6.

We have gone through this ritual for as long as I can remember, and it has become quite the spectacle now that I've grown taller and my grandfather has started shrinking. At some point, I realized that my grandfather was actually quoting scripture, reciting a blessing handed down from God himself.

God gave this blessing to Aaron to bestow upon the Israelites. The same Aaron who had helped the Israelites build a golden calf to worship. And the same Israelites who would go on to wander in the wilderness for forty years, after failing to take the Promised Land as God had commanded. Regardless, God remained faithful to them, promising to bless and keep them; and ultimately, God remained faithful to *us* when this blessing was fully realized on the cross.

By his obedience, Jesus paved the way to mend our broken relationship with the Father, to give us the opportunity to be so close to him that "his face [can] shine upon you"—to open us up to receive the grace and peace he offers.

So often, we think of blessings from God in terms of prosperity—material possessions, worldly comforts. In this blessing, God doesn't necessarily promise that lake house you dream of, yet what he offers is no less tangible. Jesus was born as a fully flesh-and-blood human. A real person whose blood poured out. He's a real savior whose outstretched hand pulls us to himself, whose shoulders carry our burdens, and whose arms are unceasingly available for a welcoming, loving embrace.

— *Margaret Pope*

February 10

Why are you cast down, O my soul,
   and why are you disquieted within me?
Hope in God; for I shall again praise him,
   my help and my God. (Psalm 43:5)

You would not be a human being if you did not carry around a certain amount of sadness. Sadness comes from any number of sources. There are the things you've done or things that have been done to you. There is the omnipresence of suffering in a world beset by sin. There is the melancholy that exists for no apparent reason.

Repressing sadness, though tempting, is always a bad idea. Although you may want to run from sadness, it will track you down in other forms: rage, anxiety, or a kind of alienating superficiality. Repression does internal harm, and more often than not, harms those around you with its acted-out ramifications.

There is a fairly famous poem by 13th-century mystic poet Rumi. It's called "The Guest House." It acknowledges the reality, and even the gift, of sadness:

> This being human is a guest house.
> Every morning a new arrival.
> A joy, a depression, a meanness,
> some momentary awareness comes
> as an unexpected visitor. (Coleman Barks, translator)

Rumi continues that these unexpected visitors have "been sent...from beyond." All things come from God. That's why, with the psalmist, we can say to our downcast souls, "Hope in God; for I shall again praise him, my help and my God."

Heavenly Father, thank you for being our help in times of hurt or despair or need. Please open the eyes of our hearts to see you at work in our lives today, through Jesus Christ our Lord. Amen.

— Paul Walker

February 11

> [Martha] had a sister named Mary, who sat at the Lord's feet and listened to what he was saying. But Martha was distracted by her many tasks; so she came to him and asked, "Lord, do you not care that my sister has left me to do all the work by myself? Tell her then to help me." But the Lord answered her, "Martha, Martha, you are worried and distracted by many things; there is need of only one thing. Mary has chosen the better part, which will not be taken away from her." (Luke 10:39-42)

The story of Mary and Martha can easily fit into a narrative of all of the unfair stories in the Gospel. Like the workers in the vineyard (Mt 20) or the prodigal son (Lk 15), we can put Mary in the category of the one who is not *doing* anything and yet is still God's beloved. And if that song makes your heart sing, then go ahead and belt it out.

But Mary was not doing nothing. She was hearing everything. Even her position, seated on the floor at the feet of Jesus, suggests the position of rabbinical students at the feet of their holy teacher. When Jesus tells Martha that Mary has chosen the better part, he is telling us that Mary has chosen to hear the Story. Mary is taking the time to learn who Jesus is. And she is learning that those late-to-the-grapes employees and that derelict younger brother are her people. And that Jesus is her savior.

We all want to defend Martha. Because, like her, we believe that if we can just keep moving, then we will not have to face the horrible and beautiful truth. We will not have to hear the Story. If we scrub all of the grime from the stovetop, perhaps we can also scrub away our addictions, affairs, and hurtful ways. Perhaps we can make ourselves clean.

And who could blame us? We live in a Martha culture. We define ourselves by the cleanliness of our houses and less by the cleanliness of our hearts. The former feels tangible and doable. But the latter feels like an impossible task. How could we ever live without sin?

We cannot. But we can count on and learn from the sinlessness of Jesus, who came to save us from ourselves.

51

Jesus famously said that the poor will always be with us. Well, so will that dirty kitchen.

So take a metaphorical (or an actual) seat on that unswept kitchen floor. Stare up at the One who calls you beloved. The dishes will still be there in the morning.

— *Sarah Condon*

And the peace of God, which transcends all understanding, will guard your hearts and your minds in Christ Jesus.
   Finally, brothers and sisters, whatever is true, whatever
is noble, whatever is right, whatever is pure, whatever is
lovely, whatever is admirable—if anything is excellent or
praiseworthy—think about such things. Whatever you
have learned or received or heard from me, or seen in me—
put it into practice. And the God of peace will be with you.
(Philippians 4:7-9 NIV)

These words are often said as a part of a benediction, or blessing, at the
end of church services, sending the congregation out of the building with
a reminder that there is a peace beyond their understanding that protects
them. "Transcends all understanding." For those of us who find comfort
in knowledge and understanding, even when it's not our own knowledge
and understanding (thank you, modern medicine), it can feel daunting that
there is something that transcends all understanding. *All* understanding.

At the same time, even those of us who long to understand may find
comfort that there is a peace that transcends all understanding. Even the
limits of our own understanding are unknown to us—we don't even know
what we don't know. Our understanding of the natural world is constantly
changing. We can be grateful for advancements in science that increase our
understanding, while at the same time standing in awe and wonder at the
unexplainable and that which cannot be understood.

Not only is this peace beyond our comprehension, but it is a peace that
will guard our hearts and minds in Christ Jesus. We don't have to know
how it works to trust that the peace of God will guard our hearts and minds.

Biblical scholars tell us that Paul likely wrote this letter from prison, and
we can picture him saying these words to himself as much as to the Philippians, willing himself to think of "whatever is true, whatever is noble, whatever is right, whatever is pure, whatever is lovely, whatever is admirable."
And, even from our own personal captivity, we can pray these things for
ourselves, too, and the God of peace will be with us.

— *Carrie Willard*

February 13

The LORD answered Moses, "Is the LORD's arm too short?
Now you will see whether or not what I say will come true
for you." (Numbers 11:23 NIV)

My rather short grandmother had this wonderful pair of salad tongs she used when she needed to reach the top shelf of her kitchen cabinets. But my child-self saw something completely different. My grandmother had a superpower: very stretchy arms! The adult me knows better—there is no magic in a pair of metal salad tongs.

In this passage from Numbers, the magic has begun to disappear for God's people. Tired of the all-manna-all-the-time menu, they start to complain, loudly. God proposes a solution. He will give them all the meat they could eat, not once, not twice, but for a whole month! Moses is nonplussed. There are 600,000 mouths to feed. How exactly is this supposed to work? Moses rather sarcastically suggests emptying the sea of fish or barbecuing whole herds of cattle or flocks of sheep. I can only imagine that there was a moment of ominous silence before the Great "I AM" broke it with a question: "Is my arm too short?"

God doesn't ask if Moses is up to the task. God hasn't asked Moses to do anything, except to make the announcement that "the Lord will give" and to see what happens. It isn't Moses's attention to detail, smart planning, or skillful use of the resources available to him that has provided for and repeatedly saved God's people. It is God.

We figure out pretty quickly that life is full of stuff well beyond our reach or ability to accomplish. The problem is, our inability doesn't make that stuff go away, and worst of all, it can't make death go away. Fortunately, as Moses learns over and over again, our inability isn't a problem for God. Those same hands that were nailed to the cross, as Ephesians 2 tells us, were the very same ones that "raised us up with him and seated us with him in the heavenly places in Christ Jesus." On the cross, death was proclaimed dead and was replaced with life forever—no salad tongs required!

— *Joshua Retterer*

February 14

> And if I have prophetic powers, and understand all myster-
> ies and all knowledge, and if I have all faith, so as to remove
> mountains, but do not have love, I am nothing. If I give
> away all my possessions, and if I hand over my body so that
> I may boast, but do not have love, I gain nothing.
>
> Love is patient; love is kind; love is not envious or boast-
> ful or arrogant… Love never ends. (1 Corinthians 13:2-4, 8)

This passage is often read at weddings, but verses 2-4 are not really romantic. They're about empty performances. And there are certainly performances in marriage. Who doesn't want to be the sanctified spouse in the picture-perfect relationship? But Paul says that no matter how well we perform, we are *nothing* if not anchored by love.

What are the ways you perform? The early Christians in Corinth were spouting prophecies, bragging about spiritual gifts, and most dramatically, suffering persecution ("hand[ing] over my body") in order to reap personal acclaim. It's no coincidence that in its earliest usage, the Greek word *eucho-mai* meant "pray," but it also meant "boast."

Today, we boast about successful careers, higher education, well-behaved children, and political "righteousness." No sooner have many of us awoken than we are scanning headlines, arming ourselves with information to show off: "Didn't you hear about…?" "I read that…" But what are we doing, really? Often, we are trying to be impressive. We are looking for someone to say, "Wow! You know your stuff." We are looking for love.

In today's verse, Paul writes of a love deeper than admiration, deeper, even, than romance. This is a love that loves regardless of status and cir-cumstance. This love endures when prophecies cease, when current events become obscure trivia, when our houses of sticks fall to the ground.

This love is God, who is patient, and kind. God envies your obsession with everything that distracts you from Him, but God won't be easily angered. God humbled Himself in the form of an innocent man who was killed for the forgiveness of sins. God keeps no record of wrongs. And when you reach your lowest point and no longer have the energy to keep up the performance, God will be there: protecting, persevering, neverending.

— *CJ Green*

February 15

Cain said to his brother Abel, "Let us go out to the field."
And when they were in the field, Cain rose up against his
brother Abel, and killed him. Then the LORD said to Cain,
"Where is your brother Abel?" He said, "I do not know; am
I my brother's keeper?" And the LORD said, "What have
you done? Listen; your brother's blood is crying out to me
from the ground!" (Genesis 4:8-10)

In his novel *East of Eden*, John Steinbeck makes use of this tragic Bible story.
A character named Adam gives his father a stray puppy for his birthday,
and his father loves that dog! His brother Charles saves up his money to
give his dad a German-made pocket knife, but he never sees his dad use it.
Overcome by melancholy and jealousy, Charles savagely beats his brother
Adam almost to the point of death.

Cain, like Charles in Steinbeck's novel, cannot seem to handle the fact
that God, for reasons not clearly presented, prefers his brother Abel's sacrifice (vv. 4-5). Cain not only beats his brother—he kills him.

Genesis 4 is a dark mystery, and I don't pretend to divine all its secrets.
While Cain's treachery is clearly on display, the passage also manages to
paint brilliantly a picture of what alienation feels like. Alienation feels like
a lack of love from the one whose love we crave the most. Alienation feels
like "not enough," like our gifts and contributions don't measure up. Alienation can lead to murderous anger and bitter regret.

Cain's brother's blood "cries out" to God, yet God in His mercy puts a
special mark on Cain to protect him (v. 15). It will take some time for the
blood of another "brother" to atone for all our grievous sins. Christ our
Brother will put a new mark on us, not the mark of Cain but the mark of
the cross. Christ assures us that, regardless of what we feel in our most
alienated moments, the Father truly does love us.

— *Larry Parsley*

February 16

As a father has compassion for his children,
  so the LORD has compassion for those who fear him.
For he knows how we were made;
  he remembers that we are dust. (Psalm 103:13-14)

Much of the Episcopal burial service, as well as the core of the liturgy for Ash Wednesday, is focused on the principle that we are made of the dust of the earth, and will return to it when we die. Someone I knew refused to have anything about "dust to dust" read at her funeral. That fact said a lot about her life as she understood it.

On the contrary, this is the psalm I want read at *my* funeral. Why? Because it outlines the gospel and describes the true nature of God. He is always merciful and gracious, He removes my transgressions as far as the east is from the west, and He has compassion for me in my limitations. God is not surprised by my sin or my weakness. He remembers that I am merely dust. Sure, "fearfully and wonderfully made" (Ps 139), but nevertheless, I am but dust.

What would it mean for me to remember on a daily basis that "I am but dust"? Would this not be a most helpful prayer for the kind of humility I desire as a follower of Jesus? Might it help me to admit my sin and failure more quickly, and avoid getting caught in the paralyzing mire of guilt and shame?

He remembers that I am dust. Can I? *Lord, have mercy.*

— *Mary Zahl*

February 17

"No one has ascended into heaven except the one who descended from heaven, the Son of Man. And just as Moses lifted up the serpent in the wilderness, so must the Son of Man be lifted up, that whoever believes in him may have eternal life." (John 3:13-15)

There is something quite paradoxical about the way of God. It contravenes our expectations. We tend to think that the way to health and healing is to run away from suffering and distress, to simply avoid the dark corners of our lives and "always look on the bright side of life" (*Life of Brian*, 1979). But Jesus says just the opposite. The key to breaking out of the wheel of sorrows—and its recidivistic cycle—is to acknowledge the negativity in our lives. Recognizing the illness is the very occasion for the cure.

In the above passage, Jesus points back to Moses and a grim period in Israel's history. Lost in the wilderness, they were being attacked by a deadly plague of snakes (Num 21:4-9). As the bodies began to pile up, Moses put a snake on a staff, and everyone who looked to this snake was kept safe. The cause of despair was the path toward healing. It's like when Pamphilus, in Thornton Wilder's novel *The Woman of Andros*, saw "how strangely life's richest gifts flowered from frustration and cruelty and separation."

The cross of Christ forces us to look head-on at life's sins and cruelties. To see not some abstract tragedy, but our selves, our sins, our sorrows, our tragedies, our failures, our core problems, united to Jesus in his hanging on a tree. To see in that moment the sins of humanity united to the very being of God, who is love. God is not indifferent to our sorrows, or removed from them, or helpless to confront them. Instead, God became the Man of Sorrows to redeem and save.

— *Todd Brewer*

February 18

> Beloved, let us love one another, because love is from God; everyone who loves is born of God and knows God. (1 John 4:7)

I love this insight from the late author/pastor/theologian Eugene Peterson: "I have developed a strong allergy to the word 'dysfunctional' when applied to persons... It's a word useful for describing machines, not persons." When we value others for what they can do rather than for who they are, then "Love, the commanded relation, gives way to considerations of efficiency." To one another, we become human doings rather than human beings.

When life becomes a problem to be solved, or a goal to meet, or a dream to achieve, or a kingdom to establish, then inevitably people become the sum of their functionality. This is a mistake of dystopian proportions, not to mention a rebellion against God's way of "doing" things.

John famously reminds us that we love only because God first loved us. Thankfully, He loved and loves us without reference to our "function" and despite our inefficiency. This is a happy reminder for many of us whose functions have been either strained or sidelined and whose efficiency is in neutral or possibly reverse.

> *O God, you have taught us to keep all your commandments by loving you and our neighbor. Grant us the grace of your Holy Spirit, that we may be devoted to you with our whole heart, and united to one another in self-giving love; through Jesus Christ our Lord. Amen.*

— *Paul Walker*

February 19

"The LORD your God, who goes before you, is the one who will fight for you, just as he did for you in Egypt before your very eyes, and in the wilderness, where you saw how the LORD your God carried you, just as one carries a child, all the way that you traveled until you reached this place." (Deuteronomy 1:30-31)

Unlike the Israelites, most of us are not currently lost and wandering through an actual desert. Yet it's easy to see that the thoroughfares of our lives are indeed littered with their own unique wildernesses. Because of sin and the Fall, every last one of us is lost, lonely, hurting, thirsty, and *searching*. We are, like the Israelites, helpless as little children. We are also, like the Israelites, in the habit of taking our survival into our own hands.

In the darkest thickets of my own wilderness, I look to be carried through by another person, like my husband. When he cannot fully come through, I turn to something like food, drink, entertainment, or online shopping—anything that might make the thorny brambles, the arid nothingness of the wild, more endurable. Yet none of these things can suffice.

This passage from Deuteronomy, and God's intimate care for the Israelites throughout their very real, very barren desert, puts even the strongest of spouses and stiffest of cocktails to shame. God names our pitiful state, and he says he's got this. He says he is going before us, clearing the path for our weary legs; he says we can drop our limp fists, he will do the fighting for us; he says that when we are out of gas, out of life, when we are full-stop out of hope, he will do the hoping for us. He will carry us all the way through. And it will be as easy for him to do all this as a father lifting a small child.

Standing in the terrible midst of your own wilderness, can you remember how God has previously carried you? If not—if the mud is thick around your ankles—then look to the cross for your certain rescue. Remember the proof in Jesus that God loves you, goes before you, fights for you, and provides for you. Know that because of the resurrected Christ, *he is in the midst* of carrying you.

— *Charlotte Getz*

How long will you assail a person,
  will you batter your victim, all of you,
    as you would a leaning wall, a tottering fence?
Their only plan is to bring down a person of prominence.
  They take pleasure in falsehood;
they bless with their mouths,
  but inwardly they curse. *Selah*

For God alone my soul waits in silence,
  for my hope is from him.
He alone is my rock and my salvation,
  my fortress; I shall not be shaken. (Psalm 62:3-6)

"Vulnerability" is a buzzword in the psychology sphere these days. TED Talks and social science bestsellers promote the need to stand honestly before our friends, families, coworkers, and teammates—to *own* who we are with courage. To do so, the experts say, is to be brave, and will foster the belonging we so desperately crave.

It certainly is brave to be vulnerable, if you're the psalmist, because it's not far from social suicide. "Vulnerability" is not *risking* injury—it is *assuring* it. Nobody but God is worthy of your trust. To live in the world of relationships is to be shaken, to be toppled, to be battered by those around you. All of you, the psalmist says, speak pleasantly face to face, but secretly "take pleasure in falsehood." *Schadenfreude* runs rampant.

Where, then, are we left? We live our lives inevitably surrounded by (and dependent upon) gamers, schemers, liars, and climbers—people just like us.

This psalm is all about low expectations. It basically says that nobody, nowhere, at no time, can provide the absolute sense of trustworthiness and belonging you seek. "Those of low estate…those of high estate…they are together lighter than a breath" (v. 9). While the parades of strength continue unabated from the cradle to the grave, they are as expendable as the air you're breathing now, a puff of smoke. Nothing but God is worthy of your trust.

Don't be vulnerable, then, in order to be strong. That's a fool's errand. Be vulnerable because your weakness lies in strong and trustworthy hands. "On God rests my deliverance and my honor; my mighty rock, my refuge is in God" (v. 7).

— *Ethan Richardson*

February 21

Therefore prepare your minds for action; discipline yourselves; set all your hope on the grace that Jesus Christ will bring you when he is revealed. (1 Peter 1:13)

Terminator 2: Judgment Day (1991) is far superior to *The Terminator* (1984). Considered to be one of the best sequels ever made, its use of computer-generated imagery changed everything for moviemakers. If it wasn't for Skynet's T-1000 in *Terminator 2*, the Marvel Cinematic Universe would simply not exist.

The plot of the second (and third, and fourth, and fifth, and sixth *Terminator*, or any tangential installment) is like the first: Peril arrives from an unavoidable future controlled by computers and war machines seeking to destroy humanity. That James Cameron, Linda Hamilton, Arnold Schwarzenegger, and so many of us cannot restrain ourselves from "the Terminator loop" suggests that, in life, the future feels precarious at best. It is not hard to see why. The auguries of our current *anno Domini* imply that a future of our own making, one as monstrous as the one controlled by Skynet, is in fact coming for us, and is coming to destroy us.

But the Spirit of Jesus will not leave us alone. In 1 Peter, the apostle delivers a divine word from the future to address our present dismay. He says the future is inevitable. The day of divine judgment awaits each and every one of us.

According to Peter, there is no secret about what's going to happen on that day. He says we already know. As an ambassador of our Eternal Judge (aka the Friend of Sinners), the apostle assures us that just as God's grace and peace have been multiplied to us in this life, there is even more where that came from. He promises that there is "a salvation ready to be revealed" and more "grace that Jesus Christ will bring you when he is revealed."

Peter's good news about the future is a bulwark against any accusatory shape-shifting android sent to us by the evil powers of this world. The future is *all grace*. It is one lavish gift, and *Jesus Christ will bring it to you when he is revealed.*

— *Stuart Shelby*

February 22

"Let anyone with ears listen!" (Matthew 11:15)

As a preacher, I take comfort in the fact that, even with his best material, Jesus often bombed. He frequently encountered stiff resistance from the audience. Folks would look down at their cell phones and move on with their lives, unaffected by his words.

In what history has since judged to be a pretty darn good speech, Jesus used the words "*Let anyone with ears listen.*" When someone does not have ears to listen, they simply will not listen. You can marshal your best communication skills, make your most persuasive arguments, use expressive hand motions, raise the volume to eleven, and still they will not hear you. We all have a confounding predisposition to remain deaf to the truth about ourselves, and about God.

I remember when my youngest daughter first realized that I had a glass eye. I explained to her how, years ago, I had lost my eye in a car wreck. This information blew her seven-year-old mind. She had no category in which to place this troubling new reality: "How can that be? You mean you really can't see anything at all with that eye?" "No, honey. Not a thing." Then she asked, "But what if you really tried?!"

Not all problems in life can be fixed by trying harder. That's part of what it means to be human. Spiritually, we are blind. We are deaf. Trying harder does not change our basic incapacities when it comes to our most difficult problems in life. More effort will not make us "see" or "hear" God. In relation to God, we remain blind and deaf, no matter how hard we try.

In the New Testament, the worst cases of deafness were with people who could not hear the Word of God Himself, the Son of God, speaking words of truth *directly to them.* If Jesus himself could not get through, who could? Our problem in relation to God is generally much worse than we think. We can't hear God by trying harder. Our incapacity is so profound that we can't perceive God even by ramping our efforts "up to eleven" (*Spinal Tap,* 1984). Something else must happen. Someone must intervene on our behalf. Our hope lies completely in the God who unstops deaf ears and opens blind eyes.

— *Drew Rollins*

February 23

David danced before the LORD with all his might; David was girded with a linen ephod. So David and all the house of Israel brought up the ark of the LORD with shouting, and with the sound of the trumpet.

…David returned to bless his household. But Michal the daughter of Saul came out to meet David, and said, "How [glorious was the king of Israel today], uncovering himself today before the eyes of his servants' maids, as any vulgar fellow might shamelessly uncover himself!" David said to Michal, "It was before the LORD…that I have danced… I will make myself yet more contemptible than this, and I will be abased in my own eyes; but by the maids of whom you have spoken, by them I shall be [glorified]." (2 Samuel 6:14-15, 20-22)

The ark is dangerous, because the glory of God is there. Once, the Philistines captured the ark in battle and suffered so greatly from its presence that they sent it home to Israel on a driverless cart. Israel's priests come before it only with utmost caution, vested, purified, at the right time and saying the right things. No one else is to touch it. There is no freedom before the ark. It must be handled in a manner befitting its solemn, invisible glory.

David's handling of the ark is not solemn. He has not purified himself and is no priest, but he dons a priest's garment and prances about before God and everyone, his wife Michal included, leaving nothing to the imagination. David's freedom, his utter, reckless abandon, is shameful to her. It is not glorious, like the majesty of a king one should barely catch sight of; David is lewd and far too visible.

It is a curiosity of Christian art that every gory bit of the crucifixion can be shown, except for the Lord's naked flesh. We wear the death of the Son around our necks, but the shame of his splayed body is too much for us. Like Michal, we feel that keeping peace with the Almighty requires that some things be kept hidden, out of sight. They cannot be seen, cannot be said, perhaps cannot even be thought. Both God and our body of sin must be veiled, as with a priest's linen apron, or Jesus' imaginary loincloth. Only then are we safe.

When David dances before the Lord, the veil of glory is removed, and David is not ashamed. Like a child sprinting around the house after his bath, he is free in his Father's presence. To Michal and all who seek God in glory, this is contemptible; but to the servants of servants, to the lowest of the low, to those who hide themselves in shame, it is hope and faith. So David dances, getting low, lower all the time, low until he is the spitting image of his promised Son, by whom David—and you, with all the low—shall be glorified.

— *Adam Morton*

February 24

[I]n the place where it was said to them, "You are not my people," it shall be said to them, "Children of the living God." (Hosea 1:10)

Romeo and Juliet were doomed from the start. At the infamous balcony scene, the young lovers, exchanging gushy romance, question the power of their family's surnames. "What's in a name? that which we call a rose / By any other name would smell as sweet," says Juliet, before asking Romeo to exchange his last name for her love. Without his family name, Romeo would be the same person, right?

In the book of Hosea, God disagrees with Juliet. He intervenes in the prophet Hosea's marriage, and declares the names of his three children. The first is named Jezreel, after a city where Israel will experience a great defeat. It's like a Frenchman naming his child Waterloo, or a Virginian naming her child Gettysburg. The second child is named Lo-ruhamah, meaning "no mercy." The third child is named Lo-ammi, meaning "not my people."

In these names, God announces his frustration with Israel. Israel made a longstanding commitment to their God, one that had been in place for nearly a thousand years, and Israel was not faithful to their end of the deal. They have begun to import and worship idols, and God likens it to infidelity. So God uses Hosea's marriage as a reflection of that broken promise, and the product of Hosea's infidelity is defeat, rejection, and no mercy. And yet, the passage also ends with a promise: The names will be changed. Jezreel will become a place of future victory, God will forgive broken promises, and the people will once again be welcomed as "Children of the living God." These names will one day change and mean their opposite.

God knows your name, and he knows the unfaithfulness that comes along with it. He knows your defeats, and he knows your family history. He knows your bad reputation, and he knows where your name is mud. It's only through God's love, more potent than the romance of Shakespeare's famous lovers, that our names lose their baggage. To quote The Rock (not St. Peter, but professional wrestler Dwayne Johnson), "it doesn't matter what your name is!"

— Bryan Jarrell

> "Or suppose a woman has ten silver coins and loses one. Doesn't she light a lamp, sweep the house and search carefully until she finds it? And when she finds it, she calls her friends and neighbors together and says, 'Rejoice with me; I have found my lost coin.' In the same way, I tell you, there is rejoicing in the presence of the angels of God over one sinner who repents." (Luke 15:8-10 NIV)

Is there any better feeling than finding something that has been lost? It's often better than obtaining something new: Not only can you hold the item in your hand again, but the mental itch of The Missing has been scratched in a most satisfying way. For those of us who have ever lost a child, even for only a moment, we know that every second is agony. The moment the child is returned to our arms, we feel like we might never let them go. We call our neighbors and friends to rejoice that what was lost has now been found.

In the same way, each one of us is so, so precious to God. Jesus says there is *rejoicing in the presence of the angels* over the found one. This verse brings to mind the scenes in NASA documentaries and movies, when the engineers in mission control, all short-sleeved business shirts and pocket protectors, high-five each other, exchange hugs, and wipe surprising tears from their eyes when their mission is a success. There is rejoicing in the relief of a mission safely accomplished.

"In the same way, I tell you, there is rejoicing in the presence of the angels of God." Each one of us is sought and found by God's love, and we can rejoice in that.

— *Carrie Willard*

February 26

"So it was not you who sent me here, but God; he has made me a father to Pharaoh, and lord of all his house and ruler over all the land of Egypt." (Genesis 45:8)

A couple of things stand out to me about this passage. The first is that it is soaked in tears: Joseph's, primarily, which both precede and follow verse 8, and his family's. In his younger years, Joseph so angered his brothers that they left him for dead after he recounted to them his dreams—dreams in which he became more powerful than them. Turns out those dreams came true, as he has since ascended to a senior leadership role in Egypt. Years of famine have impelled the brothers to seek grain from the man who controls its distribution: their long-lost brother, who is now brought to tears by their mere presence. Verse 1 says that "Joseph could no longer control himself...and he cried out." Cried out so loudly, in fact, that the whole house of Pharaoh could hear him. *Awkward!* But so overwhelmed by love is Joseph for the family who betrayed him that he cannot—nor does he care to—conceal his emotions.

This is what grace does to a heart: changes it, leaving it raw, and open, and unconcerned with appearing put-together or composed or anything but *real*. Joseph had been saved by the grace of a God who found him and led him safely to Egypt. In my own life, tears have often been an indicator of the Spirit at work, moving deeply within my heart beyond what words could express.

The other thing that stands out in this passage is the rightful recognition of who's in charge. Joseph knows, even in his position of power, that he is not the "master of his fate" or "captain of his soul." Those roles are above his pay grade, for it is and always has been God who engineered circumstances to bring him to this exact moment. With God ultimately in command, as Julian of Norwich says, "How can anything be amiss?"

These tears, and this recognition of who is really in control, come from a kinglike figure here in the form of Joseph but point to another King, who not only wept but bled, who not only revealed his emotions but allowed himself to be stripped of all dignity. "Not my will, but yours," Jesus said in the garden, headed to his own foreshadowed destiny, so that we could know once and for all: When it's God telling the story, we will always end up right where we should be.

— *Stephanie Phillips*

February 27

O LORD, I am thy servant;
I am thy servant, the son of thy handmaid.
Thou hast loosed my bonds. (Psalm 116:16 RSV)

This verse gives voice to one of the key and normative indicators of good religion. Everybody has "bonds," ranging from actual, visible chains, if you are a legal prisoner or a kidnapping victim; to emotional chains, invisible but as powerful and constricting as the former; to demonic chains, which are invisible even to the inner eye, although *some* (gifted) people can see them, and even you can, occasionally, when the gift is given.

Anyone remember the old TV show *Thriller*? The episode entitled "The Cheaters" is about a cursed pair of spectacles that allows the wearer to see and hear what is really going on around them. It is almost always bad news. Finally, the curious but foolish hero puts them on and looks in a mirror. He *dies* from the shock of seeing himself as he was.

There are visible bonds and invisible bonds. Either way, people can be confined by them, held back by them, even crushed by them. We can *inherit* bonds, and we can also make them for ourselves.

Good religion breaks chains and removes them. Bad religion doesn't realize the chains are there—except in *other* people—and treats us as if we don't have them. Good religion frees people. Bad religion makes us "kick against the goads" (Acts 26:14 RSV), causing us to give up (eventually) and hate God.

The God of the Bible is the One who breaks our bonds, mainly by an overwhelming forgiveness, and frees us.

— *Paul Zahl*

February 28

"Peace I leave with you; my peace I give to you. I do not give to you as the world gives. Do not let your hearts be troubled, and do not let them be afraid." (John 14:27)

William Barclay puts it this way in his book *The Facts of the Matter*:

> In the last 300 years, there have been 386 wars in Europe. And since the year 1500, 8,000 known peace treaties have been signed. Each one was signed with the intention that it should last forever, but the average length of each was a little over 2 years.

Plus, there are all of those personal peace treaties that you and I make that end up "in the sod." *I will* make peace with my parent/child/friend/boss/pastor over that argument, damn it. *I will* make peace with that fear of being overlooked/rejected/humiliated, damn it. *I will* make peace with my guilt over that thing that I did yesterday/ten years ago, damn it.

The extraordinary news of this verse from John is that the peace of God becomes real and is experienced —and is marvelous—not in spite of strife, but in the very midst of it and through it.

One afternoon 36 years ago, I was standing outside a small church in Nairobi, Kenya, frozen with fear after a flashback from Vietnam. A woman from the church approached me. She was well over six feet tall and not slen-der. She proceeded to invade my personal space and wrap her arms around me. I felt my fears falling away, just as leaves fall off the trees in autumn, and being replaced by a kind of peace I hadn't known was possible. I later learned that she was one of three wives to a local Kenyan man, that she spoke no English, and that she had sixteen children. She and I had nothing in common, except that both of our lives had been captured by the Lord Jesus Christ, who said to his disciples and to us: "Peace I leave with you... Do not let your hearts be troubled, and do not let them be afraid."

I can't wait to see that woman in heaven (when I'll understand Swa-hili). And I can't wait for you who are reading this to experience the loving embrace of the One who says to us, "My peace I give to you."

— *Jim Munroe*

February 29

"I give you a new commandment, that you love one another.
Just as I have loved you, you also should love one another."
(John 13:34)

What are the old commandments? Simply flip through Exodus, Leviticus, Numbers, and Deuteronomy, where you'll find the likes of these: "Do not wear clothing woven of two kinds of material." "Do not mate different kinds of animals." "Do not turn to mediums or wizards." These commandments are specific, weird, and—with a few exceptions—pretty do-able.

But Jesus announces a "new commandment," the very heart of his ministry. *Just as I have loved you, you also should love one another.* Sounds good, but he does not mean "treat others with kindness and respect, and smile at people on the sidewalk." He means *be prepared to die for others, even your enemies.* After all, that is how Jesus demonstrated his love.

This commandment has all the combined force of the old ones plus some. Not unlike when Jesus said, "Be perfect," or "Do not worry," this "new commandment" is pure, holy, good, and patently impossible to follow. Author Muriel Spark points this out in a brilliant passage from her novel, *The Comforters:*

> The demands of the Christian religion are exorbitant, they are outrageous. Christians who don't realize that from the start are not faithful. They are dishonest; their teachers are talking in their sleep. "Love one another...brethren, beloved...your brother, neighbours, love, love, love"—do they know what they are saying?

To Jesus, Peter swears, "I will lay down my life for you!" (v. 37), but immediately Jesus questions him: "Will you...?" (v. 38). Shortly after this, Peter fails to live up to his promise; in fact, when it really counts, he denies knowing Jesus at all.

Have you ever been forced to spend time with someone you detested? Maybe they had a particular smell you couldn't stand, or a grating voice, or maybe they had insufferable opinions. (Maybe this impossible person is you!) (Maybe it is me...) In any case, Jesus died for *that* person. But I am not prepared to. I, like Peter, am hardly prepared to die for the people I *like*.

If the "new commandment" outs us as sinners, then we have all the more reason to praise Jesus, because he loves when we do not. When we deny him, he goes to the cross. When we run away, he stays. When we resist, he loves. And "His mercy endures forever."

— *CJ Green*

March 1

Therefore, to keep me from being too elated, a thorn was given me in the flesh, a messenger of Satan to torment me, to keep me from being too elated. Three times I appealed to the Lord about this, that it would leave me, but he said to me, "My grace is sufficient for you, for power is made perfect in weakness." (2 Corinthians 12:7-9)

The Second Letter of Paul to the Corinthians is by far his most vulnerable letter. Here, the apostle pulls back the curtain and reveals his all-too-human struggles—from being afflicted and persecuted as a "clay jar" messenger of the gospel (4:7-10), to being "under daily pressure because of [his] anxiety for all the churches" (11:28). And yet apparently there was something even more challenging in Paul's life, something he identified metaphorically as "a thorn given me in the flesh," something that defied any effort on his part to solve it, or fix it, or take care of it, or get over it—something even too great for the Apostle Paul.

There has been much debate as to what exactly this thorn was for Paul—a besetting sin or struggle with depression, an addictive behavior or an impossible relationship, remnants of guilt or shame from his past—but he does not identify it. And yet Paul has done the same thing many of us would do with a "thorn given [us] in the flesh"—he has begged God to take it away, but God has not. Instead, God has assured Paul of something that is always greater than the thorns in the flesh of our lives: grace, God's one-way, unconditional love that surrounds and embraces us in every area of our lives, especially the thorny places.

God historically and definitively expressed this grace in the death of Jesus Christ, who bore a crown of thorns on Calvary, and who even now bears our thorns as well. This grace is inexhaustible, especially when it comes to the things that exhaust us and remind us that we are weak. It is often in these thorny areas of our lives that we experience again and again the sufficiency of God's grace, grace that is always more than enough.

— *David Johnson*

March 2

And behold, a woman who had suffered from a hemorrhage for twelve years came up behind him and touched
the fringe of his garment; for she said to herself, "If I only
touch his garment, I shall be made well." (Matthew 9:20-
21 RSV)

Christ's healings in the Gospels often put the spotlight on doubtful faith. In
this passage, the famous "woman with the issue of blood" is tentative and
does not wish to engage with Christ directly. She wants to come up *from
behind* and touch his garment. (Maybe she can do it without being noticed.)

Zacchaeus, hiding high in the sycamore tree at Jericho, just wants a look.
The man with the epileptic son says, "I believe. Help thou my unbelief!"

Later in the Gospels, every single disciple reveals himself to be a man
not "planted by streams of water" (Ps 1:3), and runs away. Even Peter's faith
turns to sand when he is provoked by the high priest's servants during the
Lord's trial.

And you and me? Our faith is horrendously weak, at least a lot of the
time. We can talk a good line, but when the rubber hits the road and we're
confronted with a giant, unbudgeable problem, our faith in its resolution
suffers decline, to say the least. (In other words, it's when we think, "That
particular issue is untouchable.")

You might say, though, that Christ made allowance for this. Almost all
his medical successes, and his psychological ones, too, were with highly
tentative people. Tentative people! This is a most provocative fact, since
it means that He could even, could even want to, meet the need of feckless,
faithless me.

I am 69 years old and have never believed this more.

— *Paul Zahl*

> Do nothing from selfish ambition or conceit, but in humil-
> ity regard others as better than yourselves. Let each of you
> look not to your own interests, but to the interests of oth-
> ers. (Philippians 2:3-4)

In our world, we are not only encouraged but expected to care for ourselves. Independence and self-sufficiency are highly respected ideals and make us feel good about ourselves. But in reality, besides the fact that true inde-pendence is unattainable, it also does not satisfy like giving and receiving from others.

When my husband became a pastor, our extended family came to town to celebrate his ordination. We were proud of him for his hard work in sem-inary and for his accomplishments. One day during this visit, my mother-in-law asked me to step into the other room, and there before me, all shiny and new, was a beautiful table that I had been wanting. She had purchased it for *me* as a gift for *his* ordination! I shed the kind of tears that only a truly unexpected and undeserved gift can bring.

Christ did not give himself what he deserved, and he deserved better than what we take for ourselves. Paul says that Christ, "though he was in the form of God, did not regard equality with God as something to be exploited" (v.6). The one who was completely entitled to take all of the power and riches for himself did not. Instead, he became a servant washing his disci-ples' feet, spending time with sinners, and dying like a criminal. He relied on God to lift him up. Paul continues, "Therefore God also highly exalted him and gave him the name that is above every name" (v.9). This same Heavenly Father, who exalted Jesus, also has our needs in mind.

The command to be humble and put others above ourselves does not equate to "do this and then you will receive that," because in Christ every-thing has already been given. It is this unconditional gift that will allow us to become more concerned with others than ourselves. As a wise pastor (okay, my husband) once said, "Receiving undeserved love is the fuel for loving others."

— *Juliette Alvey*

March 4

> But the LORD said to Samuel, "Do not look on his appear-
> ance or on the height of his stature, because I have rejected
> him; for the LORD does not see as mortals see; they look on
> the outward appearance, but the LORD looks on the heart."
> (1 Samuel 16:7)

The notion that "mortals...look on the outward appearance" is indeed terrifying, and it's absolutely true. Did you spend any time in front of the mirror
this morning? I certainly did, and I discovered afresh that age grows hair
where it shouldn't, and vice-versa. The amount of time and resources we
spend on trying to win the image game is exhausting.

But the next thing the LORD says to Samuel is even more terrifying:
"the LORD looks on the heart." Here's the reality of the human heart: "The
heart is devious above all else; it is perverse—who can understand it?" (Jer
17:9) When God looks at our hearts, he does not see something beautiful.
He sees deceit, sickness, and sin.

And yet God looks at our sin-sick hearts and loves us still. He loves us
as we are, not as we should be. And it's not a sappy, "I'm okay, you're okay"
kind of love. It's a love that says, "You're not okay, but I'm going to intervene
on your behalf, and rescue you." And through Jesus' work on our behalf,
through his life, death, and resurrection, God has forgiven us, given us his
very righteousness, and reconciled our hearts back to himself.

In *The Hammer of God*, the blessed Bo Giertz put it this way:

> The heart is a rusty old can on a junk heap. A fine birthday
> gift, indeed! But a wonderful Lord passes by, and has mercy
> on the wretched tin can, sticks his walking cane through it and
> rescues it from the junk pile and takes it home with him. That
> is how it is.

And a heart that is safe at home with God is a heart that can finally learn to
look to God with trust and faith, and turn to his neighbor in love. Remember what Martin Luther wrote in his *Heidelberg Disputation*: "The love of
God does not find, but creates, that which is pleasing to it."

— *Curt Benham*

March 5

> For in [Jesus] every one of God's promises is a "Yes." For
> this reason it is through him that we say the "Amen," to
> the glory of God. (2 Corinthians 1:20)

We have a God who makes promises and keeps promises. From the small
pains of living this side of heaven, to the large and devastating traumas each
of us is bound to encounter at some point, this truth is a safe place where
we can hide. *We are loved and kept by a God who makes promises throughout
scripture, and in his time and in his way, he keeps those promises.*

God has promised healing (Is 57:18-19). He has promised never to condemn us (Rm 8:1). He has promised peace (Phil 4:6-7). He has promised steadfast and everlasting love (Jer 31:3). He has promised to fight for us, to go
before us, to help us (Ex 14; Dt 31:8). He has promised to be our portion and
our satisfaction (Ps 16; 37:4). He has promised to never leave us, to always
be with us (Dt 31:4; Mt 28:20). He has promised to carry us, to sustain us,
to give us strength (Is 41:10). He has promised us eternal life where there
will be no more tears, no more suffering (Jn 10:28; Rev 21:4).

In his time, in his way, because of Jesus, all of these promises are a
wild and improbable *yes*. What are you struggling with today that, by all
appearances, sounds like a "no" from God? Friend, by God's grace may you
cling to the certain hope that in Christ, all of God's promises to you are a
resounding *yes*.

He *is* healing you, he *is* fighting for you, he *is* loving you, he *is* your
satisfaction, he *is* with you, he *is* making all things new, and he *is* carrying
you straight toward eternity—where all his promises come to their fullest,
most magnificent fruition, where your real story actually begins. Amen and
amen to this glorious, promise-keeping God!

— *Charlotte Getz*

March 6

"Food will not bring us close to God." We are no worse off if
we do not eat, and no better off if we do. (1 Corinthians 8:8)

Food nourishes our bodies. It brings people together. Food fosters tremendous creativity. It is, as they say, one of the best things there is to eat. Ha. The rise of foodie culture has been a net win for the human palette. What is your favorite meal?

Yet food also incites an inordinate amount of hiding and shame. Maybe you're a person who has a chocolate stash. Maybe you've lied to a spouse when asked to explain a fast-food charge on your bank statement. Or maybe you've heard yourself say things like, "Oh I was *bad*, I had a brownie"; or "I'm not eating that tonight, I'm being *good*." Good? Bad? What?

Much as we enjoy chowing down, for many of us, meals double as dramas of discipline, deprivation, and self-satisfaction, or conversely, indulgence and guilt. A source of joy, yes, but also pain. No wonder we talk so much about "comfort food." Life is hard.

I remember one night during a particularly stressful period. It was late, and I was hungry. So I wandered downstairs, under the auspices of needing to turn off all the lights. What I actually did was consume an entire box of my kids' Girl Scout cookies. And then I burst into tears.

I felt better for the few minutes that I was actively downing Thin Mints, and then terrible for the rest of the night. I was looking to food for something it couldn't give me.

Paul clearly recognized the power that food could exert over hungry men and women. He knew the anxiety it could produce, especially among religious folks worried about purity. Perhaps that's why he went to pains to relativize it. Food will not bring us close to God, he writes. Full stop.

Paul understood that God relates to you and me not on the basis of calories or carbohydrates, but on the basis of his Son, this Jesus who sat down to eat with sinners, who fed those who could not feed themselves.

What's more, he promises us that the real banquet is yet to come.

— *David Zahl*

March 7

> Then [Noah] sent out the dove from him, to see if the waters
> had subsided from the face of the ground; but the dove found
> no place to set its foot, and it returned to him to the ark,
> for the waters were still on the face of the whole earth. So
> he put out his hand and took it and brought it into the ark
> with him. He waited another seven days, and again he sent
> out the dove from the ark; and the dove came back to him in
> the evening, and there in its beak was a freshly plucked olive
> leaf; so Noah knew that the waters had subsided from the
> earth. Then he waited another seven days, and sent out the
> dove; and it did not return to him any more. (Genesis 8:8-12)

One morning while reading this passage, I began to think about prayer in
a whole new way.

As Genesis 8 opens, Noah, his family, and a bunch of zoo animals have
been stuck inside the ark for five months. At last, the boat has come to rest
in the mountains. A "wind" is blowing outside (interestingly, the Hebrew
word for "wind" is also the same word for "spirit"), but inside the boat,
"Project Evaporation" is happening at an agonizingly slow pace.

What Noah does next I find fascinating. He releases first a raven and
then a dove. The raven does not return, but the dove flies and flies without finding a place to perch and eventually comes back to Noah. A week
later, Noah releases the dove again, and this time it returns with "a freshly
plucked olive leaf." One week after that, Noah releases the dove for the
third time, and this time it does not return, signaling the renewal of creation.

Prayer is like that. Sometimes we feel trapped in the dark, without even
a tiny window into the mind of God. Our prayers boomerang back in our
faces, leaving us to question whether the Spirit is truly at work. At other
times, even though we don't get the specific answer we seek, God does
bring something "green" and fresh into our dark and damp lives—not the
full answer we seek but a little, vital artifact of hope.

And then there are those glorious times when our prayer receives the
signal that our long-awaited answer has arrived. In the meantime, by God's
grace, we keep opening the window and releasing our prayers into the wild.

— *Larry Parsley*

March 8

Jesus, full of the Holy Spirit, returned from the Jordan and was led by the Spirit in the wilderness, where for forty days he was tempted by the devil. He ate nothing at all during those days, and when they were over, he was famished. (Luke 4:1-2)

This year my Lent was going to be the greatest in the history of all penitential seasons. I had pledged to go to bed every night at 9:30PM. This seemed achievable and wise. Not overly spiritual or diet-related. It was all with the goal in mind that I would be a more patient mother in the morning. I am one of those people who swear they will go to bed by 10PM, but then I discover a vortex of reality dating shows or British baking dramas and suddenly it's midnight and I've eaten an entire bag of Dove chocolates.

But not this year. This year I was going to get eight hours of sleep and be one of those mothers who bakes muffins *in the freaking morning*. Big plans. I had a vision of motherhood that included early morning yoga, perhaps some quiet time with the Lord, and constantly smiling at my progeny.

Then, on the Thursday after Ash Wednesday, the second day of Lent, our son broke his arm. And I realized that my Lent was going to consist of sleeping with a third grader to help him prop up his arm and praying to God he doesn't accidentally whack me in the face with his cast in the middle of the night. Again.

This Lent, I will be giving my son sponge baths and consoling him through a missed baseball season. So I will not be the kind of mom I had planned on becoming. But God is positioning me firmly in his own kind of motherhood for me regardless.

We always come at Lent like we are going to shape God. Like we are going to tell him all about our willpower and our devotion to him. We are, in so many ways, a bit like the devil in this passage, making Jesus an offer about us that he cannot refuse.

Only, he does refuse. God takes our plans and pushes them further this season. He pulls them apart and puts them back together. In so many ways Lent is the season when Jesus shapes us.

— *Sarah Condon*

March 9

"The LORD is my rock, my fortress, and my deliverer." (2
Samuel 22:2)

Did you ever have a Nintendo? I grew up playing the original 8-bit version.
We played *Super Mario Bros* for countless hours back then. One of the cool
things about *Super Mario Bros* (and many other video games in its wake) is
that it has secret extra boards. I'll never forget the underwater bonus level.

On a related note, do you know about the secret 23rd Psalm in the Bible?
It's not one of the famed 150 contained in the actual book of Psalms. That's
right, there's another Psalm of David at the end of 2 Samuel, in chapters
22 and 23. I think of it as basically a bonus level. The secret bonus Psalm
covers much of the familiar material found in the most recognizable Psalm
with verses like: "In my distress I called upon the LORD…" (22:7).

The opening verse reiterates that great biblical sentiment: "The LORD
is my rock, my fortress, and my deliverer." An especially interesting detail
lies in the moment in which it occurs. Even after the defeat of Goliath, the
Israelites are persecuted by the Philistines for years. 2 Samuel records four
more battles with them, long after David's famous initial victory.

As with most problems, the situation with the Philistines proves to be a
recurring one. You finally recover from an ailment only to have it reemerge,
or have a new health issue develop in its place. I remember a friend, who,
after recovering from a knee replacement, was diagnosed with melanoma.
Fortunately it was treatable, but then came a terrible fall that required
months of corrective surgery. Similarly, the Philistines are a relentless threat.

And when they come against David after that legendary initial victory,
to everyone's surprise, this time David is exhausted (21:15). The next three
battles are won, not by David himself, but by his fellow soldiers. The victory belongs to him, in a sense, but he did not win these subsequent battles
alone. So it is, in fact, with every conquest: "The LORD is…my deliverer."
God deserves the credit for every success, and not we ourselves.

Are you currently facing the reemergence of some difficulty? Perhaps
this time you need to turn to your friends for help. Ultimately God is the
one who can get you through, just as before. Only this time, perhaps you
see things more clearly.

— *John Zahl*

March 10

Weeping may linger for the night,
but joy comes with the morning. (Psalm 30:5)

It is an understatement to say that I follow the University of Virginia's sports teams. I'm obsessed, and too much of my mental health is caught up in their football and basketball programs, but that's for another devotion or session with my therapist.

The psalmist's words in this passage will always remind me of the Virginia Cavaliers' unprecedented loss as the overall #1 seed in the 2018 NCAA Men's Basketball Tournament. They were the first and only number #1 to ever lose to a #16 seed. It was a traumatic event (again, back to therapy).

But Coach Tony Bennett responded by quoting this psalm. His words were so soothing at the time because they grounded the horrible event, the horrible mistake, the horrible pain, in a larger context. As followers of Jesus, we understand this all too well—we commemorate Good Friday before we celebrate Easter Sunday. At my church, the congregation confesses our sins before receiving Communion. We acknowledge that pain is part and parcel of our lives, but that the sun (and the Son) does rise from the East.

What makes you weep today? It may well be the same thing that caused you pain yesterday and the day before. It may be something that you want comfort for and pray God will vanquish from your life.

Whatever makes you weep, remember these words of the psalmist: Joy comes with the morning. We know this because, as his friends wept at the tomb, Jesus was in that very same moment seeking them out. He was coming back for them to bring joy and the good news of his resurrection.

Don't just believe the Bible on this one. In 2019, just one season after their devastating loss, the University of Virginia Cavaliers won the NCAA Men's Basketball Championship. And there was joy even for Wahoos like me.

— *Willis Logan*

March 11

> Jesus took with him Peter and James and his brother John and led them up a high mountain, by themselves. And he was transfigured before them, and his face shone like the sun, and his clothes became dazzling white. (Matthew 17:1-2)

The transfiguration, according to Thomas Aquinas, is Jesus' "greatest miracle." Apparently it reveals the perfection of heaven, the glory of our Lord and Savior. But all that happens is that Jesus' face shines "like the sun," and his clothes become as "white as the light" (NIV).

I have never liked this passage. Reading it always leaves me disappointed, because I sense that it's supposed to be more impressive than it really seems to be. Imagine staring straight into the sun. This, we are told, is the glory of God. Honestly, I would hope the Lord is *more* than a lightshow.

Which is why I wanted to pay this scene special attention. I have found that God is often trying to teach me something in the places I am most loath to look. So I reflect on the passage. I search for the story's "second ply," and what I begin to notice between the lines is the springtime. You know this feeling. You've been inside all winter. Your toes haven't seen daylight in months; then arrives the first blast of warm air, and you step outside, and the sun, ever so gently, begins to warm your skin. There is nothing quite like the feeling of thaw. If in his glory Jesus shines "like the sun," then this is what being with Him might feel like: *relief*.

But the sun is also blinding. When you take a photo into it, the image becomes blank and white, irreversibly so. There is no editing software that can recover what has been washed out by the light. In his transfiguration, Jesus is revealed to be a photographer's worst nightmare, a dizzying flash, subsuming all darkness. And though the transfiguration itself lasts only a little while, the light has come to stay.

Essentially, an overexposed photo is just a white rectangle—like a clean slate, or a blank canvas, which is frightening for the very same reason it is exciting: It is a place of endless possibility. So maybe Aquinas was onto something, I don't know. But when dreaming of the glory of God, it's best to dream big. And let your imagination run wild.

— *CJ Green*

March 12

> We declare to you what was from the beginning, what we
> have heard, what we have seen with our eyes, what we
> have looked at and touched with our hands, concerning the
> word of life— (1 John 1:1)

We have in Jesus, as the hymn goes, a great High Priest whose name is Love
("Before the Throne of God Above"). This Jesus is a real person who, history agrees, lived and breathed and moved and died. The in-the-flesh-ness
of Jesus is one of many things that stands out to me as convincing about
the Christian faith.

God's love for us has a physicality to it. It is not obscure or intangible.
His love can be felt, seen, tasted, heard, probably even smelled. Throughout
the Bible, God's love for his people shows up as manna, a voice, a pillar of
smoke, a raging fire. In its fullest expression, it shows up as an actual person.
And there are a great many witnesses to everything this Jesus did in life, in
death, and after death. At the time, thousands of people *heard* Jesus, they
saw him, they *touched* him, they *knew* him. And because of the cross, *we*
walk around physically and spiritually united with that same Jesus—each
one of our names graven on his hands, written on his heart.

Beloved, because of the cross, God's love is every bit as touchable, see-
able, and knowable as it was when Jesus actually walked the earth. His love
is, in the words of Mary Oliver, like "fires for the cold, ropes let down to
the lost, something as necessary as bread in the pockets of the hungry." In
King Jesus, who is the steadfast, God's love for you is personal and pointed,
not broad and spread out and general. It is specific. It has an object. It is
there with you. It is warm and unwavering and selfless. It makes gestures.
It is active, held captive, always working. It delights, it is particular, and it
is *ever fixed on you*. This is the Word of *life*.

*Lord, give us the grace for today to sense your very real, very pres-
ent nearness and love.*

— *Charlotte Getz*

> So for the second time they called the man who had been blind, and they said to him, "Give glory to God! We know that [Jesus] is a sinner." [The man] answered, "I do not know whether he is a sinner. One thing I do know, that though I was blind, now I see." (John 9:24-25)

Being honest is often a hard thing to do. I don't actually mind it when someone prefaces their opinion with "Well, to be honest…" because I just don't think someone being genuine, I mean *truly* honest, is something to take for granted. If you're a people-pleaser, it's often more important to be liked than to be honest. If you're a romantic, you might sometimes prefer to live in an idealistic world than to live in the real one. Even if the truth is the very thing that sets us free, all too often, we simply "can't handle the truth."

In these two verses, the Pharisees are out to condemn Jesus for healing a blind man on the sabbath. They confront the man and try to pressure him into discrediting Jesus by saying that Jesus is a sinner. The man doesn't even try to refute their claim; he simply tells them what he knows. He has no agenda to convert the masses or debate the issues. He's just thrilled that, after a lifetime of blindness, he can see! Whether he knows it or not, his plainspoken honesty does, in fact, "give glory to God." Later, after this man is thrown out of the temple for disrespecting the Pharisees, Jesus comes to find him and tells him that he is the Son of Man, to which the man replies by believing and worshipping Jesus on the spot.

This passage tells us that Christianity is not a worldview to be argued or a platform to be pitched, but an experience to be lived. Jesus breaks into people's lives and gives sight to their blindness. What more is there to say?

One more thing: In the areas of your life that are still too painful to face, you can take comfort in the fact that, while you might not be able to handle the truth, God can.

— Sam Bush

March 14

> Every generous act of giving, with every perfect gift, is from above, coming down from the Father of lights, with whom there is no variation or shadow due to change. (James 1:17)

Grace is not always guaranteed to *work* on the horizontal plane—that is, as we attempt to generously give grace in the midst of our relationships. We can, however, be sure that grace is always *at work*. We don't get to define what this has to look like. We don't always get the privilege of discerning its results or activity. In fact, grace specializes in disappointing and confounding our expectations of what God and His people "should be."

The gospel confronts our self-righteousness and confirms the righteousness of Jesus as being ours. You're free, though you often feel like a slave. You're forgiven, though you often feel the weight of judgment. You're victorious, though you often feel like a chump. We walk by faith, not by sight, yes, but rarely in an experiential or functional manner.

Most of the time, grace is extremely impractical. In many cases, it is probably not in your best interest to extend grace toward another person— if you're like me and you desperately want life and relationships to stay safe, comfortable, and problem-free. Sometimes, we give people grace and they still don't change. Sometimes, we're gracious toward our enemies and they still retaliate. Sometimes (or maybe often), we concede in our relationships and people still take advantage of us. And we resent it, even though we know we should "count it all as joy."

God doesn't guarantee that if we "apply the gospel" to our lives, we'll always see the results we want, but He does promise that in Christ, we are always bearing fruit. Grace doesn't always fix the problem, but grace *can* use a difficult circumstance to change us.

And yet, there are times when grace leaves us broken. God doesn't always intervene when life and relationships create dissonance (though I wish He would). But Christ is alive to intercede for the forgiveness of our sins.

Ultimately, the generous gift our Father gives is the word of the gospel implanted in our hearts, working in tandem with the indwelling Spirit, articulating the incredibly ridiculous verdict that never changes: *You are absolved.*

— *Jason Thompson*

March 15

> And [Jesus] rolled up the scroll, gave it back to the atten-
> dant, and sat down. The eyes of all in the synagogue were
> fixed on him. Then he began to say to them, "Today this
> scripture has been fulfilled in your hearing." (Luke 4:20-21)

This passage in Luke is one of my favorites in the Bible. As Stefon from
SNL would say, these verses *have it all*. There is a reference to the God and
traditions of the Old Testament. There's a shout-out to a prophet. And,
most importantly, there's the acknowledgment of Jesus as the fulfiller of all
those hundreds-of-years-old prophecies. He is, quite literally, the Word(s)
brought to life.

In the Bible's best mic-drop moment, Jesus informs this crowd—his
hometown crowd, no less—that he is the long-awaited Messiah. Such a
reveal would have been (and clearly was, if you read on) jarring for the audience, who expected a stately king and instead got "Joseph's son" (hardly the
worst thing they'd called him—see Mark 6:3 for an ancient Near East burn).

Jesus is undeterred by their doubts. Following the custom of the day, he
stands to read the scrolls, but sits to teach. And his teaching is this: I AM.

I am the fulfillment of scripture. I am the Anointed One. I am the one
bringing good news to the poor, proclaiming release for the captives and
recovery of sight for the blind. I am the one letting the oppressed go free.
I am the one proclaiming the year of the Lord's favor (a time on the Jewish
calendar during which all debts were forgiven). This is good news indeed
for those who count themselves as poor, captive, blind, oppressed, or in
need of favor. Which we all are, of course.

One thing he doesn't mention from Isaiah's prophecy? The "day of vengeance of our God." There was no need to announce the coming of God's
vengeance to the people, because it was not coming to them. It was coming, instead, to *him*, to the Messiah, whose ministry—indeed, whose life—
was one long walk toward Calvary, where he was the recipient of divine
vengeance.

Fulfillment and completion. The answer to every question that matters.
Vengeance swallowed up by love. What better news could there be?

— *Stephanie Phillips*

March 16

The wise have eyes in their head,
but fools walk in darkness.

Yet I perceived that the same fate befalls all of them. Then
I said to myself, "What happens to the fools will happen to
me also; why then have I been so very wise?" And I said
to myself that this also is vanity. For there is no enduring
remembrance of the wise or of fools, seeing that in the days
to come all will have been long forgotten. How can the wise
die just like fools? (Ecclesiastes 2:14-16)

It is one of the priceless gifts of my life that I was born into a family of wise
Christian people, especially my father and grandfather. Recently, I went
with one of our sons and his young family to the gravesite where these parents and grandparents are buried. Our son spoke of them to his children.
He was visibly moved as he recalled his grandparents; what a wonderful
influence they had had on his young life. He wanted his own children to
know about them, and to remember them in this short visit to the cemetery.

But apart from photos and stories, his children did not actually know
these fine people, and my son did not know my grandparents, also buried
there. It was a salutary lesson. All of us are short-lived and will scarcely be
remembered, even if we have lived lives of exemplary Christian wisdom.

This passage from Ecclesiastes is a bit of a shock, for riches and fame are
easily targeted as "things passing away," while we think wisdom is to be
sought. None of us wants to be a fool. Yet even the wise die and are soon
forgotten. What, then, is lasting? What about my life, if anything, will last
beyond the grave?

*O Lord, show me the things which will last, and root out any
vanity in me, even my seeking after wisdom.*

— Mary Zahl

March 17

"I am the good shepherd. I know my own and my own know
me, just as the Father knows me and I know the Father.
And I lay down my life for the sheep." (John 10:14-15)

The first time I heard the term "spirit animal" was from a fellow student at seminary who asked me, with all seriousness, if I had discovered mine yet. Such is the formative terrain of the Episcopal Church!

I suppose that I have since chosen the red-winged blackbird as my own. When asked about their spirit animal, people will answer "bald eagle" or "lion" or perhaps "stallion." One animal no one has ever chosen is "sheep." Sheep are not particularly intelligent, inspiring, or independent. Sheep, being sheep, are easily led astray.

Well, Jesus has chosen your spirit animal for you! Lo and behold—you are a sheep! Me too! And so is everyone else who has ever lived. The good news is that being a sheep disabuses us of having unrealistic expectations of ourselves. And the better news for those we interact with is that we are also relieved of the high expectations we put on other people.

Sheep need a shepherd—a Good Shepherd—to take care of them. Fortunately, we can and should have high expectations of our Shepherd. He has already proved Himself by laying down His life for us.

Jesus, you are our Good Shepherd. Grant that when we hear your voice we may know that you call us each by name. Please make us follow where you lead. Amen.

— Paul Walker

March 18

For a brief moment I abandoned you,
    but with great compassion I will gather you.
In overflowing wrath for a moment
    I hid my face from you,
but with everlasting love I will have compassion on you,
    says the LORD, your Redeemer. (Isaiah 54:7-8)

Many times in scripture, God tells us that he will never leave us or forsake us. And yet that is not the on-the-ground reality of the life of the Christian. In this passage in Isaiah, the Lord is honoring our perceptions. God does not abandon his people, but it certainly seems that way sometimes. And God, in his great mercy, does not say that we are crazy for feeling that way. In fact, he says that from our perspective, that is exactly what happens. We feel abandoned—it appears that the Lord is not on the throne, and that if he is, he is apathetic to me. That is not true, but it feels true. Our feelings may lie to us, but they're still real.

Instead of God telling us that we are faithless and feckless and earthly-minded (true accusations if there could ever be any), he tells us that those feelings of abandonment are real. In our circumstances, we feel that we are often far from the Lord, that we are abandoned and that he is angry. We are not, and he is not, but for us, we are and he is. He does not call us to repent of our misleading feelings. No, he enters into them with us and reminds us of his truth.

With great compassion he will gather us. No matter our abandoned feelings, he is coming with everlasting love and with great compassion to snatch us back up. He is our Redeemer.

There is a distinct contrast in time here: Our afflictions are momentary, but his redemption is eternal. May we look up, away from despair and toward the One who saves. May we look up and know that despite our felt abandonment, he is coming, and his gathering will be everlasting.

— Ann Lowrey Forster

March 19

As they were coming down the mountain, [Jesus] ordered
them to tell no one about what they had seen, until after
the Son of Man had risen from the dead. (Mark 9:9)

A lot of people have beach scenes on the background of their phones and
laptops. I have a sunset scene from the Yellowstone River. It's like an amulet for bad times, a small way to beat back the despondency of daily life.

Nobody wants to suffer. Not even Jesus wanted to suffer. But we do
suffer. Suffering is an inevitable fact of life. I think this is what Jesus was
trying to communicate to Peter as the two of them descended the mountain
after the Transfiguration. Peter has just experienced a monumental blessing,
a splendorous foretaste of the great Happily Ever After—but now he must
go back down the mountain, re-enter the fog, and suffer the dirt and fatigue
and de-lumination that, most of the time, life just plain *is*.

But we do not suffer alone, and sometimes a prayer can go a long way,
especially if we need courage to face what's ahead. Here's one for today:

*Lord Jesus, I know that your way is the Way of the Cross, that
in your suffering came our salvation, but I admit that it still
doesn't sound too inviting right now. As I step out into this new
territory, denial sounds much easier. Not a good idea, maybe,
but easier.*

*Of all the things I fear—the uncertainty, the hopelessness, the
need of others—I am most afraid of experiencing it alone. Lord,
please give this coward the courage to follow you into the pain of
today. Please give me the assurance that you've gone there ahead
of me. Help me believe the promise you give us: "I will never leave
you or forsake you."*

— Ethan Richardson

March 20

"No one shall be able to stand against you all the days of your life. As I was with Moses, so I will be with you; I will not fail you or forsake you. Be strong and courageous…"
(Joshua 1:5-6)

The Dutch Catholic priest Henri Nouwen once joined the circus. He began as a spectator but returned again and again until the trapeze artists, the Flying Rodleighs, asked him to tour with them for a week. Nouwen learned the secret of high flying from the leader of the troupe, Rodleigh: "As a flyer, I must have complete trust in my catcher… The secret…is that the flyer does nothing and the catcher does everything… A flyer must fly, and a catcher must catch, and the flyer must trust, with outstretched arms, that his catcher will be there for him."

In this passage from Joshua, Moses has died, and his assistant Joshua must now lead the people into the Promised Land. We can only imagine how Joshua must have felt following in Moses' footsteps: inadequate, discouraged, helpless, overwhelmed. God assures Joshua, however, that it was never about Moses' wisdom, courage, or strength, but about God's presence: "As I was with Moses, so I will be with you."

In effect, Joshua is being told to trust the "catcher" who will always be there for him. God's presence is with us, too: Emmanuel, Christ Jesus, who did not forsake us when we were sinners in need of a Savior.

You may be holding onto the bar of life today, instead of trusting the grace that Christ died to bring. But in the crazy circus that is your life, the "catcher" is already there and has been there since you were conceived in the womb (Ps 139). You will not be forsaken because God has promised to be with you all the days of your life, including this one.

— *Marilu Thomas*

March 21

I lift up my eyes to the hills—
 from where will my help come?
My help comes from the LORD,
 who made heaven and earth...
 he who keeps you will not slumber.
He who keeps Israel
 will neither slumber nor sleep. (Psalm 121:1-4)

So how did you sleep last night? Did you wake up refreshed, alert, ready for the day? If you're anything like me, then, um, *no*. You tossed and turned. Maybe you woke up to pee at 1 A.M., and your arm fell asleep under your pillow, and you hit snooze thrice, then at last sat up groggily with a kink in your neck.

In theory, we spend a third of our lives asleep. It is a necessary, natural part of life, but sleep can also be hard. Sleep is the image of utter passivity. For several hours every night, we enact the posture of death. It means complete surrender, and we hate to do that. We try to control it. *I must log eight hours*, we think; *I must sleep now!* But you can set aside countless hours and still sleep fitfully. Maybe, on your worst night, no matter how much time you carve out for it, you can't sleep at all.

I have always failed at sleep. As a child I used to lay awake, counting sheep in a panic. My first truly comforting experience of God was on one of these nights. I had been taught that, waking or sleeping, God was always with me. Knowing this, I was calmed. I didn't nod off immediately but I didn't have to, either; in any case, I knew I was going to be all right.

In Genesis 2, the Lord "caused a deep sleep to fall upon" Adam, the first man; and during that sleep, the Lord fashioned Eve, Adam's partner. When we are out of control, God is in control; while we rest, God still works. He "will neither slumber nor sleep." In *The Inward Journey*, Howard Thurman tells the story of a woman who wakes and greets each morning, saying, "This is the day the Lord has made. I will rejoice and be glad in it." And at night she says to herself, "This is the night which the Lord has made. I will relax and rest in it." May you relax tonight and all nights, knowing that your Maker never sleeps. God is with you, even at night.

— CJ Green

March 22

> "Woe to you, scribes and Pharisees, hypocrites! For you are
> like whitewashed tombs, which on the outside look beauti-
> ful, but inside they are full of the bones of the dead and of
> all kinds of filth. So you also on the outside look righteous
> to others, but inside you are full of hypocrisy and lawless-
> ness." (Matthew 23:27-28)

A friend of mine loves to tell his crab story to illustrate just how out of
touch with reality he can be sometimes. He went to the doctor because he
had been experiencing heart palpitations. The doctor also found that his
blood pressure was through the roof. She asked him, "Have you been under
a lot of stress lately?" He said no, no more than usual. She asked him if he
could walk her through a usual day.

"Well," he said, "I have been taking the kids to school before work. And
I've been traveling for work lately. And I'm taking a couple night classes.
And my wife and I are planning to put in a new kitchen. And my father-in-
law's been sick..." He went on, casually, for about ten minutes. Then he
said, "But we're cooking crab tonight, my favorite!"

The doctor looked at her chart, and looked at him, and reported, "As
your doctor, I want you to know: You *are* under a lot of stress lately."
She continued, suggesting maybe his favorite food was crab because he
was one—"growing more and more in love with your boiling pot." As the
demands of his life had gone up, he kept adjusting to a more excruciating
new normal. His heart palpitations were just the latest signal that he was
almost cooked.

Your day-to-day life is one of the slyest ways to lose sight of what matters. You do not need a family crisis to increase the temperature of your
stock pot; you can do that all on your own. All you need is a free weekend
and a to-do list. It feels good to cross each item out, to take care of business.
But the thrill of your own competence easily becomes addictive and, as an
overfunctioning crustacean, you lose your feeling for the waters you were
meant for. Life in the boiling pot becomes the only life you know.

So it is with the woeful Pharisees, and why Jesus is trying to coax
them out of the righteousness game in the passage above. They're "killing
it" everywhere—professionally, socially, even spiritually—and it's killing

them. Jesus commends to these dying crustaceans all the hope they (and we) ultimately have: Let yourself out of the stockpot of your own competence and start to feel your own pincers again. Only then will you feel again what matters and who you really are: one beloved, barnacled creature in a deep, blue sea.

— *Ethan Richardson*

March 23

"I was in the city of Joppa praying, and in a trance I saw a vision. There was something like a large sheet coming down from heaven, being lowered by its four corners; and it came close to me. As I looked at it closely I saw four-footed animals, beasts of prey, reptiles, and birds of the air. I also heard a voice saying to me, 'Get up, Peter; kill and eat.' But I replied, 'By no means, Lord; for nothing profane or unclean has ever entered my mouth.' But a second time the voice answered from heaven, 'What God has made clean, you must not call profane.'" (Acts 11:5-9)

In this passage, we see the death of Peter's holiness. At least, what he thought was his holiness. Peter thought of himself as a good guy. There were rules in the Torah about what you could eat: no bacon, no cheeseburgers, and definitely no bacon cheeseburgers. Peter had followed the rules and kept kosher.

But in Acts 11, on a rooftop in the coastal city of Joppa, God tells Peter to break the rules. He shows Peter a vision of lobster rolls, wild boar, and turtle soup. And lots of bacon cheeseburgers. When he tells Peter to dig in, Peter promptly clutches his pearls: "Well, I never! Lord, you can't be serious!" Peter is wedded to his self-perception as a rule-follower.

To see oneself this way is spiritual poison. Peter was so focused on patting himself on the back for clean eating, he missed the elephant in the room (or on the plate): He was a sinner saved by grace.

Peter, so concerned with his holy diet, needed to remember who he was. The night Jesus was arrested, right before his crucifixion, Peter publicly betrayed Jesus three times. Jesus, after his resurrection, forgave him. By Acts 11, however, Peter had moved away from being a forgiven sinner to a righteous rule-follower.

How about you? If you are more aware of how many points you've scored for God, you may need to hear God tell you to break some rules. This passage invites you to remember that because of Jesus, scorekeeping is over. The refs have all gone home. You are someone about whom God has said, "I love and forgive that one." Don't run back to the law after the gospel has set you free.

— *Aaron Zimmerman*

March 24

> Again the anger of the LORD was kindled against Israel, and he incited David against them, saying, "Go, count the people of Israel and Judah." So the king said to Joab… "Go through all the tribes of Israel…and take a census of the people, so that I may know how many there are." (2 Samuel 24:1-2)

> Satan stood up against Israel, and incited David to count the people of Israel. So David said to Joab… "Go, number Israel… and bring me a report, so that I may know their number." (1 Chronicles 21:1-2)

These passages recount the same event, which is fated to always be the Bible's second most famous census. The two stories are alike except in a few details, one of which is startling. In 2 Samuel, it is the Lord who incites David to count the people. In 1 Chronicles, it is Satan.

How can that be? How can God (or Satan) incite David to act and then, as we see later in each chapter, David get the blame? These are not hypothetical questions; they describe things that actually happen, not only to David but to us. The two accounts tell us what Bob Dylan sang: "Well, it may be the devil or it may be the Lord / But you're gonna have to serve somebody."

We would hope we could at least tell them apart, because we think knowing makes all the difference, but it is not so. In the midst of suffering, we will never be able to tell God's hand from that of Satan or any other agent, nor would it make much difference if we could. In these situations, God is so deeply hidden that he appears as his opposite; he opposes us.

The difference between God and all others is finally shown, not merely in God's unfathomable power, but specifically in his mercy. David prays to fall into the hands of God rather than of humans, for God has promised himself to David. Even though he punishes, he will relent according to his word. Where God has made you a promise, he is no accuser, no enemy, no threat, but your savior, simply and only.

— *Adam Morton*

March 25

> After this, when Jesus knew that all was now finished, he said (in order to fulfill the scripture), "I am thirsty." (John 19:28)

When Jesus cries out on the cross, "I am thirsty," he is saying, in the simplest and most profound way, that he completely identifies with all of the different ways in which you and I thirst.

When I was in the fourth grade and my sister was in the second, the core of our relationship was not sacrificial, self-giving love. One afternoon after school, she and I were having a fight in our house. At one point, I punched her in the stomach, and she opened her mouth to cry. Without thinking, I reached down and grabbed a spray can sitting on a table. It was a chemical called DDT that killed bugs in the garden. It was so poisonous that, years later, it would be banned.

As my sister began to cry, I stuck the can in her face and sprayed DDT into her mouth. At that moment, my mother appeared in the room. She grabbed my sister, ran out into the street, flagged down a car, and raced off to the hospital. Thankfully, my sister would be fine, but at the time I didn't know that.

I went into my room, sat down on my bed and waited. I waited for the end, which I knew was not far off. After a half-hour, the front door opened. I heard my father's steps on the stairs. I knew that the apocalyptic second coming was about to happen; the final judgment was at hand.

My father walked into my room. He saw the sorrow and the guilt and the despair on my face. Then he did something that has permanently affected my life. He simply opened up his arms. I burst into tears and ran toward him. He folded me in his embrace.

My father understood how I thirsted for grace, and he opened his arms. But I know whose arms those really were. Those were the arms of my Lord, stretched open on the cross. And it was the voice of my Lord, telling me that I was forgiven, and that I was loved.

Come unto me, says the man on the tree, all you who are thirsty, and I will give you the living water of redeeming love.

— *Jim Munroe*

March 26

Consequently, faith comes from hearing the message,
and the message is heard through the word about Christ.
(Romans 10:17 NIV)

This verse serves as a road sign: *this way to faith!*

Where does faith come from? It comes from "hearing the message." It comes by receiving God's promise. This verse is a direct rebuttal to the claim that faith is the one human contribution to our salvation. Faith does not come from making the right choice, nor does it come as a result of grabbing hold of God's hand. This is because faith is not something that we are humanly capable of. The only thing that can give us any conviction that God is real and that He is with us is God saying, "I love you." This Word, the life-giving message of Christ, is the only thing that will stir any kind of conviction. Thus, all you have to do is hear the gospel. And the gospel is the birthplace of faith.

The ears, Martin Luther said, are "the only organs of the Christian." His point was that hearing is the most passive of the senses. While the watchful eye and the grabbing hand both suggest a more aggressive mode of action, the ears simply receive whatever comes their way. Their lack of filter leaves them completely vulnerable to their surroundings and, in our modern age, they often take a beating. Chances are your ears pick up jackhammers and sirens more frequently than trickling waterfalls and whispery breezes. The world is full of noise, what Ambrose Bierce once called "a stench in the ear… the chief product…of civilization," and we are at its mercy.

As Christians, we experience a God who is not seen but heard. Through scripture, we *hear* his Word (or, rather, His two words of Law and Gospel). This is what Martin Luther was getting at: that to be human is to be one to whom God speaks. And now that we've finally taken a brief moment to listen, what do we hear Him say? Do not be afraid. God is real and He is with you. Jesus Christ has died so that you may live fully and freely. He has removed your transgressions once and for all. Nothing will ever stop Him from loving you. In a noisy world, this word of comfort, the Word of Christ, is all I want to hear.

— *Sam Bush*

March 27

Your eyes are too pure to behold evil,
  and you cannot look on wrongdoing;
why do you look on the treacherous,
  and are silent when the wicked swallow
  those more righteous than they? (Habakkuk 1:13)

Putting God on trial is not an uncommon idea. Holocaust survivor and writer Elie Wiesel witnessed three rabbis in a concentration camp holding a *"beth din,"* a Torah tribunal, to see if God was guilty of abandoning his people. C. S. Lewis wrote a book of essays called *God in the Dock*—conjuring the image of God in the defendant's chair. But Habakkuk beats everyone to the punch. His three short chapters are an accusation against God's goodness and justice. Responding to the prophecy that God would bring judgment against Jerusalem through the wicked Babylonian empire, Habakkuk basically says this to God: "You say that you are good, but you're giving a wicked empire the spoils of Israel. That doesn't seem very good to me!"

Perhaps the most famous story of God on trial is Fyodor Dostoyevsky's Grand Inquisitor parable from his novel, *The Brothers Karamazov*. Dostoyevsky imagines that Jesus returns during the Spanish Inquisition, and the Church captures him and subjects him to inquiry. The charges are many: abandoning his people, not feeding the hungry when he had the power to multiply bread, allowing humanity free will to make choices that lead to great suffering. After the Grand Inquisitor finishes the list, he demands a defense. Jesus, wordlessly, stands and kisses the Inquisitor straight on the lips.

Habakkuk didn't have the benefit of seeing Jesus' death and resurrection, when God the Son stood trial against the accusations of the Pharisees. Sometimes we don't see God's full plan in action, but we read in Habakkuk that he can handle our frustrations and accusations while his plan unfolds. It is good news that you can come to God with your frustrations and accusations, and God doesn't turn away. Always remember that the death and resurrection of Jesus, God's gentle kiss to our inquisition, means that all of our suffering can eventually be redeemed.

— *Bryan Jarrell*

March 28

"O my God, incline your ear and hear. Open your eyes and
see our desolations, and the city that is called by your name.
For we do not present our pleas before you because of our
righteousness, but because of your great mercy. O Lord,
hear; O Lord, forgive. O Lord, pay attention and act. Delay
not, for your own sake, O my God, because your city and
your people are called by your name." (Daniel 9:18-19 ESV)

How is it that a prayer written thousands of years ago feels like it was written for today? Daniel's world was just as much of a mess as ours, and we can
join him in this desperate, urgent plea.

In this chapter, after consulting the prophecies of Jeremiah, Daniel per-
ceives that the exile of the Israelites is about to end, so he turns in hope to
prayer. Daniel boldly pleads with God to hear, forgive, pay attention, and
act. He emphasizes that God's people bear his name, reminding God of the
vested interest he has in the lives of his people. But he also confesses that
they have done nothing to deserve rescue and appeals to God's mercy.

All of this could be said today as we look at the world around us and
long for God's restoration. Like Daniel, we look to the end of our exile, to no
longer being sojourners on this earth, and to being brought back into God's
presence. We "groan inwardly while we wait for adoption, the redemption
of our bodies" (Rm 8:23).

Unlike Daniel, though, we are on this side of Jesus' death and resurrection, holding onto His victory over sin and death and the hope that gives
us beyond our circumstances. We have the promise of Christ's return to
deal one final blow to the Enemy and restore everything to how it should
have been all along. *Come, Lord Jesus!*

— *Margaret Pope*

March 29

He is like a tree
  planted by streams of water,
that yields its fruit in its season,
  and its leaf does not wither.
In all that he does, he prospers. (Psalm 1:3 RSV)

Frank Lake, the English psychiatrist and charismatic Christian, once wrote, "We are not meant to be self-contained, but channels of the life and energies of God Himself. From this point of view, our wisdom is to let the bottom be knocked out of our humanity, which will ruin it as a container at the same time it turns it into a satisfactory channel." My wife Mary Zahl remembers Frank saying that more than once when we were with him.

A person's thriving, over a long, persisting life, requires a sort of death to your self-contained ego, in order, as Frank Lake said, for your being to be refreshed by the welling Spirit of God the Creator. This is actually true, for static or objectified understandings of the self generally end in desiccation and death.

People used to say that my father-in-law, Mary's dad, was the man described in Psalm 1, for he was "like a tree planted by streams of water." When he died, the minister conducting the service, who had known Mary's dad for many years, said that he was the most trusted man in West Orange County, Florida. What a remarkable thing to be said of you!

The point is this: A good man or woman needs to be planted in soil that will feed and nourish, neither causing him to sink nor causing him to dry out. This person is constantly renewing, not withering, welling up eternally—unquantifiably. He or she exists next to the running water of the never-static Spirit of God.

— *Paul Zahl*

March 30

> Philip said to him, "Lord, show us the Father, and we will
> be satisfied." Jesus said to him, "Have I been with you all
> this time, Philip, and you still do not know me? Whoever
> has seen me has seen the Father. How can you say, 'Show
> us the Father'?" (John 14:8-9)

Genuine spiritual growth seems to be marked by a deepening awareness of
our spiritual blockheadedness. We just never fully *get it*. No one ever has,
evidently, judging from the performance of even God's best and brightest
students. Take Moses, for instance, whose eyes drink in a panoply of divine
wow-moments: the burning bush, the ten plagues, the Red Sea halved, Sinai
as one massive bonfire. Yet still he prays, "Show me your glory" (Ex 33:18).
Really, Moses? As if you haven't seen enough glory?

Or centuries later, there's Philip. Having seen Jesus pile miracle upon
miracle, having witnessed smoking-gun evidence that Jesus is in the Father
and the Father is in him, still he utters this foolish statement: "Lord, show
us the Father, and we will be satisfied."

From Moses ("show me"), to Philip ("show us"), to our hankering today
for God to show us a sign, awe us with a miracle, give us a sneak peek behind
the celestial curtain, there lurks this same notion: If only we could see a little more of God than what he's already shown us, then our curiosity would
finally be satisfied and our faith confirmed.

To all such desires, Christ's response remains the same: "Whoever has
seen me has seen the Father." The hands and feet of God are the hands and
feet of Jesus. The mouth that speaks, the ears that listen, the heart that
loves, are the mouth and ears and heart of Jesus. The sole face that God
shows to us is the face of Jesus. And far from being merely "enough," that
is everything.

We don't really know God apart from Jesus, since "in him the whole fullness of deity dwells bodily" (Col 2:9). He is God's complete self-disclosure.
Jesus reveals to us the fullness of God. And the good news? That fullness
means one thing: that God is *with us*, on our side, as a human who was dead,
and buried, and raised to life for us.

— *Chad Bird*

March 31

> God may perhaps grant them repentance leading to a knowl-
> edge of the truth, and they may come to their senses... (2
> Timothy 2:25-26 ESV)

To call a thing what it is and see it aright is a gift from God.

Our fleshy eyes and ears do not perceive things correctly. Quite the opposite. Left to ourselves, we see things as we want to see them, or even as we have to, in order to make life bearable. As Jack Nicholson told us, we can't handle the truth! And so our wills and minds turn, twist, and distort things in all manner of ways. As the bumper stickers wisely warn, don't believe everything you think. We simply do not naturally perceive things as they actually are.

And so we come to the central question of repentance. We often think of repentance as something we should do apart from God, on our own, as the precondition for faith. We are to repent, then believe the good news. Repentance gets twisted to mean something like being sufficiently sorry for being sinners, and it's up to us to be sorry for the way we are. Right?

What if we have a fundamental misunderstanding of repentance, and that even repentance is a gift from God? What if repentance is granted to us by Him, so that we may "come to [our] senses" and begin to behold what is truly true? This is the way the Book of Common Prayer understands it. When God absolves and frees us, He may perhaps grant us "true repentance, amendment of life, and the grace and consolation of His Holy Spirit."

What if the Word leads us to a knowledge of the truth by giving us a new set of lenses to see things correctly? What if this is what is meant by the Bible's repeated invitations to *behold, awake, arise,* and *hear*? Even our repentance is not of our own doing.

What a gift, to be led to the knowledge of what is true, that we may come to our senses and see what the Lord has done.

> *Awake, O sleeper, and arise from the dead, and Christ will shine on you. (Eph 5:14 ESV)*

— *Gil Kracke*

April 1

> For Jews demand signs and Greeks desire wisdom, but we proclaim Christ crucified, a stumbling block to Jews and foolishness to Gentiles, but to those who are the called, both Jews and Greeks, Christ the power of God and the wisdom of God. For God's foolishness is wiser than human wisdom, and God's weakness is stronger than human strength. (1 Corinthians 1:22-25)

In the crucifixion of Jesus, this world's whole matrix of norms and judgments is revealed for what it really is: blind, corrupt, and barbaric, utterly worthless in its judgment of worth. Human wisdom values the powerful and rich, but God values the weak and the poor. Human wisdom values those who are winners, those who marry the right person, who attend the right school, get the right job, own land, and don't go to jail.

By contrast, God's wisdom appears insanely foolish, the exact opposite of what we would want or expect. God values losers: lazy, unsuccessful people whose lives don't add up to much of anything, people who can't hold down a job, who can't sleep because of stress, who struggle to get out of bed, whose debts far exceed their income and whose guilt far exceeds their righteousness.

God does not operate according to the world's standard of worth, but on the basis of grace given to the *unworthy*, those who do not deserve anything. To God, we are not what we do or have done or will do, but we are loved beyond measure. In Christ, there is an amazing freedom to be completely oblivious to worldly judgments, to not follow the trends or live in fear of the performance evaluations we receive every day.

Our worthiness before God shields us from the judgments of the world—"God's weakness is stronger than human strength"—providing calm amid the storm. When the world says we are worthless losers who will never amount to anything, and holds our failures irrevocably against us, God says otherwise. When we fail to live up to worldly ideals of coolness or status, we are comforted by a God who couldn't care less about the cover of *Vogue* or *GQ*. In the shelter of God's foolishness, we are free to look foolish and walk on the path of abundant mercy, following our crucified savior into eternity.

— *Todd Brewer*

April 2

> Then Jesus cried again with a loud voice and breathed his
> last. At that moment the curtain of the temple was torn in
> two, from top to bottom. The earth shook, and the rocks
> were split... Now when the centurion and those with him,
> who were keeping watch over Jesus, saw the earthquake
> and what took place, they were terrified and said, "Truly
> this man was God's Son!" (Matthew 27:50-51, 54)

I have always been captivated by this account in Matthew. This centurion
witnessed deaths and crucifixions on a daily basis. Yet in a matter of hours,
he went from nailing Jesus to a cross, to proclaiming him as the Son of God.
What about the events of this day made such a dramatic impact on him?

He had likely made a host of puzzling observations: the quiet dignity of
Jesus, the mercy he poured over the very people who rejected him—"Father,
forgive them!" And yet the incident that took the centurion to his knees
was creation's literal groaning. Night had fallen *in the afternoon*. Then the
earth shook so powerfully that rocks split, graves were opened, and the
massive temple curtain was torn in two.

Have you ever experienced an earthquake? I have—a 7.1 magnitude
temblor that rocked my family from 100 miles away. My husband and I
were settled on the couch when the ground beneath us began to roll. The
roof and walls squealed as if on the verge of splintering. The doors and our
hanging lights swayed back and forth as if we were on an ancient ship in
the throes of a storm. Land that was supposed to be fixed suddenly turned
fluid. I have never felt so small, beneath a force so far beyond my control.
Maybe the centurion experienced a similar upheaval; tossed from his tiny
throne by the ground itself. Maybe he realized just how little he knew, so
he fell at the mercy of something much greater than himself.

God often reveals himself in ways that are massively inconvenient and
deeply disruptive to our self-revolving worlds. Beloved, have you—like
the centurion—seen God breaking down your kingdom? Are you ready to
give in? To fall on your feeble knees in full surrender to King Jesus? His
name is mercy. His name is love. He is *for you*. And he will move the earth
to reach you.

— *Charlotte Getz*

April 3

The words of the Teacher, son of David, king in Jerusalem:
"Meaningless! Meaningless!"
says the Teacher.
"Utterly meaningless!
Everything is meaningless." (Ecclesiastes 1:1-2 NIV)

No one has expressed the inner logic of the book of Ecclesiastes better than French novelist Georges Bernanos: "In order to be prepared to hope in what does not deceive, we must first lose hope in everything that deceives."

The Teacher, Solomon himself, declares his conclusion from the beginning. Everything we do is *hebel*, he says: *meaningless, fleeting, absurd, empty, frustrating, pointless, vain*. Then, for twelve chapters, he calls it out: He's been there, done that, seen it all, seen it crash and burn. Fame, fortune, achievement, power, pleasure, work, and wisdom… We seek eternity in heaps of ash and we never lay hold of it.

"Under the sun" (1:3, 9, 14)—under the aspect of temporality, within the immanent frame, after the Fall—nothing is new, everything is old and dying and passing away. "[T]he Christian religion," C. S. Lewis said, "does not begin in comfort; it begins in dismay…and it is no use at all trying to go on to that comfort without first going through that dismay." We need have no fear of missing out; we're all on the same sliding board, and a "common destiny" (9:2) awaits us at the bottom of the ride. Solomon reminds us—no, he relentlessly pushes our faces in it—that life may be enjoyed, but it can never be fully grasped.

Yet we yearn for eternity. God has placed it in our hearts (3:11) and we glimpse eternity as through a keyhole. We sense that this life is only a vestibule; the finite entryway to an infinite reality beyond. Prisoners in time, we are bent, broken, and bewildered. God's plans in eternity are not only beyond our control, they escape our understanding.

I have reached the age where there are fewer days ahead than there are behind. I still have plans and dreams and desires, ambitions of achievement and success. I can't help it; none of us can. But I will not make a dent in the universe. Solomon achieved an empire and became a broken man. It was a necessary brokenness and a difficult comfort. At the end, he remembered God (12:1), who was always there, and waiting.

— *Michael Nicholson*

April 4

"But go to my brothers and say to them, 'I am ascending to my Father and your Father, to my God and your God.'" Mary Magdalene went and announced to the disciples, "I have seen the Lord"; and she told them that he had said these things to her. (John 20:17-18)

There is a local legend of a preacher in Jackson, Mississippi. He stood up to offer a word on Easter Sunday, simply leaned into the mic and said, "It's all true," then sat down. I have heard people tell this story two ways. Some people talk about that minister like he was a lazy so-and-so with little regard for the pageantry of Easter. Such a day demands a well thought-out sermon befitting the hats, lilies, and plastic eggs! And then there are the people in the other camp. Those of us who are mystified that someone would so boldly say such a simple thing and let the gospel speak for itself.

This is exactly what I need to hear on Easter morning. I need to hear that it is actually all true. That Jesus came to rescue me. That he came to die in my place. That my sins are forgiven. Such news hits an almost unreachable spot in my heart. But Jesus manages to find it.

Resurrection rips through all of those intellectual questions that I want to throw at it: Do I have to be forgiven? Can't I just forgive myself? Why do I have to forgive others? All of those questions are just my heart's feeble barrier to keep me feeling like I have some say in the matter. Jesus rising from the dead burns that old fence right down.

I love Mary Magdalene in this moment. She is like an Olympian with a torch, running to light the next fire, racing to tell everyone this one simple thing: The light has come to stay. To love us, to die for us, and to save us from ourselves. Friends, it is all true.

— *Sarah Condon*

April 5

> ...as all die in Adam, so all will be made alive in Christ. (1 Corinthians 15:22)

If Jesus means anything, it's that God is reviving every single person and every single thing in the whole universe. Right now, we all suffer decay and loss. The resurrection says that futility isn't the end of us.

Why does Paul parallel Christ with Adam? Elsewhere, Paul calls Jesus "the image of the invisible God, the firstborn of all creation"—evoking the creation story of the first humans made in God's likeness. But Jesus is a better Adam, because Jesus is both humanity *and* God. And Jesus is both "the firstborn of all creation" *and* "the firstborn from the dead"; he has preeminent status both in and after life (Col 1:15, 18).

But it's not just for himself. When Paul compares him to Adam—who is both the mythic first human and all of humanity (the Hebrew word can mean both)—he is saying that Jesus is the same, but better, because "if anyone is in Christ, there is a new creation: *everything* old has passed away; see, *everything* has become new!" (2 Cor 5:17).

"All" comes up so many times in the New Testament: "All things" come from the Father, through the Son (1 Cor 8:6). Because we are alienated from God, God is at work through Jesus to gather up and reconcile "all things" back to God (Eph 1:10, Col 1:20). And because everything comes from and through God, Jesus is said to "fill all things," "making all things new" (Eph 4:10, Rev 21:5). And ultimately, everything that Jesus does is "so that God may be all in all" (1 Cor 15:28).

These promises can seem pretty otherworldly in the here-and-now. But since God is the one doing the remaking, God can make it tangible, too.

God, today, show me one way that you are making everything new, including me.

— Kendall Gunter

April 6

For while we were still weak, at the right time Christ died
for the ungodly. Indeed, rarely will anyone die for a righteous person—though perhaps for a good person someone
might actually dare to die. But God proves his love for
us in that while we still were sinners Christ died for us.
(Romans 5:6-8)

There is a tendency to think we need to "get our act together" in order for
God to love us. While this is a common, even pervasive tendency, theologically, it is the exact opposite of the truth of the gospel, which could not
be any more clearly expressed than in this passage from Paul's letter to the
Romans. "Christ died for the *ungodly*," Paul wrote. "God proves his love
for us in that *while we were still sinners* Christ died for us."

While we were still liars, thieves, adulterers, murderers, and addicts,
Christ died for us. While we were still grumblers, gossips, idolaters, embez-
zlers, and hypocrites, Christ died for us. While we were still slanderers,
traitors, infidels, atheists, and agnostics, Christ died for us. While we were
still narcissists, cynics, consumerists, coveters, and fornicators, Christ died
for us. Christ died for all of us sinners, no exceptions, to prove God's love
for all of us sinners, no exceptions.

When it comes to a relationship with God, the truth is that none of us is
ever able to "get our act together"; rather, we need help from God. The gospel has *nothing* to do with "the Lord helps those who help themselves" and
everything to do with "the Lord helps those who cannot help themselves." The
good news of the gospel is that God, who is indeed "a very present help in
trouble" (Psalm 46:1), did not and does not wait for us to do what we cannot
do, but instead proved, and proves even now, the truth that we are loved
as we are right now, not as we should be or could be, but as we actually are.

The late preacher and writer Brennan Manning had a mantra along these
lines: "God loves you unconditionally, as you are and not as you should be,
because nobody is as they should be." This gospel of God's unconditional
love in Jesus Christ is good news for the ungodly, and therefore good news
for me and you.

— *David Johnson*

April 7

[W]hen I am afraid,
   I put my trust in you. (Psalm 56:3)

David lived a life full of opportunities to be afraid. I think that's why, in this verse, he uses the word "when" instead of "if." It's just one of the many reasons we all love David: He's honest about the scary messes he finds himself in.

David places a definite hope in God, because, once again, he has found himself in an impossible situation—the third one this week! Hope is all he's got! Sister Wendy Beckett once wrote that, in light of God's love and goodness, "Hope accepts all disaster, understands it as disaster, but knows that fundamentally it is irrelevant... Body and soul may feel we are wasting our time. Hope smiles and ignores them."

Now, I don't picture David with a big grin on his face while writing this particular psalm. This isn't about denying reality or pretending not to be afraid when we really are. This isn't about grit—there are way too many things to be afraid of for that to work for very long. This is something different: a hope that refuses to comply with fear's demands. Fear isn't hopeful, nor does it engender trust. Hope is only viable if the object of our trust is able to follow through—and that definitely doesn't describe me. But it does describe God.

Hope requires a faith that we don't have most days, if we're honest. Fortunately, we know from Hebrews that the Source, the Author of our faith, is God (12:2). The hope we place in Him won't disappoint because it can't, whether we are feeling it at the moment or not. And that's worth smiling about.

— *Joshua Retterer*

April 8

"It is I, Jesus, who sent my angel to you with this testimony for the churches. I am the root and the descendant of David, the bright morning star."

The Spirit and the bride say, "Come."
And let everyone who hears say, "Come."
And let everyone who is thirsty come.
Let anyone who wishes take the water of life as a gift…

The one who testifies to these things says, "Surely I am coming soon." Amen. Come, Lord Jesus! The grace of the Lord Jesus be with all the saints. Amen. (Revelation 22:16-17, 20-21)

I have a habit of reading the last few lines of a novel before I start. I'm not sure when I began this practice, but my wife thinks it's crazy. I simply want to know where the journey is headed before I invest the time to read a whole book. In my mind, knowing the destination makes the journey more interesting.

If you were to start at the end and read the last few verses of the Bible before reading anything else, you would get a major spoiler. You would see the destination of God's relationship with humanity. The last verses of the Revelation to John disclose the whole story. Jesus is the root and descendant of David, the bright morning star, and he offers the water of life as a gift.

All of Holy Scripture leads to this proclamation: The grace of God is poured out for all who thirst for it. From our first moments east of Eden, humanity has longed to drink from the living water of God. For all of human history, we have wandered and searched for something—anything—to quench our thirsty souls. We know this to be true in our own lives as well. We are like travelers wandering in a desert, desperate to drink. We continually chase after each new oasis, but it always turns out to be a mirage.

Spoiler alert: There is one who offers relief. To all who thirst, Jesus says, "Come!"

— *Connor Gwin*

April 9

Thus the service of the house of the LORD was restored.
And Hezekiah and all the people rejoiced because of what
God had done for the people; for the thing had come about
suddenly. (2 Chronicles 29:35-36)

The Protestant reformers under King Edward VI sometimes referred to
their reforming king as "our Hezekiah," for Edward was zealous to tear
down "Romish idols" and to put up pulpits and pulpit preachers for the
purposes of the Word of God. And as in the time of the original Hezekiah,
the thing came about suddenly.

(It also got *overturned* suddenly, when Edward died and "Bloody Mary"
became Queen. But ultimately Edward's work was confirmed and sustained.)

The point for you and me is that a good thing can come about suddenly.
A bad thing, or bad actor, can also exit suddenly. We don't have to suppose that every good change in life is a long, hard slog, and that the tortoise
always conquers the hare.

An evangelist friend of ours frequently talks about "your suddenly,"
which she ties to "God's suddenly." What she means is that God has to
wait for no one, and for no necessary preparation, in order to act. And that
applies to anything, whether it's the removal of an obstruction or the provision of a fresh new circumstance.

Sometimes, to myself, I chide my evangelist friend, believing her to be
over-optimistic and over-positive. But no, in fact! She is on solid ground.
God turned it all around in 2 Chronicles, within a matter of days. That
turn-around became one of the most splendid moments in the entire history of Israel.

Anyway, don't rule it out. Pray—at least try it once—for a *sudden* deliverance, a *sudden* answer.

— *Paul Zahl*

April 10

> "A man had a fig tree planted in his vineyard; and he came looking for fruit on it and found none. So he said to the gardener, 'See here! For three years I have come looking for fruit on this fig tree, and still I find none. Cut it down! Why should it be wasting the soil?' He replied, 'Sir, let it alone for one more year, until I dig around it and put manure on it. If it bears fruit next year, well and good; but if not, you can cut it down.'" (Luke 13:6-9)

"Why should it be wasting the soil?" asks the vineyard owner in this strange parable, pointing to his barren fig tree. The accusation translates beyond agriculture. We all to some extent harbor anxiety about wasting money, opportunities, or especially time.

Maybe you feel like you wasted good years on a relationship that didn't work out. Maybe you feel like you wasted your education studying something you didn't really care about. Maybe you feel like you wasted much of your adult life being angry or depressed or, well, wasted. Maybe you wasted yesterday afternoon scrolling through social media. Whatever the case, the feeling isn't a good one.

Into this scenario steps the gardener, the only one who actually knows anything about fruit production. "Give it one more year," he intervenes, and then proceeds to fertilize the soil with *waste itself*, otherwise known as manure. Curious!

In her book *The Art of Memoir*, Mary Karr recalls looking through hundreds of rough draft memoirs: "With every manuscript I've ever edited—even grown-assed writers'—the traits a writer often fights hardest to hide may serve as undeniable facets both of self and story." The waste is what makes the book, you might say.

If you feel like you've wasted something important, or are doing so currently, or are afraid you will do so in the future, then hear this today: In God's economy of your life, there is no waste. In fact, that which you deem unimportant or ugly or shameful might be the means of your eventual bearing of fruit.

For what is the cross but an apparent waste? This Jesus, who had so much potential, cut down at his prime.

And yet the stone the builders rejected has become the cornerstone. Which means that nothing, no matter how wasteful it appears, is beyond the reach of God's intervention and redemption.

— David Zahl

April 11

[T]he Spirit helps us in our weakness; for we do not know how to pray as we ought, but that very Spirit intercedes with sighs too deep for words. And God, who searches the heart, knows what is the mind of the Spirit, because the Spirit intercedes for the saints according to the will of God. (Romans 8:26-27)

I have always struggled to maintain a spiritual routine. That is, the morning "quiet time"—a time of stillness in which you read your Bible, light a candle, journal prayers, etc. Recently, I was relieved to discover that I am not the only one struggling; when I confessed my shame over not being able to establish this routine every day, some friends admitted they also felt burdened by the expectations around the morning quiet time. I'm fairly certain many of us do.

I'm also fairly certain (read: positive) that God does not limit His presence with us to an hour of silent Bible study at sunrise. In her delectably rebellious book *The Very Worst Missionary*, Jamie Wright demands to know why "quiet time" always has to be *quiet*: "If my life is loud, why can't I just be *loud* with God?"

The point of a "quiet time" is to spend intentional time with God. While stillness before our Creator is a wonderful practice, sometimes our lives don't allow for that luxury. But even here, there is hope to be found. Wright continues: "I will listen for God's voice in the wilderness, and at the water park, and under McDonald's indoor play structure, because that is my daily *loud time* and God is faithful to meet me in the chaos."

We serve a God who is with us day in and day out, a God who so desires our frail human presence that He sends the Spirit to intercede for us when we are too tired and weak to know how to pray. We can show up disheveled, disorderly, and maybe even disinterested, and God will meet us there. He is there when we are wiping runny noses, cooking leftovers, and just trying to keep our sanity. He will accept our "quiet time" and our "loud time."

He is faithful to meet us in the chaos.

— *Sarah Woodard*

> Yet even now, says the LORD,
>> return to me with all your heart,
> with fasting, with weeping, and with mourning;
>> rend your hearts and not your clothing.
> Return to the LORD, your God,
>> for he is gracious and merciful,
> slow to anger, and abounding in steadfast love,
>> and relents from punishing. (Joel 2:12-13)

There's a healthy skepticism about the supposed deathbed conversion of Oscar Wilde to Roman Catholicism. Critics of the day noted that noted that Wilde's decadent life frequently flouted Victorian standards. But in his dying years, Wilde befriended a young priest who reported that, hours before his death, Wilde received Last Rites and assented to the teachings of the Church in sound mind. Many wondered whether such a conversion would really do him any good on "the Day of the Lord."

More than any other prophet, Joel is concerned about the Day of the Lord. That day, says Joel, will not be pleasant. Locust plagues, invading armies, destruction: It's all coming, says Joel. And it's not just coming for Israel's enemies—it's coming for Israel, too. They are not immune to the judging fire of God. If anything, they are more culpable for knowing God's law and still ignoring it!

Yet God says this through Joel: "[E]ven now…return to me with all your heart…rend your hearts and not your clothing." God is inviting last-minute repentance. He's endorsing, in a way, deathbed conversions. It's never too late, says God, to voice a word of apology.

Whether we'll meet Oscar Wilde in the communion of saints is between the man himself and God. And yet, in his famous poem, "The Ballad of Reading Goal" (pronounced "red-ing jail"), Wilde seems to be toying with the theology of deathbed conversion. During his own infamous imprisonment, he witnessed the hanging of a man condemned for murdering his wife. Reflecting on this condemned man's apparent conversion, he penned these lines:

And he of the swollen purple throat
   And the stark and staring eyes,
Waits for the holy hands that took
   The Thief to Paradise;
And a broken and a contrite heart
   The Lord will not despise.

— Bryan Jarrell

April 13

Just after daybreak, Jesus stood on the beach; but the disciples did not know that it was Jesus... When Simon Peter
heard that it was the Lord, he put on some clothes, for he
was naked, and jumped into the sea. (John 21:4, 7)

This amazing sequence happens toward the end of John's Gospel.

Bored, seven of the disciples have paddled out to the Sea of Tiberias
for a night of fishing, with no luck. They spend the hours under the stars,
waiting, and also naked, because why not? Then, as the sun rises, they hear
the voice of a man on the shore. He tells them to drop their net one final
time, and they do. Two things happen very quickly: They haul in a full net
of fighting fish, and they realize the figure on the shore is Jesus.

The other disciples begin rowing back to the beach, but Peter is so overcome with emotion that he throws on some clothes, because modesty, and
flings himself overboard. He has lost all practical reasoning faculties. He
abandons the catch of a lifetime and leaves his friends to do all the work.
The fish are the last thing on his mind.

There is a classic YouTube video that stars a little girl whose parents
surprise her with a trip to Disneyland, probably her lifelong dream. She
is so excited that she breaks down in tears and begins wailing. She loses
her sense of time and place, asking, "Is it my birthday?" This is the kind of
elation I imagine Peter feels upon seeing his formerly dead best friend and
long-awaited Messiah standing over on the beach.

Have you ever felt so full of joy that you just lose control? Maybe you
were in love and couldn't sleep a wink, or maybe a beloved relative showed
up at your door unannounced. Maybe, when you were a child, your parents surprised you with a trip to Disneyland—who knows? Whatever it
was, take a moment to savor the memory, and know that it is only a trace of
the "fullness of joy" (Ps 16:11) promised by God, in our Savior Jesus Christ.

— CJ Green

April 14

Nehemiah said, "Go and enjoy choice food and sweet drinks, and send some to those who have nothing prepared. This day is holy to our Lord. Do not grieve, for the joy of the LORD is your strength." (Nehemiah 8:10 NIV)

This chapter portrays two versions of church. First, when Ezra reads scripture aloud, the people hear only the law. They fall to the ground and weep in contrition. Ezra is what we might today call "a fire-and-brimstone preacher," one of the originals, in fact. By contrast, Nehemiah offers a different kind of ministry. He pushes the legalistic voice aside and says: "Do not mourn or weep" (v. 9). He tells the people, in spite of their shortcomings, to get up and realize that God is (and will continue to be) a source of joy and strength, not to mention grace and comfort.

One of the members of my former parish was left in the care of her three capable older siblings when she was 11 years old. Her parents had to leave town for a few days. Just minutes after she saw them head to the airport, a sneaky idea popped into her head. She went inside and took her mother's car keys when nobody was looking. She then climbed into the front seat, turned on the car, put it in reverse, and proceeded to back out of the driveway. She drove up to her best friend's house, just up the street, picked up her friend, and then they did what any free-thinking 11-year-olds would do: They headed straight for McDonald's.

But on the way to McDonald's, in a surreal moment, she passed her aunt, this girl's mother's sister, who was very much not out of town. Quickly, the dots were connected and the aunt realized what she'd just seen, and this girl realized what she'd just been seen doing. So she turned the car around and drove straight home...where she found her three older siblings waiting in the driveway. They were not amused. She spent the next few days like Cinderella, doing everybody's chores and being reminded that she was "in trouble." She had not heard from her parents directly, though she was told they had been informed about what had happened.

When her mom came home, and when she saw her daughter, she said: "Honey, did you ever make it to McDonald's? Let's go." And just the mom and the daughter went off and had a little meal together at McDonald's. God is like that, the original gracious parent.

— John Zahl

April 15

"Can you draw out Leviathan with a fishhook,
  or press down its tongue with a cord?
Can you put a rope in its nose,
  or pierce its jaw with a hook?
Will it make many supplications to you?
  Will it speak soft words to you?
Will it make a covenant with you
  to be taken as your servant forever?
Will you play with it as with a bird,
  or will you put it on leash for your girls?" (Job 41:1-5)

Let me tell you an old story, perhaps one of the oldest.

Sometime near the beginning, the gods were threatened by an enemy—scaly, serpentine, and redolent of the watery deep—and among them rose up one who, through great labor, conquered and slew it. This young, strong god cut the dragon into pieces and so established order within creation, and became king. The Greeks told of a battle between Zeus and Typhon. In Babylon, they spoke of Marduk's triumph over Tiamat, the coiled embodiment of primordial chaos. The Bible, too, knows this story, because the whole ancient world knew it. One may catch sly references and fragments of it in Genesis, the Psalms, Daniel, Revelation—and here, in Job. Leviathan is no ordinary animal, but just such a monster, so terrible that even the gods fear him.

Job rages against God's injustice, his infuriating tolerance for disorder. When the Lord speaks from the whirlwind to answer the complaint, his concluding argument is merely a description of Leviathan: "On earth it has no equal" (v. 33). As frightening as Leviathan is, the monster is not God's enemy. Instead, he is a pet, a creature—mighty to be sure, but one who cannot oppose God's order. He is not chaos, and God delights in him, just as he delights in Job.

Each of the two is unique, unlike any other on earth. Each is a servant of God. Each has his own private words with the creator. It may surprise us that God is not at war with such monsters, but this is the unlikeliest of good news. The Lord who made the monsters also made you, and though you too rage and sow chaos, your creator's almighty peace cannot be overcome·

— *Adam Morton*

April 16

As they came near the village to which they were going, he
walked ahead as if he were going on. But they urged him
strongly, saying, "Stay with us, because it is almost evening
and the day is now nearly over." So he went in to stay with
them. When he was at the table with them, he took bread,
blessed and broke it, and gave it to them. Then their eyes
were opened, and they recognized him; and he vanished
from their sight. (Luke 24:28-31)

When these disciples (whom New Testament scholar Richard Bauckham
says were likely a husband and wife) were walking toward Emmaus, they
were walking away from an exciting and bewildering turn of events. Jesus
had been crucified, but now his body was nowhere to be found. Angels had
appeared to some from their group and told them Jesus was alive.

We don't know why these disciples were traveling away from the heart
of the story that was unfolding. Maybe they were on their way to handle
some sort of pressing business. Maybe they were returning to their homes
and jobs. Maybe their babysitter needed to be paid. Whatever the reason,
I imagine the disappointment they might have felt in having to leave Jerusalem, where Jesus had died and been entombed. Something really big had
happened and was still happening, and they weren't able to stick around
to see what would come next.

But Jesus met them in their walking. He met them and spoke to them
in ways that made them want more, so they asked him to stay with them as
night fell. When they gathered around their table to share a meal together,
Jesus broke and blessed the bread, and they finally recognized him. Their
disappointment was transformed to delight.

Sometimes I feel like I'm walking away from where the spiritual action is.
I know this sounds silly because the spiritual action is all around us, all the
time. But if I miss church one Sunday or if I haven't studied and meditated
on scripture in a few days, I worry I might not see God at work in my life.
I might be disappointed that I'm not where I'm supposed to be. The truth
is that I am right where I need to be, and there is no place I can go where
God is not. May Jesus show himself to us today, and may our disappointment be transformed to delight.

— *Charlotte Donlon*

> Jacob was left alone; and a man wrestled with him until daybreak. When the man saw that he did not prevail against Jacob, he struck him on the hip socket; and Jacob's hip was put out of joint as he wrestled with him...
>
> So [the man] said to him, "What is your name?" And he said, "Jacob." Then the man said, "You shall no longer be called Jacob, but Israel, for you have striven with God and with humans, and have prevailed." (Genesis 32:24-25, 27-28)

Some may argue that the greatest athlete of the 20th century was Jim Thorpe, or Muhammad Ali, or Michael Jordan. But in my view, Bo Jackson is the standard by which all others should be judged. He is the only athlete ever to play as a first-ballot pick in the MLB All-Star Game *and* make the NFL Pro Bowl. But Bo Jackson's career ended abruptly. The reason? A blow to the hip. Arguably the best athlete in the last 100 years was sidelined by the same injury that cripples Jacob in the above passage from Genesis. A minister I know once called Jacob's affliction a "wound of grace."

God has great plans for Jacob, but in Jacob's current situation, the night before he expects to have a climactic battle with his brother Esau, the Lord makes sure to slow him down a tad. The wound of grace is a wound that God uses to let Jacob know that triumph does not depend on his conniving or athletic prowess.

Here, Jacob is renamed Israel, which can be rendered as "The Overcomer." He strove against both God and men, and still prevailed, although he was left with a severe limp and, likely, arthritis. Jacob became "the Father of the Twelve Tribes," and when we look at his full narrative, we see that he was indeed an "overcomer" but went forward with a bit of "hobble in his giddy-up."

Bo Jackson surely had friends praying for the complete healing of his hip, but those prayers were not answered with a "yes." Jackson's hip didn't get better. Jacob's didn't, either. But these head-scratching "wounds of grace" point to our Savior, whose "power is made perfect in weakness" (2 Cor 12:9). He was wounded for our sake, so that one day, we might be made whole. Like Jacob, we may think it is up to us to "overcome," but thankfully God, in Christ, had other, better plans.

— *Howie Espenshied*

April 18

For I do not understand my own actions. For I do not do what I want, but I do the very thing I hate... Wretched man that I am! Who will deliver me from this body of death? Thanks be to God through Jesus Christ our Lord! (Romans 7:15, 24-25 ESV)

When I was in college, a Bible study I participated in posed the question: If you imagine God looking at you, what expression does he have on his face? It has always stuck with me, prompting me to recognize how warped my perception of God tends to be.

If I, like Paul, do not understand my own actions, and can't even get my act together enough to "do what I want" instead of doing "the very thing I hate," how can God look at me with anything other than the same frustration and disappointment that I feel myself? If I'm keenly aware of my wretchedness, how can God possibly be pleased with me? My perception of Him is tied so closely to how well I think I'm fulfilling the law. I begin to believe the lie that God's love for me is conditional.

Fortunately, that is where my view of God is deeply flawed. God "knows our frame; he remembers that we are dust" (Ps 103:14 ESV). He knows we are weak, gravitating toward self-destructive habits and wallowing in our sin. But because Jesus has delivered us "from this body of death" by His own death, God sees us clothed in the righteousness of His Son and looks at us with an expression of unconditional love, complete acceptance, and unwavering mercy, rejoicing over His children who once were lost but now are found.

— *Margaret Pope*

April 19

I have indeed received much joy and encouragement from your love, because the hearts of the saints have been refreshed through you, my brother. For this reason, though I am bold enough in Christ to command you to do your duty, yet I would rather appeal to you on the basis of love...
(Philemon 7-9)

As a pastor, I have heard and experienced the profound pain of conflict. I have seen congregations split over small points of theology, musical choices, or the use of certain vestments. A constant undertone of anger can lead a couple, once madly in love, to eventual divorce. Life is filled with these sad stories: treasured friendships, deep relationships, shattered by the pain and anxiety of conflict. The question is this: Is there anything we can do about it?

Philemon is a short epistle that St. Paul wrote as an old man, most likely while living under house arrest in Rome. Paul could not go anywhere, but people could come to him. One of those who came was Onesimus, a runaway slave. It seems that Onesimus had stolen something from his master, Philemon, and when this was discovered, he fled for his life. Paul knew that under Roman law, Onesimus' actions could be punished by death. So Paul wrote a letter to his friend Philemon, and in verses 4-7 he *imputes* righteousness to Philemon. Oftentimes, in the midst of conflict, being able to see the other person through the same lens as Jesus makes a profound difference and can transform real situations.

As I say, this is called "imputation": seeing something in someone that may not actually be present. St. Paul reminds Philemon of who he is in Jesus Christ: a person of tremendous faith, generosity, and encouragement. Whether he is or not is not the question. In Jesus Christ, Philemon is all of those things, which enables St. Paul to appeal to Philemon to treat Onesimus generously and as a brother.

Requirements usually only broaden the conflict. But imputation, the ability to see and call out the character of Jesus in another person, is a healing word, which enables people to do the impossible: to help heal their breaches with others.

— *Jacob Smith*

April 20

> So Gad came to David and said to him, "Thus says the LORD, 'Take your choice: either three years of famine; or three months of devastation by your foes, while the sword of your enemies overtakes you; or three days of the sword of the LORD, pestilence on the land, and the angel of the LORD destroying throughout all the territory of Israel.' Now decide what answer I shall return to the one who sent me." Then David said to Gad, "I am in great distress; let me fall into the hand of the LORD, for his mercy is very great; but let me not fall into human hands." (1 Chronicles 21:11-13)

A few verses prior to this passage, King David had emerged victorious from many battles. He wanted to know how powerful his army was, and so he ordered a census to be taken of all of the troops. David's pride and lust for power angered God, and, as a result, David had to atone for his sin by choosing one of three forms of punishment: three years of famine, three months of war, or three days of devastation by the "sword of the LORD."

While the severity of punishment might seem to us to be vastly incommensurate to the offense, what is most striking about this passage is David's choice. He did not choose famine, a natural disaster which would be hard to endure but would have avoided violent bloodshed. He did not choose war, even though he had over one million able fighters. Instead, he chose to be punished by "the sword of the LORD," which would involve *both* natural disaster and bloodshed. His reason? "[H]*is mercy is very great.*"

Foundational to David's understanding of God was his deep knowledge of both God's justice *and* God's mercy. Although he knew both to be always and equally true, David's words reflected the characteristic of God that was more salient to him: God's mercy is deep and wide. This is what we see, two verses later. God has mercy on David and his people, and he orders the angel, wielding the sword of the LORD, to stop (vv. 15-16).

We do not always like to be reminded that God is righteous and just, and that the wages of sin is death. But we are loved by God, "whose property is always to have mercy" (Book of Common Prayer). His mercies are new every morning. No matter your circumstances, may you have David's trust to fall into the hand of our God who saves, *for his mercy is very great.*

— *Bonnie Poon Zahl*

April 21

"Do not judge, so that you may not be judged. For with the judgment you make you will be judged, and the measure you give will be the measure you get. Why do you see the speck in your neighbor's eye, but do not notice the log in your own eye?" (Matthew 7:1-3)

I find obedience to this command to be very elusive in my life. It's tricky, and I can never quite get the hang of it. So often, I find myself judging people before I even realize what I'm doing. In the moment, it just seems like a normal assessment or observation. I think I'm seeing the real, flesh-and-blood person, but I'm really viewing a distorted caricature I have created in my mind. For me, that individual's faults have literally become who they *are*.

Sin truly lies waiting to ambush us (Gen 4:7), and the worst assault is our blindness to what we're indulging. Judgment is unconscious most of the time. Yet even when I *do* know exactly what I'm doing, I often can't stop. There is something intoxicating and pacifying about that moment when I look at my neighbor and feel in my heart, "I'm glad I'm not like that."

How do I resolve this tension? I don't want to judge, but I do. I want to see the real person in front of me, but I can't. Thanks be to God that Christ incarnate literally embodied and fulfilled the command to "judge not" (see Jn 8:11).

Christ crucified was judged with a harsher measure than we judge one another, and you were crucified with Him. You are hidden in Him. You were judged and found innocent; therefore, the record of *not judging your neighbor* is perpetually and eternally yours. Even while you secretly thank God you are not like others, the Spirit graciously assures you that you are like His Son.

— *Jason Thompson*

April 22

Strengthen the weak hands,
   and make firm the feeble knees.
Say to those who are of a fearful heart,
   "Be strong, do not fear!
Here is your God.
   He will come with vengeance,
with terrible recompense.
   He will come and save you." (Isaiah 35:3-4)

Are your hands weak today? Are your knees feeble? Physically and metaphor-ically speaking, most days mine are both. I love Isaiah 35 because, beginning to end, it so beautifully illustrates an out-of-this-world redemption for people like me who often feel weak and feeble—it speaks of a place where the blind will see, the deaf will hear, and water will gush forth in our wilderness places.

Here is what Isaiah *doesn't* say about our limitations: make yourself stronger, heal yourself, save yourself. No, Isaiah's message in this passage is that we have not been left to our own devices. Our salvation is not on our own brittle backs. In fact, our salvation isn't anywhere near the pitiful spheres of our own reach.

Our deliverance is entirely dependent on a God who desired to be with his people with such intensity that *he* would do every bit of the heavy lift-ing. A God who hated sin so deeply that *he* would come with vengeance on our behalf. Isaiah tells us that *God*, in full authority and grace, will do the saving. This scripture, one of many Messianic prophecies in the Old Testament, foretells of Jesus, our rescuer, hundreds of years before his birth.

If you read this passage in its full context, Isaiah tells us that God loves us so completely, that with the Messiah as his instrument, he will undo and remake every last wrong that has parched our world, starting with our hearts. One fine day, we will live on this renewed earth with glad singing; and everlasting joy will crown our heads. Dear one, I pray that you would find an abundance of comfort and hope in the *now*—feeble knees and all—knowing and imagining the unspeakable wonder and glory that's in all our futures, all because of what Jesus has done. Can you imagine what it will be like to feast together with Christ at the head of the table?

— *Charlotte Getz*

April 23

> He said to him the third time, "Simon son of John, do you love me?" Peter felt hurt because he said to him the third time, "Do you love me?" And he said to him, "Lord, you know everything; you know that I love you." Jesus said to him, "Feed my sheep." (John 21:17)

My husband thinks Peter is the greatest gift to us among the characters of the New Testament. He always says that Peter makes him feel so much less alone. Peter is impulsive and immature; he spouts off at the mouth. But Christ says that on this very imperfect rock, he will build his church.

On the night of Jesus' crucifixion, Peter denies Christ three times. We're often told this story to highlight Jesus' omniscience: He knows Peter is going to deny him, he predicts it, and it comes to pass. But stop and think. Peter has followed Christ for years and then completely abandons him. Not just once, not even just twice, but three times a denier. Can you imagine living with that guilt? How in the world—why in the world—would Christ build his church on such a feckless rube?

Christ did not come to save the righteous, and he does not mean to fill his church with them either. Christ looks at each sinner, sees us to our core, and redeems his own completely. After his resurrection, Christ pursues Peter. He asks him if he loves him. Peter says yes. And then he asks him again. And then a third time. Not just once, not even just twice, but three times a lover of Christ. How painful for Peter. But how good of our God. He gave Peter an opportunity to redeem each denial. Christ could have left it unsaid. He could have wiped the slate without a word. But, though painful, there is such beauty in this complete and public renovation of Peter's soul.

Our resurrected Lord wasn't seeking affirmation from his disciple. He was going after Peter and providing this painful, beautiful interaction for Peter's sake—and for ours, so that we may feel less alone. Jesus' redemption of Peter's three denials goes all the way to the details, and Peter is compelled to affirm Christ three times. Redemption is often painful, but it is always complete. God builds his church on sinners, sinners he will fully redeem.

— *Ann Lowrey Forster*

April 24

"For if you keep silence at such a time as this, relief and deliverance will rise for the Jews from another quarter, but you and your father's family will perish. Who knows? Perhaps you have come to royal dignity for just such a time as this." (Esther 4:14)

We all long for a day when we might be in such positions of power and influence that our actions would have great consequences for God's kingdom. Yet most of us feel that our lives are so very ordinary, and so very far removed from the kind of extraordinary position that Esther was in.

In this verse we see the critical moment when Esther realizes who she has become: She is someone with power. She has power over the lives of Jewish people living under the rule of the Persian king, to whom she is married. But that moment does not exist in isolation. Before this moment are all the other moments in her past that have led her to that point: moments of grief over losing her parents, of uncertainty and pain from being in exile, of hope and fear from being chosen to live in the palace, of nervousness from having to hide her identity, and of excitement from being crowned the queen. She has come to her royal position *for such a time as this* because of a long chain of events, choices, actions, and experiences that were part of God's plan for her and her people.

God uses every moment of our lives to shape us, and he does so for our sake and for the sake of the people around us. The ordinary moments of your life are no less valuable and purposeful to God's work than Esther's moment of realizing her immense power and the significance of the choices that she would make. No moment is hidden from God's sight, and no moment is wasted. Your joys *and* your sorrows, your moments of faithfulness *and* of faithlessness, your actions *and* inactions, are all a part of your prayer: "thy kingdom come, thy will be done, on earth as it is in heaven."

— *Bonnie Poon Zahl*

April 25

> Now the Berean Jews were of more noble character than
> those in Thessalonica, for they received the message with
> great eagerness and examined the Scriptures every day to
> see if what Paul said was true. (Acts 17:11 NIV)

When Luke describes this group of people as having "noble character," he doesn't mean that they were especially dignified or that they looked like Jane Austen characters. He means that they exhibited noble behavior, that they were open-minded, fair, and thoughtful. These people searched scripture for clarity, wisdom, and understanding, with a voracious appetite. Luke is supporting the idea that the Bible can be understood rightly, not only by scholars but by ordinary people like you and me. He is saying that, when reading the Bible, knowledge and expertise take a backseat to heartfelt interest and curiosity. The Bible is a wonderful thing to read with an eager mind because you never know what God will show you.

Jewish sages used to say that scripture either reads us or is worthless. With that in mind, the term "Bible Study" is a bit misleading because when we read the Bible we are not actually the ones at work; rather, God is at work in us. In fact, I'd like to start a petition to change the term "Bible Study" to "A Self-Examination and Encounter with the Living God." Because when God's word and Spirit move in us, the Bible does two things. First, it forces us to look at ourselves and realize that we, despite our best efforts, are not God and that we are deeply in need of His mercy. And second, it helps facilitate the flip-side of that coin, which is, of course, receiving His boundless mercy.

You, dear reader, are receiving the same words this "noble" group of people was receiving. You are swimming in the same spiritual waters as they did. And whether you are dipping your toe in with hesitation or diving right into God's faithful promise, He is at work in you right now as you read this little verse. May He reveal what needs to be revealed to you today.

— *Sam Bush*

April 26

> And Jesus came and said to them, "All authority in heaven
> and on earth has been given to me." (Matthew 28:18)

Faced with the burdens and responsibilities of adulthood, and looking around at a world that sometimes seems to be burning itself to the ground, a friend of mine likes to ask: "Where are the grown-ups?"

I suppose my generation are the "grown-ups" now. I am of that age where we take care of others rather than being taken care of ourselves. These days, it is often we who make the decisions that have real stakes for others, who decide which path we will all go down. If we don't do something about the problems we see around us, who else will?

But this is easier said than done. There are too many problems that are too complex. So often, we either know what needs doing but can't bring it about, or we don't know what to do at all, or we end up misusing the authority we have.

Which of us can bring about order from the disorder, peace in the midst of the violence, a truly and lastingly better world? Who in this generation has the goodness, the wisdom, and the power? The answer is no one. "For mortals it is impossible" (19:26).

But this verse speaks of another way. We are so prone to misusing our authority, it's true. But what if the authority belongs not to you or me, but to one who once walked among us? What if the authority lies with the one who loved the outcasts and the unclean, who came not to be served but to serve, and who looked upon every person he met with infinite mercy and understanding? What if authority lies with the one who looked upon even his murderers with compassion and forgiveness (Lk 23:34)? What if the one with the authority is Jesus of Nazareth?

If you are tired, if you are weary, if you are worn down with responsibility, take your burden to the man from Galilee. In him you will find hope for a better world, and rest for your soul.

— *Simeon Zahl*

April 27

Then Joshua son of Nun sent two men secretly from Shit-
tim as spies, saying, "Go, view the land, especially Jericho."
So they went, and entered the house of a prostitute whose
name was Rahab, and spent the night there. (Joshua 2:1)

We're not told why, of all the places the two men could have gone, they
wound up inside the home of a woman in the sex industry. But it seems
highly improbable that they were there to talk religion. What a surprise it
must have been, therefore, to encounter a prostitute who was not only into
theology, but one who was a closet believer in the God of Israel.

Rahab informs the spies that she knows all about the Lord's drying up
of the Red Sea, their conquest of foreign powers, and that the Holy Land
will soon be Israel's inheritance. Not only that, but she makes this bold confession: "The LORD your God is indeed God in heaven above and on earth
below" (2:11). Regardless of what Rahab does for a living, she does indeed
live "by faith" (Heb 11:31).

Her life story is testimony to God's humorous upending of all expectations. Rahab has led an unclean life. Yet this sex worker, who's also an ortho-
dox theologian, ends up saving the skin of these two young men, rescues her
entire family when Jericho's walls come tumbling down, eventually becomes
the bride of an Israelite, and finds her way into the Messiah's family tree.

This is indeed the Almighty's way of poking fun at our all-too-com-
mon divinization of moralism. He goes around saving sinners, not applauding the sanctimonious. Rahab the prostitute joins the ranks of Noah the
Drunk, Abraham the Liar, Jacob the Cheat, Moses the Murderer, David
the Adulterer, and the host of others in the league of failures that populate
the people of God.

Rahab is the patron saint of all of us with sketchy pasts (or presents).
Her story is a hopeful and beautiful reminder that there is no place outside
the limits of God's grace, and no person outside the bounds of his love.

— Chad Bird

April 28

Jesus wept. (John 11:35 KJV)

In our culture, you can feel like a real failure if you're unhappy—because if you're unhappy, obviously it's your own fault. Maybe you're not eating right or getting enough sleep. Maybe you haven't been praying and/or meditating, or you're being too negative. You need medication. So much advice, no matter how good it may be, usually leaves us feeling like we're doing something wrong—and thus, even unhappier.

The literary critic A. Alvarez once argued that unhappiness is not a problem. "[P]roblems imply solutions," he wrote, "whereas unhappiness is merely a condition of life which you must live with like the weather." It comes and goes. There are rainy days. And there are things you can do to make the rainy days more bearable. But to think you can change the weather is to think you are God.

Today's Bible verse is famous for its brevity. In the King James Version, it is the shortest verse in the Bible. It occurs after the death of Jesus' friend Lazarus: Jesus arrives four days too late, observes the mourning family and friends, and is moved to tears. As Nikos Kazantzakis describes it in *The Last Temptation of Christ*:

> All the blood went to [Jesus'] head, his eyes rolled and disappeared, only the whites remained. He brought forth such a bellow you'd have thought there was a bull inside him…he uttered a wild cry, a strange cry, something from another world.

This is a powerful depiction of grief, but I am 100% sure this is not the only time Jesus wept. Historians agree: He was a real person, after all. Emotions—the whole spectrum of them—are facts of life. There were plenty of days when Jesus' serotonin levels dipped and languished. He got cranky. He got upset. Sometimes he lurched along in sadness.

Jesus wept. By the grief of this world, he was broken so that you can give yourself a break. You don't have to cheer up today. You don't have to beat yourself into happiness. Here is a prayer for your unhappy days:

> *O God, today I would like to be happy. Of course I would. But since I am not, help me see you even though the world seems gray. I know you are here. I trust you. Amen.*

— CJ Green

April 29

> And after you have suffered for a little while, the God of all grace, who has called you to his eternal glory in Christ, will himself restore, support, strengthen, and establish you. To him be the power forever and ever. Amen. (1 Peter 5:10-11)

"A little while" sounds like good news in this passage, but I am slightly wary of God's idea of time, since a thousand years is like a day to him (Ps 90:4). Adults often tell children, "Almost done!" I remember my parents sometimes saying, "Already halfway there!" and I would think to myself, "I have to go through all that again?" Whether it was a chore, schoolwork, or a painful procedure at the doctor or dentist, it could feel like forever.

In the middle of suffering, nothing feels like "a little while." Adults try to encourage children in this way because we can see it from the other side of the suffering. With certain childhood struggles behind us, we can honestly tell a child, "Don't worry, it's almost over! It will get better!" Children have not experienced this for themselves, and so they have to take our word for it.

We are like children who cannot see the wonderful future that God describes. We don't understand eternity because we have not yet experienced it. So we trust in the Father who gave us his only Son, and let him be crucified on the cross, to take onto himself all of the world's sin and suffering. From the other side of this, God promises, he will one day "restore, support, strengthen, and establish" us in eternal glory with Christ. Then we will be able to look back at our lives and say to God, "Oh yes, now I see what you meant by 'a little while.'"

— *Juliette Alvey*

April 30

An account of the genealogy of Jesus the Messiah, the son
of David, the son of Abraham. (Matthew 1:1)

There are plenty of famous books with unforgettable opening lines. Some
are short and catchy, like "Call me Ishmael" from *Moby Dick*. Some are
lengthier and more sage-like, such as *Anna Karenina*'s "Happy families are
all alike; every unhappy family is unhappy in its own way." A first line, of
course, is crafted to hook readers and reel them into the story.

And then there's the New Testament. It begins, "An account of
the genealogy..." Not exactly unforgettable. And 17 more verses full of
"so-and-so begat so-and-so," along with their tongue-tying Hebrew names,
does little to fan the flames of a reader's curiosity. The fault, however, is
not Matthew's. He didn't flunk Writing 101. His original audience, by verse
17, would already have been on their feet, applauding the author. In less
than twenty verses, he somehow pulled off a summation of the hope that
had loomed on the Israelite horizon for more than a thousand years—and
finally arrived in the bulging belly of Mary.

God's promise of new life for the world, as it unfolded over the centuries, was rooted not in esoteric speculations or mystical rituals, but sperm
and egg and womb, moms and dads and babies. Every marriage, every con-
ception, every child born into this world brought us closer to The Child.
So to read Matthew's genealogy is to climb the Gospel Family Tree, from
root to trunk to branch, and, perched high atop it, to gape in wonder at
how the story is told.

It is also our story, our world's story, the narrative of the God who not
only served as the ghost writer for this drama, but who wrote himself into
the story through the ink of flesh and blood in the incarnation. He became
Emmanuel, God with us. God with us in our own families, happy or otherwise. God with us in our stories of laughter and tears, in babies born and
grandparents buried, in dreams achieved and lives imploded. Whatever
twists and turns our stories take, they are now part of God's story, for he
is one of us. And, in the metanarrative of Christ's story, all our stories build
toward the dénouement in which—to paraphrase Tolkien—"everything
sad will come untrue."

— *Chad Bird*

May 1

[Jesus], though he was in the form of God,
  did not regard equality with God
  as something to be exploited,
but emptied himself,
  taking the form of a slave,
  being born in human likeness.
And being found in human form,
  he humbled himself
  and became obedient to the point of death—
  even death on a cross. (Philippians 2:6-8)

I have always loved flowers. As a young child, I would pick all the spring flowers in my parents' garden. The flowers only, not with stems. So in a few minutes the garden would be void of color: reduced to empty green stalks.

Finally, one spring, my father had an idea. "We are going to the flower store," he said. And off we went to the local nursery. We brought home a large flat of pansies: yellow, purple, white, maroon. Together we dug a rectangle in the lawn. "This is *your* garden," he said. "For you only."

We planted the pansies together. As we worked, he explained to me that these plants were different from the tulips and daffodils I had denuded each spring: When you pick those, that's it. No more flowers. But with the pansies, after you pick one flower, another blooms in its place. The more you pick, the more there are. This was *magic* to me. A miracle! In my six years on earth, all I had known was that things depleted: The more you took away, the less there would be. The last cookie in the cookie jar was *the end* of cookies. The last Christmas present you unwrapped on Christmas morning was *it*, for 364 days!

I can still feel the wonder and disbelieving delight at this news about the pansies: The more you take from them, the more they give.

So that day, I filled every empty jam jar and juice glass I could find with multi-colored pansy flowers (this time with stems) and put them all around the house. And, lo and behold, the *novum*—the new thing my father had told me—was *true*. Within a few days, my pansies in the garden were full of blooms again!

The more they give up, the more they give. This perfect occurrence in nature, in our everyday world, reflects the good news of Jesus, who gave himself "to the point of death—even death on a cross."

— *Nancy Hanna*

May 2

Then he began to speak to them in parables. "A man planted a vineyard, put a fence around it, dug a pit for the wine press, and built a watchtower; then he leased it to tenants and went to another country. When the season came, he sent a slave to the tenants to collect from them his share of the produce of the vineyard. But they seized him, and beat him, and sent him away empty-handed." (Mark 12:1-3)

There was a time in my life when I was desperately in need of help. I didn't see it, of course, but everyone else did. Family, friends, acquaintances—you name it. Of course, I thought I was doing just fine, thank you very much. So when these offers for help came, I rebuffed them at every turn. Help looked like judgment, which of course it was, and I recoiled.

This is the situation of the tenant farmers in the parable. Well, it's not quite their situation, but it's close enough. The owner sends his representatives to the workers of the farm for his allotted share of the crops, and the farmers will have none of it. They are perfectly fine without the owner, thank you very much. They'd rather be on their own, so they beat, abuse, and kill to keep things the way they were.

The hearers of the parable, the ones who understood that Jesus spoke about them—they desperately needed help. They had forgotten about God's mercy for sinners. They were religious snobs and had deceived themselves into thinking they were perfectly fine. Who needs a doctor when you're healthy (Mk 2:17)?

The more God tried to intervene, the more viciously they rebuked him. Their Deliverer had come, and the Pharisees and scribes saw judgment. Jesus shined a light on the established system of thought, and his aid was viewed as a threat. And so they had him killed.

There is a fine line between help and threat, between diagnosis and judgment, salvation and damnation. And yet we desperately need help. The struggles of life, both within ourselves and within the world, repeatedly remind us of our infirmity. The Physician we need is always right in front of us, staring us in the face. He speaks words of life, comfort, and peace to the dead, afflicted, and weary. We all need help, and Christ has come to our rescue.

— *Todd Brewer*

May 3

When the day of Pentecost had come, they were all together
in one place. And suddenly from heaven there came a sound
like the rush of a violent wind, and it filled the entire
house where they were sitting. Divided tongues, as of fire,
appeared among them, and a tongue rested on each of them.
All of them were filled with the Holy Spirit and began to
speak in other languages, as the Spirit gave them ability.
(Acts 2:1-4)

Imagine a team of eyewitness reporters on the day after Pentecost, standing
on the street outside the Upper Room, interviewing the witnesses: *Can you
please relate what you saw? Witnesses said they heard a loud rushing sound
of some kind. Can you confirm?*

But how does one properly describe the descent of the Spirit? I feel certain the witnesses to Pentecost grappled with this very question. As Luke
records it here in Acts, the participants seem to struggle to capture what
it sounded like, looked like, felt like.

I can picture those charter members of the First Church of Jerusalem
responding to reporters this way. *Well*, they would say, *imagine a gale-
force wind, coming not from the north, south, east, or west, but from above,
breathing new life into each person in the room. Or how about this: Imagine one single flame, you know, like the pillar of fire that led God's people of
old in Exodus. But this single flame separates out and rests on each one of us,
purifying and energizing our souls.*

Regardless of how we might define the experience, we know one of
the unmistakable evidences that the Spirit has arrived is that the church
becomes a *chatterbox*. The Spirit loosens our tongues and enables us to
embed our stories of grace into diverse places and cultures and languages,
"speaking about God's deeds of power" (v. 11). And so, we pray, once again,
Come Holy Spirit!

— *Larry Parsley*

May 4

For it has been reported to me by Chloe's people that there are quarrels among you, my brothers and sisters. What I mean is that each of you says, "I belong to Paul," or "I belong to Apollos," or "I belong to Cephas," or "I belong to Christ." Has Christ been divided? Was Paul crucified for you? Or were you baptized in the name of Paul? (1 Corinthians 1:11-13)

In the late 1970s and early 1980s, a strange naming trend crept through the music world. A New York disco group called itself Kleeer. A few years later an outfit known as Videeo had a disco hit. Soon MTV was playing clips from a hair metal group named Ratt. I asked a friend what was behind novel spellings. He quipped, "Well, you always got to add a little something."

The same sentiment applies to the Corinthians. Paul is upset that they're adding something to the gospel. It was Jesus plus "I got baptized by this person." Today we add other pedigrees: the right family, the right politics, the right affiliations. We're always looking for something more to add so that we might *be* something more.

Sadly, the stratagem tends to backfire, in life just as much as religion. Even if it's something good, like who baptized you, the impulse to add something more creates something less—less unity, less cohesion, less love.

Furthermore, when we make the spiritual life into a matter of *more more more*, we turn God into something he's not. Martin Luther famously remarked, "Men fast, pray, watch, suffer. They intend to appease the wrath of God and to deserve God's grace by their exertions. But there is no glory in it for God, because by their exertions these workers pronounce God an unmerciful slave driver, an unfaithful and angry Judge. They despise God, make a liar out of Him..."

Our insistence on the tyranny of *more* constitutes a refusal to believe that God's approval of us in Christ is full and final. So where are you clamoring after more? Where is more being demanded of you? The gospel is not about adding anything, but being added to something. It does not have to do with lining up your affiliations but about the God who is undividedly loyal to you despite your disloyalty to him. Who, instead of saying *More*, says *Mine*. Or *Miiine*.

— *David Zahl*

May 5

> They heard the sound of the LORD God walking in the garden at the time of the evening breeze, and the man and his wife hid themselves from the presence of the LORD God among the trees of the garden. But the LORD God called to the man, and said to him, "Where are you?" (Genesis 3:8-9)

One of the oldest patterns in human relationships surfaces smack dab in the beginning. It is the "pursuer-withdrawer" dynamic, our tendency to move away from a loved one who is trying to pull us closer.

It can take all sorts of shapes, but give a cursory glance at human relationships and you will see this pattern at work: When a mom carves out a mother-daughter night, and the daughter asks if she can bring a friend. When a boss initiates a "staff togetherness" lunch, and half the staff sneaks out. When a husband provides his wife with the ninth installment of his armchair lectures on home economics, and he watches (yet again) the lights go out in her eyes.

The pursuer-withdrawer dynamic happens because, for good reason, the person being pursued expects *judgment* rather than connection. The withdrawer may genuinely want the exact same thing as the pursuer—to connect with their parent or partner, to love their job—but their suspicion is that the pursuer is not bringing good news, but bad news: more advice, more grievances, more *to do*. Sadly, when we are pursued by these tactics, we hide.

You could say that the Bible itself is a *collection* of these stories, where God's pursuit of his people leads to withdrawal, leading to more pursuit, and more withdrawal. We withdrew in Eden, we withdrew in Gethsemane, and I suspect you will withdraw in some way today.

Yes, the pursuer-withdrawer dynamic is alive and well with God. The more the withdrawer withdraws, the more the pursuer pursues. But there is one important distinction. While the rest of the world's lovers may pursue with any number of selfish needs and vindictive motives, this Pursuer simply seeks *you*. Today's passage may be only the beginning of the story, but the chase is on.

— *Ethan Richardson*

May 6

We make our own plans,
but the LORD decides
where we will go. (Proverbs 16:9 CEV)

I take a daily walk from my house through the Grounds at the University of Virginia. Rarely do I alter my routine; I like to note the changing seasons along the settled path. I like the familiarity of the four miles, and I don't listen to music or podcasts, as I usually use that time to puzzle through some interior issue, to think about a sermon, or just to be open to what comes to mind.

The other day, I came upon a pedestrian detour. Due to construction, walkers and runners were shunted off the main road and through a less traveled part of Grounds. At first, I was annoyed, but having taken the road less traveled, I decided I would make that my new normal! There were more trees, less traffic, and yet undiscovered (by me) architecture. Who knew?

Well, life has a way of detouring all of us. It might be a health issue, a job change, or a relationship bust-up. Or on the positive side of the ledger, it might be the birth of child or an unexpected windfall. The point is that we are not the ones in charge of charting our own paths.

What is true is that God is with every single person, and He makes good out of bad for everybody. That's His nature, that's His history (e.g. the cross), and that is His current and future activity. In other words, I look forward to seeing what detours become happy new circumstances. Today's scripture tells us, "We make our own plans, but the LORD decides where we will go." And we can be certain that where He has decided to take us is decidedly good.

> Grant, O Lord, that the course of this world and the course of my day may be governed by your providence, and that I may joyfully serve you in confidence and peace, through Jesus Christ our Lord, who lives and reigns with you and the Holy Spirit, one God, for ever and ever. Amen.

— Paul Walker

May 7

And I pray that you, being rooted and established in love,
may have power, together with all the Lord's holy people,
to grasp how wide and long and high and deep is the love
of Christ, and to know this love that surpasses knowledge—
that you may be filled to the measure of all the fullness of
God. (Ephesians 3:17-19 NIV)

A friend of mine has been in a wheelchair since the age of three. One afternoon, in the middle of her brother's sports game, she set off on a particularly precocious solo adventure up a very steep hill. The hill was too steep
for her parents to climb to ask her to cease these dangerous wanderings, so
they stood watching down below. And they were still watching when she
flipped over backwards. She lay on the hill, strapped into her chair, which
was made of heavy metal. Battery acid had leaked out of it and would soon
burn right through her skin.

My friend tells the story as a funny anecdote of the "fastest she ever
saw her dad run." He sprinted up that hill to unstrap his daughter, carry
her down in his arms to a water fountain. Frantically, he rinsed her in this
tiny basin, and after that, she was safe.

As a typical, bored little sister, she had simply been going for an adventure, testing her luck against the hill. And her dad had allowed her the
freedom to wander. Yet at a moment's notice, he burst into action to save
her from a danger incomprehensible to her young mind.

This story reminds me of the old hymn: "How deep the Father's love for
us; how vast beyond all measure…" Our Heavenly Father is always sprinting
up the hill. His love is vast beyond measure, because we do not yet know
the dangers we put ourselves in, yet God saves us every time.

But lest we think our Heavenly Protector only acts heroically in
moments of crisis, let's also remember the *mother* at the bottom of the
hill, who bathed, dressed, toileted, fed, cleaned, lifted, and transferred my
friend in and out of her chair into beds and sofas every day. Like her, God
also nurtures and nourishes every second of daily existence. This type of
every-moment love, every-need love, is certainly vast beyond all measure.

— *Anonymous*

> For my part, I am going to bring a flood of waters on the
> earth, to destroy from under heaven all flesh in which is
> the breath of life; everything that is on the earth shall die.
> But I will establish my covenant with you; and you shall
> come into the ark, you, your sons, your wife, and your sons'
> wives with you. And of every living thing, of all flesh, you
> shall bring two of every kind into the ark, to keep them
> alive with you... (Genesis 6:17-19)

The Flood story is very uncomfy, for two main reasons. First, it contradicts contemporary geology and genetics. And second, it seems to undermine God's goodness.

Whenever I read it, I mainly try to imitate Jacob, and wrestle with God about it (Gen 32). What makes the most sense to me is to view the Noah story as a "type" pointing to Christ (1 Cor 10:6, 11). Since Jesus said that Moses wrote about him (Jn 5:46), and since the Flood story is attributed to Moses, the Flood can be about Jesus, just like the whole Bible (Lk 24:27).

So where is Jesus here? According to Peter, he's the ark, and in baptism, we're kept safe inside him (1 Pt 3:21).

But what about all those people who died? Or, if the story is a type, then what about everyone who dies now? Does God care about them?

Soon after his ark analogy, Peter tells us something strange: "the gospel was proclaimed even to the dead" (1 Pt 4:6). Stranger still, that idea made it into the Apostles' Creed: Jesus "descended into hell." And what was he doing there? Declaring the good news, apparently. In the late 100s, Clement of Alexandria makes it clear: "the Lord descended to Hades for no other end but to preach the Gospel." He goes on: "For it is not here alone that the active power of God is beforehand, but it is everywhere and is always at work" (Stromata VI.VI).

The Noah story still disturbs me, and I think it always will. But Jesus enacts what the Song of Songs declares about him: "Many waters cannot quench love, neither can floods drown it" (8:7).

— *Kendall Gunter*

May 9

Taste and see that the LORD is good;
  blessed is the one who takes refuge in him. (Psalm 34:8 NIV)

Babies, who are very bad at most things, are experts at tasting. Everything ends up in their mouths—from the magazine you were just reading to the doorknob of the pediatrician's bathroom. Thankfully, most of us outgrow this particular trait of treating the world as our (literal) oyster. But we can also be grateful that someone, somewhere along the line, retained enough sense of adventure from toddlerhood to taste and see artichokes, pineapples, and sea scallops. A perfectly ripe peach can taste like a gift given directly from heaven, and there are some among us who daydream about a "just right" avocado.

In the wake of the attacks on the World Trade Center on September 11, 2001, cooks from *Gourmet* magazine gathered to cook for first responders. After Hurricane Harvey, home cooks stirred and baked in their own kitchens to feed their flood-weary neighbors. We show our love for one another by feeding each other.

Taste and see that the Lord is good: Jesus fed the crowd of five thousand, instructed his disciples to eat what was put in front of them, broke bread with them on the night before he was crucified, and ate breakfast on the shore after his resurrection.

Christians around the world gather regularly at Communion tables to remember Jesus' death and celebrate his resurrection with bread and wine. For some Christians, that is the only meal that they will share with others all week. For others, it is the only meal they will eat that isn't complicated by disordered eating. For all of us, it is a meal that we can taste and see, and know that the Lord is good.

This might be why table blessings are such an important part of many Christians' lives. This one is a favorite of mine:

> *For food in a world where many walk in hunger,*
> *For faith in a world where many walk in fear,*
> *For friends in a world where many walk alone,*
> *We give you humble thanks, O Lord.*

— Carrie Willard

May 10

[H]e forgave us all our trespasses, erasing the record that
stood against us with its legal demands. He set this aside,
nailing it to the cross. (Colossians 2:13-14)

I've been a fly-fisherman for a long time now. I know most of the basic flies.
But when it comes to variations of the same or similar dry flies, I'm lost. I
know what a caddis is, but what is an x caddis again? Hackles? Parachutes?
Emergers? I've got books and flashcards and online tutorials, but when
I'm on the water, trying to identify the hatch and choose the right fly, I'm
befuddled more times than not. Although the flies may look "close enough"
to me, the trout, especially brook trout, know the difference. The "x" in the
x caddis will mean the difference between landing 5 or 6 fish and getting
skunked. That's why I like to fish with my more advanced friend, Tommy.
I'll just throw what he's throwing!

Thank you for reading all about my fishing. (We all need our diversions!)
You have your own diversions and your own inabilities to master even the
things you love to do. Thankfully, the gospel is not like fly-fishing! The
gospel is easy. A newcomer to the faith told me she was also new to playing
golf, so she looked forward to learning about both the faith and golf. My
response: CHRISTIANITY IS WAY EASIER THAN GOLF!

That's because there is nothing to master about the gospel; it has already
been mastered for you in the death and resurrection of Jesus Christ. The
gospel is not about what you do, but what has been done for you. Deep
breath...tension draining out of your neck and shoulders...there's nothing
difficult about that!

*Thank you, Father, for what you have done for us in the death
and resurrection of Jesus Christ. Help us to know that our sin
is put away once and for all so we might live in gratitude and
freedom. Amen.*

— Paul Walker

May 11

Take delight in the LORD,
and he will give you the desires of your heart. (Psalm 37:4)

The book of Psalms feels, to me, to be all over the place. This is why I love it. Most of these psalms are attributed to David, a shepherd before he became a king before he became a hunted man. He lived in extremes: one minute bedding his neighbor, the next ordering the execution of her husband; a few months later expecting a child, only to be grieving that child not long after.

I can relate.

Not to the specific events—luckily—but to the particular way David's life and its failings oriented him to God. Who among us hasn't desired something we don't have, or wished harm upon our perceived enemy, or experienced grief, or felt targeted? And what David did was bring all of this to God. The psalms are full of lament, of desperation, of highs and lows. They scatter across the emotional spectrum and reveal a heart that cannot escape its Maker.

This psalm, as they go, is pretty sedate: There aren't any exclamation points or question marks, no shouts or pleading. It must have been written during a calm moment in David's life; for what it's worth, he admits in verse 25 that he's old. While I personally find comfort in David's more erratic moments (and the fact that they were included as canon), I also take solace in his certitude here.

When I was younger, the phrase "desires of your heart" meant, for me, things like a prom date or a new car. Later, it was a husband and kids. Now, it's a moment to myself in the bathroom. In any case, what I know now is that my desires, like David himself, can be erratic. And not always oriented to what God wills for me. Maybe you can relate?

But, also like David, we can bring all of this to God: our desires, and our lament at not receiving them. The broken parts of ourselves, the disappointments, the extremes. Laid bare, we find that we cannot escape our Maker, and the space between what we want and what he wants for us narrows.

Against all odds, *God* becomes our desire. And then we realize: We can always have what we want.

— *Stephanie Phillips*

May 12

As he went ashore, he saw a great crowd; and he had compassion for them, because they were like sheep without a shepherd; and he began to teach them many things. (Mark 6:34)

If someone ever tells you they know all the answers, they're either deluded or lying. God has all the answers, for sure, but people? We have provisional insights that never fully resolve and a litany of examples of doing what we know we shouldn't. We think we are throwing a baseball, when we are actually holding a boomerang. We are, in the words of Jesus, sheep without a shepherd. We are entirely helpless if left to ourselves.

In the famous third act of Thornton Wilder's play *Our Town*, a deceased character laments that to be a human is to "move about in a cloud of ignorance; to go up and down trampling on the feelings of those…of those about you. To spend and waste time as though you had a million years. To always be at the mercy of one self-centered passion, or another… Ignorance and blindness." We grasp at whatever answers we can find, trading fashions and fads with ease. New ideas become common wallpaper at the moment we move on to the next big thing. We need a shepherd to guide us, a foundation on which to build and have some certainty.

It is striking how much of Jesus' life was spent being kind to others. When he sees the aimless crowd, he does not turn away from them in apathy or irritation. Nor does he condemn them for their ignorance. Instead he has compassion on their weakness. This radicalness of Jesus is easy to miss. He sees their frailty and loves them all the more, opening his mouth to give them hope, peace, and assurance. While we blindly pursue love, liberty, and happiness, he reaches out to us to give all that we need. We hear his word of life and hold fast in faith to the one thing we know to be true. Our shepherd speaks and we listen, following where he leads.

— *Todd Brewer*

May 13

May I never boast of anything except the cross of our Lord
Jesus Christ, by which the world has been crucified to me,
and I to the world. (Galatians 6:14)

One of my favorite articles from *The Onion* has the headline "Unambitious
Loser with Happy, Fulfilling Life Still Lives in Hometown." By contrast,
I told my parents before I started middle school that I would be moving
across the country. I judged all of the people I knew who stayed. "What losers," my 18-year-old self would smirk and think. And I did move across the
country, for about three months. I went to a small, showy college out west,
and was terrified of the drug scene, and 9/11 happened my first month of
school, and so I moved back home that spring semester. I showed up at the
University of Mississippi humiliated, with no friends, and sporting bright
pink hair. I was like my own warning label.

Thankfully, Jesus sees warning labels like runway lights. He flies right
in. It was then that I found Jesus again. Or rather, he found me. Loneliness
drove me through the doors of a small church with some old ladies who
became my first college friends. I learned to pray in community as an adult.
Most of all, I learned that Jesus had changed who I was and who I felt like
I had to be. God had to help me learn early (and often) that I had been crucified with Christ. And boasting about anything other than his love of me
was just going to leave me empty inside.

"Boasting" seems like a weird thing to encourage. But really, we boast
about ourselves all the time, exhaustively. Social media, work meetings, and
PTA meetings are boasting opportunities. But boasting in God's love for us,
is something altogether different. I failed at my worldly boasts. It turned
out I was a loser too. And that was kind of a relief.

— *Sarah Condon*

> He said to me, O mortal, eat what is offered to you; eat
> this scroll, and go, speak to the house of Israel. So I opened
> my mouth, and he gave me the scroll to eat. He said to me,
> Mortal, eat this scroll that I give you and fill your stomach
> with it. Then I ate it; and in my mouth it was as sweet as
> honey. (Ezekiel 3:1-3)

The scroll that the prophet Ezekiel eats—yes, God asks him to *eat* it—is a scroll of judgment, God's long list of "lamentations and woes" for the stiff-necked people of Israel. Doesn't sound like the sort of thing that would go down easy. It certainly doesn't sound like it would be "sweet as honey."

Sometimes, though, especially when you find yourself in a room full of deception or fakery, it can be really good to hear a person talking sense. It can, in fact, be "sweet as honey" when you are confronted with the whole truth about something. Even if the truth is unsavory, something you've lived with (but not discussed) for a long time, even if it marks *you* specifically as the guilty party. It can be a relief to have it standing before you—no more and no less than what it is. What Ezekiel is forced to swallow down is the honest-to-God truth.

Tasting the truth is more than just refreshing: It is the taproot to real, lasting love. Love isn't really complete if it relies on half-truth and misdirection to achieve its end. Love, as Walker Percy described it, comes from those who "know the worst of us and don't turn their faces away."

God has not turned his face away. He is sending Ezekiel off to plead to yet another "rebellious" and "obstinate" generation of these his chosen people. God tells Ezekiel it will most likely be a futile task but to do it anyway. And so, to see God's truth—the full picture—also allows him to see God's undeterred love. Without the truth, there is no grace.

While I often pray that God would make me less bitter, maybe this is a more appropriate prayer:

> God, grant me the courage to welcome the ugly truth today. I
> know that, because of what has been promised in its wake, the
> truth will taste as sweet as honey.

— *Ethan Richardson*

May 15

Therefore confess your sins to one another, and pray for
one another, so that you may be healed. The prayer of the
righteous is powerful and effective. (James 5:16)

Hug the cactus. This is how Robert Downey, Jr., once described the need
to directly embrace the hard stuff in our lives. It's the opposite of sweeping
something under the rug.

Confess your sins, says James. So far, so good. I can confess my sins
to God all day long. But then James adds something else: "to one another."
Oof. This is hard. Telling another actual human being my sin is hugging
the cactus.

Coming clean sucks. It means admitting fault. Being wrong. Acknowledging that you are not perfect, not the smartest person in the room, not
"making good choices." It means revealing you are something other than the
person you want people to see. It means showing someone your mugshot,
not your glamour shot.

The reason we can do this, as Christians, is because we know that, ultimately, we have already died and risen with Christ. God is fresh out of
condemnation. We're like criminals who have been granted immunity. We
can come clean because there's no fear of judgment. On the cross, Christ
has already dealt with that.

Sometimes, though, that feels a little abstract. Which is where James'
wisdom comes in. Confessing our sins to each other makes it feel real. It
enfleshes grace. It's the difference between hearing, "That's OK, I forgive
you," and getting a running-to-meet-the-Prodigal-Son-come-home embrace
from our loving Father.

So we confess our sins to one another. In that vulnerable moment of
shared honesty, one sinner beholding another, there is healing, James tells
us. The other human to whom we confess displays God's grace to us.

Who is a safe person to whom you can confess your sins? Where do you
need healing?

— *Aaron Zimmerman*

May 16

O sing to the LORD a new song,
  for he has done marvelous things.
His right hand and his holy arm
  have gotten him victory. (Psalm 98:1)

Who here wants recidivism, and who wants newness? Well, we usually *get* recidivism, which is the compulsive repetition, within and issuing from ourselves, of unwanted acts, attitudes, and words. One *desires* to change, especially when the consequences of our repetitions—especially in rela- tionships—produce loss and retribution. But it's "Easier Said Than Done" (The Essex, 1963).

A precious value of biblical religion is the experience of new life and renewed hope. That newness is spectacularly expressed in St. Paul's words about the New Birth: "Therefore if any man be in Christ, he is a new crea- ture: old things are passed away; behold, all things are become new" (2 Cor- inthians 5:17 KJV).

It is not so rare a thing for an individual to feel so renewed—especially by merciful absolution after a period of dark despair—that the only just description we have of it is "Born Again."

I don't think we need to shy away from such a bold expression. Sure, it's 'tarred' with cultural associations that feel corny, and maybe even obnoxious. But everybody wants it! I submit to you that everybody wants to be born again, in the sense of starting over again, in the sense of Ebenezer Scrooge at the end of *A Christmas Carol*, in the sense of midlife adults who *Look Back in Anger* (John Osborne, 1956).

I am not ashamed of wanting to proffer sufferers the hope of a new song. I've been given it once or twice myself, and in the words of Jimmy Webb, addressed to a human, "I owe you / More than I could ever pay." That's how I feel about the Lord.

— *Paul Zahl*

153

May 17

This is what the LORD of Hosts, the God of Israel, says to all the exiles who were carried away from Jerusalem to Babylon: "Build houses and settle down. Plant gardens and eat their produce. Take wives and have sons and daughters. Take wives for your sons and give your daughters in marriage, so that they too may have sons and daughters. Multiply there; do not decrease. Seek the prosperity of the city to which I have sent you as exiles. Pray to the LORD on its behalf, for if it prospers, you too will prosper." (Jeremiah 29:4-7 BSB)

The U.S. Census Bureau reported in 2009 that only half of American families could afford a "modestly priced" home in their state. These "modestly priced" homes are on average the cheapest twenty-five percent of homes. That means the other half can afford to purchase no home at all.

In an ironic sense, a house of one's *own* ("exclusively belonging to one's self") by default has to be one that you *own* ("to possess and have command of"), rather than one that you *owe on* ("to have to repay"). But we do not have to be refugees or immigrants to know the sinking feeling of having no command over our living situation. We are in debt to an apartment complex or to a landlord, or to the bank, or to the series of historical events that led to ownership or to the lack of it. We are constantly grasping for our *own*, in a world that is *God's*.

The above passage is from Jeremiah's letter to the Jewish people in the midst of their housing crisis, their exile in Babylon. Here are the instructions for a nation in captivity: They should not worry over whether it is worth it to plant a garden on someone else's land; they should fix their drafty, leaky apartments. They should not diminish themselves in a foreign city. The Lord whispers of rootedness, fruitfulness, and fertility. In His cities, all renters and refugees are invited to take off their shoes and enjoy the land as if it *were* their own. The Lord doles out love and hospitality to new arrivals and established residents alike. Because the Lord our God's acceptance is not constrained by property lines or borders or social classes or races or credit histories. The Lord our God cares for us, just as He cares for the birds of the sky and flowers of the field, who pay no rent or mortgage: beautifully and freely.

— *Maddy Green*

> But God said to Jonah, "Is it right for you to be angry about the bush?" And [Jonah] said, "Yes, angry enough to die." Then the LORD said, "You are concerned about the bush, for which you did not labor and which you did not grow; it came into being in a night and perished in a night. And should I not be concerned about Nineveh, that great city, in which there are more than a hundred and twenty thousand persons who do not know their right hand from their left…?" (Jonah 4:9-11)

There is nothing more infuriating than ingratitude.

God asked Jonah to do him a simple favor: Go to Nineveh and tell them I'm unhappy about their wickedness. Of course, that's never an easy message to deliver, especially on behalf of an all-seeing and all-knowing God. But guess what, God *is* all-seeing and all-knowing. It's not like he can be outrun.

Well, Jonah begs to differ. He sets sail in the wrong direction, and God sends a storm after him. Fearing the right hand of God, Jonah asks to be thrown overboard. A guy dumb enough to believe he can outrun God probably belongs at the bottom of the sea. But then, with his left hand, God sends a big fish to swallow Jonah and vomit him on the shore.

Jonah gets the point and eventually delivers the bad news to Nineveh. And Nineveh repents! Jonah has done what God asked him to, and the city is saved.

But Jonah is furious. *I almost died trying to deliver this message, and God just changed his mind?* In the midst of this temper tantrum, God doesn't give up on Jonah. He sends him a shady bush and lets him rest beneath it. The next day, to teach him a lesson, God causes the bush to wither, and Jonah, again, is furious, prompting God's explanation above. That's where the book ends.

Why does God waste his time on this guy? Jonah makes a series of horrible choices, and God bails him out at every turn. He gets swallowed by a fish, sees a major city repent, and watches an entire bush grow out of the ground in a single day. And still, he is so angry that he wants to die. Jonah doesn't know his ass from his elbow or, more biblically, his right hand from his left.

And yet, despite having just returned 120,000 lost sheep to his flock, God won't give up until he gets one more.

— *Michael Sansbury*

May 19

For we are God's handiwork, created in Christ Jesus to do
good works, which God prepared in advance for us to do.
(Ephesians 2:10 NIV)

I don't know about you, but to me, some days just feel hard. Of course, there
are the *really hard* days, in the midst of illness, grief, or change. And when I
think about all of the big problems of the world—ecological, political, sys-
temic—I don't even know where to begin.

But often, even just the day-to-day normalcy of to-do lists and relationships and work feels plenty hard enough. It doesn't help that I tend to put
pressure on myself to do all the things, right now, and to do them all perfectly. Life quickly becomes an exhausting cycle of feeling overwhelmed,
insufficient, and just plain tired.

But when I read these words from Ephesians, I am reminded that it is
not my striving that will make me lovable. It is not accomplishing all of the
tasks on my list that will make me *enough*. I am God's handiwork—God's
creative work, God's poetry. I am a work of art, and so are you. Reading
these words slows me down, in a good way. They invite me to pause, to
take a deep breath, and to feel—even for just one second—my inherent
belovedness.

God has made us just as we are, and has laid good work before us. We
do not have to seek it out. We do not have to strive to make the biggest
impact possible. Because of Christ, it is enough to simply be *you*, imperfect
and yet deeply loved.

— *Lindsey Hepler*

May 20

For [the LORD] is like a refiner's fire and like fullers' soap;
he will sit as a refiner and purifier of silver, and he will
purify the descendants of Levi and refine them like gold
and silver, until they present offerings to the LORD in righteousness. (Malachi 3:2-3)

Most people are familiar with the image of a metalsmith's purifying forge,
a heat that burns away impurities in precious metals. Less familiar is the
profession of fuller.

A fuller is the last person in the process of turning wool into a fabric.
Wool fiber was spun into thread, then woven into a sheet. That sheet would
still have a natural oily residue from the sheep, dirt from the weaver's hands,
and it would be delicate from the weaving process. A fuller would take the
sheet and thoroughly clean it. They would fill a large, shallow bucket with
soap and water, take off their sandals, and stomp on the fabric, becoming a
DIY washing-machine agitator. The process could sometimes take all day,
but the fabric treated by a fuller became remarkably clean and white. Once
the fuller was done cleaning the sheet, they would stretch the garment on
a frame to dry, then the fabric could be used for making clothes.

Malachi's prophecy in today's reading is directed to the priestly class of
Israel. They were abusing the system by offering second-rate animal sacrifices, divorcing their wives, and importing unfaithful practices from other
religions. Through Malachi, God says that "a messenger of the covenant"
is coming to purify the priestly class, like a refiner's fire and a fuller's soap.
(Hint: The next book of the Bible features John the Baptist!)

In a similar way, God finds our impurities and removes them. Sometimes,
that process feels like firing and fulling, like the heat of the metalsmith and
the stomping of the cleaners. On the other side of God's work, however,
we find that we have been made as white as a fuller's garments, that our
failures, weaknesses, and frailties (what the Bible calls "sins") have been
mysteriously removed. Thanks be to God that he is willing to get his hands
and feet dirty to clean us up.

— Bryan Jarrell

May 21

I can do all things through him who strengthens me. (Philippians 4:13)

In 1999, the rapper Ice Cube penned the famous line, "You can do it, put
your back into it." Though frequently misinterpreted, it has faithfully
served as our national motto ever since. It is simply the American way to
believe that we can achieve anything through our own willpower. Nothing
is impossible as long as we work hard enough.

But what happens when you blow out your back? What happens when,
for whatever reason, your efforts are simply not enough to, say, finish an
assignment, repair an estranged relationship, or get out of bed in the morning? In these moments, doubling down and putting your back into it can
often make the matter worse and eventually lead to a debilitating breakdown. The English playwright Ben Jonson once said, "Many might go to
heaven with *half* the labor they go to hell." It's true, isn't it? We may believe
that the way to God is in our striving, but oftentimes, our striving leads
to our undoing.

This verse declares that the source of all true strength is God. He is
capable of doing anything, even the things you didn't think were possible.
In fact, God's promise is always that which is humanly impossible. Faith
is a double-sided coin in that way—one side confessing "I can't," and the
other side proclaiming "He can." Because of God, what once was a wall is
now a wide-open door that leads you to a place you never would have gone
on your own terms. Not only is He your daily supplier of strength, but He
is strong enough to face any problem that is too big for you to face today.

P.S. I'm kidding about the national motto, by the way, which just so
happens to be "In God We Trust."

— *Sam Bush*

May 22

The heavens declare the glory of God,
 and the sky above proclaims his handiwork.
Day to day pours out speech,
 and night to night reveals knowledge.
There is no speech, nor are there words,
 whose voice is not heard. (Psalm 19:1-3 ESV)

There's a hymn adapted from this psalm, written by Joseph Addison and set to Haydn's *Creation* tune. It starts with the words, "The spacious firmament on high…" and describes how the sun, moon, and stars tell the earth the story of her creation. So what if there's "no real voice nor sound" that comes from these orbs? Even in their silence, they "utter forth a glorious voice, / For ever singing, as they shine, / 'The hand that made us is divine.'"

This psalm, and the poetry of the hymn, remind us of the scope of creation, and the comfort that the sun and the moon and all of the stars have existed long before the psalmist, and will exist long after we leave our footprint on the earth, and through all of the changes of our understanding of planets and space and nature. When we forget or fail to sing the story of our birth, the spacious firmament will continue to sing, as they shine, that "The hand that made us is divine."

For those of us who worry over God's creation, including God's creation of ourselves, it is a comfort to read these words from the psalmist and the poet, who remind us that the sun and the moon reflect the glory and love of God in creation, even without real words or voice.

The hand that made us is divine.

— *Carrie Willard*

May 23

For I am the LORD who brought you up from the land of
Egypt, to be your God; you shall be holy, for I am holy.
(Leviticus 11:45)

Maybe it's the ring slipped onto our grandmother's finger on her wedding
day. Maybe it's a stuffed animal that our child cuddled. Maybe it's a military medal that graced our father's dress blues. We all probably have some
physical item which is imbued with an importance invisible to others but
unmissable to us. We wouldn't sell it for the world. It's an icon of a narrative
we ourselves are a part of. In and of itself, it may be worth little or nothing.
But we have set it apart as a treasure of incalculable value. In the language
of the Bible, we have sanctified it. Made it holy.

It's fascinating—in a twisted sort of way—to observe how words can be
transmogrified to mean the exact opposite of their origin. "Holiness" often
implies a self-congratulatory quality, as if it's a spiritual status acquired by
hard work, a level we've reached that all the "unholy" people have not. Or
it's an insult, as in "holier-than-thou." In the scriptures, however, holy is a
word of divine love.

When the Lord liberated his people from Egypt, he made them holy.
When Jesus frees us from the prison of shame and guilt and death, he makes
us like himself. When we hear, "You shall be holy," we hear a declaration.
It's like the bestowal of a name, "You shall be called Veronica, or Jim, or
Nathanael." God says, "You shall be called Holy. I'm declaring you to be that
way. You have an importance that may be invisible to others but is unmissable to me. You are a treasure of incalculable value to me."

Holiness is always a divine gift, never a human achievement. We are that
"physical item," that creation of God, imbued with an importance over which
the angelic choirs sing. When God says to us, "You shall be holy," that's just
another way of him saying, "You shall be mine, my beloved, my own, my
cherished people now and forever, for I have sanctified you."

— *Chad Bird*

May 24

Then [Jesus] withdrew from [his disciples] about a stone's throw, knelt down, and prayed, "Father, if you are willing, remove this cup from me; yet, not my will but yours be done." (Luke 22:41-42)

To make a request of God is a strange act. In a world of calculation, prayer stands in stark contrast; its efficacy cannot be calculated, nor does proper training directly correlate with results. In his short essay "The Efficacy of Prayer," C. S. Lewis writes, "Simply to say prayers is not to pray; otherwise a team of properly trained parrots would serve as well as men..." He goes on: "You cannot pray for the recovery of the sick unless the end you have in view is their recovery."

In this passage from Luke, Jesus pleads for relief at the feet of the Father. Woven into his prayer is the longing for resolution and the shadow of what resolution may mean. How can we possibly pray with the end in view, as Lewis suggests, when the future seems so bleak? Especially when God's will seems disastrous, our cup of pain is still filled to the brim, and the pesky roots of doubt run deeper than peace?

And yet, we find a strange comfort in the Garden of Gethsemane, where the request of the holiest and most deserving human being went unanswered—Jesus Christ, whose greatest petition was not met so that our greatest need could be. The Lord, who pled from a stone's throw away, has drawn near to us and emptied the cup of judgment for our redemption. Our cries for help have been answered in the form of a corpse on the cross, an empty tomb, and a Savior whose fixed view has always been our recovery.

— *Sam Guthrie*

May 25

Now to him who is able to keep you from falling, and to make you stand without blemish in the presence of his glory with rejoicing, to the only God our Savior, through Jesus Christ our Lord, be glory, majesty, power, and authority, before all time and now and forever. Amen. (Jude 24-25)

The Bible is hard to read. I don't understand a lot of it, and what I do understand I often don't like. In this short letter's 25 verses, there's the condemnation of false teachers, whom Jude calls libertines. Then there's a warning, that God destroys turncoats and wantons and blowhards. Stay away from all these people, Jude says, and alert anyone who tends their way!

Amid the intimidating, fearful talk of "fire," "chains," and "darkness," which "certain intruders" must suffer for ages—Jude can only conclude his letter the way he begins: with deference to God's power, totally outside human agency. In his salutation, he addresses his letter to "those who are called, who are beloved in God the Father and *kept safe* for Jesus Christ," wishing that "mercy, peace, and love be yours *in abundance*" (vv. 1-2).

So why all this talk about such severe judgment, about eons of punishment? Why does Jude's talk of grace slide so quickly into a moral tirade?

Jude's problems also seem trivial to me, being so distant in time and space. But in my own time, certain divisions agitate me and deserve real alarm about the harm they can inflict. (I mean, for example, social prejudice that keeps people at odds, or militant atheism that undermines the value of life, or theological discord that drives family members apart.)

I find myself in the middle of life, like the middle of Jude's epistle. I'm somewhere between hearing good news—about security, leniency, calm, and care—and hoping for it to be realized. And in that space between, life is full of scandal and confusion. What I need again and again is this transcendent, alien hope that, despite all the pitfalls around me, the one who is able to keep me from falling is not myself but God.

— *Kendall Gunter*

May 26

> When I remember you in my prayers, I always thank my
> God because I hear of your love for all the saints and your
> faith toward the Lord Jesus. I pray that the sharing of your
> faith may become effective when you perceive all the good
> that we may do for Christ. (Philemon 1:4-6)

Paul's letter to Philemon is just a handful of verses, leaving readers to spec-
ulate about the behind-the-scenes details. Apparently Onesimus is a former
servant whose relationship with Philemon had been broken in some way
and so Paul takes it upon himself to ask them to receive Onesimus back in
the community as a beloved brother. In terms of economy of words, it's the
opposite of Romans. This is Paul not as apostle, not as prophet. This is Paul
as coach, referee even, seeing a need and taking it upon himself to make
things right. This is Paul way down deep in the weeds of life.

This letter isn't written to a collective: the Romans, the Colossians, the
Corinthians. This is the Letter to Philemon. Just one guy. This is a letter
written to just one guy because of Paul's love for just one guy. Think about
it—Paul cared enough for Onesimus that he wrote what would become
this book of the Bible, just to help him. When you step back for a bigger
perspective, this little letter shows that God can do with our lives more
than we will ever see. God can do more with our lives than what can be
put into words.

Not only is it a bold promise, it's counterintuitive, countercultural even.
We say that we should practice what we preach, but Paul here in Philemon
demonstrates something different. Paul is saying, "God will do more through
you than I can say. The Living God will enlist you into practicing even more
than I could ever preach." The good we do in Christ, Paul says, it's always
going to be more than we can say.

As a preacher, I stand in the pulpit every week and I try to find the
words to get people to practice what I preach. But the good news that Paul
proclaims in this short letter is that Christ, who is not dead, can catch us
up into more good than any of us can put into words, because death does
not enclose our lives.

— Jason Micheli

May 27

> Now Israel loved Joseph more than any other of his children,
> because he was the son of his old age; and he had made him
> a long robe with sleeves. But when his brothers saw that
> their father loved him more than all his brothers, they hated
> him, and could not speak peaceably to him. (Genesis 37:3-4)

If you are thinking that the Bible is the story of virtuous parents with sinless progeny, think again. Consider some of the lead characters in the book of Genesis: Cain and Abel, Noah's sons, Jacob and Esau. All had contentious relationships with each other, some to the point of death. Each was vying for parental or divine love or attention, consumed by jealousy or deviously vengeful.

What is it about our siblings that can drive us to such lengths? It seems we can't get enough love. We are bottomless pits in terms of the amount of love we need just to function in a world that tells us we are unlovable. If being young, thin, wealthy, and smart are the gifts of favor, then we feel the condemnation of aging, thickening, dwindling resources, and degenerating brain cells. Life can be judged unfair by any standard. When someone, especially a sibling, who has the same genes and "nature" as we do, seems to be getting more than their share of love, our insecurities flare up, leaving us feeling angry and jealous.

What is the point of this story in Genesis? To illustrate that God knows who we are and how we behave. We are envious, spiteful, prone to feeling unloved and inadequate, and constantly comparing ourselves to others. But later, Joseph tells his brothers, "Even though you intended to do harm to me, God intended it for good" (Gen 50:20). In every relationship, there is more than meets the eye because God is there. You can trust that Jesus Christ has redeemed you from the rivalry rat-race and that, unlike many earthly parents, he does not play favorites.

— *Marilu Thomas*

May 28

The integrity of the upright guides them,
  but the crookedness of the treacherous destroys them.
    (Proverbs 11:3)

Sit up straight! Don't slouch. I heard this a lot growing up. So much so that I have this deep fear of developing a hunchback and that I will eventually walk around only able to look at my feet. As I age, my body reminds me it's aging as well; I've come to realize how important my posture is, literally and figuratively.

How does one remain upright in a world where, according to St. Bob Dylan, "everything is broken"? The demand of the law is back-breaking; it brings us to our knees and deforms us (or perhaps it reveals how deformed we already are). So how does one unburden oneself? How does Fannie "take a load off"? It's impossible, because daily demand comes not only from the outside-in but also from the inside-out.

Our nonalignment knows no end; in the final analysis, we humans always trend toward crookedness. We've known it for a very long time. Greek mythology envisioned Atlas, punished by Zeus, forced to hold the weight of the sky on his back. Bearing up under the weight of our own existence (and the oughts and the shoulds), we can feel like God is punishing us with the admonition to "be all we can be." Exhausted, depleted, and angry at ourselves, we often isolate like sick dogs who wander off alone to die.

But then the kindness of God leads to *metanoia* (a rethinking of our thinking, i.e. repentance). "The integrity of the upright" turns out to be something we receive. Putting on Christ, who assumed a perfectly God-pleasing posture, we are gifted with and grafted onto a life that is not our own.

Do you hear God's word today? "Sleeper, awake! Rise from the dead, and Christ will shine on you" (Eph 5:14). You are a child of the King who has adorned you with His uprightness and integrity. In Christ, God's best is yours.

— *Matt Magill*

May 29

You should not have entered the gate of my people
  on the day of their calamity;
you should not have joined in the gloating over Judah's disaster
  on the day of his calamity (Obadiah 1:13)

The German word "*schadenfreude*," pronounced "shah-den-froi-duh," has no English equivalent. It's a word for the emotion one has when one takes pleasure in another's misfortune. It's the feeling you get when the rival sports team has an unfortunate loss, or when your frenemy PTA parent has to move away for a spouse's job. Maybe you've taken pleasure in a politician losing an election or a business competitor losing a contract. *Schadenfreude* may not be a word in every language, but the feeling is universal.

The book of Obadiah is the shortest in the Old Testament, and it is a story of *schadenfreude*. When Jerusalem fell to the Babylonian Empire, Israel's neighbor to the south, Edom, was overjoyed. Edom's rivalry with Israel went all the way back to the book of Genesis, and the two nations were frequently in conflict. Obadiah tells us that the Edomites cheered on the Babylonians, helped them sack Jerusalem, and killed fleeing refugees. God's word through Obadiah to Edom is harsh—*everything that happened to Jerusalem will happen to you, too*. The God of the universe has witnessed Edom's *schadenfreude*. It's of no surprise then that the Babylonians march south and conquer Edom once they're done with Jerusalem.

One imagines a God of *schadenfreude* would be quite sadistic, taking pleasure in human misery from his heavenly throne with a bucket of popcorn in his lap and a cold beer on his side table. Thankfully, the heavens are different. God says that he takes no delight in the death of sinners (Ezek 18:23), and we look no further than the gospel for the fullest evidence of that claim. In Jesus' death and resurrection, God intervenes in the world of time and space to cure human misery, not take pleasure in it.

There is no *schadenfreude* in the heavenly realms. God knows your suffering and is resolving it right now as we live and breathe.

> *God, we ask that you hasten your return and set all things right;*
> *and today, disabuse us of the pleasure we find in the sufferings*
> *of enemies.*
>
> — *Bryan Jarrell*

May 30

A Samaritan woman came to draw water, and Jesus said to
her, "Give me a drink." ... The Samaritan woman said to
him, "How is it that you, a Jew, ask a drink of me, a woman
of Samaria?" (Jews do not share things in common with
Samaritans.) Jesus answered her, "If you knew the gift of
God, and who it is that is saying to you, 'Give me a drink,'
you would have asked him, and he would have given you
living water." (John 4:7-10)

Flannery O'Connor's story "Revelation" opens with a woman named Ruby
Turpin stuck in a doctor's office. She mentally pigeonholes everyone in the
waiting room—a spoiled child whose nose "ran unchecked," a "white-trashy"
woman wearing "gritty" clothes, and a well-kept "stylish lady" with whom
Ruby rushes to converse. Meanwhile, Ruby's husband, Claud, "lifted his
foot onto the magazine table and rolled his trouser leg up to reveal a purple
swelling on a plump marble-white calf." (Ruby's pride in her genteel manners is perhaps misplaced.)

Don't we all walk into a room and pick out the people "like us" (and the
people not like us)? O'Connor's setting is deliberate; a doctor's office is the
one place where achievements won't help us a bit. One day, the doctor will
find something wrong with your body—or, heav'n forfend, find something
to critique about your "lifestyle." An uncomfortable awareness of our infirmities can, ironically, intensify our compulsive need for moral identities—
the "stylish" group, the Dartmouth parents, or the "good" political party.

But in John 4, Jesus seeks out the least stylish person in the room: the
first-century equivalent of the runny-nosed kid. He asks the Samaritan—
thought to be unclean—to give him a drink. This inverted favoritism targets
moral outcasts. The woman had been through five husbands and lives with
a prospective sixth. She promptly deflects to a debate on Judeo-Samaritan
Issues. But Jesus dodges the Issues and cuts straight to the heart of human
sin. Like a doctor's diagnosis, this is good news. Even if you're right about
politics, or education, or parenting—or at the top of the social pyramid
at the doctor's office—you have your own version of the "five husbands"
problem somewhere in your past or present. Our infirmities, like Claud's
leg ulcer, "will out." But the Doctor is ready for you, and he has a total cure.

— *Will McDavid*

167

May 31

I am confident of this, that the one who began a good work among you will bring it to completion by the day of Jesus Christ. (Philippians 1:6)

In the midst of dire news headlines, good work is still happening in the world. It is happening in our cities and countries by way of community-building and legislation. It is happening in our families as babies are brought home from the hospital, or as a prodigal child is welcomed home in forgiveness and love. It is happening in our minds and spirits when we have a breakthrough in therapy. Good work is happening all around, and it is an honor that we get to be a part of it in so many ways.

However, we have not yet seen the *completion* of the good work in the world. We end each day well aware of the ways that our world is still very much incomplete: We could always use more therapy; our families are still holding onto heartache and resentment; and our cities and countries are wracked with cycles of poverty and inequality. In this verse from Philippians, we read that God will bring the good work to completion by the day of Jesus Christ. It is not yet the day of completion, and that truth hurts daily.

Thankfully, the fate of the good work among us is eternally and fully in the hands of God. If we were the ones to either start the good work or bring it to completion, our egos would mess up the entire operation. Luckily for us, God begins the good work, and God completes it.

So today, as you consider these words of St. Paul to the Philippians, be comforted that the whole world does not, in fact, rest on your shoulders. We are graciously given the invitation to be a part of the good work that God is doing, but we do not start the work nor do we complete it. That power and honor rests solely on the shoulders of our suffering Savior, the One who met our broken world face-to-face with the ultimate Good Work: a sacrifice that concludes our story of pain with mercy and, finally, redemption on the day of Jesus Christ.

— *Amanda McMillen*

June 1

Now the whole group of those who believed were of one heart and soul, and no one claimed private ownership of any possessions, but everything they owned was held in common. With great power the apostles gave their testimony to the resurrection of the Lord Jesus, and great grace was upon them all. There was not a needy person among them, for as many as owned lands or houses sold them and brought the proceeds of what was sold. They laid it at the apostles' feet, and it was distributed to each as any had need. (Acts 4:32-35)

Over the last half dozen years, I've had the privilege of mentoring a boy who lives near my church. Since my kids are college-aged and beyond, hanging out with him has kept me in touch with fun stuff like throwing a football, shooting baskets, building crazy structures with Legos, and assembling SpongeBob jigsaw puzzles. We make a good team on puzzles: He has great visual memory for where a discarded piece might be, and I contribute the strategy. I'm teaching him that, when confronted with the chaos of random pieces, he should locate the corners.

I think it is sound advice, not just with jigsaw puzzles, but also with the debris of daily life. That original Jerusalem church in Acts would face so much chaos, with persecution from outside and dissension and deception inside. Still, in the jumble of challenges, God somehow helped them find the corners—a deep belief in the resurrected Christ, a profound experience of "great grace," an uncharacteristic unity, and an uncommon generosity. For a time, it seemed that, in their midst, you couldn't find a needy person or an obscenely greedy person. May such "great grace" fall upon us all.

— *Larry Parsley*

June 2

I saw all the deeds that are done under the sun; and see, all
is vanity and a chasing after wind. (Ecclesiastes 1:14)

Sorry for the rather morbid question—especially if you're reading this in
the morning—but when you're on your deathbed, what do you think will
matter to you? When your life is coming to an end, or when it feels like your
life is coming to an end, what matters? The fact that you never finished that
PhD? The fact that you got that much-deserved promotion at work 25 years
ago? That your high school team was three points away from winning state,
and you missed the field goal? That you never got even with that one guy?
The fact that *the* deal went down the tubes?

No. At that point in your life, none of those things will matter. None of
them. Only one thing will matter, only one question will be asked: "Who
will deliver me?"

King Solomon came to some conclusions about what's really important.
The son of King David, he had devoted his entire life to gaining wisdom. He
had seen it all, he had done it all, and he had owned it all. But in the midst
of his success, he wasn't really happy. His assessment: It's all smoke. It's all
vapor. "Vapor of vapors!" It all comes and goes so quickly.

On my deathbed, I will need more than vapor. It would be really nice
to have some people there who I love and who love me. But they can't go
with me, and they can't deliver my soul to safety either.

Here's the one thing that will ultimately matter:

…you have died, and your life is hidden with Christ in God.
When Christ who is your life is revealed, then you also will be
revealed with him in glory. (Col 3:3-4)

Jesus is not vapor. He is our only hope in life and in death. He is a sure
anchor, and a very present help in time of need (Ps 46:1). And when you
reach for him, he won't float off in the wind. When you reach for him, you'll
find that he's been holding onto you all along. He will never leave you nor
will he forsake you, and nothing will snatch you out of his hand. Not even
death.

— *Curt Benham*

> To another he said, "Follow me." But he said, "Lord, first let me go and bury my father." But Jesus said to him, "Let the dead bury their own dead; but as for you, go and proclaim the kingdom of God." (Luke 9:59-60)

In the early 20th century, an English philosopher named Alfred Whitehead said, "Apart from religion, expressed in ways generally intelligible, populations sink into the apathetic task of daily survival, with minor alleviations." Does your own life ever feel like this? No matter where you work or what you do all day, being alive can often feel like treading water. With all of its compartments—work life, family life, social life, spiritual life—it often feels like life itself is impossible to keep balanced.

This passage reveals how Jesus approaches our "tasks of daily survival." A man expresses a desire to follow Jesus but asks to bury his father first. Burial at this time in Judaism often involved a year-long period, starting from the time the body was first buried until the bones of the deceased were placed in an ossuary box. Jesus' response is hardly a shining example of pastoral care to a man who's clearly grieving the loss of his father, but he sees that this man is using his father's death as an excuse to put off following Jesus just a little bit longer. As the old Yiddish proverb goes: "We always keep God waiting while we admit more importunate suitors." When Jesus says, "Let the dead bury their own dead," he is talking about spiritual deadness. He's saying, "You think you're treading water right now—keeping everything in your life in place—but you are actually lying at the bottom of the ocean."

Here, we see that God is an all-or-nothing God. He doesn't want just a piece of you. He's not going to ask how your "spiritual life" is going (as if that were a thing). He wants your entire life and everything it entails. Jesus is the Lord of all, which means that he is the Lord of the parts of your life that aren't all together—your addictions, your failures, your doubts, your fears. He wants your entire life because he cares about your actual life. And he doesn't want it when you're ready; he wants it now.

Thanks be to God, who breaks into our lives today and each day—with each of our unique struggles—to give us rest, because he has done everything that needs to be done. Thanks be to God that while we gave nothing, Jesus paid it all. How's that for balance?

— *Sam Bush*

June 4

The Lord is not slow about his promise, as some think of slowness, but is patient with you, not wanting any to perish, but all to come to repentance. (2 Peter 3:9)

The film *Batteries Not Included* is required viewing for anyone who talks about Jesus. It is one of those 80s movies that made my parents worry about me living in New York City. Everything is gritty and kind of dangerous. You think that the movie is about these apartment tenants who are struggling against the man to keep their building from being torn down. At first, it feels almost inspirational! The people seem so different from one another and yet here they are coming together for a greater good! Only, their plans fall apart and they fail.

It is tiny robots from outer space that save them. Yes, you read that right. Tiny, unexplained machines rescue them. It is hard as a Christian to watch this movie and not think about the Lord. God would be fine without us. He is divine. He does not need us. We are, in some ways, not even on his planet. We are, in so many ways, a liability. And yet, he comes from out of nowhere on a mission to make us safe.

Grace is always the miracle that comes from outside of ourselves. God wants all of us folded into his loving embrace. He wants repentance from us not because he needs it but because we do. Because he longs to save us.

That something would come from beyond this place to save us is a staggering idea. And yet that is the only way that salvation works. And that is precisely the promise we get from Jesus.

— *Sarah Condon*

June 5

[H]e measured off a thousand cubits and then led me through water that was ankle-deep. He measured off another thousand cubits and led me through water that was knee-deep. He measured off another thousand and led me through water that was up to the waist. He measured off another thousand, but now it was a river that I could not cross, because the water had risen and was deep enough to swim in—a river that no one could cross. He asked me, "Son of man, do you see this?" ...

"Swarms of living creatures will live wherever the river flows. There will be large numbers of fish, because this water flows there and makes the salt water fresh; so where the river flows everything will live." (Ezekiel 47:3-6, 9, NIV)

Some years ago, I worked for a small civil engineering company in Northern Virginia. We used to assess whether a little blue line on a map represented a stream, and thus a significant restriction on building, or just a ditch that occasionally had water in it. We would go out to the site with a checklist and look for clues—for example, fish.

In this passage, Ezekiel has a vision, and in it he sees water coming from the temple, but he doesn't see a river. He sees what is called a wadi, a dry bed that floods when the rains come. Rivers are powerful symbols of life. To ancient people, rivers had gods in them. But a wadi has no god. It means nothing, because you cannot rely on it for life. Sometimes it flows, and sometimes it is dry as a bone. Ezekiel sees barely a trickle. But a little farther on, and it's ankle deep. Farther, and up to the knees. Then the waist, and then too deep to touch bottom; and everywhere it goes, it gives life to the dead. This thing that should have no god in it, and no power, has more life in it than the sea.

We who trust in God are a wadi, not a river. We are a dry stream; but there is a trickle of water that proceeds from the temple of God, a trickle so slight that it could go all but unnoticed for ages. It looks like nothing because it's just a word—not thunder, or fire from heaven, or armies or wealth or glory—but a quiet word that sounds like this: "Your sins are forgiven." And

173

the only sign that it is true is the blood and water flowing from the side of the one who says it (Jn 19:34), and a trickle of that water splashed on your head in his name. Now you who were scattered and alone are many. You swarm. And now the water is ankle deep—no, waist deep, no, too deep to touch bottom, and it is a raging river, this little word, and wherever it goes, wherever you speak it, there will be life, and many fish.

— *Adam Morton*

June 6

So [Hagar] named the LORD who spoke to her, "You are El-roi"; for she said, "Have I really seen God and remained alive after seeing him?" (Genesis 16:13)

She was a runaway. Young, scared, defenseless. As if that weren't enough, the baby in her belly was fathered by a married old man whose jealous spouse had made her life a living hell. Hagar hadn't asked for any of this. She was no gold-digger who'd winked her way between some rich old codger's sheets to woo him away from his wife. In fact, it was his wife's idea in the first place! Old Sarah told old Abraham to make a baby with her maid because God was dragging his feet about giving them their own promised son. Then, once Hagar was pregnant and started acting a little high and mighty, Sarah conceived disgust for her and eventually impelled her to flee.

It all seems like an episode from *Game of Thrones*—minus the dragons.

So there was Hagar, on the run, at the end of her rope, in a godforsaken place. In other words, she was in the ideal location for heaven to pay her a visit. "[T]hough the LORD is high, he regards the lowly," says the poet (Ps 138:6). To paraphrase Luther, the lower down we are, the better God sees us. He sees Hagar. Visits her. Blesses her. And fills her with hope again. So she gives this gracious God a gracious name: El-roi, "the God who sees."

Hagar, the patron saint of the used-up and thrown-away, is the only person in the Old Testament to name God. She, and the divine name she chose, are vivid reminders that God is never blind to our pain, our shame, our tears. He is the God who sees. He saw Hagar. He sees us, even when it feels like we're buried so deep in the darkness of depravity, depression, addiction, divorce, or bankruptcy that even divine eyes can't penetrate the blackness enveloping us.

Hagar was shocked that she remained alive after seeing God. Oh, dear Hagar, it gets even better. When the Lord sees us, we not only remain alive: We are vivified, enlivened, filled with divine life. Because El-roi not only sees us; he loves us into life and hope again.

— *Chad Bird*

June 7

"Now when these things begin to take place, stand up and raise your heads, because your redemption is drawing near... Be on guard so that your hearts are not weighed down with dissipation and drunkenness and the worries of this life, and that day does not catch you unexpectedly, like a trap. For it will come upon all who live on the face of the whole earth. Be alert at all times, praying that you may have the strength to escape all these things that will take place, and to stand before the Son of Man." (Luke 21:28, 34-36)

Few questions are guaranteed to produce anxiety faster than "Are you ready?" Are you ready for the exam? For the big game? Are you ready to get married? For the baby to arrive? Ready for the court date? Ready for the empty nest? Are you ready for retirement? Are you ready for...today?

Most of us, if we're honest, do not feel ready for anything—at least in the sense of being "prepared." And those of us who think we are ready usually aren't. A wise person once said that if you wait until you're ready to do x, y, or z, you'll wait forever.

The question of readiness inspires panic because it creates in us a sense that our efforts will possibly not be enough, that there's not enough time left before some impending change or judgment.

In today's passage Jesus counsels his disciples to "be on your guard" and "be alert at all times" for the Second Coming. He doesn't want them weighed down by worry or distraction. He wants them ready. Is this his way of conveying that classic sign "Jesus is coming—look busy"? Shape up or ship out? I don't think so. Because it's not doom on the horizon but redemption!

The judgment of the Son of Man is indeed coming, but that judgment isn't like others. The judgment of God in Christ is forgiveness. Authoritative, God-initiated, God-sustained, God-fulfilled forgiveness. This pardon does not depend on your own perceived preparedness but on the trustworthiness of the Judge.

You may not be ready for anything else in life, but on account of the one whose "words will not pass away" (Lk 21:33), you stand perfectly primed for the only impending judgment that counts. So lift up your heads and let your hearts rejoice: No matter how you may feel at this moment, you are ready.

— *David Zahl*

June 8

While Jesus was in Bethany in the home of Simon the Leper, a woman came to him with an alabaster jar of very expensive perfume, which she poured on his head as he was reclining at the table. When the disciples saw this, they were indignant. "Why this waste?" they asked. "This perfume could have been sold at a high price and the money given to the poor." Aware of this, Jesus said to them, "Why are you bothering this woman? She has done a beautiful thing to me. The poor you will always have with you, but you will not always have me." (Matthew 26:6-11 NIV)

For someone who's been telling his followers to feed the hungry and give away all of their belongings, this seems like an odd thing to say. It's also a bold thing to say: "The poor you will *always* have with you." There's no strategic plan to rid the world of poverty in ten years. However, there *is* a very strategic plan in place that will lead to Jesus' crucifixion in a few minutes. But back up—the poor will always be with us?

Jesus seems to be telling his disciples that in spite of their best intentions and right actions, this world will never be perfect. Jesus is also telling his disciples that his life is about to end. And just in case he wasn't abundantly clear, Jesus plays his crowd favorite of turning the world upside-down, elevating the erstwhile shamed woman into the hero of the hour.

It has become cliché to say that someone "meant well," but that's almost always a veiled insult. Nobody says that someone "meant well" when someone actually *did* well. And yet Jesus' words over the woman who anointed him with oil tell us that no act of love is wasted. Even if it only appears that "she meant well" to the well-meaning but quick-to-criticize disciples, her act of love toward Jesus was not wasted.

This passage brings to mind the words of Henri-Frédéric Amiel, a nineteenth-century Swiss moral philosopher: "Life is short. We don't have much time to gladden the hearts of those who walk this way with us. So be swift to love; make haste to be kind." Your impulsive acts of love and kindness are not wasted, even when rule-minders might make you feel that they are.

— *Carrie Willard*

June 9

For the message about the cross is foolishness to those who
are perishing, but to us who are being saved it is the power
of God. For it is written, "I will destroy the wisdom of the
wise, and the discernment of the discerning I will thwart."
(1 Corinthians 1:18-19)

If you grew up in an oppressive religious environment, there's a good chance
you've had to "deconstruct" your faith in order to keep it. That's what I've
done anyway: taking apart the beliefs I received and trying to analyze, sort,
and reassemble them as something I can stomach.

This method of "deconstruction" came from a twentieth-century French
philosopher, Jacques Derrida. (Stay with me.) For him, it was a way of protecting minority voices, of opposing absolutism, of dismantling dominant
ideas by pointing out internal incoherence. What's more interesting to me,
and more relevant to everyday life, is where Derrida got his idea. He got it
from another modern philosopher, who got it from Luther.

In Luther's Heidelberg Disputation, he wrote against pretended wisdom. Anyone considered moral or powerful had gotten it all wrong, he
said. They were "theologians of glory," believing God was only in obvious
progress and success. "Theologians of the cross," however, could see God's
activity where it really was—in the worst parts of life, "destroy[ing]" (literally, *deconstructing*) established power and knowledge. God didn't delight
in people's pain and humiliation, but God delighted to identify with people
there, first and finally in the cross.

Yet Luther didn't come up with this idea either. He got it from Paul,
here in 1 Corinthians. And Paul in turn got it from Isaiah. God's work won't
be contained by what's polite, convenient, or presentable. God "destroy[s]
the wisdom" of those things, because they try to ignore God's real activity,
and its friendship with shame and confusion and failure. And that's where
God is, in Jesus, on the cross.

This history of "deconstruction" helps me orient my faith in "secular"
contexts. But even more than that, it actually addresses my experience.
Against my intuition, and against what I'd have done, God tells it like it is,
and meets us where we are, and shows up where we don't expect.

— *Kendall Gunter*

178

June 10

But Moses said to the LORD, "O my Lord, I have never been eloquent…" Then the LORD said to him, "Who gives speech to mortals? Who makes them mute or deaf, seeing or blind? Is it not I, the LORD? Now go, and I will be with your mouth and teach you what you are to speak." But he said, "O my Lord, please send someone else." (Exodus 4:10-13)

I've never been big on conventional heroes—the Captain Americas or Neil Armstrongs of the world. To me, the most compelling figures in literature and life are those that are flawed or vulnerable in some meaningful way, and I'm pretty sure God shares this proclivity, at least if the Bible is anything to go by.

Moses is one of God's great anti-heroes. Despite lowly origins, he grew up in the royal court of Egypt to become what one can only infer was a cocky, hot-blooded young man—the sort who neither doubts his own righteousness nor his ability to fix things. But then he murders an Egyptian and is forced to flee for his life. Through the next forty years in rural anonymity, he passes from excessive confidence to profound self-doubt. By the time God visits him in a burning bush, Moses is hardly inclined to see himself as the heroic type.

And yet God nevertheless charges him with the epic task of confronting Pharaoh and bringing the Israelites out of Egypt. Moses naturally wonders, "Who am I?" and peppers God with a litany of quite sensible misgivings. Despite God's reassurances, Moses still isn't having it. Then, as if the burning bush thing wasn't enough, God proceeds to turn Moses' staff into a snake, then back into a staff, and then covers Moses' hand with leprosy before healing it again. After all this, as we see in the passage above, Moses *still* pleads inadequacy and begs God to "send someone else."

Who can't relate? Who doesn't after all feel inadequate and fearful when confronted by the vast problems of this world or by our own weaknesses and failings, not to mention by the awesome mystery of God? But in this Exodus story, God reminds Moses that we are never the real heroes anyway. And just as God took a murderous "basket case" like Moses and made him the deliverer of his people and conduit for the Torah, God takes even us and breathes life and purpose and the strength of love into our dreary lives. We're still anti-heroes, to be sure, but we're God's anti-heroes, and God's not done with us.

— *Benjamin Self*

June 11

[T]hey shall beat their swords into plowshares,
   and their spears into pruning hooks;
nation shall not lift up sword against nation,
   neither shall they learn war any more;
but they shall all sit under their own vines and under their
      own fig trees,
   and no one shall make them afraid;
for the mouth of the LORD of hosts has spoken. (Micah 4:3-4)

In the very last book of the Old Testament, when Micah is retelling the old prophecies of the restoration of Zion, he slips in a curious stanza about the end of all wars. All weapons will be refashioned into gardening tools, he says. Every man will have his own fig tree, and no one will be afraid.

I've had this magical vision written on my wall ever since the Arab Spring in 2011. I have prayed these verses for our brothers and sisters in Syria enduring a decade of violence. In the very land where fig trees grow, where Jesus and his disciples roamed, children are weary of war. This weariness stretches everywhere, through the Congo and Korea, the past and the future, through trenches and bullet proof vests.

Returning to these verses now, the prophecy speaks loudly even into my daily existence this side of eternity.

When weapons are fashioned into plowshares, we will reap life instead of death. Shootings will cease and all people will be nourished.

When nations will not train for war anymore, no grieving mother will have to receive a folded American flag; no caskets will be lowered into the ground in Arlington.

When each person will sit under his own vine and fig tree, we will all be restored to the garden of Eden, where our needs will be met, cool shade will be cast, and our toil in the land will be over.

And there, no one will be frightened. Our anxieties will be faded memories. No fear of unmet need will prevent us from seeing God's abundant grace and accepting it joyfully.

Lord, make it so. Amen.

— Maddy Green

June 12

Then Jesus cried again with a loud voice and breathed his last. At that moment the curtain of the temple was torn in two, from top to bottom. The earth shook, and the rocks were split. The tombs also were opened, and many bodies of the saints who had fallen asleep were raised. (Matthew 27:50-52)

There is a song by the band Journey called "Wheel in the Sky"—it's a fantastic song—and the key lyric repeated over and over again is "The wheel in the sky keeps on turning." Or if you prefer Season One of the TV show *True Detective*, "Time is a flat circle." Both have the same implication—life is a series of tedious, inevitable, empty events. All that is, is all that was. Your life is the product of an endless and infinite chain of cause and effect, over which you have no control and the sum of which is nothing but the indifferent rhythm of nature. "The wheel in the sky keeps on turning...the wheel in the sky keeps me yearning."

Christianity says something different precisely because of the death of Jesus on a cross. At his death, the Temple curtain is torn, from top to bottom, and the divide between heaven and earth is forever breached. An earthquake happens and the dead are raised.

These apocalyptic events signal that the course of history is fundamentally disrupted. By his death, the world is turned upside down and reoriented toward a new goal. A new age has dawned unlike any other. The death of Christ is the new hinge upon which all of humanity turns.

The cross is the stick that is thrown into the spokes of the wheel in the sky, and with it, our sins and the burdens of our past. As Paul says repeatedly, if anyone is in Christ they are a new creation—"The old is gone, the new is here!" (2 Cor 5:17 NIV). By Jesus' death, life is given to the dead, grace is given to the unworthy, and forgiveness is given to sinners, creating a new future and making all things new. Nothing will ever be the same again.

— *Todd Brewer*

June 13

> They devoted themselves to the apostles' teaching and fellowship, to the breaking of bread and the prayers.
>
> Awe came upon everyone, because many wonders and signs were being done by the apostles. All who believed were together and had all things in common; they would sell their possessions and goods and distribute the proceeds to all, as any had need. (Acts 2:42-45)

If this were the only snapshot we had of life in the early church, we probably wouldn't trust it—especially if we've logged more than a handful of hours in a local church. And of course, it is not. In this book of Acts, we soon witness church people lying and cheating, negotiating bitter divisions, and struggling with false teaching and false prophets.

Still, in our passage, we get a glimpse of some of those magical moments that I hope all of us have experienced at one time or another in a local church: this rich sense of friendship mingled with prayer, this ravenous hunger for the gospel, and the sheer joy of breaking bread with one another, whether we are celebrating communion or divvying up a potluck. I pray you've belonged to a place that is animated by the silent conviction that nobody who sits in one of our pews is going to go hungry while the person sitting next to them has a stocked pantry back at home.

Yes, sadly, church does not always work that way. But when it does, as it did in our passage, it is not surprising that God's unmistakable grace keeps drawing outsiders in (v. 47). May God fill our lives with more of the gracious 'magic' that only the Spirit can bring.

— *Larry Parsley*

June 14

I will greatly rejoice in the LORD,
    my whole being shall exult in my God;
for he has clothed me with the garments of salvation,
    he has covered me with the robe of righteousness,
as a bridegroom decks himself with a garland,
    and as a bride adorns herself with her jewels. (Isaiah 61:10)

Chief among my real-world concerns as a kid was how I dressed. I'd heard adults say, "Dress to impress," and I took that to heart. Consider the long-treasured clothing itinerary I dreamt up at age 9 for a 1985 trip to Disneyland:

Monday: Jams and red tank top
Tuesday: Izod with shorts
Wednesday: Shorts and Spuds MacKenzie shirt
Thursday: Jams and polo (Vans)

Not unlike Tamatoa—the glam-rock coconut crab in *Moana* who sings "I'd rather be shiny!"—I have often found myself on a futile search for acceptance, affirmation, and influence, even through something as seemingly trivial as clothing.

In true "What Not to Wear" fashion (pun intended), and through the use of His Law, God shows us that when we seek to "clothe ourselves" in this way, we exacerbate our spiritual nakedness. The burden of clothing ourselves is *the* fashion emergency that has our Father stooping low to give us His Son, who was stripped naked so that we might, at long last, be covered.

With fruit juice still on their lips, our oldest ancestors hid their nakedness with clothing that cost animals their lives. Out with the old and in with the new: God's garments are intended to "show off" His glory and resurrection. The Divine Dresser helps fashion-disasters like you and me wear "the garments of salvation." Trust and believe this: Hope, humility, a sense of humor, and gratitude are always in style. And no matter what you see in the mirror, God sees you as the perfect model to wear His designs. You are an integral part of the beauty that "brings forth its shoots" and "will cause righteousness and praise to spring up" (v. 11).

You're a model. You know what I mean. You do your little turn on the catwalk!

— *Matt Magill*

June 15

"Go therefore and make disciples of all nations, baptizing
them in the name of the Father and of the Son and of the
Holy Spirit…" (Matthew 28:19)

I once read this verse and concluded that in order to be faithful, I had to
buy a plane ticket, learn a foreign language, and convert as many Muslims
as possible. Of course, evangelization is a big part of the Christian faith, but
I'm no longer sure that that's all the Great Commission is about. There is a
lot here that does not necessarily demand our patronage of the airlines. In
fact, when we read this passage through the lens of a personal burden, we
may be distracting ourselves from a more startling idea.

The setting: a mountain in Galilee. The resurrected Jesus has met his
disciples there. He does not tell them, "Make disciples of the teachable, the
intelligent, the people with magnetic personalities." He says, "Make disciples
of *all nations*." In the Greek, "nation" relates closely to "ethnicity," which
was especially notable for a time when gods were associated with specific
places and people groups. The Jews had their own God, and the Romans
had theirs, and the Persians had theirs. Each god, or pantheon of gods, dealt
with an exclusive group.

But Jesus means to take everyone under his wing, and he will not be
stopped by the boundaries of ethnicity or geography. In the Great Commission, Jesus describes his ideal group: everyone. "The disciples" are not an
exclusive class. No one is left out, not the poor, the sick, the young, the old,
the weird, the excessively normal. Not even you, with your failures, and
ugly secrets, and all of those dumb things you said at the party last night.

Every day, we sort ourselves into little nations based on political beliefs,
wealth, clothing, body type, taste in music. So today, when you encounter
a stranger from a strange land, bear in mind that they, like you, are God's
beloved. God wants *that person* to be included. And remember, too, Jesus'
final promise: that no matter which nation we come from, He is with us
always, to the end of the age.

— *CJ Green*

June 16

There are many who say, "O that we might see some good!
 Let the light of your face shine on us, O LORD!"
You have put gladness in my heart
 more than when their grain and wine abound.
I will both lie down and sleep in peace;
 for you alone, O LORD, make me lie down in safety. (Psalm 4:6-8)

Some people call this a "night psalm." David, on the run from his enemies, must be having trouble sleeping, and for good reason! As the psalm opens, David calls out urgently for God to be "gracious" in hearing his prayer (v. 1).

As king and spiritual leader of Israel, David feels bound to instruct his subjects on how to get right with God. He cautions them about their deceitful words and rebellious anger, and he calls them to practice silent meditation as they lay on their respective beds (v. 4).

With all this drama going on, however, how will David ever get some sleep himself? Yet, as the psalm draws to a close, the same David who passionately seeks God's intervention and vigorously upbraids his enemies now receives in his heart the spiritual equivalent of warm milk and cookies. David prays for the light of God's face, and seems to get his answer as a God-given "gladness" nestles deep in his heart. Now, at last, David is finally able to roll over and sleep in peace (v. 8) under God's protective hand.

— *Larry Parsley*

June 17

> "Go, gather all the Jews to be found in Susa, and hold a fast
> on my behalf, and neither eat nor drink for three days, night
> or day. I and my maids will also fast as you do. After that
> I will go to the king, though it is against the law; and if I
> perish, I perish." (Esther 4:16)

A note about the book of Esther: The name of God is not mentioned once. Pretty interesting, given that it was included in the Bible, right? Take a look for yourself if you don't believe me. I love that God shows up in this story anyway, his invisible hand the guiding force of the narrative—just like in our own lives.

When I was younger and heard about Esther, the teaching was focused on the "big" things she did for the kingdom of God by stepping up for the Jewish people. And, certainly, being instrumental in the saving of an entire race would qualify as big. Victorious, even! But first? She must take this very small step of entering the king's chamber—less a victorious march than a trepidatious step toward potential death.

There's not a lot that's glamorous about risking execution, but that's exactly what Esther will be doing if she approaches the king—and the passage tells us she's happy to look for another way out (take this cup from me, anyone?) before she assents to the plan. She knows she can't do it alone— she needs her people, and her unseen God.

"If I perish, I perish," Esther assents, unknowingly pointing forward hundreds of years to the One for whom there was no *if*. Esther, it turns out, did not perish, but succeeded in entreating the king to save the Jews. Fast-forward hundreds of years to the One who *did* perish, and in so doing saved all of humanity by his unseen but ever-present hand.

— *Stephanie Phillips*

June 18

Jesus answered, "Very truly I tell you, no one can enter the kingdom of God unless they are born of water and the Spirit. Flesh gives birth to flesh, but the Spirit gives birth to spirit. You should not be surprised at my saying, 'You must be born again.' The wind blows wherever it pleases. You hear its sound, but you cannot tell where it comes from or where it is going. So it is with everyone born of the Spirit." (John 3:5-8 NIV)

We can no more see transcendent reality than a corpse can see the sunrise or feel the evening breeze. We are dead to the kingdom of God. Jesus did not come to reform us; he came to resurrect us. When we are raised, it is not by our own power but by the Spirit who breathes life into dirt and dry bones.

We can no more constrain the Spirit than we can grasp the wind. Meteorology cannot pinpoint precisely where the stream of air rustling the leaves begins, nor where it ends. Neither do we "harness" the wind, though we can hoist a sail and journey where it takes us.

A sailboat cannot sail directly into the wind. Either we harmonize our direction and desire with the will of the wind, or we get nowhere. So it is with everyone who is born and borne by the Spirit. The finite soul, like a sailor on the vast ocean, moves in and toward the infinite God, traversing the infinite for eternity, moving forever from beauty to ever greater beauty, always into boundless love and endless joy. Even now, underneath the chaos and turbulence of this life, sometimes we sense a current and a direction, a horizon we are moving toward and beyond, toward something new and wonderful.

— *Michael Nicholson*

June 19

Then I acknowledged my sin to you,
    and I did not hide my iniquity;
I said, "I will confess my transgressions to the LORD,"
    and you forgave the guilt of my sin. *Selah*

Therefore let all who are faithful
    offer prayer to you;
at a time of distress, the rush of mighty waters
    shall not reach them.
You are a hiding place for me;
    you preserve me from trouble;
    you surround me with glad cries of deliverance. *Selah*
    (Psalm 32:5-7)

It's second nature to hide from or minimize our own sin. We can hardly bear to acknowledge our transgressions to ourselves, much less to a perfect, all-knowing God. Yet when it comes to candid repentance, these verses in Psalm 32 promise marketable results: *deliverance.*

Mercifully, our God is in the business of grace, redemption, and remaking, not of crushing adjudication. This is the reception we find upon casting ourselves into his arms whenever we fall short (which, you might know by now, happens often).

In her song "Selah," hip hop artist Lauryn Hill sings:

The choices that I've made have been nothing but mistakes
What a wasted use of space...
In all of my religion, I've fortified this prison
Obligated to obey the demands of bad decisions
Please save me from myself, I need you
Save me from myself, please save me from myself so I can heal
And then he came...

The word *Selah* is sometimes translated as *stop, listen,* or *forever.* In this song, it is an interruption—"And then he came"—*stop*—*listen.* She's talking about Jesus, the antidote, the ultimate interruption to our hideous curse and the awful demands of all our bad decisions.

I have not seen heart-change in my own life by doggedly resolving to be better, but rather by surrendering my many faults and failures to the care of Jesus. "Take this from me. I don't want it anymore. I cannot keep running this race. *Save me from myself.*" This—not a well-crafted plan for self-betterment—is our anthem as sinners. *Take this from me.* And Jesus' response goes just like the Vance Joy song: "This mess was yours, / Now your mess is mine."

Dear one, repentance is not something to hide from; in fact, it is your *hiding place*, where you will be surrounded by glad cries of deliverance, where you will walk free. *Selah!*

— *Charlotte Getz*

June 20

"I have said this to you, so that in me you may have peace. In the world you face persecution. But take courage; I have conquered the world!" (John 16:33)

I am a sucker for de-motivational posters—you know, the ones with the photos that ooze inspiration but have messages that are less-than-inspirational. There's one that depicts an Olympic hurdler, leaping his way to the gold, presumably. The tagline reads, "Obstacles: No matter how many you overcome, there's still an infinite number waiting." We all face hurdles—in relationships, parenting, our occupations—that call out for us to overcome them. Yet even as we conquer these obstacles, new ones arise.

This is why Jesus' words in today's verse are so affecting. They run opposite to the messages of "overcoming" found on modern airwaves and contemporary bookshelves. Jesus' subversive message of peace and courage comes through antithetical means. Instead of giving us swords and spears with which to take down the bastions of Satan's domain, the primary posture of those "in the Lord's army" is one of prostrate, desperate faith. We "overcome" simply by resting in *his* overcoming.

Jesus' words to us are not a summons to triumph over daily obstacles by the centrifugal force of pulling on our own bootstraps. Rather, his good news invites us to submit to and rejoice in his already-accomplished victory on our behalf.

We are not the fighters. We are not the overcomers. He is. Jesus, in word and deed, is the true and better Overcomer. He identified himself as the One who overcomes all. All darkness, death, and sin quakes as the Savior subdues all in order to accomplish his purposes in us and for us (Jn 1:4-5). And this is no "might be," "I hope so," "maybe" possibility. It is true right now, even in your season of darkness, that Christ has overcome the world, overcome everything that is opposed to the light, to beauty, truth, and grace.

— *Brad Gray*

June 21

> "And why do you worry about clothing? Consider the lilies
> of the field, how they grow; they neither toil nor spin, yet
> I tell you, even Solomon in all his glory was not clothed
> like one of these. But if God so clothes the grass of the
> field, which is alive today and tomorrow is thrown into
> the oven, will he not much more clothe you—you of little
> faith? Therefore do not worry…" (Matthew 6:28-31)

I worry about literally everything. I worry about finances, my health, my safety, my future, keeping the house spotless (though we have three kids), making sure I parent perfectly, whether we'll have enough money when we retire, whether we will ever be debt-free, etc.

And when I read this passage, it doesn't alleviate my anxiety. It heightens it. This word comes to us for one specific purpose: to definitively diagnose that we are, in fact, *of little faith* and can do nothing about it. Note that Jesus nowhere in this passage tells us how we can remediate our sad condition.

We who are of little faith have yet a greater hope: one who was belittled on the cross and raised to *become* our faithfulness. We can't *not* be what God tells us not to be, and neither can we *not* be who he says we are in Christ.

If God's care for us were contingent on our faithfulness to Him, we would all be in serious trouble. The law of God essentially declares, "Be faithful to God or die." A better word, though, informs us that *Jesus* was faithful to the point of death, and therefore God cares for us more meticulously than He does for the individual blades of grass, more gracefully than He does for the birds of the air.

The good news is that our capacity to worry can never exceed His commitment to us. Christ was condemned for our anxieties that we might be credited with His faith in God.

— *Jason Thompson*

June 22

My friends, if anyone is detected in a transgression, you who have received the Spirit should restore such a one in a spirit of gentleness. Take care that you yourselves are not tempted. Bear one another's burdens, and in this way you will fulfill the law of Christ. (Galatians 6:1-2)

The late, great Warren Zevon wrote the 1976 rocker "Poor Poor Pitiful Me." He wrote it ironically, and in it, he "complained" about an excess of female attention. His version (not Linda's!) is well worth a listen.

The temptation to self-pity is a strong one. One's pain is one's pain, and it is real, obviously. When people come to see me and try to shuffle off their struggle as illegitimate because others have it worse, I always attempt to validate whatever it is that brought them in to see me. Just counting one's blessings *at the expense of* expressing one's pain never works in the long run. So-called comparative suffering is no real help. You need more.

There is a counterpunch to this, though. It can be helpful, when lost in one's own pity party, to be reminded that no one person has the corner on pain. The adage "misery loves company" can be interpreted in two ways. Yes, it's good to know that we are not the only ones who suffer. But it is also helpful to be comforted by another's company. Perhaps this is why the Apostle Paul says, "Bear one another's burdens, and in this way you will fulfill the law of Christ."

Ultimately, Christ became miserable for our sake, suffering for our sins. He has carried the final burden.

Lord Christ, you went to the cross to bear my burden. I ask you, even now, to take that burden anew and give me your peace that passes understanding. Amen.

— *Paul Walker*

For thus says the LORD:
Your hurt is incurable,
   your wound is grievous.
There is no one to uphold your cause,
   no medicine for your wound,
     no healing for you…
For I will restore health to you,
   and your wounds I will heal,
       says the LORD… (Jeremiah 30:12-13, 17)

One thing has become abundantly clear to me as I've gotten older: left to my own devices, my "hurt" really is incurable. I don't know about you, but I've looked to all manner of things in an attempt to self-medicate amid the gaping brokenness of a fallen world. I've turned to wine, to Mexican food, to television, to gossip, and when I was younger, to boys. Escape, escape, escape. Feel better, feel better, feel better. Some of us are so skilled at avoiding this pain that we've convinced ourselves we're fine. Others of us are more manic about the whole thing, gripping, searching, clawing for anything at all that might bring light to this cavernous darkness. We are yet disbelieving that, like Jeremiah says, there really is no earthly medicine for our wounds. But if you let go of your rickety guardrails for a minute, can't you see he's right? That none of your attempts at self-fulfillment have satisfied your unrelenting need? Can't you see that your wounds are just too grievous?

In the above passage, God tells the Israelites that he himself will be the medicine for their otherwise incurable hurts: "For *I* will restore health to you, and your wounds *I* will heal."

Like the African-American spiritual goes:

There is a balm in Gilead
To make the wounded whole;
There is a balm in Gilead
To heal the sin-sick soul.

God sent Jesus as the utmost Balm of Gilead. What does this mean for our hurts on an average day? In Jesus, we have a friend whose name is Love, whose name is Comfort, whose name is Hope, and he is always with us. His is a hand to hold, a lap on which to lay our heads. He graciously walks alongside us through the minutes and years of suffering, improbably crafting that suffering into something beautiful, something new, something altogether redeemed. In the arms of Jesus, we are ultimately carried home, welcomed back like beloved children. There will be no more hurt, there will be nothing left to grieve. And we will feast alongside our Maker and our Savior, finally and fully *healed*, finally and fully *whole*.

— *Charlotte Getz*

June 24

> As he passed by, he saw a man blind from his birth. And
> his disciples asked him, "Rabbi, who sinned, this man or his
> parents, that he was born blind?" Jesus answered, "It was
> not that this man sinned, or his parents, but that the works
> of God might be made manifest in him." (John 9:1-3 RSV)

In the account of this miraculous healing, there is a 'front-story' and a
backstory.

The 'front-story' is of an adult man who was born with a major disability, a 'birth defect,' which Christ fixes.

The backstory concerns the cause of the man's disability. Had his parents done something wrong that caused their son to be born blind? Or had
the son somehow erred, maybe in the womb or in an earlier life—to speak
'Eastern' for a sec—and had *that* mistake caused, by way of retribution or
karma, this terrible physical consequence? The world in which Jesus was
operating wanted to know. His disciples wanted to know.

Christ changed 'the narrative' completely. He offered a backstory,
behind the 'front-story,' which confuted the disciples' way of looking at it.
The only true backstory would have to be *God's* Backstory. The cause of
the man's blindness was God's plan, 25 years or so after the man's birth, to
unveil His healing character through His incarnate Son on that particular
day. We could ask a thousand questions about symptoms, causes, and timing, but the answer Christ gave is, "That's the Way God Planned It" (Billy
Preston, 1969).

Apply this to yourself. I can give you a thousand guesses, surmises, and
suggestions concerning why my life's the way it is and why it's turned out
the way it has. But the only *bona fide* insight, at least from the Gospel of
John, is that God planned it that way. Ultimately—though not necessarily in the moment of the pain at its worst—that insight, concerning God's
transcendent plan and timing, is consoling to the max. May I recommend it?

— *Paul Zahl*

June 25

Now to him who by the power at work within us is able
to accomplish abundantly far more than all we can ask or
imagine, to him be glory in the church and in Christ Jesus to
all generations, forever and ever. Amen. (Ephesians 3:20-21)

In his speech for the American Film Institute Life Achievement Award, Steve Martin said, "I always wondered, What exactly *is* a comic genius? ... Is it someone who always gets a laugh or whose every movie is a hit? But after all these years of work and luck and mentors and compatriots, successes and failures, elation always balanced with an equal amount of insecurity, self-doubt, good audiences, tough audiences, surprise hits and surprise misses—I finally realized what a comic genius is. A comic genius is someone who decides never to go into comedy."

In effect, Steve is saying that if he had set out to be a comic genius, without any problems, it would have worked out differently. If we want to be a genius, it is probably because we believe it will protect us from the pain of life and the limitations of being human. Steve, however, received more than he asked or imagined *because* of the unforeseen doubts, insecurities, misses, and failures that we experience as powerlessness.

This prayer in Paul's letter to the Ephesians opens us up to recognizing "the power at work within us," to thinking outside not just our box, but our universe. We want to accomplish and achieve, but we are like ants on a mission to a rained-out picnic; we don't know what we don't know. Jesus Christ, however, can see the whole mosaic of time as well as our short moment on this earth in the long arc of his eternal existence with us.

What could be, as Paul says, "more than all we can ask or imagine"? I would venture a guess that it would be somehow about love and acceptance. Christ knows that we will not find that in Lifetime Achievement awards, the approval of others, or piles of cash. But through his death and resurrection, he achieved the ultimate act of love and acceptance and, because of that, your lifetime is safe in his hands.

— *Marilu Thomas*

June 26

> Therefore, let those suffering in accordance with God's will
> entrust themselves to a faithful Creator, while continuing
> to do good. (1 Peter 4:19)

Every Christian needs a doctrine of suffering, and Peter gives it to us here in his characteristic style: a few punchy clauses. Each and every one of us will suffer. We need to know what to do with that reality. Thus, God gives Peter these words to give to us.

First, we learn that we do not suffer capriciously. Whatever the reasons for it may be, our suffering is not outside of God's care for us. This can be painful—why would a loving Father allow such suffering? But not one heartache of ours is wasted. God is making us more like Christ. All is in accordance with his will.

Secondly, we learn that we have one job, and that is the care of our souls. Peter is not speaking of our temporal bodies but our eternal souls. My own body is much afflicted: I have autoimmune spinal arthritis involving much physical suffering. Peter isn't telling me to "let go and let God" and not visit a doctor or attempt treatment. Peter knows that suffering threatens our souls. How do we care for our souls? We "entrust" them to our faithful Creator. Because our Creator is faithful, we can trust ourselves to him.

Finally, we are to continue to do good. Is this a prescription to reduce suffering by obedience? Absolutely not. This is an exhortation that even in the midst of suffering, as we entrust ourselves to God, we have the privilege of still doing good. We do not have to pause our lives and suffer. God does not will for us to only experience the hard. He also wants us to, in the midst of inevitable suffering, enjoy our privilege of being co-creators and co-redeemers. The order here is important, though—doing good without trusting God will only lead to guilt and shame. But doing good in the light of trust in God is a great privilege.

Sufferer, know that God loves you and nothing is outside of his will. Trust your soul to him, and then enjoy the privilege we have to participate in his good works on earth.

— *Ann Lowrey Forster*

June 27

Jesus, looking at [the rich man], loved him and said, "You lack one thing; go, sell what you own, and give the money to the poor, and you will have treasure in heaven; then come, follow me." When [the rich man] heard this, he was shocked and went away grieving, for he had many possessions. (Mark 10:21-22)

There is an ever-growing list of demands on our lives that constantly holds us back from feeling any sort of "enoughness." Just when we think we are doing something right, the law always arrives in its shining armor to tell us that there is one more thing to do in order to be "righteous"—to feel like we've done enough. A spouse did the laundry, but did they wash the dishes or take out the trash? An old friend shows up to church for the first time but is bombarded with ways to serve. Our attempts to show support and solidarity for any cause are met with a list of additional things we must do; otherwise, we are not doing enough.

In the Gospels, the rich man (or rich young ruler) asks Jesus what a person must do to inherit eternal life. Jesus responds by giving him a list of things to do. The ruler, probably joyfully, lets Jesus know that he has done everything on that list. But then Jesus gives him one more thing to accomplish. Jesus gives him an impossibility. The man walks away "grieving."

However, Jesus does not stop there. A couple verses later, he gives us the good news: *what is impossible to us is possible to God* (v. 27). We see this when we continue to read through the Gospels and encounter the death and resurrection of Jesus. We might be discouraged by our own inabilities to do good and become righteous, but we do not have to walk away sad and defeated. Our God does not arrive donning expensive shining armor with a to-do list in hand. Instead, we have a suffering servant who arrives in ordinary clothes on a donkey. It is that Jesus who heads towards the cross and makes us righteous through his death and resurrection. We are able to continue participating in whatever good work is laid before us, because we rest, not in our own, but in Jesus' finished work.

— *Bryant Trinh*

He was indeed so ill that he nearly died. But God had mercy
on him, and not only on him but on me also, so that I would
not have one sorrow after another. (Philippians 2:27)

I imagine Paul sitting by his friend's bedside, wondering for the hundredth
time that day whether that next ragged breath Epaphroditus took would be
his last. I'm sure Paul shed more than a few anxious tears in his prison cell.
It wasn't that he was surprised by his own suffering; he'd known that was
coming before his ministry had even started (Acts 9:16). Paul understood
his own sufferings had a purpose, but seeing his friend get an extra helping
of it felt like it would cost him more tears than he had left.

Paul never wanted to be mistaken as a superhero. He was a physically
fragile human being—just like his readers were. Dr. Frank Lake, the British
psychiatrist and theologian, once wrote that Christians

> and their leaders are not only sinful people but to some degree
> sick people. They all have their infirmities, their ailments, their
> diseased and ill-functioning parts. Their minds and hearts, spir-
> its and bodies, their feelings and their wills are also, by basic
> Christian definition, "fallen." To share in the human condition
> is to participate in a fallen humanity. (*Tight Corners in Pastoral
> Counseling*, 1981)

A big part of that participation involves a body prone to suffering, and
Paul's body knew all about that. Even the first moment he met Jesus, he fell
off his horse and was struck blind! So powerful was this experience that
everything, even his way of suffering, changed.

Later, he wrote about "always carrying in the body the death of Jesus,
so that the life of Jesus may also be made visible in our bodies" (2 Cor 4:10).
Once blinded, Paul couldn't unsee what Christ had done. His very real suffering became a "slight momentary affliction" in comparison to the "eternal
weight of glory" (2 Cor 4:17).

— *Joshua Retterer*

June 29

> One night the Lord said to Paul in a vision, "Do not be afraid, but speak and do not be silent; for I am with you, and no one will lay a hand on you to harm you, for there are many in this city who are my people." He stayed there a year and six months, teaching the word of God among them. (Acts 18:9-11)

Modern-day Corinth is a land of windswept ruin. Standing in the places where Paul preached, you can see to one side, across the water, the snow-capped mountain of Delphi—infamous seat of the oracle of Apollo—and to the other side, the massive acropolis and crumbling temple to Aphrodite. The pagan god of light and truth to the one side, the pagan goddess of love to the other. Paul's missionary journey took place between these great mountaintops—these giants of earthly power—in a port city that was rife with corruption and need. Corinth must have seemed an intractable place.

Paul had come to Corinth to preach the word of God, but in the above verse, the Lord speaks of a completed work—"there are many in this city who are my people." The Lord has, in fact, already done what He has sent Paul to do: move the hearts of the people. What great and glorious news for Paul! It is no longer up to Paul, in his human efforts, to convert the citizens of Corinth. Paul is to keep on speaking—"do not be silent"—in the sure and certain knowledge that the Lord's power and grace has already come before him, entering the hearts of the Corinthians to await the Lord's messenger. Paul's only work is to keep on speaking the story of Christ to the world in need. The Lord has done the rest.

The Lord is a greater prophet, a greater light-bringer, and a greater lover than any pagan god, no matter how grand their temples. This is the Lord's promise to all Christians: "Do not be afraid, but speak and do not be silent; for I am with you." And not only is He with us, He has already established "many in this city who are my people." He has claimed others around us as His own, marking each of us as His children by the blood of His son. The Lord does not need temples on mountaintops, for He builds his temples in the hearts of His believers. What wondrous love is this, indeed.

— *Derrill H. McDavid*

June 30

"I have said these things to you so that my joy may be in you,
and that your joy may be complete." (John 15:11)

"Nip it in the bud!" That was one of Don Knotts' iconic lines from *The Andy Griffith Show*. Knotts played Barney Fife, Deputy Sheriff of Mayberry, a hyper-zealous "Bloodhound of the Law" whose greatest joy was to catch someone in an infraction. He would frantically spout codes and ordinances, blow his whistle, and yell, "Break it up! Break it up!" When he caught someone in the act, it was obvious that some deep need for approval was being met.

We tend to think that God finds His greatest joy in enforcing the law. What joy it must give the Almighty to intervene whenever someone is having too much fun. This was made painfully clear to me soon after I was ordained a priest. My wife and I were invited to a backyard pool party. We were new to town and excited to make new friends. When we arrived, the party was going strong. Folks were casually dressed, relaxed, swaying to the music. Lots of laughter, drinks, and good times. But when we walked into the backyard, a friend of the host stepped forward and announced, "Hey, everybody, the priest is here! Hide your beer! Ha ha ha!" We'd arrived to join the party, not to kill it! But their impression of clergy, and probably of God, was that we were there to "nip it in the bud!"

The people who spent time with Jesus thought just the opposite. He was repeatedly accused of creating a party where none was allowed, of eating and drinking with sinners, of breaking the religious rules. He was accused of having too much fun. Those who came to know Him best found a joy they had not previously thought possible. The ultimate purpose (*telos*) of His coming, His ministry, His teaching, His life and death, was to bring joy. That's hard to believe. But what wonderful news! C. S. Lewis wrote, "Joy is the serious business of Heaven." Jesus is serious about this. His purpose was not to "nip it in the bud" but to complete our joy.

— *Drew Rollins*

July 1

Take delight in the LORD,
and he will give you the desires of your heart. (Psalm 37:4)

We're built for desire. Setting aside the more prurient desires that would make a person blush to read aloud to their grandparents (or grandchildren), our online carts overflow with desires. We keep wishlists of books we want to read, recipes we want to try, and movies we can't wait to watch. Advertisers seem to know this, targeting our desire for just the right pair of shoes or the perfect outdoor furniture. We've barely begun to vocalize a desire before our devices have already found four attractively photographed versions of it to delight our eyes. We know desires, and so does the marketing department.

The desires of our heart, though—they haven't developed an app for that yet. We ourselves might not know those deep desires, even if we've spent some serious time thinking and praying about them. But we are promised that if we take delight in the Lord, he will give them to us. We may have even received our heart's desires before, but because they didn't arrive on our doorstep delivered by FedEx, we might not have recognized them as such.

The friendship that came into our lives when we most needed it. The out-of-season hymn that our child hums on the stairs when he had no way to know that's just what we needed to hear. The niece that brings your sister back into your regular rotation of phone calls. The windfalls of grace and mercy that we didn't know we needed until we received them.

Take delight in the LORD, and he will give you the desires of your heart. With a small adjustment of our perspective, we might be able to see the fruits of those desires where we hadn't been looking.

— *Carrie Willard*

July 2

> "Come to me, all you that are weary and are carrying heavy burdens, and I will give you rest. Take my yoke upon you, and learn from me; for I am gentle and humble in heart, and you will find rest for your souls. For my yoke is easy, and my burden is light." (Matthew 11:28-30)

In the summer of 1999, I saw Paul Simon in concert in North Carolina. He opened with the classic song "Bridge Over Troubled Water," singing three words that resonated with every person in that audience: "When you're weary…" Everyone in the sold-out venue immediately hushed and listened to that gorgeous song of hope for the weary.

The end of the eleventh chapter of the Gospel According to Matthew is one of the most comforting passages in the entire Bible. It is a personal invitation from our Savior to come directly to him "when you're weary." Why? So you can receive God's gift of rest, a gift Jesus freely offers with no catch: "I will give you rest."

All of us find ourselves weary at times. Some of us live in a state of unceasing weariness, weariness that may undulate in its intensity but never really goes away. All of us have experienced, to one degree or another, what Abraham Lincoln once said when unspeakably weary in the midst of the Civil War, while also battling depression and grieving the death of his eleven-year-old son Willie: "Nothing touches the tired spot." And yet the good news of the gospel is that there is actually something that *can* touch the tired spot, or rather Someone who can. Jesus offers to carry your burdens. Jesus is tender with weary people—"I am gentle," he says. Jesus does not offer a motivational speech to the weary; he offers grace, the yoke that is easy because he carries it himself.

On Good Friday, Jesus took the yoke of the burdens of the world, including yours, upon himself in the form of the cross. The cross is the universal "bridge over troubled water," where Jesus both atoned for your sins and fulfilled the law in your place. And even now the Risen Jesus offers rest "when you're weary," rest that can touch the tired spot—rest for your soul.

— *David Johnson*

July 3

And the LORD said to Moses, "How long will this people despise me? And how long will they refuse to believe in me, in spite of all the signs that I have done among them? I will strike them with pestilence and disinherit them, and I will make of you a nation greater and mightier than they." (Numbers 14:11-12)

Every parent has experienced that moment when even young children exercise a lawyerly expertise. They catch us in our own words. We made a promise—perhaps seriously or perhaps just to get them out of our hair for a while—and now we're trying to weasel our way out of it. But our prosecutorial attorney-child is having none of that. They place Mom or Dad on the stand and deal with us as a hostile witness, throwing three words back in our face: "But you promised!"

That, in essence, is how Moses deals with God when, more than once, Israel's Parent is ready to hit "reset" and start all over. It happened after the golden calf debacle. It happened when Israel refused to enter the Promised Land. God basically says, "Listen, Moses, I'm done with these stiff-necked, stone-hearted ingrates. I'm going to wipe them out and start all over with you." And Moses responds, "But you promised! You promised a covenant with their forefathers. You promised to bring them into a new land. You promised to be their God and to keep them as your people. Are you a God who keeps his promises or not?"

Of course, God is caught in his own words. And, truth be told, he is happy to be caught. Unlike human parents, our heavenly Father eagerly anticipates having his own words used against him. That's why he let those words fall in our laps. That's why he made those promises. We talk back to God with his own words.

Us: "I've broken every law you ever uttered, but you promised to forgive me."
God: "I do."
Us: "I've totally messed up my life, but you promised to love me anyway."
God: "I do."

Us: "I can't forget all the stupid, destructive, shameful stuff I've done, but you promised to forget it."

God: "What stupid, destructive, shameful stuff? All I remember is that nothing makes me happier than calling you my child."

— *Chad Bird*

July 4

The wilderness and the dry land shall be glad,
   the desert shall rejoice and blossom;
like the crocus it shall blossom abundantly,
   and rejoice with joy and singing. (Isaiah 35:1-2)

Sometimes it seems like God sends mixed messages. In Isaiah 34, we read of a God "enraged against all the nations…[who] has given them over for slaughter…" But then Isaiah 35 upends that narrative of despair with a stirring vision of rebirth—a promised day when the desert itself will blossom and rejoice.

As a teenager, I lived in Saudi Arabia. We used to take camping trips into a desolate part of the Arabian Desert known as the Rub' al Khali, or "Empty Quarter." One year we drove out there specifically because we'd heard that a rare occurrence was underway—that crocuses were blooming. We searched and searched and found only *one crocus*, astonishingly beautiful and seemingly out-of-place. Those who've lived in deserts know the joyous celebration of rain, of how quickly a desert can spring to life, and how blessed such occasions are precisely because they are so desperately longed for and so rare.

To me, the desert offers a perfect metaphor for the spiritual life, because even in our often materially rich circumstances, we still live aridly, we still thirst, we still long for the thrill of God's presence. And it's a metaphor with even greater resonance when viewed in the broader Judeo-Christian context. Richard Rodriguez reminds us in *Darling: A Spiritual Autobiography* that "Christianity, like Judaism, like Islam, is a desert religion…born of sinus-clearing glottal consonants, spit, dust, blinding light." The Christian calendar even contains, as he puts it, two "desert" seasons—Advent and Lent—"penitential preludes to the great feasts of Christmas and Easter."

The desert imagery evokes a dual sense of trust and longing. Like the great prophets and poets of the Old Testament, we too look to collective memory for strength and guidance, leaning in arid times on God's long record of faithfulness. But in such contexts, when it might be tempting to fall back primarily on dogma—which Rodriguez says "strives to resemble the desert" as a kind of "fossil of the living God"—let us also look with Isaiah to the promise of new life, trusting that God is with us even in the most barren of places, and that God's kin-dom is forever gathering beneath the surface, ready to burst forth once more.

— *Benjamin Self*

July 5

The saying is sure and worthy of full acceptance, that
Christ Jesus came into the world to save sinners—of whom
I am the foremost. (1 Timothy 1:15)

My NIV translation of this verse uses the word "worst" in the place of
"foremost." While "worst" has a better ring linguistically, "foremost" gets to
the deep dark heart of the matter: St. Paul's claiming to be the A-1, numero
uno, big kahuna offender of all offenders.

Before Paul came to know Jesus, he persecuted Christians. Yet in this
letter to Timothy he doesn't say, "Christ came to save sinners—of whom I
was the foremost." No, Paul says that even then, as one of the greatest evan-
gelists in the history of the church, he remained the chief of sinners. He is
reminding us of the unevangelized rooms in our hearts that are perpetually
in need of redemption.

I too am the *foremost* of sinners. Forget the outright offenses, like my
proclivity toward "addictive behavior," delusions of grandeur, relentless
dissatisfaction with reality, and the inexplicable willingness to believe I
have everything under control (despite abundant evidence to the contrary).
It goes deeper than that.

Even my sincerest repentance is underwritten with a desire for great-
ness—not for God's glory, but for my own. When it's me in the confessional,
at the root of much of my repentance is not just a longing for holiness, but
an ambition to become greater. I even need to repent of the motives beneath
my repentance.

Dear one, there is good news. What remains in the dark *remains in the
dark*; but the more we recognize the reach of our sin, the more we will see
Christ entering that darkness, bringing light and light and light everlasting.
Sin causes death, but death is the precursor to every resurrection.

— *Charlotte Getz*

July 6

But I am a worm and not a man,
  scorned by everyone, despised by the people.
… Dogs surround me,
  a pack of villains encircles me;
  they pierce my hands and my feet. (Psalm 22:6, 16 NIV)

In several places in scripture, animals put humans to shame. When we read about the diligence of the ant in Proverbs (6:6), we are immediately convicted of our sloth; the psalmist indicates that even a sparrow has sense enough to rest at God's altars (84:3). Jesus would say the same in the Gospels, pointing to birds as a picture of perfect trust in God. Furthermore, God makes Nebuchadnezzar live like an ox for seven years to dismantle his pride (Dan 4).

Jonah, too, was swallowed by a fish as an indictment of humankind. In that submariner slapstick narrative about a reluctant, runaway prophet, we find that sin disrupts and reverses God's order. God created people to exercise dominion over "the fish of the sea" (Gen 1:26). Men do not belong inside fish.

This imagery ultimately highlights the absurdity of human pretenses. The serpent convinces our first parents they can become like God without God, but the attempt can only make us monstrous. Paul aptly summarizes this in Romans 1: "Claiming to be wise, they became fools; and they exchanged the glory of the immortal God for images resembling a mortal human being or birds or four-footed animals or reptiles" (vv. 22-23).

Thankfully, there's a greater foolishness that saves: God, in Jesus, became a worm surrounded by vicious dogs that pierced His hands and feet, so that, for eternity, we could surround the Lamb who was slain for our redemption.

— *Jason Thompson*

July 7

"Take care that you do not despise one of these little ones; for, I tell you, in heaven their angels continually see the face of my Father in heaven. What do you think? If a shepherd has a hundred sheep, and one of them has gone astray, does he not leave the ninety-nine on the mountains and go in search of the one that went astray? And if he finds it, truly I tell you, he rejoices over it more than over the ninety-nine that never went astray. So it is not the will of your Father in heaven that one of these little ones should be lost." (Matthew 18:10-14)

What is always striking to me about this parable is that it is not concerned at all with *why* the sheep has strayed away from the herd. Because if the parable suggested why the sheep became lost in the first place, then this would be a parable about correcting your bad habits, or not losing sight of what's important, or some other tangible thing you can do to keep the faith: *Buck up! Try harder! You wandered before and you better make sure it doesn't happen again.* But if any explanation is offered for why the sheep strays, it is simply the fact that it is a sheep, and wandering away is what sheep tend to do! Humans, too, are itinerant and in need of a shepherd.

A lost sheep tends to die without the protection of a shepherd; you never find packs of wild sheep roaming the countryside. When sheep inevitably wander away, God is the good shepherd who pursues and rescues them. The restoration of the one lost sheep does not depend upon the sheep's ability to turn or repent or even muster up some semblance of contrition. No—what matters is not the measure of our sorrow, but the measure of God's mercy. It doesn't depend on our own will to turn to God, but on God's will to save. We wander all the time, and God is determined to always bring us back, even from the dead.

— *Todd Brewer*

July 8

We are afflicted in every way, but not crushed; perplexed,
but not driven to despair; persecuted, but not forsaken;
struck down, but not destroyed… (2 Corinthians 4:8-9)

When legendary *New York Times* crossword puzzle guru Will Shortz was asked to account for the abiding popularity of his section, he said something interesting. So many of life's problems defy clear-cut solutions, he noted, that it's very satisfying to achieve momentary perfection via a collection of immaculately aligned correct answers.

People love crossword puzzles, in other words, because life is perplexing. We move from decision to decision, most of which are not between Good and Bad, or Right and Wrong, but Kind of Okay vs. Possibly Alright.

Unfortunately, being a Christian does not absent a person from this plight. We thought we knew what God was doing, then something unexpected happened, and our clarity vanished.

Maybe the job we lobbied so hard for turned out to be a bust. Or the school we thought was perfect for our child chewed them up. Or the relationship we thought was "the one" didn't pan out. We find ourselves back at the drawing board, genuinely baffled. And yet, that bafflement can be an occasion for faith just as much as for doubt.

I remember when a friend and his family spent five months in a hospital with his daughter suffering from potentially terminal heart disease. Her courageous comportment, even up to accepting death in prayer, affected many in the hospital. She eventually recovered, thank God. As they were leaving the hospital, my friend thanked the staff for all they had done. The head physician replied, "No, I want to thank *you*. The presence of your family has transformed this place."

My friend said simply, "Maybe I have finally learned to stop asking why God allows problems and difficulties and started asking what God's plan is right in the middle of them." Beautiful.

Perhaps another name for the God who dwells in perplexity, who uses confounding circumstances to bring us near, is the Crucified God. Perhaps the perplexity of our lives—how could *this* happen?—is meaningful insofar as it illuminates the perplexity of the Cross—how could *that* happen?

And perhaps that is why perplexity doesn't need to drive you to despair today. It points instead to the one who *was* driven to despair, afflicted, forsaken, to ensure that you will never be.

That much is clear.

— *David Zahl*

July 9

O LORD, my heart is not lifted up,
  my eyes are not raised too high;
I do not occupy myself with things
  too great and too marvelous for me.
But I have calmed and quieted my soul,
  like a weaned child with its mother;
  my soul is like the weaned child that is with me.
O Israel, hope in the LORD
  from this time on and forevermore. (Psalm 131:1-3)

The power of music became known to me afresh when a friend asked recently, "Have you ever noticed how easy it is to use music to manipulate your emotions?" I was gobsmacked. At once it was clear to me that I'd been doing this my whole life. Scrolling iTunes playlists, or dialing into a radio station, I find that just beneath the question "What do I want to listen to?" lurks the question "How do I want to feel right now?"

I turn to music for comfort when peace eludes me, for excitement in daily monotony, and for confidence to meet familial or vocational demands. Ultimately, I find no respite on the sea of desire; I need a song that can calm that sea, even if most songs clock in at a mere three minutes.

King David surely knew the power of music. As a sinner, his heart was indeed "lifted up," and as king, he "occupied himself with things too great for him." He undoubtedly reveled in the "marvelous"; and yes, even "a man after God's own heart" knew valleys of darkness where he could neither calm himself nor quiet his own soul. So how could he write and eventually sing these words with integrity?

Psalm 131 is an antidote to the burden of managing your emotions. This song, in just three verses, describes the undeserved, pure gift of a new reality in Christ, which upends our exhausting (and futile) searches for satisfaction and emotional stability. Follow the direction of Bob Marley and "Put It On." May God clothe your naked need today.

— Matt Magill

July 10

You must understand this, my beloved: let everyone be
quick to listen, slow to speak, slow to anger; for your anger
does not produce God's righteousness. (James 1:19-20)

My wife and I had just begun our first day at an Airbnb. A sign on the
door warned us that there'd be some light construction work during the
week, and to be prepared for some sporadic noise. "No big deal," I thought.
"It won't affect us."

St. James must have heard me, because soon there was an orbital cement
grinder running full-bore on the patio next to ours. It went on for six hours,
not six feet from my laptop. My coffee was rippling in its mug like we were
in the T. Rex scene in *Jurassic Park*.

It would be an understatement to say that my initial reaction was anger.
Thankfully, James' advice to be "quick to listen" wasn't really hard for me
to obey—the grinding sound was literally not avoidable. So at least there's
that!

James is right that anger is quick. It's reptilian, one of those automatic
reactions that feels more physical than mental. But anger is also all about
the expectations you carry with you. When you expect reality to conform
to your version of it—with your vacations, your kids, your daily routines—
you are setting yourself up for serious bitterness. On the other hand, if your
expectations are lower, perhaps you would be surprised to find that the
cards you've been dealt, despite the noise, aren't so bad.

This is all great in theory. But I don't see how on earth I could, on vacation, expect less than a relaxing time. I simply can't free myself of some of
my expectations. That's just the way the human species seems to be wired.

So what can I do when what I *should* do is impossible? Perhaps first, I
notice my anger. I notice where it's coming from and what it's doing to me.
And then I ask God for help: *God, help me to deal with this new reality I
wasn't ready for.* Perhaps this is the spirit of "meekness" that James is talking
about. And perhaps after that—and this would be the most surprising—I
may find that God is saying something through this godawful noise.

— *Ethan Richardson*

July 11

[Jesus] came to his hometown and began to teach the people in their synagogue, so that they were astounded and said, "Where did this man get this wisdom and these deeds of power? Is not this the carpenter's son? Is not his mother called Mary? And are not his brothers James and Joseph and Simon and Judas? And are not all his sisters with us? Where then did this man get all this?" And they took offense at him. But Jesus said to them, "Prophets are not without honor except in their own country and in their own house." And he did not do many deeds of power there, because of their unbelief. (Matthew 13:54-58)

What are we to make of the fact that Jesus, the Son of God, "did not do many deeds of power" in his hometown of Nazareth, "because of their unbelief"? Does this mean that He might be unable to do powerful deeds in or for us when we lack faith? This connection can be a slippery slope, and a dangerous one, but Jesus' experience here must be demonstrating something about the relationship between faith and power.

It strikes me that a key fact here might be that the people of Nazareth *think they already know Jesus.* They have known him since childhood, and interact daily with his family. It is their arrogance, or lack of humility, that limits his power, and even prevents them from believing in him.

Is it not easy to see this in ourselves, too? When we are overconfident, when we think we know what is right and good, we can fall into playing God; but when we are humble, or even desperate, it is more natural to reach out in faith—to One who knows us better than we know ourselves.

— *Mary Zahl*

July 12

Praise be to the God and Father of our Lord Jesus Christ, the Father of compassion and the God of all comfort, who comforts us in all our troubles, so that we can comfort those in any trouble with the comfort we ourselves receive from God. For just as we share abundantly in the sufferings of Christ, so also our comfort abounds through Christ. If we are distressed, it is for your comfort and salvation; if we are comforted, it is for your comfort, which produces in you patient endurance of the same sufferings we suffer. And our hope for you is firm, because we know that just as you share in our sufferings, so also you share in our comfort. (2 Corinthians 1:3-7 NIV)

Hand-me-downs vary widely in quality and desirability. If you are the baby in the family, you may remember hand-me-downs with a tinge of irritation, those more than 'gently used' garments that your older sibling wore back when they were actually in style. On the other hand, sometimes a grand-parent will present you with a different kind of hand-me-down—a vintage engagement ring perhaps, something which bears great financial value as well as incalculable sentimental value.

The "comfort" which the apostle Paul is handing down in our passage definitely falls in the latter category. It is not some cheap and shopworn advice to people negotiating affliction—"hang in there," "keep on smiling," etc. It is rather an elixir of priceless vintage, a kind of spiritual strength passed on from someone who has been through the wars and by God's grace is still intact. Indeed, this comfort ultimately traces itself back to the Christ who suffered for us and whose grace is always available to us. That is the kind of hand-me-down we welcome gladly.

— *Larry Parsley*

July 13

[T]hen the LORD God formed man from the dust of the ground, and breathed into his nostrils the breath of life; and the man became a living being. (Genesis 2:7)

In this ancient passage, God, like a sculptor, gathers the dirt in his hands and shapes the first man from it. He breathes his own breath into Adam's lungs, gives Adam life from God's own life. Through these steady actions, we see how dedicated God is to each one of us; the human body is precious and hand-crafted. And no matter your shape, size, weight, or height, you are sustained by the breath of the divine.

Day to day, of course, you may not feel so glorious. You may feel more like a robot that is constantly malfunctioning. I know I do. Like Kramer from *Seinfeld*, I seem to always hit the doorframe when I pass through it, or stub my toe on a table leg. My limbs seem out of control. My emotions are even less compliant. When I look in the mirror, I'm not always happy with what I see. Inundated with media of the beautiful and handsome, it is easy to feel ungainly by comparison, not-enough.

In the ancient world, only the strong survived. In Sparta, the physically weak were killed by their mothers, and disability was a disgrace. In ancient Greece, physical perfection and beauty indicated a heightened morality. Our world still entertains this ideology, but it's far from Christian; Christianity values the opposite. Jesus blessed the poor, the meek, the sick, and the suffering. And body image was so unimportant that the scriptures never even mention what Jesus looked like. His skin color, muscle size, fat level, choice of clothes: Apparently no one cared enough to write this stuff down.

All that mattered was that he had *a* body and that it was broken for us. Through this sacrifice, Jesus crushes the serpent that whispers shame into our ears. In shame, Adam and Eve covered their naked bodies with fig leaves; gently Christ says you have nothing to hide.

My prayer for today is that you will take a deep breath, let go of whatever devilish fig leaves you cling to—even for a moment—and live.

— *CJ Green*

July 14

To you, O LORD, I cry.
For fire has devoured
   the pastures of the wilderness,
and flames have burned
   all the trees of the field. (Joel 1:19)

Reading the prophets is like watching a dystopian thriller: The land is des-olate, food is scarce, people are dead or exiled, and hope is far away. On a movie screen, all those disasters are entertaining, sometimes. In scripture, on the other hand, they're depressing and puzzling. Why all the locusts, invasions, sackcloth, and wailing?

I have never experienced grief like what Joel describes here, in large part because my life has been comparatively stable. But another factor also con-tributes, I think: Contemporary Americans don't have any way to lament, not in the full-bodied way that we hear Joel's audience did. What's funny, though, is that while I envy their freedom of emotional expression, the LORD tells them it's got to be more than that: "rend your hearts and not your clothing" (2:13). *Don't just show me you're sorry; mean it!*

I want to be that sincere, especially to God, but distractions and appe-tites, not my conscience, are what "rend" my heart, pulling me in differ-ent directions. Acknowledging this about myself shows how unstable my actual life is, at least on the inside. But long before I've glimpsed myself as I am, God sees me fully. Just as Jesus yelped, "they know not what they do," and suffered under us still (Lk 23:34), so the Spirit sees that "we do not know how to pray as we ought," and groans for us, more deeply than words (Rm 8:26).

And not only us, but the whole cosmos is in pain: In the next verse, Joel writes, "Even the wild animals cry to you because the watercourses are dried up." Amid personal crises and climate crises, disasters that reek damage beyond what we can even know, none of the Bible's most moving passages can fix it. But they do bring comfort.

The LORD will never ignore us, even our most half-hearted sighs.

— *Kendall Gunter*

July 15

And Jesus said to him, "What do you want me to do for you?" And the blind man said to him, "Master, let me receive my sight." And Jesus said to him, "Go your way; your faith has made you well." And immediately he received his sight and followed him on the way. (Mark 10:51-52 RSV)

In the relation between God and earthlings, we properly put the emphasis on the God-part rather than on the earthling-part. This is because people are invariably subjective and mercurial, while God by definition is stable and unchanging. God's good will, in other words, can be counted on in all circumstances; while *our* good will, on the other hand, is a tumult and a roar, like "My Ever Changing Moods" (Style Council, 1984).

So we do well to focus on the God-part within the engagement of faith.

But, and it's an important but, Christ praised the faith of individuals. He praised it in the case (above) of blind Bartimaeus, who called upon the Lord with brazen persistence. He praised it in the case of the woman with the issue of blood, in the case of the centurion whose servant was grievously ill, in the case of Zacchaeus the tax collector hiding up in a sycamore tree, in the case of the Syrophoenician woman whose daughter was very sick— and I could go on and on. You can't read the Gospels and ignore the faith of the people who came to Christ for healing and got healed!

What does this mean for you and me? Well, we probably won't find what we are looking for, *à la* U2 (1987), until we are given the faith and *oomph* to really, earnestly, and persistently look for it. The healing doesn't just come to us. (Wish it did.) We have to seek it, even crawling on the earth if necessary. I've done that myself. And it worked.

— *Paul Zahl*

July 16

> What then should we say? That the law is sin? By no means! Yet, if it had not been for the law, I would not have known sin. I would not have known what it is to covet if the law had not said, "You shall not covet." But sin, seizing an opportunity in the commandment, produced in me all kinds of covetousness. Apart from the law sin lies dead. I was once alive apart from the law, but when the commandment came, sin revived and I died, and the very commandment that promised life proved to be death to me. (Romans 7:7-10)

Once, when I was at a music festival, the host/sponsor took the stage to try to ignite the crowd. Multiple times and with crescendoing volume, she asked us if we were having fun. When the response was lackluster, she belted out, "You're in my house here! The only rule in my house is that you've GOT TO HAVE FUN!"

The host was just doing her job, but she made me want to leave, despite the good music, weather, food, drink, and company. Rarely do people like to be told what to do and how to feel. Often, a command will produce the opposite result. For instance, does being told to relax actually result in relaxation? Once you notice this dynamic, it is startling to realize how much everybody likes to tell everybody else what to do!

This is also how the law of God works. God's law is holy and righteous, but it does not produce the fruit of holiness and righteousness in us. Instead, the scripture tells us that it produces sin and death. As the Apostle Paul says in today's passage, "the very commandment that promised life proved to be death to me."

Thankfully, our Christian faith is not ultimately about what we are to do. Rather, it is about what Jesus Christ has already done for us on the cross. "For God has done what the law, weakened by the flesh, could not do" (8:3).

We thank you, heavenly Father, that you did for us what the law could not do, by giving us your Son. Give us grateful hearts today, through Jesus Christ our Lord. Amen.

— *Paul Walker*

Now the man knew his wife Eve, and she conceived and bore Cain, saying, "I have produced a man with the help of the LORD." Next she bore his brother Abel. Now Abel was a keeper of sheep, and Cain a tiller of the ground. In the course of time Cain brought to the LORD an offering of the fruit of the ground, and Abel for his part brought of the firstlings of his flock, their fat portions. And the LORD had regard for Abel and his offering, but for Cain and his offering he had no regard. So Cain was very angry, and his countenance fell...

Cain said to his brother Abel, "Let us go out to the field." And when they were in the field, Cain rose up against his brother Abel, and killed him. (Genesis 4:1-5, 8)

It can be very tempting to read the Old and New Testaments like a before-and-after home makeover: No one understood the space before the designers came in! What's with the old carpets and wallpaper? Was this even a real house?

But the truth is, the love and forgiveness of Jesus stretches all the way back to those first few sinners who come stumbling out of Eden.

I always struggled with the story of Cain and Abel—especially after I had children. It seemed so bleak to me that after everything Adam and Eve have been through, they would raise one child who murders another.

Until I understood the gospel, I could not coalesce the God of the Hebrews with the God of my Memaw. But as I came to understand the redemption of the cross as a once-and-for-all-time action, I began to see Jesus everywhere. I even started to see him in these painful early stories.

Make no mistake, Jesus is present when Cain kills his brother Abel. I believe Jesus holds the hand of Abel as he takes his last breath. And since we know that Jesus does not hesitate to keep company with the most violent of offenders, I believe that he places his hand on Cain's shoulder as God pronounces his curse upon Cain. Because Jesus knows this would not be the final word for this violent and failed family story.

Some years ago, a friend shared a quote with me that I think about all the time. The Lutheran pastor Ben Maton once preached, "All heaven will go quiet as Cain and Abel embrace." We cannot forget that even scripture does not get the final word. Heaven does. And the forgiving face of Jesus will meet us there, new and old sinners alike. And when we encounter our own life's "Abel," because we all have one, I have no doubt that heaven will fall quiet then, too.

— *Sarah Condon*

July 18

By the first day of the first month they had come to the end
of all the men who had married foreign women. (Ezra 10:17)

The book of Ezra tells us about the Jews returning from exile to Jerusalem. They are finally going to be God's faithful people, living in God's gifted land, perfectly fulfilling all of God's rules. However, we find that the men of Israel have already taken foreign wives and had children with them. This is a clear violation of Mosaic Law according to both Exodus 34 and Deuteronomy 7.

Sadly, as we read in Ezra 10, they attempt to realign themselves to God through legalism. Can you imagine the horror of these foreign women and their children who are divorced and disowned in the name of being good? Can you imagine the tremendous guilt of the Jewish husbands, who abandon their families in the name of religious purity, rule-following, or, as some say today, "being right with God"?

If we are honest, all of us have hit some painfully low moments while trying to follow the rules. I once counseled a woman who had hardly slept for over thirty years. Every night she tossed and turned at the memory of her newborn daughter, conceived out of wedlock, being taken from her and put up for adoption in order to maintain the family's appearance of being "right with God."

The Law produces within us two types of grief. St. Paul wrote that "godly grief produces a repentance that leads to salvation and brings no regret, but worldly grief produces death" (2 Cor 7:10). "Worldly grief" was the response of the Jewish men in Ezra; it means trying to create a quick fix. It only leads to your death and the death of others, because our can-do attitude becomes intertwined with human sin. But "godly grief" is the response of faith. In godly grief, we turn everything over to Jesus and trust that *he* will redeem the situation.

Ezra 10 is a tough place to find inspiration. However, it is a great place to be reminded that in the midst of our massive screw-ups, the ones that really affect ourselves and others, we can fix our eyes on Jesus, who has fulfilled the Law on our behalf and given us the freedom to face our shortcomings with faith and strength. We know that whatever happens, behold, he makes all things new.

— *Jacob Smith*

July 19

> "Therefore I tell you, do not worry about your life, what you will eat or what you will drink, or about your body, what you will wear. Is not life more than food, and the body more than clothing? Look at the birds of the air; they neither sow nor reap nor gather into barns, and yet your heavenly Father feeds them. Are you not of more value than they? And can any of you by worrying add a single hour to your span of life?" (Matthew 6:25-27)

I feel personally attacked by Jesus in these verses. I always have. From my earliest memory I can recall thinking, "Boy, wouldn't it be nice to not worry!" Of course, I could never make it happen. Like trying not to think of a pink elephant when someone says "don't think of a pink elephant," trying not to worry by telling yourself not to worry is nearly impossible. It is even worse when someone else tells you not to worry. If you have ever struggled with anxiety or panic attacks, you know what it feels like when a well-meaning person tells you, simply, not to worry.

So what are we to make of this injunction from Jesus? Unlike that well-meaning person, Jesus is speaking a deeper truth here. He is not simply telling us to get over our worry. He is reminding us of the way the world actually works. Worry and anxiety take us out of the present moment and into a world that does not exist. When we worry, we put our feet on the shaky ground of a future (or past) constructed in our own mind. Jesus reminds us, through the image of birds, that we did not make the world, and we do not sustain it. We did not cause ourselves to take our first breath, and we cannot add a single hour to our lives by worrying.

This truth is humbling. Instead of holding on tighter and trying to white-knuckle our way out of anxiety ("Jesus said not to worry, Jesus said not to worry, Jesus said not to worry"), we can open our hands and hold on loosely. Our heavenly Father feeds the birds of the air. Are we not of more value than they? Jesus speaks directly into our hearts: *You are of infinite value, and my grace is enough.*

— *Connor Gwin*

July 20

For the LORD has ransomed Jacob,
  and has redeemed him from hands too strong for him.
They shall come and sing aloud on the height of Zion,
  and they shall be radiant over the goodness of the
    LORD...
Then shall the young women rejoice in the dance,
  and the young men and the old shall be merry.
I will turn their mourning into joy,
  I will comfort them, and give them gladness for
    sorrow. (Jeremiah 31:11-13)

When Dr. Brené Brown asked research participants what experiences left them feeling the most vulnerable, she was surprised to find that it wasn't shame or fear, but joy. When we feel joy, it is often accompanied by a feeling of impending doom, a fear that there will be a price to pay. After all, "there is no such thing as a free lunch," right? We try to minimize our vulnerability by awfulizing or catastrophizing in order to prepare ourselves for the proverbial dropping shoe.

But there is no way to prepare for life on life's terms. Vulnerability is a position of faith, admitting we have limitations and liabilities. Come what may—joy or sorrow—our lives are in God's hands, not ours.

In this passage, the prophet Jeremiah is trying to encourage the captives in exile. He reminds them of God's promise to redeem them from the "strong hands" of oppression by sending them a Messiah. They will be restored to peace, honor, joy, and plenty. "I will turn their mourning into joy, I will comfort them, and give them gladness for sorrow." Hanging onto the promises of God, we can experience the grace of joy without penalty. Christ died to pay your debt, to catch the other shoe for you, and to turn your mourning into joy.

— *Marilu Thomas*

July 21

"For God so loved the world that he gave his only Son, so that everyone who believes in him may not perish but may have eternal life." (John 3:16)

I have been to Baton Rouge, and if you asked me if I flew there, I would say yes. But technically, that is not true. I did not, with my best efforts, fly to Baton Rouge. I could try. I could flap my arms as hard as I could. I could get out on the runway at the Charlottesville airport, sprint my fastest, beat my arms in the air, and leap off the ground for all I'm worth. And for all that effort, I would still be at the Charlottesville airport, out of breath, and a yard or two from where I took off, unless, that is, the authorities had already escorted me off the premises.

Of course, I did not fly to Baton Rouge. The airplane on which I sat, while doing absolutely nothing, flew to Baton Rouge. In terms of the kingdom of God, flapping your arms with your best effort gets you nowhere. Jesus is the plane who flies you there. All you do is sit back and do nothing, and simply believe that He will do it.

Jesus tells us the kingdom of God is seen not through the law, or our best efforts, but simply by belief. Believing in Him. That's all. If the law had been our ticket, we would have punched it long ago. If moral elbow grease was what was required, then we would have gotten 'er done by now. Ironically, the one thing required—belief—can be the hardest thing for us to accept.

> Give us faith and trust in you, Heavenly Father. Make our striving to cease and our joy in what you have done for us in your Son increase. Amen.

— Paul Walker

July 22

I have been crucified with Christ; and it is no longer I who
live, but it is Christ who lives in me. And the life I now
live in the flesh I live by faith in the Son of God, who loved
me and gave himself for me. (Galatians 2:19-20)

The first time I heard these verses, I was in eighth grade, and it was my
first time at youth group. I remember how DeGarmo & Key and DC Talk
were blaring as I walked into the room.

By turns, Paul's powerful Epistle to the Galatians confounds us as much
as it relieves us. But what mostly comes to mind when I read this verse
today is something else. It is the way one of the college interns named Amy
connected with me and a hundred other students that night at youth group.

Amy delivered a word about the life-changing power of the gospel. First,
though, she talked about how hard it can be to find your way in college,
"but it's a whole lot easier than high school, or middle school especially." She
went on to describe middle school as the wasteland that I had experienced.
She said she knew what we were dealing with; *then* she quoted these verses
from memory. Rather than talk about what she wanted to do for God with
her "one wild and precious life," or anything as serious or devout as her "call
to the international mission field," she simply reached back across a decade
to make a connection with a room full of kids, and showed some compassion.

"This life I now live in the flesh" ain't easy. Middle school, high school,
and so many other moments in our lives, have proved this to us. Thanks
be to God for Amy, and Crissy, and Mark, and Terri, and Frank, and Kris-
tina, and Virginia, and whoever it was who knew our names and looked us
in the eye when they told their stories. When they showed up in our lives,
the Spirit of Jesus made contact with us.

In the words of the song we sang back then, the Lord "opened the eyes
of our hearts." May we continue to trust that wherever it takes us, "this life
I now live in the flesh" is the threshold of meeting Him, "the Son of God,
who loved me and gave himself for me."

— *Stuart Shelby*

July 23

> Is it a time for you yourselves to live in your paneled houses,
> while this house lies in ruins? ... [T]hus says the LORD of
> hosts: Consider how you have fared. You have sown much,
> and harvested little; you eat, but you never have enough;
> you drink, but you never have your fill; you clothe your-
> selves, but no one is warm; and you that earn wages earn
> wages to put them into a bag with holes. (Haggai 1:4-6)

Maybe you remember Maslow's hierarchy of needs. He imagined a layered pyramid where the needs for a good life were ranked, bottom to top, from most to least essential. At the bottom were physiological needs: water, food, and warmth. In the middle were safety, security, and meaningful relation-ships. At the top was "self-actualization" and the freedom to be creative.

When Haggai arrives on the scene, the people of Israel are a long way from self-actualization. The bedraggled community had returned to their homeland after seventy years of captivity in Babylon. Water, food, warmth, wages: The community was working hard to acquire these basic needs and was not making progress. God intervened through Haggai, telling the peo-ple their priorities were all wrong. They were building nice, paneled houses while the temple lay in ruins from its destruction seventy years prior. The people had forgotten to make God a priority.

God does something bold with Maslow's hierarchy: He reveals himself as the essential need, the primary necessity required for life. As Jesus will later teach, "But strive first for the kingdom of God and his righteousness, and all these things will be given to you as well" (Mt 6:33). Our food, our safety, our clothing, our work... As important as these are, the foundational level of our spiritual pyramid is God himself. Everything else comes second.

What do you *need* right now? Ask God for it. Thank him for the other ways he's provided already. After acknowledging his providence and asking for help, wait and see how everything plays out. Perhaps you'll find, like the Israelites of Haggai's day, that God is true to his word. That he is ready to provide, and is worthy of the priority he claims.

— *Bryan Jarrell*

July 24

Peter said to them, "Repent, and be baptized every one of you in the name of Jesus Christ so that your sins may be forgiven; and you will receive the gift of the Holy Spirit." (Acts 2:38)

A few nights a week, I find myself lying in bed, desperate to fall asleep, with a head full of thoughts that won't let me rest. You know how it goes: There's the to-do list from the previous day, many un-checked items lingering. There's the to-do list for tomorrow that goes onto the next page because of aforementioned un-checked items. There's the replaying of the conversation that could have gone better. There's the inner critic, who accuses and destroys. Then there's the realization that you have to get to sleep *right now*, because if you don't, then tomorrow is shot too. (This thought always prolongs the whole process, of course.)

And then, sweet rest. It happens *to* you, certainly not *because* of you. Your mind surrenders to the need of your body and you finally fall asleep. You wake up the next morning and you don't remember how or when it happened, but you thank God it did!

Repentance is similar. Repentance has never been a word that I've liked. It sounds very fire-and-brimstone-y. I probably wouldn't use the word when first explaining Christianity to a friend who doesn't know Jesus.

But repentance is a sweet and restful thing. It is a blessed giving-up. It is the moment when we realize that we cannot carry the load of the law, that our rule-keeping hands of control are not serving us, that the to-do list is crushing, and that we are desperately tired. In repentance, we are simply made aware of the myriad ways that we need a savior.

Thankfully, repentance is Holy-Spirit-induced. I would certainly not give up control if I had my way! Like with sleep, we are brought to the act of surrender. And we are met in this moment, in this giving up of control, with mercy. Through repentance, we find ourselves face-to-face with our compassionate and suffering Savior, the one who lifted that burden from our shoulders and placed it on His own as He carried the heavy cross to the top of that hill. And in exchange, we are given what we are so desperate for: sweet, sweet rest.

— *Amanda McMillen*

July 25

The spirit of the Lord GOD is upon me,
  because the LORD has anointed me;
he has sent me to bring good news to the oppressed…
They will be called oaks of righteousness,
  the planting of the LORD, to display his glory.
They shall build up the ancient ruins,
  they shall raise up the former devastations;
they shall repair the ruined cities,
  the devastations of many generations. (Isaiah 61:1-4)

Isaiah is my favorite book of the Bible because everything in it points to Jesus. His birth (chapter 11), death (chapter 53), and life are all addressed in prophetic fashion. The anticipation is building toward the coming Messiah, who himself answers the prophecies by quoting these verses centuries later, in Luke 4.

There are a few groups of people addressed in this passage, and none of them are occupants of society's upper echelons. We have the oppressed, the brokenhearted, the captives, the prisoners, and the mourners all getting shout-outs, and in a prophecy foreshadowing the Beatitudes, we hear what they'll receive from God's Anointed One: good news, healing, liberty, release, favor, comfort, garlands, oil of gladness, a mantle of praise. We also hear what they'll be called: oaks of righteousness.

Jesus is the reason this good news exists, that this directional turnaround occurs. But for every gift he bestows upon those willing to identify themselves as members of the above lowly groups, he will pay the price personally. As we head toward our own destinies as oaks of righteousness, he heads toward a different tree, the cross. The cost of our glory is his.

This is not the end of the story, of course, but it is a truth worth sitting with: The good news of the gospel is only good because Jesus chose to pay the price for it.

When I was twenty-something, circumstances converged to place me at a stadium in New Jersey, hungover and in need of a shower, face-to-face with a prominent evangelical writer and speaker. She grasped both of my hands in hers. "Hello, beloved," she said to me. "Aren't you just lovely?" I wanted to protest and tell her that, indeed, I was not. But she was so *sin-cere*. Maybe she knew something I didn't.

Her talk that morning was on this passage in Isaiah. When she got to the part about rebuilding and restoring, she pointed out that this wasn't a demo job: God was working with ruins, which meant that he was using raw material already there. As I sat there, hungover and regretful, I marveled at a God who changes names and brings good news to the ruined, grasping our empty hands with his scarred ones, and calling us Beloved.

— *Stephanie Phillips*

July 26

Grace, mercy, and peace will be with us from God the Father and from Jesus Christ, the Father's Son, in truth and love. (2 John 3)

Grace, Luther wrote, "must be sounded in our ears incessantly because the frailty of our flesh will not permit us to take hold of it perfectly and to believe it with all our heart." He was commenting on Paul's greeting in Galatians, and it works here, too, with 2 John. Grace is one of the first things we hear in these letters, thankfully. I need it.

I need it especially since John quickly moves onto imperatives. He commands that "you must walk in" love and truth. "Be on your guard," he warns us, "so that you do not lose what we have worked for." He wants us to stay focused so that God won't take away our reward in the end. And he orders us to shun anyone who would distract or lie to us. That's a lot of pressure, and a fair amount of paranoia, too. *Am I doing this right?*

I feel this way reading most of the Bible. It seems there's a lot of demand, with only a little bit of reassurance. When I compare myself to the demand, I find I can't love people as I need to, and I become exhausted by constantly trying to discern the absolute truth.

But when I read John's salutation, I gain a little hope: Scripture isn't only demand. That's certainly there, but at the core of scripture, in its first and final word, it is relaying God's favor, leniency, and calm, which "*will be* with us" regardless of what we do. Some things may be rewards, but grace, mercy, and peace are unconditional gifts.

— *Kendall Gunter*

July 27

Unless the LORD builds the house,
   those who build it labor in vain.
Unless the LORD guards the city,
   the guard keeps watch in vain.
It is in vain that you rise up early
   and go late to rest,
eating the bread of anxious toil;
   for he gives sleep to his beloved. (Psalm 127:1-2)

I functionally do not believe the basic notion of this passage. In the abstract, I may *think* I like it. God puts emphasis on rest rather than activity or productivity. But in practice?

I saw the extent of my delusion on a recent vacation. I *love* vacation. I love the idea of leisure, of pleasurably doing nothing. In reality, though, I don't know how to relax. I'm constantly trying to find ways to do nothing *well*, to do nothing *productively*. I want to read a bunch of books, listen to the right podcasts, have meaningful conversations with long-estranged friends. And of course I want to fit in some long-overdue—but pleasurable—exercise. Who doesn't?

Two days in, I was on course for a perfect, pleasurable—and yes, productive!—getaway. I had three books open and a sandy pair of running shoes drying on the lanai from my first two morning jogs on the beach. Little did I know that a third run would never happen. I hadn't run two consecutive days in ten years, and so I woke up on Morning 3 with a strained Achilles and an ankle the size of a dinosaur egg. For all intents and purposes, my vacation was grounded. I was literally beached, forced to just sit there.

I'm realizing that while I say I believe in grace, there's always the caveat that I must *earn* it. This makes me a functional Pelagian, someone who believes that, while God may grant grace to his beloved, that grace is merited only after 16 hours of "working hard for the money." What is your caveat?

Thankfully, running yourself into the ground leads you to…the ground. That's inertia. And when you're grounded—forced to rest your swollen body and your bruised ego—God's blessed time extends out like the horizon in a Corona commercial, and your eyes start to see things differently. What once was a prize to be earned becomes a gift already given.

— *Ethan Richardson*

July 28

If we confess our sins, he who is faithful and just will forgive us our sins and cleanse us from all unrighteousness. (1 John 1:9)

For as long as I can remember, I have absolutely hated wearing necklaces—especially ones that touch my skin directly. It is really an unfortunate sensory quirk of mine. After a particularly difficult few months of life, I began to search for something that I could wear daily to remind me of the hope that I have in Christ, and a cross necklace was just not going to work for me. After a lot of looking around, I bought a very thin gold bracelet. Instead of being smooth, this particular bangle has been dented and hammered by the jeweler. There is no part of the bracelet that has not been changed by the blows that were inflicted upon it.

Like my bracelet, there is no part of my being that has not been shaped by the Fall. I often forget that all of my emotional, psychological, and behavioral limitations are tethered together by the Garden of Eden. Here, in 1 John, the call to confession is not only a clear call to confess my wrong behavior and hurtful actions, but it is also a call to acknowledge again that sin is indeed a condition that I was born with, not simply a set of behaviors that I engage in. When we confess our sins, we concede that *sin* is a pervasive malady of unrighteousness and that our only hope is a radical treatment that does not just relieve symptoms, but provides a complete cure of the disease.

This is why we need a God who is both faithful *and* just. God's faithfulness will always ring hollow when we consider it apart from the violence of the cross. There, justice was satisfied once and for all, while God remained faithful to his promises. Unrighteousness was an immovable obstruction between us and any possibility of existence with the tenderness and attentiveness of our perfect heavenly Father. By the merits of his blood, Jesus imputes to us righteousness that scours the sin from our lives and the life to come.

— *Ginger Mayfield*

July 29

Now the LORD said to Abram, "Go from your country and
your kindred and your father's house to the land that I will
show you. I will make of you a great nation, and I will bless
you…"

So Abram went, as the LORD had told him; and Lot
went with him. Abram was seventy-five years old when he
departed from Haran. (Genesis 12:1-4)

Perhaps you remember the classic *Saturday Night Live* skit, "Bad Idea Jeans."
In a parody of a now-forgotten Dockers commercial, several men casually
stretch their legs as the camera zooms in on their pants. We overhear their
conversation, a series of laughably terrible ideas.

"We're gutting our apartment. Ripped up the floors, pipes, wiring—having everything completely redone!"

"You're renting right?"

"Yeah."

BAD IDEA flashes on the screen.

Second only to the eating of a certain apple, the Calling of Abram ranks
as the original Bad Idea of the Bible. Uprooting at the age of 75—a time
of life when most people are moving closer to their kin, not farther away—
would have been daunting enough. But to do so in the hopes of conceiving
a child, even without the infertility that had long afflicted Abram's wife
Sarah… Well, "foolish" would be a nice way to put it.

Still, Abram takes God at his word.

Essayist Andrew Sullivan once defined faith as "a long sacrifice of pride."
In reference to the thief on the cross, psychologist Frank Lake called faith
"a desperate gaze in a counterintuitive direction." In the Calling of Abram
we see another aspect of what it means to live by faith: to doubt what seems
obviously true about you. What the world considers a bad idea may, when
seen through the eyes of faith, turn out to be anything but.

And yet, before we make Abram into an exemplar, his faith proves as
short-lived as his patience. Before the end of the chapter, he's spinning lies
about his wife, and soon he'll give up waiting on God and, with Hagar, take
matters into his own hands.

Time and again, Abram doubts God's promise of provision. And yet, time and again, just as He does with us, God takes Abram by the hand and reminds him of the promises that will never waver, however frail Abram's faith in them may be. His blessing was poured out on the weak-willed then, just as it is today. Thank God for bad ideas!

— *David Zahl*

David said, "Mephibosheth!" He answered, "I am your servant." David said to him, "Do not be afraid, for I will show
you kindness for the sake of your father Jonathan; I will
restore to you all the land of your grandfather Saul, and
you yourself shall eat at my table always." He did obeisance
and said, "What is your servant, that you should look upon
a dead dog such as I?" (2 Samuel 9:6-8)

After years of fleeing and fighting, David has secured the throne of Israel.
He's expanded its borders through conquest and won prestige for the little
backwater kingdom. Overnight, Israel has become a regional superpower.

In the ancient Near East, a ruler of David's stature would consolidate his
ascendance by liquidating all of his rivals. But rather than eliminating possible future rivals, David searches out a way to demonstrate his gratitude to
God for bringing peace to the kingdom. He has experienced the kindness of
God and now wants to transmit that kindness to another unlikely recipient.

The death of his dearest friend, Jonathan, son of the former king Saul,
still haunts David, and so he seeks out Jonathan's son (and David's theoret-
ical rival) Mephibosheth. He is found and David instantly summons him
in order to restore ancestral lands and invite him to eat at his table for the
rest of his life. Mephibosheth is overwhelmed by David's generosity—no
doubt he anticipated assassination and erasure but instead found incorpora-
tion into David's family. He dined as though he were one of the king's sons.

Each of us carries our own shame: problems or embarrassments, maybe
a difficult family history, or demerits proving how imperfect we are. They
wear on us because we fear they'll serve as badges to identify us for purging
from the kingdom that God is growing.

But David's greater Son, Jesus Christ, is seeking you out, not to elimi-
nate you, but to invite you to share table fellowship with him forevermore.
Mephibosheth was no dead dog in David's eyes or in God's. And neither
are you. Don't think of or talk about yourself this way—exult instead that
God wants to instate you into the royal family.

— *Ian Olson*

July 31

May the God of hope fill you with all joy and peace as you trust in him, so that you may overflow with hope by the power of the Holy Spirit. (Romans 15:13 NIV)

What is hope? Hope is a future-oriented feeling that is predicated on the belief that things will work out the way we want them to. Hope is an engine that keeps us moving forward towards a future that feels like it is worth getting to. Hopelessness, by contrast, is the feeling that nothing will work out. It makes us feel directionless and motionless, as if the internal engine that keeps us going has blown. It shrinks our vision of possibility. When we cannot see the future, we want to abandon the now.

It is easy to feel hopeful when the future feels within our grasp—when we can arrange our environment and have control over our actions and choices so that we can easily draw the path between now and the future. But how can we be hopeful when our circumstances or our own inadequacies and weaknesses seem to thwart every attempt we make at drawing a path between now and the future?

In Paul's simple prayer from Romans, he asks God to fill us with *joy* and *peace*. This is a psychologically astute prayer. Research shows that positive emotions are able to broaden our horizons, generating new creative energies and openness towards the world. Paul's petition is that we would experience these positive feelings while we trust in God, and in doing so, that we would overflow with hope. But Paul also understood that when we are hopeless, we cannot generate feelings of joy and peace ourselves. That is why his prayer is for God to fill us with what we cannot generate for ourselves.

If your horizon has shrunk, turn to the God of hope, and trust Him to send you His Holy Spirit, who has the power you do not.

— *Bonnie Poon Zahl*

August 1

So when they had come together, they asked him, "Lord, is this the time when you will restore the kingdom to Israel?" He replied, "It is not for you to know the times or periods that the Father has set by his own authority. But you will receive power when the Holy Spirit has come upon you; and you will be my witnesses in Jerusalem, in all Judea and Samaria, and to the ends of the earth." (Acts 1:6-8)

When we were kids, there was this one year my little brother decided he simply could not wait to find out what my parents had gotten him for his birthday. After careful reconnaissance, he discovered where his gift was hidden away. He crept into that closet one night after everyone had gone to bed and unwrapped a box that held a gleaming Dallas Cowboys helmet. My parents eventually found out, after discovering my brother's terrible job of rewrapping the present.

It doesn't really matter what age you are: It is hard to wait for the gift, especially when you're not exactly sure what the gift is. In this passage from Acts, the gift that Peter and the apostles longed for was the best kind of kingdom they could envision at that point: a kind of Jewish Camelot, with Jesus as King Arthur, and the eleven of them sitting around as Knights of the Round Table.

What the apostles could not have imagined, at least at that point, was that when they finally opened the gift, it would be nothing less than the gracious presence of Christ, not *beside* them but *inside* them, through the ministry of the Holy Spirit. This gift would bring a new power that would be employed not in kicking the Romans out of Israel but in announcing throughout the Roman Empire and beyond the new reign of God's grace. Whether Peter and his friends could have realized it or not (and whether we realize it or not), this is a gift worth waiting for.

— *Larry Parsley*

August 2

He has filled me with bitterness...
my soul is bereft of peace,
    I have forgotten what happiness is (Lamentations 3:15, 17
    RSV)

Sometimes I hear it said that God doesn't promise us happiness, just the "ability" to face unhappiness with equanimity. In other words, keep your expectations low when praying for relief and change in your situation, and concentrate, rather, on peace within and acceptance without.

I think that can be a counsel of despair. It is what famous Stoics like Marcus Aurelius and Seneca used to recommend. The former persecuted Christians, and the latter committed suicide. As a form of wisdom, it lacks hope, and mainly it lacks faith in God.

Jeremiah, who wrote the Book of Lamentations, was a brilliant, unhappy prophet. But he didn't *like* being unhappy. In my study at the churches where Mary and I served, I always had hanging on the wall Rembrandt's painting of Jeremiah contemplating the fall of Jerusalem that resulted in the Exile. The painting is as deep as *The Deep Blue Sea* (Terence Rattigan, 1952), and I don't regret its forever presence with me during decades of parish ministry.

But I hope he is happy now. Jeremiah, I mean!

Happiness is a gift from God, and yes, it is both inward and outward. But God wants us to have it. He wants us in position to love another person and be loved by that person. He wants us to hear good music—like Katrina and the Waves. He wants us to *not be alone*.

Please don't lower your expectations of God in relation to your personal happiness. Lift them. He is perfectly capable.

— Paul Zahl

August 3

Yet you are holy,
   enthroned on the praises of Israel.
In you our ancestors trusted;
   they trusted, and you delivered them.
To you they cried, and were saved;
   in you they trusted, and were not put to shame. (Psalm 22:3-5)

Have you ever watched a movie for the hundredth time and wished for a different ending, even though you knew it would end the same way it did the other 99 times? This is how I feel whenever I read about the Israelites in the Old Testament. I get my hopes up and think, "Okay, now they're following what God told them to do!" But no, they always go astray. It is frustrating to see them constantly shooting themselves in the foot. I wish I could grab them by the shoulders and shake some sense into them! "Don't you see? It would go so much better for you if you would just do what God says!"

It is easy to pick on ancient Israel, but whenever I find myself making the same mistake for the millionth time, I realize I am no different. I am very good at ignoring my own pep talks, not to mention God's word. I know what's best for me, but I am not able to do it.

These verses, attributed to David, are about Israel trusting and crying out to God. It's interesting that in the middle of his suffering, David looks to his ancestors. But how does looking to the people of the past bring hope in our current suffering? Is it exemplary behavior that we can imitate? No: Their hope, and ours, is in the way God pulled them out of despair over and over again. Hope was and is in the Deliverer, who never fails to keep his promises.

Though the curse of sin seems never-ending in Israel's history and in our own lives, it does not have the final word. These verses are preceded by the words which Jesus will repeat from the cross, "My God, my God, why have you forsaken me?" (Mt 27:46). And the final word in this psalm is the final word for us and for the Israelites—simply, "he has done it" (v. 31). It is finished. God has delivered you, saved you, and will never let you be put to shame. He did what he promised through Jesus Christ, who bore the sin of the world: past, present, and future.

— *Juliette Alvey*

> When they had gone ashore, they saw a charcoal fire there, with fish on it, and bread. Jesus said to them, "Bring some of the fish that you have just caught." So Simon Peter went aboard and hauled the net ashore, full of large fish, a hundred fifty-three of them; and though there were so many, the net was not torn. Jesus said to them, "Come and have breakfast." (John 21:9-12)

I've always wondered what it would be like to have breakfast with Jesus. Would I serve Him or would He serve me? Would He lead the conversation or would He want me to? Would He be proud of me or a little disappointed? These are just a few of my questions. Then I read the passage at hand, and my heart leaps with joy.

Let me set the scene for you. After the death of Jesus a few days earlier, Peter finds himself depressed, especially since he disowned Jesus at his darkest hour. So he goes back to what's comfortable: fishing! Peter is good at it, and being out on the open water seems to relax him. Yet he and his fellow fishermen haven't caught one fish, and all he can think about is his denial of Jesus.

As they make their way back to dry land, the fishermen see a man on the beach and exchange a few words with him. As they draw near, John, the youngest of them all, realizes who it is and yells out, "It is the Lord!" (v. 7). Now this is when the story gets interesting. Peter rushes to meet Jesus on the seashore, but before he can even get a word out, Jesus says, in verse 12, "Come and have breakfast." No rebuke, no stern look, not even a wagging figure. Just an invitation to a meal. Now, we don't know all of what they chatted about around that campfire that morning, but "it's a safe bet" that Peter repented and Jesus forgave (cf. vv. 15-19).

Ah, what good news for sinners. "Come and have breakfast." Friends, the same good news is for you today. No matter what yesterday looked like (or didn't), we repent, believe the gospel, and listen to this sweet invitation from Jesus. As it says in Revelation, "Listen! I am standing at the door, knocking; if you hear my voice and open the door, I will come in to you and eat with you, and you with me" (3:20).

— Jonathan Adams

August 5

"No one has greater love than this, to lay down one's life for
one's friends." (John 15:13)

In my early twenties I spent a summer working as a cashier at a Dollar General. One day a heavily-bearded fellow in sunglasses looked straight at me
as I was ringing him up and said, "Greater love has no man than this: to lay
down his life for his friends." Awkwardly, I mumbled back, "Uh…good
quote, man."

These are powerful words but not easy ones. In the preceding verse,
Jesus had issued a version of his great love-commandment, synthesizing all
the law and prophets. Here, we get a glimpse of what that love demands.
The stories of martyred saints throughout history fill us with inspiration
and conviction: We feel that some great power of love is at work in them, and
instinctively seek to honor them, even as we hope never to have to emulate
them. I think of the young couple who, in August 2019, died shielding their
2-month-old child in the El Paso Walmart shooting. If that's not a powerful
image of Christ-like love, I don't know what is.

There is immense tragic beauty in someone dying for others, a beauty
that inspires believers and nonbelievers alike. Think of all the self-sacrificial film heroes: Gandalf and Frodo, Harry Potter, Iron Man, Groot, John
Coffey, Aslan, Neo, that racist dude from *Gran Torino*… Perhaps nothing
is more compelling to the human soul than the image of someone giving
up their life out of love for others, and that's precisely the type of love
that Christ establishes as the ideal in this verse. This is no mere affection
between friends or lovers—this is *agape*, the expansion of the self to include
the needs and concerns and desires of others as equal to our own. This is a
call to love friends and enemies alike perhaps more than we love ourselves,
even to the point of death. It's an insanely high bar.

Don't feel up to it? Neither do I. It's one thing to say, as Peter did, that
we will gladly lay down our lives. It's quite another, as Peter found out, to
actually do it.

But the good news is that Christ provides the initiative. At several
points in this long sermon from John, Jesus makes that explicit, saying "*I
have loved you… I have called you… I chose you… I appointed you…*"
He speaks of sending an "Advocate". I used to believe that love was some

coldly rational decision we make, day-in and day-out, but no. Love is not something we control. It involves difficult choices and sacrifices, to be sure, but the strength to love is most of all a gift of the Spirit, who is with us today and for all time.

— *Benjamin Self*

August 6

> But David said to the Philistine, "You come to me with
> sword and spear and javelin; but I come to you in the name
> of the LORD of hosts, the God of the armies of Israel, whom
> you have defied. This very day the LORD will deliver you
> into my hand..." (1 Samuel 17:45-46)

"We are outgunned, outmanned, outnumbered, outplanned," sings George
Washington in the musical *Hamilton*. He may be referring to England's
armies, but the sentiment applies to anyone who has confronted an overwhelming adversary.

The account of David's battle with Goliath is usually understood as
the archetypal underdog story. From it we take inspiration to confront
the Goliaths in our lives with courage and faith—whether they be actual
persons (or nations) set against us or the looming giant of something like
cancer or depression.

If guts to emulate David is what you need today, run with it! God-given
audacity can move mountains.

Unfortunately, the nature of fear is that it overwhelms and paralyzes.
The Goliaths in our lives almost always win, often before the battle begins.
In times marked by defeat, it might do better to focus not on the combatants
themselves but the type of combat. Each side of this conflict, we are told,
selected a champion who would do battle on behalf of their people. David
and Goliath fought vicariously, as representatives.

David represents the side that had lost heart, whose cowardice was about
to do them in. The Israelites could think of a million reasons why victory
was impossible, not even worth trying. These were the colonists who viewed
Washington's revolution as a fool's errand. The taxes weren't *that* bad.

Yet it is to people such as this that David's unlikely victory applies: those
lacking courage and confidence, who, when faced with threat, cower in fear
and wrap themselves in excuses. Those loyalists who stayed home rather
than engage the British, yet who would wake up the morning after York-
town subject to the same liberties and citizenship as those who had fought.

Likewise, the victory secured by the Son of David belongs to you, today,
right now, in the midst of whatever Goliaths you are facing. So what are
you waiting for? Raise a glass to freedom!

— *David Zahl*

I will go before you
  and level the mountains,
I will break in pieces the doors of bronze
  and cut through the bars of iron,
I will give you the treasures of darkness
  and riches hidden in secret places,
so that you may know that it is I, the LORD,
  the God of Israel, who calls you by your name. (Isaiah 45:2-3)

Years ago I led a youth mission trip to Costa Rica and was also on the verge of an emotional breakdown. On my first night in this unfamiliar country, frantic because I did not speak the language and exhausted from preparations, the father of my host family opened his Bible. He pointed to the above verse and said God was giving it to me. In the moment, all I could see was verse 3: "I will give you...*darkness.*" Uh, thanks but no thanks, guy. I was already lousy with darkness. Hard pass.

The Lord is speaking here to the Persian King Cyrus. Initially, God puts on a big show about how he's going to basically make it rain for Cyrus in his ministry. And then without even switching gears, he's like, "Oh yeah, by the way, I'm also going to give you...*darkness.*" Yet a less frenzied read reveals that hidden within the darkness will be...*abundance.* Technically speaking, "treasures of darkness" equated to certain types of spoils and riches that were kept underground. Yet I cannot help but latch onto the metaphor here, the uncomfortable truth that God's gifts often come wrapped in suffering, pain, and helplessness. Once upon a time, our God transformed a tomb into a womb where his crucified Son would be reborn and resurrected.

Beloved, God has not promised you a life without suffering. Perhaps you are all too aware of that fact. But he has promised the riches of resurrection hidden within the cold, hard graves of our despair. In your loneliness, grief, and sorrow, may you find an abundance of comfort in this Jesus who is both in you and with you. In your weakness, may you find the wealth of God's strength—to level your unclimbable mountains, to break through your doors of bronze, to cut through your bars of iron. On your very worst day, may the King of Love who calls you by name open your eyes to hidden riches, amazing grace still improbably pouring down.

— *Charlotte Getz*

August 8

One day he got into a boat with his disciples, and he said
to them, "Let us go across to the other side of the lake." So
they put out, and while they were sailing he fell asleep. A
windstorm swept down on the lake, and the boat was filling with water, and they were in danger. They went to
him and woke him up, shouting, "Master, Master, we are
perishing!" And he woke up and rebuked the wind and
the raging waves; they ceased, and there was a calm. He
said to them, "Where is your faith?" They were afraid and
amazed, and said to one another, "Who then is this, that
he commands even the winds and the water, and they obey
him?" (Luke 8:22-25)

Whenever I read this story, my own feelings about choppy water get the
better of me. I've thrown up on enough deep-sea fishing trips to make this
story sound awful. But being on a boat was not for the disciples what it is
for me. Several of them actually *were* fishermen. On a boat they were *capable*—it was how they made their living.

With this in mind, it seems to me that there are a couple details to note
about Jesus' frustration with the disciples' "lack of faith."

The first is that our bouts of faithlessness, the storms of chaos in which
God may seem asleep or totally absent, tend to happen where we are most
capable rather than least. They come within "our line of work," in the are-
nas where we "should" be able to handle it. That may sound odd, but it's
much easier to "give it to God" when you have no choice, when life throws
something at you that you have no skills or knowledge to manage. It is much
harder to "rest in faith" in the areas of our lives where we are (or at least
have appeared to be in the past) supremely capable.

The second and related point is this: that while we frantically pull in
the ropes and bail the water and follow the protocol, Jesus, the "author and
perfecter of our faith" (Heb 12:2 ASV), is fast asleep. The model of true
belief is as passive as a baby in a rocker.

There is much more out of our control than we'd like to admit, and sometimes, chaos must arrive in our offices, our houses, and our daily routines
to jar us loose from the capable people we believe ourselves to be. Only

then can we see the depth of our need, and rouse the Sleeping Man who has been there all along. Thankfully, despite our faithlessness, he awakens to console his "capable" companions, who find, to their surprise, that "he commands even the winds and the water."

— *Ethan Richardson*

August 9

"So keep up your courage, men, for I have faith in God that it will be exactly as I have been told. But we will have to run aground on some island." (Acts 27:25-26)

I moved to New York City from Alabama in July of 2005. The next April, my dad called and told me that his accountant had just finished my taxes and I owed $10,000.

My panic was met by his anger. He told me I never should have moved so far away, that it was irresponsible of me to have made such a decision, that I would have to move back. Meanwhile, I sat at a desk feeling like a small girl getting in trouble. Shame enveloped me. What had I been thinking, walking away from the only home I'd ever known into the wilds of the city?

After we hung up, I went to a friend's office and, through tears, explained the situation. I don't remember what he said other than that it was supportive and comforting. Days later, another accountant corrected what had been an error on the part of my dad's accountant. I had a stay of execution, or, in this case, permission to remain aboard.

While in New York, my faith was transformed by grace. I made lifelong friendships. Later that year, I met my now-husband. But it took this experience, and others like it, to show me what the above scripture shows as well: *sometimes sh#t happens.*

No one would cite this as a theological truth, so allow me to clarify: I once believed the bad things that happened in life were, without exception, a form of "discipline" or "punishment" for sin. And to be sure, there are consequences for our sins. But sometimes, God allows such things to happen, but *not* in order to punish us (or to force us back to—gasp—*Alabama*).

The point is that this is where, as always, God shows his faithfulness. Not necessarily through the storm lifting, our wallets filling, or avoiding shipwreck (I remained marooned on the island of Manhattan for four more years, FYI, and my wallet was virtually empty the whole time). He remains with us where we are. This is the great gift—not smooth circumstances, but divine presence. And it is usually only here, at the end of ourselves, where we can see that his presence is the one thing we needed—and always had.

— *Stephanie Phillips*

August 10

> I opened to my beloved,
>> but my beloved had turned and was gone.
> My soul failed me when he spoke.
> I sought him, but did not find him;
>> I called him, but he gave no answer.
> Making their rounds in the city
>> the sentinels found me;
> they beat me, they wounded me,
>> they took away my mantle,
>> those sentinels of the walls. (Song of Solomon 5:6-7)

Why am I in such pain? Why doesn't God help when I ask?

No one can resolve these questions. But I keep pestering God, and I keep asking these questions without getting answers. Which is an undesirable outcome.

And desire is what Solomon's Song of Songs is all about. Two lovers call to one another in the throes of passion, over and over, one moment with fervent intimacy, the next with agonizing distance. Which is where the speaker finds herself in the above passage. She has turned to her beloved, ready to embrace him, and he is not to be found.

For a long time, Jews and Christians have usually understood "him" as God and "her" as God's people: Israel, the Church, the individual believer, by turns or all at once. It's the last one, the single person, that seems most relevant to us.

St. Gregory of Nyssa, an ancient theologian with a lot to say about desire, preached on the whole Song throughout Lent. Explaining this passage, he writes that the believer who wants God but can't feel that God's there is like the lover who is frustrated, devastated even, by her beloved's absence. Being disappointed and distressed feels like getting bruised, especially because this feeling of abandonment seems endless. Will God ever be there again? Or will I always be wanting? But Gregory turns this feeling on its head: Because God is infinite, beyond everything I can imagine or hold, I can't stop wanting God. There will always be more of God to want, to long for and love. And as he reminds us, God *is love*—the very love that I receive in order to love God and other people.

Does that help, really? In the middle of despair, words often don't. But in the aftermath of hopelessness, thinking this way has helped me make sense of how God is still good, still loving me, even when God seemingly gives no answer.

It also places me firmly alongside Jesus, our beloved, who became so fully human that he too felt what the psalmist felt: "My God, my God, why have you forsaken me?" In that dark moment, Jesus endured our sense of neglect, too. And three days later, he showed it wasn't the whole story.

— *Kendall Gunter*

August 11

Now the man who had been healed did not know who it was, for Jesus had disappeared in the crowd that was there. (John 5:13)

The Gospels are full of glorious stories of Jesus healing painful infirmities. Here, Jesus has just enabled a man, who had been lame for 38 years, to get up and walk. Despite this astonishing miracle, the focus of the story is actually the people's pedantic and legalistic treatment of the sabbath. But there is also this interesting throwaway line: Jesus had disappeared.

When I was growing up, there were these kitsch bracelets that were very popular in the check-out lines of Christian bookstores. They said, "WWJD," and they were meant to remind the wearer to constantly ask him or herself, "What Would Jesus Do?" The thought was that in remembering, we would go and do likewise. They were a great stroke of genius by the devil. The unattainable law was written on our wrists to enact a million tiny deaths throughout the week. We will never do what Jesus does, and with this throwaway line, John brings that into sharp relief.

I haven't performed any miracles lately, on the sabbath or otherwise. I cannot even keep up with the laundry. But you better believe that when I do have a moment of victory, I am not retiring into the crowds, disappearing into the multitude. I may try to do my crowing in a demure, Southern-lady manner, but crow I will. Sinless Jesus doesn't need the lauding of man. What would Jesus do? Disappear into the multitudes. What would we do? Wait for the reporters to call.

In the Christian's union with Christ, we gain eternity. We become heirs. We are brothers and sisters of the Savior. We are baptized into his death and his resurrection. In Christ, we have defeated the devil, even his bracelets. But think on this for a moment: God grants us every iota of Jesus' earthly righteousness, even his dismissing of adulation. In Christ, we can disappear into the crowd—because the work is finished.

— *Ann Lowrey Forster*

August 12

Sing aloud, O daughter Zion;
   shout, O Israel!
Rejoice and exult with all your heart,
   O daughter Jerusalem!
The LORD has taken away the judgments against you,
   he has turned away your enemies.
The king of Israel, the LORD, is in your midst;
   you shall fear disaster no more. (Zephaniah 3:14-15)

If you only read this passage from Zephaniah, you'd think the small book was happy and cheerful. It is not. The preceding three and a half chapters are full of some of the most scathing words of judgment in the Bible. During the reign of King Josiah, the Law of Moses had been forgotten, and cultic prostitution and child sacrifice were common substitute religious practices. It was so bad that when a book containing the Law of Moses was found in the temple's treasury, nobody even knew what it was!

The words of Zephaniah are dire: Judah and Jerusalem are destined for destruction. But the book concludes with a word of hope: "you shall fear disaster no more." Bad things are coming, says Zephaniah, but God hasn't abandoned his people, and there will be a time when Jerusalem and Judah will thrive again.

I once heard a son eulogize his father, who was a pastor, with a kind-hearted story. The son recalled when, as a new driver, he had gotten into a traffic accident, and as the police were sorting out the matter, they placed him in the backseat of their squad car. His father soon arrived and, seeing his son in the back of the police car, his heart was broken. Forgetting the damaged car, the insurance matters, and his family's reputation, the father went to the police with a simple request: "Let me sit with my son." The officers obliged, and the father slid into the back seat of the squad car with his son to reassure him that everything would be okay. The father joined his son in the seat of the sinner. To nobody's surprise, this son grew up to be a pastor, too.

Even amidst some of the Old Testament's harshest words of judgment, the gospel is proclaimed. The worst of the worst is not a barrier to God's love, and that includes your worst too. If God loves Israel in all her failures and foibles, he can love you. Let us give thanks to God that his love is not dependent on our best, and is ever available to us in the backseat of our own personal squad car.

— *Bryan Jarrell*

August 13

O LORD, you have searched me and known me.
You know when I sit down and when I rise up;
  you discern my thoughts from far away.
You search out my path and my lying down,
  and are acquainted with all my ways. (Psalm 139:1-3)

Life often feels like a prolonged interview. We fix ourselves up, hoping to make a lasting impression on those we encounter. We stifle our oddities and accentuate our strong suits—if anyone knew the depths of our brokenness, they'd surely run for the hills! And while this strategy protects us from rejection, it also guarantees we'll never be fully and truly *accepted*. Pay no attention to the man behind the curtain!

All too easily our relationship with God slips into the same paradigm. Approaching His throne in self-consciousness, we assume God only sees what we want Him to see. The refreshing truth of Psalm 139, however, disarms our defenses. The God of the Universe is fooled by no curtain. He sees every corner of our being, knowing us better than we know ourselves. He knows us fully yet loves us completely.

We can explore the depths of this truth for years and never exhaust its amazing power, so examine what this means for you. It reminds me of the climactic scene from *The Fisher King* (1991), when protagonist Parry reveals his deep knowledge and love for Lydia.

"I've known you for a long time," he tells her. "I know that you come out from work at noon every day and you fight your way out that door... I walk with you at lunch... And I know that you get a jawbreaker before you go back into work. And I know you hate your job and you don't have many friends. I know sometimes you feel a little uncoordinated, and you don't feel as wonderful as everybody else. Feeling as alone and separate as you feel you are... I love you. I love you. I think you're the greatest thing since spice racks."

We are known to the bone and loved all the way through. It is this love—the everlasting love of the Father—that frees us to drop all pretense.

— *Charlie Meyer*

[Jesus] sat down opposite the treasury, and watched the crowd putting money into the treasury. Many rich people put in large sums. A poor widow came and put in two small copper coins, which are worth a penny. Then he called his disciples and said to them, "Truly I tell you, this poor widow has put in more than all those who are contributing to the treasury. For all of them have contributed out of their abundance; but she out of her poverty has put in everything she had, all she had to live on." (Mark 12:41-44)

The best bit of marriage advice I've ever received sounds like some of the worst. "Let's stop treating our [spouses] as if they were adults, and let's start treating them like small children," is what Swiss author Alain de Botton advises. Say what? Personal experience tells me that people hate being talked down to. *I* certainly don't like it. *Respect* is what sustains a relationship.

When we blanch at being condescended to, though, we forget how generous we are with children. If one of my kids throws a fit about going to bed, my wife and I don't take it personally. We view it as a sign of how tired he is. Likewise, if my son comes home from school acting surly, I assume something happened there that upset him, not that he has it out for me. We are, in other words, incredibly generous in our interpretation of small children. Unfortunately, such generosity of spirit often gets lost in the day-to-day trenches of adult life, usurped by scorekeeping and reciprocity. Instead of interpreting our loved ones' motivations generously, we assume the opposite.

In today's passage, Jesus commends a widow's sacrificial generosity. Small as the amount itself may be, the gift comes at a cost to her very security. Would that we all would give so freely and fearlessly! Who is the most generous person you know? Would others use that word to describe you? Do you find it easier to be generous with your money or with your judgments?

The widow's mite is more than a picture of Christian charity. It is a picture of how God gives—of the generosity he not only endorses but embodies. Jesus is, as Francis Spufford put it, "what it looks like to love deliberately without self-protection."

Our God is not stingy. He holds nothing back, not even his blood. We are his (small) children after all.

— *David Zahl*

August 15

> But now that faith has come, we are no longer subject to
> a disciplinarian, for in Christ Jesus you are all children of
> God through faith. As many of you as were baptized into
> Christ have clothed yourselves with Christ. There is no
> longer Jew or Greek, there is no longer slave or free, there
> is no longer male and female; for all of you are one in Christ
> Jesus. And if you belong to Christ, then you are Abraham's
> offspring, heirs according to the promise. (Galatians 3:25-29)

I have yet to preach a sermon after which, on the way out of the church, some well-meaning person does not comment to me that I should "smile more." And there are endless comments on my hair (too short), my clothing (too loud), and my height (too tall). It's happened so much that I rarely have the energy to get angry. It is the plight of professional womanhood. And my friends who are doctors, lawyers, and academics all get the same treatment.

So I laugh whenever someone tells me that we are beyond gender roles. I laugh until I cry when someone comments that we live in a post-racial society. We very much see the differences in each other, and some days, it feels like it's all we can talk about.

Paul tells us that we are all one in Christ Jesus. And as much as I long to cling to what makes me unique, I actually find a great deal of rest in this passage. The idea that no one would comment on my appearance or gender is kind of a huge relief. It turns out that Jesus only comments in forgiveness and love. And the very human categories we fall into are not qualifiers for whether or not God loves us. After all, we are the ones who have deemed certain people as lovable, valuable, and beautiful. But this is clearly not the character of God.

I also love that this passage unites me to those who, in worldly terms, are very different from myself. Through the unearned love of Jesus Christ, we are given a powerful gift that unites us. And these days, it feels like there is so little that does.

— *Sarah Condon*

August 16

And the LORD spoke to Aaron: Drink no wine or strong drink, neither you nor your sons, when you enter the tent of meeting, that you may not die; it is a statute forever throughout your generations. (Leviticus 10:8-9)

Christians excel at *really* misinterpreting the Bible. That is, if "proper" interpretation focuses on historical context and the individual psychologies of writers. These factors are important and enrich our understanding, but it's worth noting that that's not how Jesus read. Instead, "beginning with Moses and all the prophets, he interpreted to them the things about himself in all the scriptures" (Lk 24:27). Or as he boldly told the Judeans, "If you believed Moses, you would believe me, for he wrote about me" (Jn 5:46). If Sunday School taught me anything, it's that the answer is always "Jesus," even when the question seems totally remote.

The above passage is about ancient Hebrew sacrifice and ritual purity, so it isn't too difficult to relate it to Jesus. The writers of the New Testament tell us he's our high priest, even the sacrifice a priest offers. But what does the teetotaling commandment from these specific verses have to do with Jesus?

Origen, writing in the third century, connects it to something Jesus promises us in the Gospels: "I will never again drink of the fruit of the vine until that day when I drink it new in the kingdom of God" (Mk 14:25). In his life, before his Passion, he ate and drank loads, with "tax collectors and sinners" of all people. But at the Last Supper, he gave it up, because he, like the ancient priest Aaron, was going to make a sacrifice, and that sacrifice was himself. Even now in his ascension he's abstaining, because wine is for celebration, but he feels the pain that the world and each of us suffers and inflicts. He feels it and goes to the Father for us with it. That's the job he's chosen for now, until kingdom come.

— *Kendall Gunter*

August 17

Although heaven and the heaven of heavens belong to the
LORD your God, the earth with all that is in it, yet the
LORD set his heart in love on your ancestors alone and
chose you, their descendants after them, out of all the peoples, as it is today... For the LORD your God is God of
gods and Lord of lords, the great God, mighty and awesome, who is not partial and takes no bribe, who executes
justice for the orphan and the widow, and who loves the
strangers, providing them food and clothing. (Deuteronomy
10:14-15, 17-18)

Against the backdrop of polytheistic cultures in the ancient Near East,
Old Testament writers were telling the story of a very different God than
the other gods that people worshipped. This was not just a god who could
influence fertility, command the weather, or guarantee success in conquer-
ing enemies. Greater than the gods who could control the natural world,
this God was the source of all things. He created the heavens and the earth,
and even "the heaven of heavens" belonged to him.

One might think this God to be too great, too mighty, and too awesome
for humans to approach. Yet we are told that this God also *loves* people, not
just for a short time, but for generations after generations—even if people of
some of those generations would become unfaithful. Not only did this God
love people; he had special love for the orphan and the widow, whose hearts
have known loss and grief, who feel forgotten by those around them. He
had special affection for those strangers whom others might have shunned
because they were unfamiliar or different, who felt lost or unwelcome in
the places or circumstances where they found themselves.

The God of gods and Lord of lords has special love for you. We are all
like the orphan and the widow when we feel brokenhearted, lonely, or left
behind; in all of these times, God has special love for us. When you feel
unmoored, unknown, or unappreciated, you are like the stranger whom
God welcomes in to share the warmth and comfort of his home. He calls
you *friend*.

— *Bonnie Poon Zahl*

August 18

If I must boast, I will boast of the things that show my
weakness. (2 Corinthians 11:30)

In a culture of perfectionism, in which meticulously curated images are how
individuals cultivate their personal branding, Paul's statement is the equivalent of posting a closeup of the monster zit growing on the end of his nose.
Zits may happen, but goodness gracious, we don't photograph them for all
the world to see. Blemishes and scars, weaknesses and shames, all fall into
the "cover them up" category.

Not so with the apostle Paul. He's going to brag about them. A back
mangled by Jewish lashes and Roman rods? Yes, sir. Scars from being stoned?
Oh, yeah. Shipwrecked? Been there, done that. Imprisoned? More than once.
Sleepless nights, starving, thirsty, cold, without shelter? All on my resume.
And, to top it all off, a thorn in the flesh, a messenger of Satan, that, despite
repeated attempts to get God to take it away, is still there, tormenting him?
Yes, that too. Paul is a walking, talking nightmare of a terrible, horrible, no
good, very bad ministry. Or so it would seem.

Quite shockingly, he says that in all his weaknesses and wounds and per-
secutions, he is content (12:10). Not only that, but he'll boast about them.
Why? "[S]o that the power of Christ may dwell in me" (12:9). Paul came
to the hard and inescapable conclusion that, slowly and painfully, every
follower of Jesus learns: The more there is of us in us, the less there is of
Christ in us. So God pulls out the drain at the bottom of our lives to empty
us. Our pride. Our vanity. Our perfectionism. Our the-world-revolves-
around-me egoism. Our grandstanding. Our virtue-signaling. God has his
ways of emptying us, as he emptied Paul, so that he might suffuse that void
with the power of Christ and the fullness of the Spirit.

When we are weak, then we are strong, for in the Father's backwards
way of dealing with us, our weaknesses are but his door through which to
walk into our lives with love, with power, with mercy, and with peace.

— *Chad Bird*

August 19

For freedom Christ has set us free. Stand firm, therefore,
and do not submit again to a yoke of slavery. (Galatians 5:1)

In late 2019, according to the United Nations, there were over 40 million
people entrapped in what is called modern-day slavery. Such individuals may
be subjected to debt bondage, forced labor, forced prostitution and marriage, and other forms of brutal exploitation. These figures are completely
dismaying. They should cause anyone to doubt their faith in the good nature
of humanity. They should cause us to kneel in prayer, because if you are a
Christian, you believe that human beings are meant to be free.

But we need not look too far to find the forces of subjugation at work.
In his novel *The Fall*, Albert Camus remarks, "Every man needs slaves like
he needs clean air. To rule is to breathe, is it not?" Even the most destitute
among us, Camus says, will attempt to subjugate our children, spouses, and
close loved ones, perhaps even ourselves. A bleak perspective, you might say,
but I think he's right. We attempt to impose order by domination, bossing
people around, and letting ourselves get bossed around.

What are you enslaved to? Maybe there is some addiction, or a relationship, or an ex-relationship that has crippling power over your better senses.
Maybe the voice of a demanding parent speaks loudly in your head. Maybe
you are enslaved to money, work, to the dream of one day being "successful."
Maybe you are enslaved to a fantasy of yourself.

Freedom in the most basic sense means you can do what you want. And
if you're anything like me, that sounds scary as hell. We might prefer to
stay subservient, under the thumb of guilt, obligation, and a fantasy world,
because despite its misery, it feels safer.

Hear, then, Paul's command: *Do not give in*. Remember that God loves
your actual self and is not the voice of demand in your head. You do not
need to atone for your sins. Christ already did that. You do not need to
be a hotshot. You do not need to dominate anything or anyone, not even
yourself. You need only God in Christ, who has hidden you safely within
Himself to set you free. Do not give in. Enjoy your freedom. St. Augustine
said it best: "Love, and do as you will."

— *CJ Green*

August 20

> Never be rash with your mouth, nor let your heart be quick
> to utter a word before God, for God is in heaven, and you
> upon earth; therefore, let your words be few. (Ecclesiastes
> 5:2)

Whenever we see the word "therefore" in the Bible, we can be sure that the writer is making an important link, one that is worth focusing on. What then can be the link between God's being in heaven, us on earth, and our words being few?

Years of living with my family has meant that I have been exposed to many (mostly wonderful) movies, and *many* words about these movies. One of the most helpful images I have taken in from this exposure is the "God's-eye view" camera angle. This is when the camera pulls back to show us the scene from a distance. It is fascinating to pay attention to such a camera move, because the director is always saying something about the "big picture" in the lives of the characters. The opposite of a close-up. Think Alfred Hitchcock's *The Birds* (1963).

When I stop talking and ask for the "God's-eye view" on my life, I am often given a fresh perspective on whatever concern I currently have. But the key point here might be to "stop talking," because we cannot talk and listen at the same time. Caught up in my own words, even in prayer, I fail to listen, and hence, fail to see as God sees.

> *Lord, forgive me for valuing my words over yours. Help me to*
> *stop talking so that you might give me the "God's-eye view" on*
> *my life today.*

— *Mary Zahl*

August 21

"See, I am sending you out like sheep into the midst of wolves; so be wise as serpents and innocent as doves." (Matthew 10:16)

No matter where you are today, Christ is "sending you out."

The bad news is this: The wolf seems to have the high ground. Because of this, strength will always seem like the safer bet, and the appeal of taking control will know no end.

The zero-sum game of the old kingdom invites us to become wolves. Bob Seger agrees: When you "feel like a number," you are experiencing the dehumanizing effects of a world where "more for you is less for me." It's hard not to look for the high ground and start picking off some sheep. The Brothers Grimm were onto something when they wrote, "The wolf…went straight to the grandmother's bed, and devoured her. Then he put on her clothes, dressed himself in her cap, laid himself in bed and drew the curtains."

In *Teen Wolf* (1985), a father tells his son that he hoped the curse of the wolf would pass him by. His increasingly fanged and hairy son replies, "Dad, it didn't pass me by. It landed on my face!" Our trend toward wolfishness necessitates real introspection.

The good news is this: God loves *all* of you. God forgives the wolf you are and numbers you among His sheep. In Christ, God has called us innocent and has gathered us together to enjoy both provision and protection. Nothing can separate us from the love of God in Christ Jesus. This Good Shepherd's love assures us that the wolves within us, and the wolves around us, are no problem for a God who has everything to give and holds nothing back.

— *Matt Magill*

August 22

Not that I am referring to being in need; for I have learned
to be content with whatever I have. I know what it is to
have little, and I know what it is to have plenty. In any and
all circumstances I have learned the secret of being well-
fed and of going hungry, of having plenty and of being in
need. I can do all things through him who strengthens me.
(Philippians 4:11-13)

In his book *The Youngest Day*, Robert Capon compares life to being on a
bus. There are many stops along the way, but the longer you are on the bus,
the more you begin to see that the Bus Company knows what it's doing:

> After enough transfers, breakdowns, evictions, and even will-
> ful refusals to stay aboard, you develop, if not a satisfaction
> with the way the bus line is run, at least an astonishment that
> it runs as well as it does. If you can remember not to waste
> your time wishing you were somewhere else, it's amazing what
> can happen.

Wasting your time wishing you were somewhere else is a potent and devilish
temptation meant to cheat you out of the joy of just being where you are.
*I'll be happy when I get the next stop. If only I hadn't gotten off at this stop,
I would be in a much better place. How did I end up sitting on this row with
these people?* I'd like to remind you today that the Driver knows what He's
doing and where He is going. He paid for your ticket onto the bus with His
own blood. I've always disliked the ditty "God is my co-pilot." There is no
"co" about it; you are just along for the ride, a ride that has been planned
and prepared for you with unimaginable love and attention.

Perhaps this is what the Apostle Paul means when he famously says,
"We know that all things work together for good for those who love God,
who are called according to his purpose" (Rom 8:28).

> *Thank you, God, that you are in charge of everything, including
> me. Please give me trust in you and in your plan and purpose
> for me today and always, through Jesus Christ our Lord. Amen.*

— *Paul Walker*

August 23

My soul is satisfied as with a rich feast,
   and my mouth praises you with joyful lips
when I think of you on my bed,
   and meditate on you in the watches of the night;
for you have been my help,
   and in the shadow of your wings I sing for joy. (Psalm 63:5-7)

During the 25 years that I've been a Christian, I've had a somewhat diffi-cult relationship with joy. I experience joy, but it's elusive. It comes and goes. It can be euphoric or barely discernible. I don't always understand what joy feels like, what it looks like, where it comes from, or how to keep it from disappearing. I feel like a child trying to catch bubbles blown from a plastic wand. When I'm finally close enough to reach one, it pops as soon as I touch it.

But this psalm gives me a sense of what it means for joy to be anchored in the goodness of God. It tells me that joy and satisfaction are fastened to the work, nature, presence, and protection of God.

These verses make sense when I consider my experiences during wor-ship. When I gather with others who share my faith, hear the word of God preached, and remember God's saving grace during Communion, I feel immense joy and respond by singing praises to our Creator and Sustainer.

Some days I wish I could find this same joy while I'm vacuuming or running errands or avoiding making dinner. I wish I could find it when I'm having an argument with my husband about my inability to quit buying books or when I'm frustrated with my children for leaving their unfinished laundry in the washer and the dryer and on the floor in front of the washer and the dryer.

And some days, this joy finds me. It arrives during a conversation with a friend. It arrives when I'm waiting for an answer to a prayer and I realize I'll be okay with any response. It finds me when I catch a glimpse of the sunset with its shades of orange, pink, and purple sprayed across the sky. It has even found me in the darkness, while I'm in bed, unable to sleep. I know that the wings of God surround me, even though I can't see them.

— *Charlotte Donlon*

August 24

> At that time the festival of the Dedication took place in Jeru-
> salem. It was winter, and Jesus was walking in the temple,
> in the portico of Solomon. So the Jews gathered around him
> and said to him, "How long will you keep us in suspense? If
> you are the Messiah, tell us plainly." (John 10:22-24)

All too often, our lives are suspended between two things, at least when
we're thinking of questions like, "Should I buy this house? Should I marry
this guy? Will my tests come back positive? Will I get that job offer?" Many
times it feels like these questions can make or break your life.

In this passage, the Jews have been long awaiting a Messiah to bring
them out of oppression. They've been in suspense for centuries! And here
comes a man who has given sight to the blind, walked on water, and fed
5,000 people from just a few loaves and fish. He's talked a lot about his heavenly Father and the new kingdom coming. But the people are done playing
games. They want a straight answer, so they say, "Enough! Are you the
One we've been waiting for?"

And he eventually gives them what they want: "The Father and I are
one" (v. 30). And what happens next? They pick up stones again to stone
him. Why? "[F]or blasphemy," they say, "because you, though only a human
being, are making yourself God" (v. 33). Jesus puts it plainly, and they just
can't take it because it's not the answer they wanted.

All too often, we're waiting for a sign from God while assuming that,
should we get a sign, we will obey it. That's a big assumption. It's an
assumption that ignores the human story—which is a story of rebellion,
of continued disobedience, of constantly trying to control what is uncon-
trollable. This assumption, that whenever you face a decision, it's as easy
as knowing right from wrong, is not based on your own life or the Bible.

There will be times when you don't hear a voice, when you feel much
more like you are suspended in midair than held in the palm of God's hand.
And in that moment, Jesus is with you still, for one time *he* was suspended
in midair, his palms loosed of control and stretched out on a cross. And
because of that, you are not responsible for "making or breaking" your life,
because he was broken for you.

— Sam Bush

August 25

What then are we to say? Should we continue in sin in order
that grace may abound? By no means! How can we who
died to sin go on living in it? Do you not know that all of
us who have been baptized into Christ Jesus were baptized
into his death? Therefore we have been buried with him by
baptism into death, so that, just as Christ was raised from
the dead by the glory of the Father, so we too might walk
in newness of life. (Romans 6:1-4)

There is a way to read these verses as though human beings had the power
to decide whether or not to sin. I can imagine someone waking up one
morning and saying to themselves, "I am not going to continue in sin today."
I have probably said similar things many times before. We often view sin
as individual actions we control. Following that logic, we think, "I should
sin less." It is a good thought, to be sure, but we can never quite stick the
landing.

On the days when I proclaim that I will not sin, I often break my own
promise before breakfast is finished. How can this be? It comes back to the
misplaced agency we give to humans when we read these verses. Dead people don't make decisions, and we are all dead in our sin.

But we are also born again in Christ. The newness of life in which we
walk is not some higher plane of existence where we are not sullied by the
dirt of the world. The newness of life we are given is a clear view of how
the world *actually* works and who is *actually* in charge. We cannot increase
the grace of God just as we cannot decide to stop sinning. We are dead men
and women made alive through the death of Christ.

Should I continue in sin? As if I had a choice! I am a dead man with a
bound will. Thank God that I have been (and will be) born again and again
and again through Jesus Christ.

— *Connor Gwin*

August 26

If I say, "I will not mention him,
  or speak any more in his name,"
there is in my heart as it were a burning fire
  shut up in my bones,
and I am weary with holding it in,
  and I cannot. (Jeremiah 20:9 RSV)

When you have something to say, even something to say that you believe is a word from God, you have to ask yourself whether your own anger is part of the quotient, and whether your passion to speak is tainted by a desire to draw attention to yourself in a selfish way. Even in the purest of cases, you can say a right and proper thing but say it in the wrong spirit. I'll bet this has happened to you.

At the same time, if you get too psychological about it, you might end up *never* speaking out, for fear of coming from the wrong place.

This is a constant problem in ministry, and to be honest, I find this to be a chronic problem in my own ministry. Having let myself get carried away a few times in the past, I check myself now even more than is probably necessary, and 'edit,' heavily, most comments that finally come from my pen or my mouth. Then you end up sort of cancelling out or diluting the essence of what you believed was given you to say.

The bottom line of prophecy in the Jeremiah-religious sense is that your word, when it is given by God, simply *has to come out.* You have no choice. It has to come out. And God should be trusted to help you through... your martyrdom.

— *Paul Zahl*

August 27

Then they sent to him some Pharisees and some Herodians to trap him in what he said. And they came and said to him, "Teacher, we know that you are sincere, and show deference to no one; for you do not [look on the appearance of humans], but teach the way of God in accordance with truth. Is it lawful to pay taxes to the emperor, or not? Should we pay them, or should we not?" But knowing their hypocrisy, he said to them, "Why are you putting me to the test? Bring me a denarius and let me see it." And they brought one. Then he said to them, "Whose [image is this, and whose inscription]?" They answered, "The emperor's." Jesus said to them, "Give to the emperor the things that are the emperor's, and to God the things that are God's." And they were utterly amazed at him. (Mark 12:13-17)

All things belong to God. That remains true no matter how much of our little pile we pay in tax (or for that matter, tithe) and how much we spend on beer and deep-fried Twinkies at the state fair. So what, exactly, is the point of this odd exchange?

Caesar's tax is paid in Caesar's coin, which is stamped with Caesar's head. To a Jew scrupulous about graven images, that coin represents danger—doubly so if, in good pagan style, the reverse displays a seated goddess. The coin is an offense, and so the questioners demand that Jesus work out a dispute they cannot resolve among themselves: how to uphold both commandments, to worship God alone and to honor those in authority.

Despite our desire to mine his words for a decree on church and state, Jesus does not offer a political theory. He asks for the coin, displays it, and says, "Whose image?" Yes, Caesar's—but Caesar is only a human. On that coin is a human image, a human face, and out of all creation, only the human is made in "the image of God" (Gen 1:27). The questioners forget the word of the Creator, and so a simple coin shakes them.

The one who holds the coin does not forget the Maker's word, because it is his own. It is his image, his inscription; he is the divine Son, the image of the Father, and in him is the truth of God and humanity. What prevails with him is not the legality of tax and coin, but faith that trusts in the promised "image of God." That faith holds God and humanity together, inseparably, and in it there is no danger, no chance of idolatry, but all is lawful, because in Jesus, the Creator of all things is at home with us.

— *Adam Morton*

August 28

[H]ow are they to call on one in whom they have not
believed? And how are they to believe in one of whom they
have never heard? And how are they to hear without someone to proclaim him? And how are they to proclaim him
unless they are sent? As it is written, "How beautiful are
the feet of those who bring good news!" (Romans 10:14-15)

Here is the good news: God loves you and me so very much that he died the
death we deserved, all so that God could be with us forever. This gospel
is heart-stopping. The God of the actual universe deems *me* beloved. The
God of the universe became human and endured the guilt and violence of
my faults.

If the King of Love went so far as to suffer and die to promise me resurrection, what does that mean for how he feels and cares for me on a daily,
second-by-second basis? This love is true, steadfast, near, desperate. It's in
the details, and it makes no mistakes. This love stays with me when I wake
up and when I turn down my blinds at night. How the world would breathe
with freedom and delight if we all knew this love—this Jesus—face-to-face,
heart-to-heart.

A prayer for today:

> *May our hearts, Lord, overflow with your good news. May we
> generously and with wonder hold out the Word of Life to those
> around us. May we draw others to the saving grace of your love.
> You have filled this battered and broken world with awesome rel-
> ics of your beauty, splendor, goodness, and light. May the nations
> know the same everlasting love and salvation we experience on
> a daily basis. Dark and sinful and small as we are, may your
> abundant light yet shine through us.*

"How beautiful are the feet of those who bring the good news!"

— *Charlotte Getz*

August 29

> But [Rahab] took the two men and hid them. Then she
> said, "True, the men came to me, but I did not know where
> they came from. And when it was time to close the gate
> at dark, the men went out. Where the men went I do not
> know. Pursue them quickly, for you can overtake them."
> (Joshua 2:4-5)

This story reads like a scene from a Cold War-era action movie. Joshua,
leader of the Israelites, sends his spies to scope out the city of Jericho. They
take refuge with Rahab, a prostitute, who saves their lives by hiding them
on her roof, lying to the authorities, and sneaking them out of the city. In
exchange, the spies agree to spare Rahab and those of her house when the
Israelites invade.

For ancient literature, it's pretty thrilling stuff, and yet as a child I
remember being appalled by the story. I mean, she *lied*, right? Is the Bible
saying that's okay??? It's funny how rigid the young mind can be about rules.
Not to mention the old mind. It's also strange that I didn't suffer the same
agony over the fact that—in Joshua 6—the Israelites murder almost the
entire city. Still, Rahab's story begs the question: Is lying always wrong?
A *Christianity Today* article summarized the issue: "The Bible condemns
deception... Even so, when Rahab's story is told...the Bible—while not
justifying her lie—does not condemn it. The same is true of the midwives'
lie (Exod. 1:15-21) and Elisha's lie (2 Kings 6:19)." Beyond scripture, I think
we can all envision scenarios both routine and extreme in which lying might
be commendable, and yet none of this lessens the general importance of telling the truth; it only suggests that the ethical water is a tad murky.

Is lying always wrong? Who cares? Ethical purity was never the point.
We don't worship the law, nor are we saved by it. The Bible contains much
ethical teaching but is not an instruction manual. It is rather—as Rabbi
Abraham Joshua Heschel put it—the story of "God's search for man." Twice
in 1 Corinthians, that great expert in the law, St. Paul, writes that "'All
things are lawful,' but not all things are beneficial." Such a notion doesn't
lessen the importance of the law but emphasizes the strange freedom that
comes from trusting in a loving power greater than ourselves.

— *Benjamin Self*

August 30

> I will repay you for the years
>   that the swarming locust has eaten… (Joel 2:25)

A news story from early 2020 reported on the swarms of locusts ravaging Kenya. One shocking factoid sticks in my head: a single swarm can contain 40 million locusts, which can eat *80 tons* of food in a single day. That amount of food could feed 35,000 people. To make matters worse, many farmers not only lost the year's harvest, but the seed for the following year's harvest as well. What is often forgotten, as one government official pointed out, is that the damage isn't limited to the loss of food for people and their livestock but has a devastating impact on the *entire* ecosystem. The locusts consume everything that's green, effectively rendering the landscape lifeless. Recovery is measured in years, maybe decades.

In the book of Joel, God's people were experiencing successive plagues of locusts. Whether real insects or invading armies, the effect was the same—what one swarm missed, the next one ate. They weren't simply going to tighten their belts and tough it out for the rest of the season; their future was dead. You can't plant seeds that don't exist. In plain language, zero plus zero still equals zero.

Many of us have felt similarly: helpless, with a side of bleak. We may have lost in love, had career setbacks, experienced ill health, or all of the above. The future stretches out before us like a desert, lifeless and dry. We can't undo what has been done, and it doesn't feel like there is a "next." This was the collective state of God's people, and it was at that very moment that God promised to do the impossible. He promised to restore the people to the state they were in before the locusts took everything. Only one thing was certain: Something like that was going to take a miracle.

Impossible situations, ones that don't add up, are God's specialty. When sin and death left us at zero—which is the *exact* percentage we are able to contribute to the endeavor—Christ changed life's arithmetic forever on the cross. Jesus *lived* our poverty and pain, our hunger and thirst; that blood on the cross was real. It was there that the restoration of everything was done. Death can never undo it, and poverty can never take it away. In place of nothing, Christ gave us everything: a future forever with Him.

— *Joshua Retterer*

> But you have come to Mount Zion and to the city of the
> living God, the heavenly Jerusalem, and to innumerable
> angels in festal gathering, and to the assembly of the first-
> born who are enrolled in heaven, and to God the judge of
> all, and to the spirits of the righteous made perfect, and to
> Jesus, the mediator of a new covenant, and to the sprinkled
> blood that speaks a better word than the blood of Abel.
> (Hebrews 12:22-24)

We come to the Bible with the expectation of hearing God's word for us. We grasp its covers and imagine being swept away by an inspirational directive that will overcome the deadlock of our everyday problems and...we freeze as we're not sure which book to turn to. If I automatically flip to the New Testament, am I unwittingly pretending the Old isn't important anymore? If I turn to the Old Testament, are my eyes going to blur with bewilderment when I get lost in a genealogy or a priestly statute? Often, we're drawn up short by what we're looking for in scripture and the actual texture of its surface.

I think the authors of scripture knew that it can be tricky to maintain focus and apprehend what these texts have in store for us. It isn't as straightforward as breathing. We can become so aware of this confusion and disappointment that we can begin to think they're the truest things about reading scripture.

The above passage comes after an exhortation to take heart in spite of very real trials. It testifies that however we *feel* about Bible reading, prayer, or corporate worship, *this* is what's most true, most real: that in Christ and by his Spirit, we are summoned out of the muted colors and exhaustion of our everyday world and made to inhabit the space of God's never-disenchanted presence.

If we can be swept up into the presence of angels and departed saints and the victorious slain Lamb of God without our being aware of it, then it's entirely conceivable that we can benefit from reading his words even if we aren't aware of how it's benefiting us in the moment. The deepest aspects of reality may not be obvious to us at any given moment, but we don't have to comprehend the mechanics of how scripture contributes to our well-being for it to do so. May we feed on God's words, knowing he is drawing us into something deeper and more lovely than our quotidian experience would ever allow us to believe.

— *Ian Olson*

September 1

Therefore I intend to keep on reminding you of these things, though you know them already and are established in the truth that has come to you. I think it right, as long as I am in this body, to refresh your memory, since I know that my death will come soon, as indeed our Lord Jesus Christ has made clear to me. And I will make every effort so that after my departure you may be able at any time to recall these things. (2 Peter 1:12-15)

We all have them: stories that we have heard so many times that we feel like we might just throw up if we hear it again. We can recite them word for word. Yet the family member telling us the story once again is unashamed and tells it as if we've never heard it before in our lives!

In this passage, Peter admits upfront to the churches receiving his letter: Look, I know you've heard this a million times and already know it, but I intend to repeat it ad nauseum. Why? Because it is so important and so wonderful and so…*eternal* that I don't care if I annoy you or make myself look foolish.

The gospel is all about God's amazing and unconditional love for us. And who gets tired of hearing that they are loved? Does a spouse say, "Okay, I already know you love me, so you don't have to say it or show it anymore"? Never! The beauty of the gospel is that it is so deep and rich that God never runs out of creative and meaningful ways to express it to us.

And so, at the risk of sounding annoying or foolish, here it goes: God loves you so much that he gave his one and only son, Jesus Christ, so that he can be with you forever, and he will never stop reminding you. May this be one of the many times you're reminded today.

— *Juliette Alvey*

September 2

> But they soon forgot his works;
> > they did not wait for his counsel.
> But they had a wanton craving in the wilderness,
> > and put God to the test in the desert... (Psalm 106:13-14)

Toddlers are terrible listeners. Recently I watched a father try to wrangle his son at a fast-casual restaurant. Despite the numerous reminders from dad that, if he continued to climb the booth, he would eventually fall and hurt himself, the child continued to climb. When his dad blocked one pathway, the boy found a new way to climb. Still, every time the boy teetered beyond the edge, his dad yanked him back to safety.

You don't have to be three to be a terrible listener, though. Just look at the Israelites. When the going gets tough, this psalm says, there are two things which *can* help you: *remembering* and *waiting*. From the pain of your present comes hope from both sides of the time continuum: remembering your past deliverances, and waiting for future ones to unfold. It is the same as saying, "I know God has gotten me through X before, so I will wait to see how he gets me through Y." Remembering and waiting anchors the present in a wider perspective. It doesn't remove your pain, but it does contextualize it within another, more hopeful storyline.

But it isn't that easy. It isn't even that easy in this psalm. This isn't a one-time slip-up in the history of an otherwise faithful people. No, this psalm is a litany of forgetfulness, a long lament about the perennial impatience and faithlessness of God's people. Though delivered through the Red Sea, they created new gods in the desert. Though given the Promised Land, they grumbled in their tents. It is what they do. And, if you are one of God's people, it is most likely what you do, too.

Ultimately, this psalm is not about the faithfulness of God's people. It is about the faithfulness of God, who continues to provide hope for a people bent on hopeless endeavors. While we continue to miss the warning signs from the past, while we continue to try new interventions to today's tough subject, interventions that wind up making our tough times tougher, the truth remains: God has done something, and his plan is unfolding. Even though you can't stop climbing, he won't let you fall.

— *Ethan Richardson*

September 3

Now Jesus stood before the governor; and the governor asked him, "Are you the King of the Jews?" Jesus said, "You say so." (Matthew 27:11)

Prince Charles has to be the most patient man in the world. He is the eldest child of Queen Elizabeth II, and he is the longest-serving heir apparent to the British throne. He's been waiting 60-plus years to be a king. And while he's been waiting, he's acquired some titles of his own: *His Royal Highness Prince Charles Philip Arthur George, Prince of Wales, KG, KT, GCB, OM, AK, QSO, PC, ADC, Earl of Chester, Duke of Cornwall, Duke of Rothesay, Earl of Carrick, Baron of Renfrew, Lord of the Isles and Prince and Great Steward of Scotland.* He's also a nice man. My father once met him in a men's bathroom at Harvard University. Charles looked at my dad, smiled, and said, "Take every opportunity."

Jack Dawson—played by Leonardo DiCaprio—became a king at a much earlier age. In the one of the best moments in his life (except maybe for smooching Rose a.k.a. Kate Winslet), Jack stands on the prow of the *Titanic* in the movie of the same name and shouts, "I'm the king of the world!"

According to Wikipedia, there are fifteen heads of state in the world right now who use the title "king." And then there is the Kingship of Christ.

On Good Friday, Pilate asks Jesus, "Are you the King of the Jews?" Pilate anticipates that Jesus is seeking the authority of an earthly king, with an army of angels ready to do battle. What does Jesus say? "My kingdom is not of this world" (Jn 18:36 NIV). *My kingdom has nothing to do with armies or knights in shining armor. My kingdom has nothing to do with titles.*

Instead, as Jesus says elsewhere, "Let the little children come to me...for it is to such as these that the kingdom of heaven belongs" (Mt 19:14). This is the kingdom of the king who steps down from his throne to gather little children in his arms. It's the kingdom of the king who suffers on a cross as a criminal to bear our sins. It's the kingdom of the king who tells us that it's never too late, and who opens his arms to welcome us home.

P.S. For a picture of an earthly king who embodies the grace of power and love of Christ the King, don't miss *A United Kingdom*—a 2016 Oscar-nominated true-life movie about the king of Botswana.

— *Jim Munroe*

September 4

"Are not five sparrows sold for two pennies? Yet not one
of them is forgotten in God's sight. But even the hairs of
your head are all counted. Do not be afraid; you are of more
value than many sparrows." (Luke 12:6-7)

In 1998, Disney Channel released a film called *Brink!* in which an otherwise average teenager became a sponsored roller-blader. The following year
brought *Johnny Tsunami*, a movie about a young, award-winning surfer who
also happened to be exceptional at skiing and snowboarding. In *Read It and
Weep*, a girl's private journal accidentally became a best-seller. And then
there was the hit series *Hannah Montana*, about a girl who was so famous
that she led a secret double-life to evade the press. Oh, and does anyone
remember *The Lizzie McGuire Movie*, in which a perennially normal teen
becomes, overnight, an international pop sensation?

In all of these, the ultimate message is that fame and success are not as
important as love and friendship. But that doesn't really sink in. Somehow,
the fame is still attractive. Maybe we think that fame will give us love in
abundance. As Zadie Smith once wrote, "To walk into the world and meet
love, from everyone, everywhere—this is a rational dream."

Cut to the present day, when adults, like attention-starved children,
clamor for love and acclaim by exhibiting themselves on the Internet. A
friend of mine is a recovering drug addict who is all too familiar with this
type of behavior. He says that in his former life, he vowed to be either
famous or infamous, it didn't matter which. He just wanted to be known.

If you long to be known, then hear this good news. God knows exactly
who you are, and couldn't care less about the number of followers you have.
God awards no points for your singing voice, as wonderful as it may be. Or
your beautiful face, or your way with words.

And yet God cares so deeply about *you* that He has counted out every
hair on your head. He knows precisely the dimensions of your body and
the depths of your fears and insecurities. You do not need a stadium full
of strangers chanting your name—you do not even need likes on your Instagram post—because the God of the universe is…your number one fan.

— CJ Green

September 5

"Blessed are the peacemakers, for they will be called children of God." (Matthew 5:9)

The UN recognizes 195 sovereign states. There are about a dozen more self-declared states, and more than 60 territories that are ruled under larger states. Of all these, only 23 countries exist without an active military. When highlighted on a map, these unarmed states are scattered like stars, tiny island nations all over the world.

As a species of animal on this beautiful blue marble of a planet, we have drawn countless artificial lines. To organize, lead, and cultivate civilization, we have subdivided and arranged and armed ourselves. Over time, power dynamics shift, relationships are renegotiated, feelings are hurt; change is constant. This is an individual experience as much as it is a global one. Just as we grow from being cared-for infants into rebellious teenagers, into caretakers ourselves, so too does society develop to fit new situations and demands. Countries are drawn on maps, industries thrive, economies plummet again and again. From this perspective, it is a fool's errand to place our security in leadership and states that carry out violence just to stay in power. Everything is liable to change. Factions emerge, militaries conquer, borders are disputed and crossed.

But what might we learn from those unarmed states? Well, in most cases they are so small they don't stand a chance. So rather than spend and build and fight, they make agreements with larger states, for peace and protection.

Enter God's kingdom, God's economy, God's good word of grace for us. In the above passage, Jesus tells us, "Blessed are the peacemakers, for they will be called children of God." We are not called to be victors, avidly defending ourselves, our positions, our land. When we become the losers of this world, we are dear in His sight, called children of God.

What a relief this is. Though we are steeped in the myth of the arms race and a fight to the top, that is not where God is found. God calls us out of the race, out of the violence and oppression, to level ground. There, we seek peace rather than victory; we strive to make compromises with fellow children of God. And we remember that Jesus is the ultimate peacemaker, so we no longer need to defend ourselves. For we are weary of that battle.

— *Maddy Green*

September 6

So if you have been raised with Christ, seek the things that are above, where Christ is, seated at the right hand of God. Set your minds on things that are above, not on things that are on earth, for you have died, and your life is hidden with Christ in God. When Christ who is your life is revealed, then you also will be revealed with him in glory. (Colossians 3:1-4)

In his *Small Catechism*, Martin Luther wrote that baptism "indicates that the Old Adam in us should by daily contrition and repentance be drowned and die with all sins and evil desires, and that a new man should daily emerge and arise to live before God in righteousness and purity forever." Luther is, of course, echoing scripture. The Apostle Paul summarizes the call of every Christian: "Set your minds on things that are above, not on things that are on earth."

This seems easy enough on paper, but how often have we resolved to do something (set your mind on things above, eat right, stop resenting your jabroni of a brother-in-law, etc.) and immediately failed? What hope do we have that we can actually set our minds on things above? Alone, we have no hope, but Paul offers a glimmer of light through this seemingly dark pronouncement: that we have already died and been raised.

The Christian life is not one of gritting our teeth to focus on or do the right things. The Christian life is a letting-go, a dying; a loosening grip to let the grace and mercy of God rest on us and work through us. Our life is hidden with Christ and will be revealed in glory on the Last Day. Until that time we must be reminded every day (or minute or second) that the small "me," the Old Adam, the false self, has died—and the true self, the me that is known to God, has been raised with Christ. May this serve as your reminder for today (or for this moment).

— *Connor Gwin*

> But when the Israelites cried out to the LORD, the LORD raised up for them a deliverer, Ehud son of Gera, the Benjaminite, a left-handed man. The Israelites sent tribute by him to King Eglon of Moab. (Judges 3:15)

The Bible is usually silent about the physical details of its characters, so anytime we're informed someone is short like Zacchaeus, tall like Saul, or long-haired like Absalom, you can be sure the author is winking—what literary people call "foreshadowing." So it is with Ehud the southpaw. He's from the tribe of Benjamin, which means "son of the right hand." Thus, in delicious irony, God sends Israel a backwards kind of savior: a left-handed deliverer from a right-handed tribe.

But read on and things get even more ironic. By the end of Judges, the tribe of Benjamin is criminalized. Some in their number are guilty of gang rape, resulting in the victim's death, leading to civil war and the near-destruction of the entire tribe of Benjamin. So in the big picture of this book, Ehud is just all wrong: wrong hand, wrong tribe, wrong guy for the right job of saving Israel.

God, however, prefers the wrong people. He makes Sarah, a jaded 90-year-old woman, get pregnant. He sends Jonah, who's just itching for God to blowtorch Nineveh, to preach mercy to that same city. He transforms Saul, the bloodthirsty persecutor of Christians, into the apostle to the Gentiles. And, as his *coup de grâce* to all our conventionally religious ways of thinking, he points to the son of a poor family—who was raised in the boondocks, hung out with immoral riffraff, and eventually got himself executed as an enemy of the state—and calls him the King of Kings and Lord of Lords and Irony of Ironies.

Jesus, like our lefty friend Ehud, is a backwards kind of savior. The wrong guy for the right job of redeeming the world. But the Lord's ways are not our ways, for he "chose what is foolish in the world to shame the wise; God chose what is weak in the world to shame the strong; God chose what is low and despised in the world, things that are not, to reduce to nothing things that are, so that no one might boast in the presence of God. He is the source of your life in Christ Jesus, who became for us wisdom from God, and righteousness and sanctification and redemption" (1 Cor 1:27-30). With God, upside-down is right-side up.

— *Chad Bird*

September 8

By the rivers of Babylon—
   there we sat down and there we wept
   when we remembered Zion.
On the willows there
   we hung up our harps.
For there our captors
   asked us for songs,
and our tormentors asked for mirth, saying,
   "Sing us one of the songs of Zion!"
How could we sing the LORD's song
   in a foreign land? (Psalm 137:1-5)

Recently, I realized that I was probably going to have to go through life without drugs; in other words, somewhat uncomfortably. This realization has engendered a slight but powerful perspective shift, which I find captured beautifully in this psalm.

The writer conveys anxiety: He, on behalf of his people, longs for Jerusalem but at times can barely remember it; this produces a chronic discomfort. The Israelites' feeling of foreignness in a foreign land comes partly from knowing that at some point, they had something different. Worse yet, the missingness of their current world torments them, as their captors ask them to "sing one of the songs of Zion."

Substance abuse is not the only way to understand addiction. I'd wager that no one is entirely free from the temporary respite that any addiction, be it shopping or social media, provides from a loud sense of dislodging. We deeply know that something in the body is not right, and that our body within this world is not right. We then look to fix the missingness with a not-right puzzle piece. (I borrow this idea both from my own experience of addiction but also from David Tremaine's idea of addiction as an indication of an invitation from God.)

Later in the psalm, our writer pleads with Jerusalem to let his right hand be forgotten, and to let his tongue cement, should he forget it, implying that unless he continues to profess the story of his true home, he will calcify in desperation.

In other words, longing for Jerusalem is hope. Longing for Jerusalem reminds us that, once, Jerusalem existed. It reminds us that at the end of the story (God's story), though we can't find Jerusalem, God will bring Jerusalem to us, and not for the first, but for the second time.

— *Sarah Gates*

September 9

"For nothing is hidden that will not be disclosed, nor is anything secret that will not become known and come to light." (Luke 8:17)

The writer Vendela Vida was once robbed in Casablanca. Afterward, she reflected on the experience: "I don't recommend getting your bag stolen, but I do recommend that if you do, you should watch the surveillance camera. First, everyone looks better in black and white, right? Second, you become aware of how the world is operating around you in ways you're completely oblivious to."

I don't know about you, but the very idea of being surveilled has me sweating a little. Because if we're honest, we know that, were we to be caught on camera unawares, we might not like what we saw. But we might also see that there is more going on than we first realized. We may even find that Jesus' words in the above verse are not a threat so much as a beautiful promise.

Have you ever gotten really honest with a trusted friend, or a professional counselor or minister? In a *safe(!)* environment, have you brought everything to light? Speaking secrets out loud gives us the chance to see ourselves through the eyes of another—a different kind of judge, who listens, hears, and does not rebuke. They may even offer some insightful ways to understand an experience that you, alone, found damning. You might become aware of things you'd been completely blind to.

You can also confess your sins directly to God, today. He already knows everything, but confessing will help you see your actions through His eyes. As it is written in Hebrews, "before him no creature is hidden, but all are naked and laid bare to the eyes of the one to whom we must render an account" (4:13).

This is always good news. When God studies the footage, He catches not a criminal but a child. God sees you and all the things you have tried to keep hidden, and He knows you, and loves you. So come into the light. Approach the "throne of grace." Be known, understood, and forgiven.

— *CJ Green*

September 10

"There is salvation in no one else, for there is no other name under heaven given among mortals by which we must be saved." (Acts 4:12)

Do you know what your name means? My name, Samuel, means "God has heard." The name Calvin means "bald." The name Mallory means "unfortunate" (yikes!). While the meanings of names may have lost their power in our day and age, this isn't the case for Jesus. His name means "God saves" or "God is salvation."

This verse proclaims the tremendous power found in the name of Jesus. It was Jesus' name that brought physical deliverance to a lame man just one chapter prior to this verse (Acts 3:1-10)—the same powerful name that brings eternal salvation to all who call upon him. Peter emphasizes this by saying that it is the only name throughout the earth by which a person can be saved.

But, as Juliet asks in Shakespeare's most famous play, "What's in a name? that which we call a rose / By any other name would smell as sweet." She's right. A rose would smell just as sweet if its name was mildew. Likewise, Jesus would still be the Son of God if his name was George (which means "tiller of the soil") or Rufus (which means "red haired"). Jesus' name is powerful because Jesus himself is powerful.

The gospel is not a mindset or a mantra or a worldview. It is a person. The content of the gospel is only one thing, and it is Jesus Christ. You simply don't have the gospel if you don't have Jesus. There are plenty of things that can help you in life, but there's only one who can raise the dead.

Anything other than Jesus will inevitably become a set of expectations for you to fulfill. In Jesus, however, you are safe. He is not just the key that unlocks the door to the prison of self-justification—Jesus himself is your justification. Confessing that this is true is simply admitting that you cannot achieve your own salvation. It is admitting that you need a savior. And guess what? Your savior has come.

— *Sam Bush*

September 11

The LORD of hosts has sworn:
As I have designed,
  so shall it be;
and as I have planned,
  so shall it come to pass... (Isaiah 14:24)

Everyone reacts to trauma and difficulty in different ways. However, I would guess that a common experience is the feeling of being out of control. As someone who has the privilege of controlling many parts of my own day, I know that any surrender of my cherished routines creates a mixture of grief and anxiety. I suspect I am not alone in this.

One coping mechanism is practical. I try to create routines within the drastically limited scope of available options: a daily walk, a regular prayer time, certain days for different video call meetings, all in the hopes of creating a kind of cadence to the week.

But you don't need me to tell you all that: You can find that kind of establishing-a-routine information all over the Internet. The deeper insight, and the more lasting help, comes from knowing that ultimately God is in control, and we are not. You know the joke: Q) What's the difference between you and God? A) God never thinks He's you.

The prophet tells us, "The LORD of hosts has sworn: 'As I have designed, so shall it be; and as I have planned, so shall it come to pass.'" In the end, I am so deeply grateful, now and always, that God is God and I am not.

Heavenly Father, forgive me for thinking I am in control. Thank you that you direct all things. Please give me trust in you today, through Jesus Christ our Lord. Amen.

— Paul Walker

September 12

Have nothing to do with stupid and senseless controversies; you know that they breed quarrels. And the Lord's servant must not be quarrelsome but kindly to everyone, an apt teacher, patient... (2 Timothy 2:23-24)

It might sound obnoxious, but in most of my arguments with my spouse, I don't *feel* I'm right. I know I'm right. She may not admit it, but she knows it. God knows it, too. It happened just the other night: The evidence was right there in front of both of us—she was actually doing that *exact* thing that I've said time and again is particularly irritating and unfair for her to do—and if I just stopped her and said, "See! You're doing it!" I'm sure it would close the case for good. All of the litigation between us about this one thing that may-or-may-not-be-happening would be called out as *definitely happening*. Case closed. Resentment gone.

In the interest of full disclosure, that's what I did. I said it. And for whatever reason it didn't work out the way I thought it would. In fact, my wife doubled down. When I asked her, politely, why she was getting so defensive, she said that I *provoked* that response in her. Provoked!

Someone told me once, "It's better to be kind than to be right." I guess this is also what Paul is telling Timothy. Is that really true? Another person said, "When it comes to marriage, you can either be right or be in a relationship." Both seem to say there's something undeniably un-gracious about arguing someone into submission. Even if you don't care about "being gracious" all that much, I'm 96% sure proving yourself right doesn't work.

Even though this nagging detail is something she really ought to know, even though I'm *sure*, if she took it to heart, it'd *help* her, even though it would make us both a little less obnoxious—I'm learning slowly that, when the rubber hits the road, in our own home, I think it's probably better to have a defending attorney than a prosecuting one.

Lord, help me when I'm wrong. But I pray more so that you will help me, and help those I love, when I'm right.

— *Ethan Richardson*

September 13

"I loathe my life;
    I will give free utterance to my complaint;
    I will speak in the bitterness of my soul.
I will say to God, Do not condemn me;
    let me know why you contend against me." (Job 10:1-2)

When my family evacuated from Hurricane Harvey, we took a big tour of the Deep South. We visited with my parents, aunts and uncles, and family friends. But the crown jewel of our time was spent with my Memaw. My children, then six and three years old, sat in her living room playing with the toys she had for them. They told her stories about school and ate her "hidden" chocolate bars. It was incredibly comforting. When we pulled out of her driveway, unsure of what we would face back home, I looked at her and realized she was weeping. I had never seen my grandmother cry. And I begin to cry, too, because it suddenly struck me that this would be the last time I would see her. She was not sick. But she was very old. And something whispered to me, *this is it.* She would die a peaceful death a few months later. And at her funeral, my young son would say to me, "Mama, it is a good thing that the hurricane happened. Because we got to see Memaw one more time."

That may sound selfish. But I'm reluctant to write it off that way. It felt insightful. Even in the midst of total turmoil, God had cared for our family. I realized that our son felt loved by something much bigger than me.

I am often struck by people who go through much worse and often come out on the other end with an odd kind of thankfulness. Like Job, when I am going through something incredibly difficult, I often want to look to the sky and tell God to walk a mile in my shoes. Forgetting that I am actually wearing shoes He provided for me.

It is the silence of God that we find so difficult in Job's story. Because He is voiceless for so much of the story, Job (and let's be honest, you and me) begin to believe that God has forgotten. Or worse, that He does not care. But our God is doing something in every moment of our lives. It may feel silent and lonely. Hell, it may *be* silent and lonely. But that is never the end of the story. God is using all of our heartbreak to mend what is broken within us. And sometimes silence and storms and a weeping Memaw are the only way for us to hear Him.

— *Sarah Condon*

September 14

> "So the slave fell on his knees before him, saying, 'Have patience with me, and I will pay you everything.' And out of pity for him, the lord of that slave released him and forgave him the debt." (Matthew 18:26-27)

Much of what passes for forgiveness in our culture would be better termed "applied empathy." Applied empathy is what happens, often unconsciously, when we shrink an infraction down until it's small enough that forgiveness is no longer necessary. Sometimes we do this by talking about motives: "They didn't *mean* to hit that person with their car." Or perhaps we talk about upbringing: "If you only knew how bad his childhood was." Maybe we invoke society itself: "A hundred years ago, this kind of thing would've happened all the time."

Applied empathy isn't necessarily a bad thing. But it runs into trouble when the wrongdoing is so egregious that it defies reduction, when we cannot come up with—or there aren't any!—mitigating facts.

Forgiveness, as illustrated in the Parable of the Unforgiving Servant, differs from applied empathy. It is at once more radical and complete.

In the parable, a king confronts a servant who has racked up a debt of 10,000 talents, an absurd and therefore un-repayable amount—upwards of a few billion dollars today. There is no doubt about how much this man owes nor, consequently, about how guilty he is, just as there is no doubt about his ability to repay. Coins cannot be empathized out of existence.

The servant's only hope is forgiveness. To his relief, the king decides not to refinance the debt but to absorb it himself, thereby releasing the steward from the tyranny of the balance sheet.

(The steward fails to internalize the clemency, and the result is harrowing—just as it is for any of us who insist on just deserts.)

Of course a more forgiving world would be a beautiful place. And yet, if we think this kind of forgiveness is something we can live up to—or worse, something we *are* living up to—then we are lost. Because true forgiveness isn't just hard, it is miraculous.

Yet that is the miracle of the gospel. Jesus forgives *you* like this. He forgives you where others haven't. And he forgives others where you haven't. He is not interested in your fantasies about repayment and reform, nor does he minimize your debt. Instead, your loss becomes his loss—in full!

Where are you living under the tyranny of the balance sheet today? In a relationship perhaps? Have you reached the limits of applied empathy yet?

The king awaits.

— *David Zahl*

> Therefore, since we are surrounded by so great a cloud of witnesses, let us also lay aside every weight and the sin that clings so closely, and let us run with perseverance the race that is set before us, looking to Jesus the pioneer and perfecter of our faith, who for the sake of the joy that was set before him endured the cross, disregarding its shame, and has taken his seat at the right hand of the throne of God. (Hebrews 12:1-2)

Many packages of cookies, a number of pounds, one kid, and a graduate degree ago, I ran a marathon. It wasn't pretty. I had never done track, cross country, or running sports, and was always much more comfortable on ice skates than on my own two feet.

In a marathon, mile 20 is called "the wall." The idea is that from mile 20 through the finish (26.2), it is mostly psychological. You have to find it in yourself to push through to the end. I hit the wall incredibly hard. I was hurting all over and exhausted. I had nothing left in me.

But around the same time, the crowds grew thicker. There were more people cheering. A random stranger started cheering for me by my race number: "Come on, 1424, you've got this! You can do this!"

I never fully understood the power of Hebrews 12:1-2, which I had written on my racing shirt, until this moment. At mile 24.3, a complete stranger gifted me the ability to finish that race. I could pretend it had been in me all along, but it wasn't. The power to finish came from outside of me. Just like our faith comes from outside of us. It comes from Jesus, "the pioneer and perfecter of our faith."

We are all running our own crazy races in life. "Hitting the wall" is inevitable, whether it comes in the form of a health or financial crisis, unmet expectations, the death of a loved one, or something else. As we find ourselves slogging through a long, seemingly impossible race, we realize that we do not run alone. We are surrounded by a great cloud of witnesses, whether they be random strangers or close family and friends. They remind us of Jesus, who gives us the gifts of faith and life. And through the cross, he has already won the race—for all of us.

— Tasha Genck Morton

September 16

I am the LORD your God...you shall have no other gods before
  me.
You shall not make for yourself an idol...
You shall not make wrongful use of the name of the LORD your
  God...
Remember the sabbath day, and keep it holy...
Honor your father and your mother...
You shall not murder.
You shall not commit adultery.
You shall not steal.
You shall not bear false witness against your neighbor.
You shall not covet your neighbor's house...or anything that
  belongs to your neighbor. (Exodus 20:2-17)

Try telling someone he or she is a sinner. People don't like it. They say, "I'm a good person, I keep the Ten Commandments." People think the Ten Commandments are things like "Be nice; believe in God; don't cheat, don't lie, don't steal, don't kill anyone, and don't use the 15-items-or-less lane at Kroger if you have 16 items."

But when you read the Ten Commandments, you realize they are different from what people assume. Sure, they prohibit murder, stealing, and adultery. But those come near the bottom of the list. And then there are some weird ones that aren't on most people's radar screens: no idols, keeping the sabbath, no using God's name frivolously. Finally, the last one—don't covet the cool stuff your neighbor has—seems to go against the American Dream and Super Bowl commercials. "What do you mean I can't have an inexplicable desire for new throw pillows and a bigger TV when they go on sale at Target?" Murder, adultery, stealing: These are actions done in the body. I can do or not do them. But coveting? That's in the heart. That's a hard one!

But wait. There's more. I haven't even mentioned *numero uno*. "[Y]ou shall have no other gods before me."

Think about that. You have to worship God exclusively. Your life and devotion should revolve around him. Not your ego. Not your retirement plan. Not your family. Not the college football schedule. Not your religious works. Not your BMI. Not your country. Not your politics. Not your intel-lectual superiority. Not your career.

What does your heart revolve around?

The secret of the Ten Commandments is that *no one* keeps them. Except for one Person. He was from Galilee a long time ago. He kept them. And that is his gift to you.

— *Aaron Zimmerman*

September 17

I have loved you with an everlasting love;
    therefore I have continued my faithfulness to you. (Jeremiah
31:3)

Can you remember an event in your life, maybe it seemed minor, maybe it was catastrophic, that made you question whether or not you were lovable? These moments for me, from early childhood onward, flash before my eyes like some horrible montage I'd prefer to forget. Sometimes we do something that makes us question our lovability, and other times we are victims of other people's words and actions. "You are not enough," the voice in your head may jeer. "Just look at you. Work harder. Eat better. You are disgusting. Nobody really loves you. Every awful thing you suspect about yourself is true." All of this is called *shame*.

Beloved, do you—like me—walk through most of your days trying to prove to yourself and the world that you are, or could be, lovable? And are you—like me—exhausted from all that striving?

Several years ago, God began whispering the above scripture into my heart, like a tiny but mighty antidote to the curse of self-hatred. It would ring in my ears at any odd hour of the day, both in moments of shame and in moments of joy, like a song stuck in my head going round and round: *I have loved you with an everlasting love.*

God's love for us is permanent. It is unwavering. There is nothing in our capacity to change the condition of that love. When we fail: *I have loved you with an everlasting love.* When we succeed: *I have loved you with an everlasting love.* And of course in our smallest, darkest, most painful moments: *I have loved you with an everlasting love.*

Jesus' love for us is so grand, so all-encompassing, so determined to stay fixed on you and me, so *everlasting*, that he died to prove it. There is nothing we can do, better or worse, that can change this magnificent fact.

Consider for a minute how this verse speaks to your own montage of unworthiness. One day, you might find those awful scenes are being healed, transformed, altogether obliterated by this Love that has—wonder of wonders—chosen you, and stayed.

— *Charlotte Getz*

September 18

From his fullness we have all received, grace upon grace.
The law indeed was given through Moses; grace and truth
came through Jesus Christ. (John 1:16-17)

This passage is high-octane gospel, turbo-powered good news for sinners
and sufferers like you and me, like all of us, because it identifies the heart
of the gospel: the grace of God in Jesus Christ. The grace of God is the
unconditional love of God for you that has no ulterior motives, no strings
attached, no catch—God's love for you that "never ends" (1 Cor 13:8). God's
love for you is so great that it "surpasses knowledge" and cannot be measured (Eph 3:18-19). The grace of God means that God not only loves you,
but God *likes* you, too.

This is the heart of the gospel—"by grace you have been saved" (Eph 2:8).
In other words, no grace, no gospel. This grace was expressed historically,
definitively, once for all in the death and resurrection of Jesus Christ. This
"grace upon grace" has already been given, is being given, and will always
be given in Jesus Christ—not just for some, but for all of us. God's grace is
comprehensive in the best sense.

Moreover, the entire Bible is brilliantly summarized here: "The law
indeed was given through Moses; grace and truth came through Jesus
Christ." The Old Testament law was and is superseded by New Testament grace. The law of the Old Testament is what Joshua told Israel near
the end of his life: "[C]hoose this day whom you will serve" (Josh 24:15).
The grace and truth of the New Testament is what Jesus told his disciples
at the Last Supper: "You did not choose me *but I chose you*" (Jn 15:16).

This "grace upon grace" defines your life—"you are not under law but
under grace" (Rom 6:14). And this grace is inexhaustible. Every single time
you need God's grace, which is every single moment of your life, God's grace
is there for you. Grace upon grace, grace upon grace, grace upon grace. It
is God's heartbeat of love for you that has never stopped, and never will.

— *David Johnson*

September 19

"I will tell of your name to my brothers;
    in the midst of the congregation I will sing your praise."
(Hebrews 2:12 ESV)

Sunday morning. Into the little country church, worshipers stream. The sanctuary is peopled by a mom and dad and three little girls in pretty dresses, there by a widower with his old wooden cane propped against the pew, with teens and newlyweds and the random stranger filling in the gaps. The bells toll, whispered chatter subsides, and the organ begins painting the air with the colors of music.

And they sing. The little girls with their little voices. The old widower with his half-wheezing baritone. The dad who can't carry a tune in a bucket, sing-speaking the words anyway. This mix of old and young, men and women, who outside this space might have little if nothing in common, here do together a quintessentially human thing: They testify to the deepest bonds of humanity in the communion of song.

When the preacher who wrote Hebrews wanted to make it clear that Christ doesn't slough off his humanity as soon as he's completed his mission, that he truly and everlastingly shares our flesh and blood, suffers as we too suffer, dies as we too die, and is made like us in all things—to prove all this, the preacher turns to song. "I will tell of your name to my brothers," he quotes the Messiah as saying, "in the midst of the congregation I will sing your praise."

In the midst of the congregation, surrounded by his brothers and sisters in this vast choir of humanity, Emmanuel opens his own mouth to sing. He who sang creation into being sings now as a creature, too. He who, in Eden, breathed into Adam the breath of life exhales hymns to his Father as the new and last Adam.

Our Lord and our God, who is our brother and redeemer, demonstrates the deepest bonds he shares with our humanity in the communion of song. There's hardly a more striking image than picturing a worldwide choir, open-mouthed, lifting their voices on high—and in the very middle of them stands the God who became our brother, our friend, our fellow-singer and savior.

— *Chad Bird*

But I said, "I have labored in vain,
  I have spent my strength for nothing and vanity;
yet surely my cause is with the LORD,
  and my reward with my God." (Isaiah 49:4)

There are certain seasons, relationships, and events in life that can be much harder to move on from than others. We may try to "shake the dust off our sandals" to no avail. My suspicion is that it has to do with our tears: wet dust turns into mud, and whether it is wiped off or, over time, dries and crumbles, we're left with a messy residue.

The prophets aren't just familiar with this concept. They live it, writing about it in explicit, heart-rending poetry. Rarely are they allowed to make a thundering pronouncement and then cut and run; their lives are inextricably tied to the people they were sent to warn.

Isaiah turns himself inside out trying to get the people to do the right thing, but repeatedly finds himself incapable of making them do it. It would be hard not to feel like your life has been a waste when the folks you are sent to turn away from disaster insist on running *towards* it. Exhausted, Isaiah points to the real Redeemer by admitting his own failure.

Many of us like to think we are Isaiah, pouring ourselves out for the benefit of an unappreciative audience, until we realize that *we are* the unappreciative audience. This realization, in light of Christ's sacrifice and suffering on the cross, makes the second half of verse 4 all the more remarkable. The reward goes to failures like you and me: to those who shed the tears *and* to those who caused them, which is all of us. This is why it is such scandalously good news! All that mud, and all the tears that made it, are washed away by the blood of Christ.

— *Joshua Retterer*

September 21

Of making many books there is no end, and much study is
a weariness of the flesh. (Ecclesiastes 12:12)

I like to read, and I even like to read (some of) the Bible (sometimes). But
never consistently. Even when I was young, I would try reading a chapter a
day, and could keep it up for a little while. Come Leviticus, though, and I'd
be done for. Even if I were reading something that intrigued me and spoke
directly to me, like Paul's letters, I couldn't stay on track. In college, I tried
keeping a simple journal. That soon metastasized into a sprawling digital exe-
gesis, in which I attempted to interpret whole epistles with copy-and-pasted
academic commentary and hyperlinks to interlinear translations. Which is
to say, under the pressure of piety, devotion turned into homework.

Sometimes I enjoyed approaching scripture this way. I can understand
the flow of thought better when I take time to ruminate, to read and reread
at a snail's pace, to reflect on each section in light of the others. But it also
produces anxiety. Am I "rightly dividing the word of truth," or am I "con-
ceited, understanding nothing," as Paul describes various church factions to
Timothy? And even after devoting all this time to "the word of the LORD,"
why is my life still glitching?

There is always more to read. Why not read two chapters instead of one?
Why not read twice a day? Why not a commentary, or four? Why read that
novel when you could be meditating on the Bible? This endless stream of
questions is "a weariness of the flesh."

In its weariness, it is this "flesh" that finally makes God knowable. Book-
making and studying go on forever. But when the Word finally becomes
flesh, he lets himself grow weary alongside us. That Word is not a text for
us to understand but a Someone who already understands us. And Paul said
the Spirit prays for us when we don't even know what to ask for. Whatever
is good for us, God is already going ahead of us to do perfectly. So we can
fumble our way into it, acknowledging how weary we are but knowing
God's Word and Spirit are already on our side.

— *Kendall Gunter*

September 22

Then Jesus said… "Someone gave a great dinner and invited many. At the time for the dinner he sent his slave to say to those who had been invited, 'Come; for everything is ready now.' But they all alike began to make excuses… Then the owner of the house became angry and said to his slave, 'Go out at once into the streets and lanes of the town and bring in the poor, the crippled, the blind, and the lame.'" (Luke 14:16-18, 21)

Films about high school are a genre unto themselves. They're sweetly nostalgic, yet inherently tense. Think *The Breakfast Club*, *Mean Girls*, or *Grease*; my own favorite is the little-known masterpiece *The Spectacular Now* (2013). In any case, there is usually a scene depicting students at different lunch tables, or in cliques, each according to their "thing." Athletes at one table, nerds at another.

Sadly, life can feel like a high school cafeteria. If you don't have a "thing," you might not have a place to sit. We usually assume that, in the words of writer Dan Brooks, "you are a type first, and you behave accordingly." What's *your* thing? Maybe you are the funny person, or the smart, sarcastic person. Maybe you are the sensitive person. More likely than not, your "thing" changes depending on who you are with.

Late in *The Spectacular Now*, we learn that the two protagonists, Sutter and Aimee, are not who they first appeared to be. Sutter's easygoing facade shatters to reveal, beneath it, someone more damaged and vulnerable; Aimee becomes more daring than her mousy exterior implied. Only time and love can reveal the hidden pieces of them—and us.

In Luke's Gospel, the Parable of the Great Dinner relies on types. First, there are the self-satisfied invitees who think they have a better place to be. Then there are the poor, the blind, and the lame, who are just happy to get a look. But these types are actually various components of all of us. We are all a little bit self-satisfied, and a lotta bit spiritually blind and lame. Probably self-satisfaction is the very "thing" that blinds us.

Most importantly, a hidden hunger resides in everyone. The moment we admit this is the moment we become willing to see that there is, indeed, a seat at the table for us. "[T]here is still room!" the servant tells his master (v. 22). And there always will be.

— *CJ Green*

September 23

> I wrote you out of much distress and anguish of heart and with many tears, not to cause you pain, but to let you know the abundant love that I have for you.
>
> But if anyone has caused pain, he has caused it not to me, but to some extent—not to exaggerate it—to all of you. This punishment by the majority is enough for such a person; so now instead you should forgive and console him, so that he may not be overwhelmed by excessive sorrow. So I urge you to reaffirm your love for him. (2 Corinthians 2:4-8)

The apostle Paul was not, shall we say, conflict-*avoidant*. If an elephant strolled into the room, Paul would be the first to point it out. Trust me, Paul would not let you get through the entire course of pasta primavera without letting you know you have spinach in your teeth! Paul is quick, in his letters to the Corinthians and elsewhere, to call a sin a sin.

But in today's passage, Paul is just as quick to call for forgiveness. As we try to make sense of the correspondence, it appears that on one of Paul's earlier visits he was ill-treated by a man in the church (and no one called the man out for it). Paul wrote them a now-missing letter (v. 4) which apparently laid out Paul's disappointment with the Corinthian church, a letter which was painful to write and no doubt painful to read. The Corinthian church finally got around to confronting the offender.

But now Paul worries the church has gone too far. For that sinner to live through a kind of never-ending Cold War from his fellow believers could put him at risk of becoming "overwhelmed by excessive sorrow." The whole purpose of confrontation was not so that this man might live under a cloud of guilt, but rather so that he might confess and freely receive forgiveness. For those believers whose spiritual economies had been bailed out by grace, this was no time to embargo grace for sinners sitting next to them.

Paul wants his readers to know that the gospel does not banish people to perpetual stays in the 'doghouse' of never-ending guilt. Jesus, who continually makes a way for us to come back inside God's house, wants us to leave the door open for everyone.

— *Larry Parsley*

September 24

> The angel said to those who were standing before him,
> "Take off his filthy clothes." And to him he said, "See, I
> have taken your guilt away from you, and I will clothe you
> with festal apparel." (Zechariah 3:4)

The phrase "the clothes make the man" comes from *Hamlet*. Polonius, the king's advisor (who is ironically prone to giving bad advice), offers this quip to his son as his son leaves on a trip to France. Any counsel coming from Polonius is suspicious, but the sentiment has persisted over the generations: "The clothes make the man."

In today's passage, the prophet Zechariah has a vision about clothes. He sees Joshua, the high priest of Israel at the time, standing before God's angel and being accused by Satan. Why the accusation? The high priest wasn't wearing the correct clothing for his job. He should have been wearing an opulent vestment of purple and blue and gold and gems, but instead his clothes were filthy rags. It's no wonder Satan is accusing: Not only is Joshua disrespecting God by wearing filthy clothes, but it's a violation of the law of Moses!

The angel's response is telling: After rebuking Satan, the angels remove Joshua's dirty clothes and give him "festal apparel." Festal apparel is a fancy way of saying that the angelic host gives Joshua the purple and blue and gold and gem-encrusted vestment required of the high priest. God, through his angels, gives Joshua the very thing he lacks, turning him from law-breaker to law-obeyer.

To say the clothes make the man is one thing, but in Zechariah's vision, we see that God makes the clothes. He clothes his saints in white, removing their tattered and torn rags and replacing them with royal, spotless robes. That's his promise to all his people: The wear-and-tear of life on earth will be washed away, and we will all be given the gift of righteousness. Who can accuse us before God when God's own righteousness, purchased through Jesus' death and resurrection, is being worn around our necks and draped across our shoulders? God's clothes truly do make the man.

Thanks be to God that he not only sets the standards for righteousness, but also gives to his people the very righteousness he demands.

— *Bryan Jarrell*

September 25

When [the crowd] kept on questioning [Jesus], he straightened up and said to them, "Let anyone among you who is without sin be the first to throw a stone at her." And once again he bent down and wrote on the ground. When they heard it, they went away, one by one, beginning with the elders; and Jesus was left alone with the woman standing before him. Jesus straightened up and said to her, "Woman, where are they? Has no one condemned you?" She said, "No one, sir." And Jesus said, "Neither do I condemn you. Go your way, and from now on do not sin again." (John 8:7-11)

It is common knowledge that a huge percentage of communication is non-verbal. Our "body language" often speaks louder than our words. We can learn volumes about a person if we "listen" to what they are saying through their posture or eye contact or how they walk.

One of the most important questions we can ask about a passage of scripture is, "What does this tell me about Jesus or God?" In this case, what can we learn about Jesus through his body language?

John is careful to paint a most instructive portrait of Jesus in this encounter: He *straightens up* to face the woman's accusers, eye-to-eye, as it were. It must seem like he is gathering his power as he stands to face them. We sense the importance of Jesus' words delivered from his full height: "Let anyone among you who is without sin be the first to throw a stone at her."

Then, he *bends down* to allow his words to sink in, and for the accusers to depart. He is not interested in humiliating them with his stare. There is a gentleness, and even compassion, as he avoids watching their guilty escapes.

Finally, *he straightens up* once again to pronounce his words of compassion to the accused woman, eye-to-eye, with total conviction of body and voice: "Has no one condemned you? ... Neither do I condemn you." Imagine his saying these life-changing words from his stooped position. Would the impact have been the same? He knows the eyes are essential in communicating compassion, and posture in bestowing confidence.

Thank you, Lord, that you did not fear your accusers, and that you stood tall on behalf of this woman and on behalf of us.

— Mary Zahl

September 26

[The Israelites] confessed that they were strangers and
foreigners on the earth, for people who speak in this way
make it clear that they are seeking a homeland. If they had
been thinking of the land that they had left behind, they
would have had opportunity to return. But as it is, they
desire a better country, that is, a heavenly one. Therefore
God is not ashamed to be called their God; indeed, he has
prepared a city for them. (Hebrews 11:13-16)

It used to be said that polite conversation always avoids the subjects of politics and religion. Someone forgot to tell this to social media, or perhaps the
standards have changed. If Facebook or Twitter feeds are any indication, it
seems that the sum total of life as we imagine it can be reduced to a political
chess game. For many of us, politics is the modern totem upon which we
project all of our hopes, anxieties, and fears, commandeering our discourse
and our very selves. The flag demands our allegiance and promises our prosperity, as our civic duties become our civic religion.

But for the writer to the Hebrews, the political is but another manifestation of the world to which we don't belong. He places the realm of the
political under a cosmic, divine question mark, ascribing it to the realm that
is passing away. This is a striking affront, particularly for us who cannot
imagine a life without politics.

Instead, we have a heavenly inheritance, and the citizenship we possess
far exceeds any earthly nationality. We are all foreigners and wanderers in
a world which is not our home, let alone our friend. The world to which
we truly belong promises prosperity and eternal life, giving it to us by the
blood of a crucified criminal. In faith, we are grasped by the promise of grace
alone, which frees us from what pulls us away from God.

Grace pulls us toward the shore of our heavenly city. There is something better waiting for us that no election can provide, where love reigns
forever as king and we bow before his glorious majesty.

— *Todd Brewer*

September 27

When [Jesus] came back, he again found [his disciples] sleeping, because their eyes were heavy. So he left them and went away once more and prayed the third time, saying the same thing.

Then he returned to the disciples and said to them, "Are you still sleeping and resting? Look, the hour has come, and the Son of Man is delivered into the hands of sinners. Rise! Let us go! Here comes my betrayer!" (Matthew 26:43-46 NIV)

How many of us have found ourselves on both sides of this conversation?

We've all been the friend who disappointed someone we love. We fell asleep. We forgot something that was important to them. We knew exactly what to do, and we failed. And how many of us have been the disappointed friend? Our friends have forgotten our birthday, or we're suddenly the only person working on the group project. We've prayed for God to deliver us from the group project, only to realize that life is a group project. Lord, have mercy.

This is also where God, in Jesus, becomes so human to those of us who worry, those of us who are disappointed, and those of us who pray alone at a time when we most need someone to pray with us. And this is where the disciples, the very friends hand-picked by Jesus, remind us of their humanity and their frailty.

Yet Jesus does not leave them sleeping in the garden. He wakes them up and gives them another chance to try again. How many of us get woken up with another chance to try and fail again? We are often confronted with our own failures, but our Lord also gives us the gift of another chance every day.

God, help us to remember those who frustrate and those who are frustrated. We disappoint others, and we are disappointed by others, just as Jesus was disappointed at the hour he most needed his friends. We are forgiven for our drowsiness in our own faults, and given the opportunity to wake up and begin again, every day. Help us to be grateful for these opportunities to be forgiven, and to forgive.

— Carrie Willard

September 28

For surely I know the plans I have for you, says the LORD, plans for your welfare and not for harm, to give you a future with hope. (Jeremiah 29:11)

Not long ago, I woke up to a text message from a high school friend. It contained a link to a news story about a high school classmate of ours who had gotten into some very significant trouble with their local authorities. It was clear from the report that my former classmate was currently suffering greatly in body, mind, and spirit. There was a palpable pain in their mugshot, behind their vacant, bloodshot eyes.

Later that day, I pulled out my senior yearbook and looked up this same classmate. They were smiling broadly, and their face was radiant with youth (and perfectly tanned from hours spent in a crew boat on the Tennessee River). For their senior quote, they had chosen Jeremiah 29:11.

I closed the yearbook and prayed that this classmate would know that this promise was still true. It was just as true for them in the mental health facility where they had been committed as it was for them as a high school senior when they were young, confident, and most excited about their future.

In Jeremiah 29:11, we read what God says to His chosen people in a moment that was undoubtedly their worst nightmare. They had watched Jerusalem be destroyed and were now in exile in Babylon. Many of them would die in exile and never see their home again. Not only were their current circumstances devastating, but they knew that this was undeniably a mess of their own making. They had been warned repeatedly that there would be consequences for their idolatry and rebellion against God.

We know that God did in fact end the exile in Babylon, like He promised He would, but ultimately we can trust all of God's promises because He entered exile with us on the cross. There, Jesus accounted once and for all for the totality of human sin and brokenness. Because of Jesus, we can trust that in the midst of our worst nightmare (and on our best days), there is a plan for our lives. That we will be provided for, and that we can look to the future with hope.

— *Ginger Mayfield*

September 29

When I thought, "My foot is slipping,"
  your steadfast love, O LORD, held me up. (Psalm 94:18)

This entire psalm is a roller coaster. But I like this verse in particular. It reminds me of Scooby-Doo, that clumsy crime-solving dog who somehow captured every masked menace, just in time and usually by accident.

Toward the end of every episode, the meddling kids of Mystery, Inc. would set a trap, and Scoob would often trip, slip, and slide right into it. Even so, the villain would be swooped into the chaos, and justice would be served—but never the way anyone expected.

Of course, when Scooby slips, he appears to be a failure. You can imagine Fred slapping his forehead and groaning, "Oh no! Scooby goofed!" while his pet flies off down a wooded trail in a runaway cart alongside a wan zombie.

Like Scooby, I have slipped both literally and metaphorically too many times to count. So I know from experience that when you hit the ground, you can respond in one of two ways: You can either laugh and try to make it look as if you are not at all embarrassed, which is the most surefire way to show that you are, actually, mortified, or you can admit the truth—"how embarrassing!"—and have a little cry.

It is not always easy to face the embarrassing truth—the slip, the failure, the goof. But it's a lot easier when you have this scripture in mind.

To cushion our fall, we might prefer a soft pillow or a bed to land on, but what upholds us is actually something better: *your steadfast love, O Lord.* Better, because it's the only thing we've ever really wanted. And thanks be to God, it's the exact thing we've got.

Jinkies!

— *CJ Green*

> For I am not ashamed of the gospel; it is the power of God for salvation to everyone who has faith, to the Jew first and also to the Greek. For in it the righteousness of God is revealed through faith for faith; as it is written, "The one who is righteous will live by faith." (Romans 1:16-17)

I used to misunderstand this verse. When I was a teenager, I thought it meant that I should proudly wear Christian t-shirts and bracelets in the hallways of my school. That, in the cafeteria, I should be unashamed to pull out my Bible (in its sweet carrying case). I don't mean to dissuade any young people from doing these things, but I have come to realize that this is not what Paul has in mind.

In her book, *The Crucifixion*, theologian Fleming Rutledge dedicates many pages to showing how shameful the cross of Christ would have been in the first century. Even more surprising is the claim that the crucifixion of Jesus accomplished something that was almost unimaginable: The shameful cross repaired the breach between God and man. It put right that which was broken. It made the atonement that was required for the world to be whole.

We live in a secular, cynical age. Secular because we operate as though the transcendent God is not real or at least does not act in human life. Because of this, we operate with a dangerously high anthropology—we think humans can and should fix the world's problems. This leads to cynicism, because five minutes spent with humans causes one to realize that a world in human hands is doomed. The problems are too big. The hole we are in is too deep.

Into this world, God speaks the seemingly shameful truth that the world has been saved by a transcendent God. The shameful cross of Christ knocks our anthropology down a few pegs to its rightful place. We cannot save ourselves, but Christ can and did. Beyond the initial shock of the shameful cross, we find salvation and peace. Beyond the humiliation of Christ, we find humility. In that humility, we can begin to live by faith and be unashamed.

— *Connor Gwin*

October 1

Alas for those who go down to Egypt for help
  and who rely on horses,
who trust in chariots because they are many
  and in horsemen because they are very strong,
but do not look to the Holy One of Israel
  or consult the LORD! (Isaiah 31:1)

The Christian life is a journey of trust. There are many sins of which we must repent, but the question of trust—of faith—is at the root of each of them. God tells us we can always find safe-harbor with him. He is sovereign. He is our refuge. He is our home. He will protect us. He will bring us through. And yet, we surely do love a good chariot.

It is difficult to live with eternity in view—to be heavenly minded—when we all have feet of clay. Our days have real temporal struggles: illness, economic distress, parental anxiety, broken relationships, faltering careers. Add global terror and pandemic, and it is no wonder that we live in the age of anxiety.

It is the most human thing to look around to find something to fix it. When our children fall down and skin a knee, they do not look to the Lord. They look to the Band-Aid and the kiss-it-all-better of a caregiver. And we do too. We look to the federal reserve and the therapist and the latest self-help strategy or personality instrument. Isaiah has one word for us: alas.

Isaiah is remembering, and expects his audience to remember, what happened to Egypt's horses and chariots. They were all swallowed up in the sea. God gives us good things to help us here in our temporal reality. He gives us economic and emotional and relational aids here on earth, but they are all meant to point us toward our One True Savior. The horses and chariots are not the problem after all. The trust is the problem. What wipes away our tears? In whom do we trust? What is the thing that is never met with an "alas"? Perhaps Charles Wesley put it best:

Jesus! the name that calms our fears,
  that bids our sorrows cease;
'tis music in the sinner's ears,
  'tis life, and health, and peace!

— *Ann Lowrey Forster*

October 2

Now in Jerusalem by the Sheep Gate there is a pool [where
there were] many invalids—blind, lame, and paralyzed.
One man was there who had been ill for thirty-eight years.
When Jesus saw him lying there and knew that he had
been there a long time, he said to him, "Do you want to be
made well?" The sick man answered him, "Sir, I have no
one to put me into the pool when the water is stirred up;
and while I am making my way, someone else steps down
ahead of me." Jesus said to him, "Stand up, take your mat
and walk." At once the man was made well, and he took
up his mat and began to walk. (John 5:2-9)

A person can become addicted to being afflicted. We can attach our identities to wounds and maladies such that we don't know who we are without
them. Perhaps we do this because suffering lends our lives a significance or
purpose we fear it might otherwise lack. "The only thing better than being
right is being wronged" is how the saying goes. Sometimes this is called a
victim mentality and, justified or not, it can be very alienating.

The novelist David Foster Wallace once called self-pity "the great enemy
of life," not because pitiable things don't happen, but because self-pity
keeps us focused squarely on our own belly buttons. Sometimes we can
even mistake a gift for a curse, denying the good fruit so often produced
by suffering. A person mired in self-pity is a stuck person, glued to a very
strict narrative of themselves.

Jesus understands that sometimes sick people balk at healing—that pro-
testation to getting better is *part* of our infirmity. Thus, he comes to the
invalid at the pool in both his suffering and his spiritual paralysis over that
suffering, in the place where the man considers himself to be un-heal-able.
Jesus allows the man to spout his "narrative."

Thankfully, Jesus doesn't insist on the invalid having a proper attitude
before giving him his walking papers. Nor does he wait on contrition or
even receptivity before speaking restoration. What about you? Do you
want to get well? Self-pity and bitterness may keep others at bay, but they
will not stymy the Great Physician. He knows your afflictions better than
you do, and is not convinced of their immutability. He bore them, after all.

— *David Zahl*

October 3

He is the image of the invisible God, the firstborn of all
creation; for in him all things in heaven and on earth were
created, things visible and invisible, whether thrones or
dominions or rulers or powers—all things have been created through him and for him. He himself is before all things,
and in him all things hold together. (Colossians 1:15-17)

This morning I was sitting on my back porch drinking my morning joe,
playing some soft jazz and minding my own business when God showed up.
No, not physically or even abruptly but quietly, in the calm of the morning. The birds were singing in the sky, the sun was rising and gleaming,
the bugs were chirping, a distant cow was lowing, the breeze was blowing
through the trees. And in the middle of it all, I heard the sweet music of
God reminding me that He is present.

As I listened to this morning song that God made, I was reminded of
this passage in Colossians: *for in him all things in heaven and on earth were
created...and in him all things hold together.* As I write this, a pandemic has
swept across the globe, and many are suffering, but the birds are peacefully
enjoying their day, not at all worried over their portfolio or the price of oil,
not concerned if there is enough toilet paper or bottled water in the store.
Not even a little. They are just enjoying their morning and singing their
song to the Creator, the One who, despite everything, holds it all together.

Friends, God loves us far more than He does the birds of the air and
flowers of the fields. In the passage above, we are reminded that He is in
control. He is not scratching His head wondering if our worries are going
to figure out a solution. He hasn't fallen off His throne or tossed up His
hands. One day, He will make all sad things come untrue.

> *Lord Jesus, help us to trust you with our worries today. Help
> us to cast all our anxiety on you, because you care for us (1 Pet
> 5:7). Help us to take our eyes off ourselves and to listen to your
> gentle reminders through the world you have made, and to find
> peace in you. In the name of the Father, the Son, and the Holy
> Spirit. Amen.*

— *Jonathan Adams*

October 4

The hand of the LORD came upon me...and set me down
in the middle of a valley; it was full of bones...

So I prophesied as I had been commanded; and as I
prophesied, suddenly there was a noise, a rattling, and the
bones came together, bone to its bone. I looked, and there
were sinews on them, and flesh had come upon them, and
skin had covered them; but there was no breath in them.
Then he said to me, "Prophesy to the breath, prophesy,
mortal, and say to the breath: Thus says the Lord GOD:
Come from the four winds, O breath, and breathe upon
these slain, that they may live." (Ezekiel 37:1, 7-9)

To spend any length of time in this world is to come up against the limits
of our power. Who has not tried to make some corner of the world a better
place and been met with intransigent resistance? Who has not tried to make
someone they love happy and failed? Who has not poured the best of themselves into a project or dream only for it to crumble to dust in their hands?

God, however, is not like us. God is not limited by intractable situations, or stymied by hostility or indifference. God created the universe from
nothing, and there is nothing in all of creation that can constrain his plans
or resist his purposes.

But we must not think of God's power simply as a matter of brute force.
God's power also has a particular character—a warp and a weft, a weight
and a direction. Today's passage from Ezekiel gives us a glimpse of how this
particular God chooses to make use of his omnipotence. It shows us that
God's most characteristic act, the most perfect expression of his infinite
divine power, is the act of resurrection. This is a God who draws on the
power that called the stars into existence and uses it *to give life to the dead.*

If you want to encounter the awesome power of God, look to the piles
of bones around you. Look to the place in your life that has no breath in
it—the intractable situation, the hope that died, the dust in your hands.
And then have the courage of faith to invoke God's resurrection power. Call
upon the Holy Spirit, whose nature is to give life, to be poured out over the
circumstances of your life: *Come breathe upon these slain, that they may live.*

— *Simeon Zahl*

October 5

And the people of Nineveh believed God; they proclaimed
a fast, and everyone, great and small, put on sackcloth...
God changed his mind about the calamity that he had said
he would bring upon them; and he did not do it. But this
was very displeasing to Jonah, and he became angry. (Jonah
3:5, 10; 4:1)

When Jonah finally stumbled into the morally decadent city of Nineveh, he
expected to witness the full extent of God's wrath on sinners. Instead, he
was met with a surprise: The king there immediately issued an order for a
repentance of sackcloth and ashes. And God, in keeping with his promise,
pardoned over 120,000 people (and "much cattle") from their sin, relenting
from the foretold disaster. Jonah, however, is irate. He launches a diatribe
against grace, reminding God that, although he knows God is gracious and
slow to anger and abounding in steadfast love and all that, the Ninevites
certainly don't warrant forgiveness. Come on, God. I know you were merciful to me, but surely not *them*.

A popular early-2000s cartoon vegetable depiction of Jonah chides, "The
bad guys finally getting what they deserve! ... I did my job! So, fire! Brim-
stone! Whatever! You pick—right over there!" God patiently waits for the
wayward prophet to finish his foolish tirade only to (I imagine) chuckle.
Even still, Jonah admits that he'd rather die alone in the wilderness than
live to see the *Ninevites*, of all people, forgiven. Notwithstanding, in either
a well-timed joke or an act of compassion (or perhaps both), God *still* gives
Jonah grace, raising a plant to provide him shade (4:6).

Jonah demands that God act according to the constraints of the law,
while the author of the law himself chooses to bestow grace. How easy it is
to, like Jonah, condemn those whom God has forgiven! In the same timeless
VeggieTales epic, Khalil the caterpillar (a.k.a. God) sharply reminds Jonah (and
us): "Has it ever occurred to you that maybe God loves everybody, not just
you? That maybe he wants to give everyone a second chance?"

Today, may we seek to forgive as we ourselves have been forgiven, remembering that we are not the only ones that God has chosen for his mercy.

— *August Smith*

October 6

Therefore, a man leaves his father and his mother and clings
to his wife, and they become one flesh. (Genesis 2:24)

Some marriage services include a petition asking God to "make this marriage a sign of Christ's love to this sinful and broken world." Sadly, married couples often labor to make their marriage a sign of perfection and balance, a relationship to which each partner contributes equally. But balance is not the same thing as love. Frisbees are perfectly balanced; strong marriages are not. Nor are strong relationships with friends, parents, or siblings. We eventually lose in all our relationships when a balanced score becomes the goal.

Our fundamental imbalance can, by the grace of God, be one of the great joys of relationships. When my wife and I got married, we two became one in a mystic union. To my way of thinking, this means that my Lifetime Grade Point Average (LGPA) took an enormous leap the second we exchanged vows. Prior to our marriage, she enjoyed an elevated academic status. I did not. However, through the miracle of grace, we take her cumulative LGPA and combine it with mine. Through the witchcraft some call "math," the result is a combined score of a B minus. Her LGPA took a nosedive; mine rose significantly. I often remind her of this fact. It's a mystical union with the happy result of my entering the academic elite.

Is that fair? Absolutely not. But welcome to relationships. By virtue of the grace that she extends me, I find myself to be smarter, better looking, and funnier. I have made her a better dancer; she makes me a more thoughtful listener. I contribute a knowledge of various ales; she contributes a deeper knowledge of politics. I taught her to fish; she taught me long division. We find that we are more together than we were separately.

Perfect equality, fairness, and balance never made anyone's loins quiver. A married couple that has successfully attained a perfectly even score is not "a sign of Christ's love to this sinful and broken world." Balance does not encourage or inspire. Instead, we are encouraged by couples who revel in their differences, delight in the ridiculousness of a God who would bring together two such obviously different people, spouses who fully appreciate the basic otherness of one another. Those couples are signs of Christ's love to this sinful and broken world.

— *Drew Rollins*

313

October 7

> [T]he Lord has commanded that those who preach the gospel should receive their living from the gospel.
>
> But I have not used any of these rights… What then is my reward? Just this: that in preaching the gospel I may offer it free of charge, and so not make full use of my rights as a preacher of the gospel. (1 Corinthians 9:13-18, NIV)

The church teaches that the gospel is free, but this by itself says hardly anything. Free is slippery. Free is thinly veiled advertising, the first step into a multi-level marketing scheme. Free spans all the linguistic turf between "priceless" and "worthless."

Often, a gift incurs a debt, as anyone who has been trapped in a competitive gift exchange knows well. What is never given for money may nevertheless be traded for loyalty, guilt, honor, or obedience. Christians have excelled at such commerce, binding the world to the Kingdom through an exquisitely strong, invisible web of debt. We are people of obligation, always beholden to someone and eager to invite others to become equally beholden, which we call "free." Is this not our commission?

Perhaps surprisingly, it is not. Paul's great desire is for the gospel to have no cost associated with it; not for the preacher, and not for the hearer. He means to give it away, so that all who hear are truly free. Just how free? Certainly free from guilt and free from sin, because the blood of Jesus has declared it so; free from death, because the word freely preached is the word of Resurrection; free from fear, because Christ reigns and no power can oppose him. Could anyone be more free than that?

Yes. As Paul notes, the Lord has commanded that laborers should be paid, but Paul acknowledges this command only to refuse it for himself. This means he ignores the command of *Jesus*, not because he is above Christ, but precisely because he belongs to him. The one who hears the gospel of Jesus is free, because freedom is not a kind of higher debt, but the condition of life without any law at all. It is being Lord over the law, belonging to and living in Christ himself, who cannot be traded, owed, or governed—only given. That and that alone is Paul's boast: a gospel preached without any law, in the impossible freedom of Christ himself. In this word, you are free.

— *Adam Morton*

October 8

"It is enough; now, O LORD, take away my life, for I am no better than my ancestors." Then [Elijah] lay down under the broom tree and fell asleep. Suddenly an angel touched him and said to him, "Get up and eat." He looked, and there at his head was a cake baked on hot stones, and a jar of water. He ate and drank...then he went in the strength of that food forty days and forty nights to Horeb the mount of God. (1 Kings 19:4-6, 8)

Elijah, a prophet of the Lord, had just performed a miracle on Mount Carmel for the wayward, Baal-worshipping Israelites: He built an altar to the Lord with a burnt offering, doused it in water, and then prayed that God would show up. He did this so the Israelites would know the one true God. With that, the fire of the Lord fell down and "even licked up the water that was in the trench" (18:38). The people were amazed, and they believed. *Go-go-go Elijah!*

Although this breathtaking performance was accomplished through the Lord's strength, Elijah had utterly poured himself out. The whole thing was *an ordeal.* To make matters worse, following this miracle Elijah had to go on the run because of a death threat from the king's Baal-loving wife. This is where the above scripture picks up. Elijah is *done.* He is *exhausted.* He is completely out of gas and he just wants to give up altogether.

Have you been here before, feeling that you have nothing left to give but your very life? The good news for us, and the good news for Elijah, is that God is in the business of giving us the life we need when we are all but dead. He meets us with perfect tenderness in these blessed moments of surrender, often in small yet essential ways we tend to overlook: "Eat," he says, and he provides food. "Drink," he says, and he hands us water. "Sleep," he says, and he leads us to the shade of a broom tree.

Friends, in your own moments of being all poured out, may you go in grace like Elijah. Put your feet up, eat some cake, receive the finishing work—that bread of life, that cup of salvation—that has already been done on your behalf in Christ, and then go on in *God's* strength.

— *Charlotte Getz*

October 9

For God alone my soul waits in silence,
    for my hope is from him.
He alone is my rock and my salvation,
    my fortress; I shall not be shaken.
On God rests my deliverance and my honor;
    my mighty rock, my refuge is in God.
Trust in him at all times, O people;
    pour out your heart before him;
    God is a refuge for us. *Selah* (Psalm 62:5-8)

It's so easy to distract ourselves from difficult circumstances and unwanted life events. Sometimes we're able to convince ourselves that everything is just fine when everything is not. Instead of accepting the reality of our suffering and waiting in silence for our ultimate source of hope, we turn to friends or family, work, errands, busyness, social media, Netflix, Spotify, food, and drink to fill the hole that was made for hope.

The psalmist tells us that God alone is who our souls long for. And God alone offers us the protection and strength we so desperately need when everything around us and within us is falling apart.

I love how this psalm says "my hope is *from* him." I usually say "my hope is *in* him." Maybe the way I say it is accurate, too, but I prefer the psalm's phrasing. Any hope we have is *from* God. It's not anything we can create or squeeze from other sources. As God bestows on us this genuine hope, we are moved toward vulnerability and trust which form us into people who believe good things are on the other side of our distress. By the grace of God, we may be able to sit in the uncomfortable silence and wait for whatever it is that God is up to. And while you sit today and wait in silence and pour out your heart, may you become more aware, that in your suffering, you are refuged by the Triune Lord.

— *Charlotte Donlon*

October 10

My wife and I head up the small jail ministry at our church. Every time
we go, we are reminded just how rare—and immensely consoling—it is to
experience God's word without the blinding trappings of teams and tribes.
Ironic that this is easier to do in the jail than in most churches. (It's harder
to judge when everyone's in stripes.)

Every now and then, an inmate will ask if, when they get out, they
can join our church. Of course, we heartily welcome them and assure them
that we'd love to help them in any way possible once they're back out in
the "real world."

For lack of faith and lack of imagination, I always worry about what will
happen if and when these inmates *do* one day darken our door. Our church
is full of nice, loving, gospel-believing people—they would surely welcome
these new brothers and sisters—but going by first glances, the differences
are hard to deny. Our church building is all stone and brass. Our parishio-
ners wear penny loafers. There are very few (visible) tattoos.

This isn't a new problem, judging by this passage. Even Gentiles are
blinded by tribalism. Despite the message we proclaim we believe, we all
build boundaries within God's wide generosity.

The gospel, thankfully, does not have manners. It is a message for Gentiles of all colors, creeds, and stripes. I am the beneficiary of its free admission policy, and so it's never my job to protect any insiders from more
outsiders. It is my job to remember that, above all else, *I am an outsider who
was welcomed in.* Remembering this can open a fearful heart and is sure to
"glorify God for his mercy."

— *Ethan Richardson*

October 11

In the womb he tried to supplant his brother,
   and in his manhood he strove with God.
He strove with the angel and prevailed,
   he wept and sought his favor;
he met him at Bethel,
   and there he spoke with him. (Hosea 12:3-4)

In the play *Angels in America*, the protagonist is dying of AIDS when he receives a divine vocation: A heavenly messenger visits him and delivers a book of prophecy. But he doesn't want words. He needs help, tangible help, with his disease and also his anger. Where's God in his misery? Why won't God actually help? So Prior (that's the protagonist) makes up his mind to confront the Lord. Along the way, though, Prior meets his ex's dead Jewish grandmother. What she says has stuck with me. She tells Prior, "You should struggle with the Almighty! ... It's the Jewish way."

Which is sound doctrine. Struggling with the Almighty goes all the way back to the Jewish forefather Jacob—which is who Hosea is talking about in the passage above. In utero, Jacob grappled with his twin Esau. As an adult, he swindled Esau's birthright and a blessing from him, so Jacob had to flee. The night before he is to meet Esau again, he is frantic. His twin is likely still angry, enough to hurt him and his family. He begs God's help, but God appears silent. Instead, "a man" shows up and wrangles him till dawn, dislocating Jacob's hip. That's why he's renamed Israel, "the one that strives with God."

As the sun appears, the "man" forfeits. But Jacob won't have it: "I will not let thee go, except thou bless me" (Gen 32:26 KJV). In *Angels*, Prior tries this tactic, too, in his own match with an angel. And it works. But in the play, the characters call a blessing "more life." Unlike the pious but ambiguous word "blessing," you can feel "more life" immediately. You can tell when you've got it and when you don't: It's a reprieve from suicidal depression. It's being able to forgive your friend. It's surviving a fatal disease.

Like Prior, I get angry at God. I pray without reply. I read scripture and hear only demand. I go to church and feel more confused. The story of Jacob, at the heart of the history of God's people, lets us acknowledge those conflicts. We can struggle with the Almighty! And through the resurrection, God has already promised *more life*.

— *Kendall Gunter*

October 12

> "Ask, and it will be given you; search, and you will find; knock, and the door will be opened for you... Is there anyone among you who, if your child asks for bread, will give a stone? Or if the child asks for a fish, will give a snake? If you then, who are evil, know how to give good gifts to your children, how much more will your Father in heaven give good things to those who ask him!" (Matthew 7:7, 9-11)

There is a simple song with verses pulled directly from this passage that I grew up singing at least one Sunday a month for almost twenty years in the pews of my childhood church. "Ask and it shall be given unto you / Seek and ye shall find / Knock and the door shall be opened unto you," we would all sing together as we approached the altar rail for communion. As a child, this message felt like a given. Of course God will take care of me; God loves me!

As an adult, this song and scripture (and, let's be honest, my version of "care") always feel more complicated. I can easily be convinced that if God really cares for me then He will give me X thing that I am convinced I need. I can begin to rate God's care: *4/10 stars, Lord. Would not recommend.*

His care becomes contingent on my feelings. Which is probably the heart of this passage. We do not actually know what we want. Or, in my case, we want questionable things.

I would like quiet children. I would like macaroni and cheese to be healthy. Oh, and as long as I am making a wish-list, I would love to be the Queen of the Universe. But God does not always give us what we want or need, even if we ask nicely.

There is a reason that Jesus describes God as a parent in this passage. Because the best mothers and fathers do not give children what they want; they give them what they need. Mercy, consolation, encouragement, and above all, love. And if we are really honest, it is probably what we have been knocking, and seeking, and asking for all along.

— *Sarah Condon*

October 13

By this we know that we abide in him and he in us, because
he has given us of his own Spirit. (1 John 4:13 RSV)

Are people God-like? Or rather, is there a little bit of God in you and me?

The very question sounds 'Eastern,' and one's initial response is maybe to head for the hills. I mean, isn't Christian faith anchored in an understanding of humanity that accurately diagnoses our fallenness and utter self-absorption, thus marking out the *difference* between "God and man" (David Bowie, 1983)?

Well, yes and no. St. John wrote that God "has given us of his own Spirit." Something *of* Him is part of us now, not by human birth but by means of the New Birth. St. John's "mysticism"—not a bad word in itself—states that there's a little element of God in us. This is known as the Holy Spirit.

I have had too low a view of the Holy Spirit. Mary and I got to be right in the middle of the "charismatic movement" during the 1970s. We knew Michael Harper, Terry Fullam, and Frank Lake, and met in person David Watson and Graham Pulkingham. We were ministered to, deeply, by these men.

Then it dimmed a little, almost to the extent that my theology changed. Nevertheless, the power of these inspired ministers was tangible and unforgettable.

Isn't there a song by the Monkees entitled, "A Little Bit Me, A Little Bit You"? That's what I'm talking about. God understands me because He became a human being once. And I can understand Him a little because He gave me a soul that comes from Him. And "it only takes a spark to get a fire going" ("Pass It On," 1969).

Talk to Him about what's on your mind.

— *Paul Zahl*

October 14

Incline your ear, and come to me;
> listen, so that you may live. (Isaiah 55:3)

Tip number one for being a good listener: Don't interrupt the person talking. Sounds simple, but why is it so hard? Perhaps because most interruptions don't take the form of sudden interjections. They come disguised as questions, or advice, or the sharing of personal experience. "Oh, that happened to me once," we sympathize. The result tends to be a derailing of whatever is being shared. "Uh, I forgot what I was saying."

William Faulkner once wrote, "Somebody to talk to...not to converse with you nor even agree with you, but just to keep quiet and listen. Which is all that people really want, really need." Not being listened to, on the other hand, breeds anger and contempt.

Would people describe you as a good listener? Or, when someone else is talking, are you really just waiting for your own turn to speak?

The truth is, good listening is as rare as it is healing. There's always a reason not to listen to another person. Maybe we feel crunched for time. Maybe we think we already know what the person is going to say.

Yet when someone actually takes the time to listen to us—*sans* judgment—it's almost shocking. You can feel the earth shifting under your feet. The sensation of being listened to is akin to that of being loved. Anger dissipates, hearts soften. It is akin to the experience of grace.

On the flipside, when you actually listen to another person, you find out they're not as alien as you expected. They have reasons for believing, or acting, or voting the way they do—and *vice versa*. You might even start to love *them*.

How does one become a listener like Isaiah describes? Perhaps today it can begin by looking to the God who listens in infinite compassion to all the terrible listeners of the world. The God who absorbs our many words and the pain they so often cause—and then *interrupts* our self-centered chatter, not with a command to be quiet, but with a Word of grace made flesh.

Can you hear it?

— David Zahl

October 15

See, you shall call nations that you do not know,
  and nations that do not know you shall run to you,
because of the LORD your God, the Holy One of Israel,
  for he has glorified you. (Isaiah 55:5)

I was a small child, and my siblings and I had been in a fight, and my parents were doling out justice in a way that I felt was shortsighted. To me, my siblings' punishment did not fit their crimes. I seethed that my parents weren't seeing "the big picture." This got a laugh from them. I could barely see over the kitchen table.

As a child, I presumed to know everything, and as an adult, I still presume to know everything. It's an easy pose to strike. We live in what is often called "the age of information," when we know all too much: the private lives of celebrities, the details of war zones 3,000 miles away. With three clicks and a Google search, we can answer the most random questions.

Alexander Pope once wrote, "Some people never learn anything because they understand everything too soon." When we feel as if we know everything, we are more in the dark than ever: closed off, rigidly dogmatic, reluctant to see the gracious surprises each day has to offer. And what is despair but the feeling that you know everything? *I know how this goes*, you might think; *I know what today holds for me.*

But God assures you that you do not.

In the above scripture, the prophet Isaiah promises his fellow Israelites, who are trapped in Babylon, that there are "nations that you do not know." Better yet, they will "run to you." This promise reflects God's covenant with the Israelites, and through Jesus, that covenant is extended to us, to you. You have been promised a beautiful unknown, a future that will arrive at your doorstep without your having to take one step. It will run to you, not because you deserve it, but because "the LORD your God…has glorified you."

God, grant me the eyes to see over the kitchen table. To see the beauty of your gifts today. With wonder and humble acceptance, may I greet whatever comes running.

— CJ Green

October 16

"Sovereign Lord, as you have promised,
  you may now dismiss your servant in peace.
For my eyes have seen your salvation,
  which you have prepared in the sight of all nations:
a light for revelation to the Gentiles,
  and the glory of your people Israel." (Luke 2:29-32 NIV)

These are the words of Simeon, a man who was described as "righteous and devout." Luke doesn't tell us that he is an old man, but he is often depicted as old in artistic renderings of the scene in the Temple, where he says these words. We imagine that he's near death, and that the revelation of the Messiah is something he has anticipated for an entire lifetime. God revealed to Simeon that he will not die before he sees the Messiah, and the Spirit prompts him to go to the Temple on the day that the infant Jesus is presented there.

Simeon has been worrying for Israel. In Jesus, he finds relief. "[Y]ou may now dismiss your servant in peace." The world he would leave, and the realm he would enter in death, would be saved by the fulfilled promise of Jesus. His words mark the promise that Jesus was a glory not only to the people of Israel, but also a light to the Gentiles.

How many of us are waiting and worrying for consolation and comfort? Would being dismissed in peace be a relief?

The Book of Common Prayer includes these words in the orders of Morning Prayer, Evening Prayer, and Compline (to be said at the end of the day). For generations, Christians have found comfort in these words to mark the beginnings and endings of their days, as Simeon said them as a comfort at the end of his life, and at the beginning of Jesus' life.

There is comfort in Simeon's words for all of us. Those of us who worry and wait are not alone. Jesus may be revealed to us not as a baby in a Temple, but in any number of ways. And we are relieved that the salvation of Jesus is a light of revelation to the Gentiles and the glory of God's people Israel.

— *Carrie Willard*

October 17

If you put these instructions before the brothers and sisters, you will be a good servant of Christ Jesus, nourished on the words of the faith and of the sound teaching that you have followed. Have nothing to do with profane myths and old wives' tales. Train yourself in godliness, for, while physical training is of some value, godliness is valuable in every way, holding promise for both the present life and the life to come. The saying is sure and worthy of full acceptance. For to this end we toil and struggle, because we have our hope set on the living God, who is the Savior of all people, especially of those who believe. (1 Timothy 4:6-10)

It is fairly common to hear that the story of Christianity is one of many myths in the pantheon of world religions. Similarly, many people (including some of "those who believe") hold that Jesus Christ was a good moral teacher in a long line of moral teachers like Gandhi and Mr. Rogers. The problem with these two assertions is that Jesus and his Church claim the opposite. Christianity is not one religion among many but *the end of religion*. Jesus Christ was not simply a good moral teacher, but one who came to show that good morals are not enough to save us.

The Apostle Paul tells us that we are to have "nothing to do with profane myths and old wives' tales." Myths and old wives' tales were invented to teach morals and provide a lesson. This is a good thing. This is not, however, what Jesus Christ was about. Too often, church can feel like physical training. Do more, try harder, care about this or that issue. Instead, we are to train ourselves in godliness, because godliness holds "promise for both the present life and the life to come."

When we lose sight of the faith of the gospel, we end up on the hamster wheel of human myths and morals. It is never enough. There is always more to do. Only when we focus on the Savior can we realize the promise of the present life and the life to come.

We are called to only one thing: to have faith in Jesus Christ. You can step off the hamster wheel. You can drop the myths and wives' tales. You can stop the training regimen. Set your hope on Christ, and rest.

— *Connor Gwin*

October 18

For we ourselves were once foolish, disobedient, led astray,
slaves to various passions and pleasures, passing our days
in malice and envy, despicable, hating one another. But
when the goodness and loving kindness of God our Savior
appeared, he saved us, not because of any works of righteousness that we had done, but according to his mercy,
through the water of rebirth and renewal by the Holy
Spirit. (Titus 3:3-5)

In 1987, the pop group INXS reminded the whole world that "every single one of us [has] the devil inside." In the passage above, St. Paul reminds
his friend St. Titus of this very same truth. Existentially, there is very little difference between you and the non-Christian people around you. We
understand what it is to be rebellious in nature, ready to tell people off, to
quarrel with anyone who gets in our way, because we have engaged in all
the same disorderly behaviors and attitudes that our pagan neighbors engage
in. *Every single one of us has the devil inside.*

However, what St. Paul also reminds Titus is that our salvation never
comes about by our personal decisions. Instead, as St. Paul writes, God saved
us, not because of works done by us in righteousness, but according to His
own mercy. This salvation is confirmed not through subjective experience,
but rather through ordinary old water with the Holy Spirit attached to it;
that is, through baptism.

This is such freeing news because it takes the onus off us to improve as
Christians and allows us to rest in God's salvation, understanding that any
real improvement in our life is pure gift and not earned. This allows us to
relate to those around us with humility and grace, and to sympathize with
them as they deal with their own "devil inside."

— *Jacob Smith*

October 19

> Now only King Og of Bashan was left of the remnant of
> the Rephaim. In fact his bed, an iron bed, can still be seen
> in Rabbah of the Ammonites. By the common cubit it is
> nine cubits long and four cubits wide. (Deuteronomy 3:11)

Ever notice how it's almost always the little person who takes down the giant? The boy Jack chops down the beanstalk, sending Mr. Fee-fi-fo-fum tumbling to his death. In *Game of Thrones*, it's little Lyanna who sinks a knife into the ice giant. And, of course, it's young David who wields a sling to send Goliath to his grave. As if the odds aren't already stacked in the giant's favor, classical stories up the ante by pitting the extraordinarily big against the extraordinarily small. We realize the little person will not win by muscle or military prowess. Conventional means will not secure the underdog's victory.

Israel has to learn this same lesson. They initially fail. The first generation stands on the brink of the Promised Land and quails at the giants there (Num 13:28-33). They cower in fear and, as punishment, spend 40 years dragging their feet through the wilderness sands. Their children, however, face down and kill King Og of Bashan, as well as other giants. If Og's iron bed, measuring 13 feet long and 6 feet wide, is any indication of the body size of these mammoth men, you can understand why the Israelites say they feel like grasshoppers next to them (Num 13:33).

Giants, ancient and modern, real and metaphorical, always seem undefeatable. Indeed, that's their job, the point of their existence. The bigger they are, the smaller their conqueror must be. It is only after 40 years of being diminished, humbled, lowered, that Israel is ready to face the giants.

In God's storytelling way, this is all his means of preparing us for the ultimate underdog's victory. In the battle of battles, the Og of death, the Goliath of hell, the Ice Giant of sin—every huge foe of humanity is massacred not by an armored knight or a celestial Hercules. No, a naked, bleeding, defenseless, abandoned servant, strung up on a cross, takes them all down by the unstoppable weapon of self-sacrificial love.

Giants, it turns out, are no match for the God who's willing to become the smallest of the small for us.

— *Chad Bird*

> If with Christ you died to the elemental spirits of the uni-
> verse, why do you live as if you still belonged to the world?
> Why do you submit to regulations, "Do not handle, Do not
> taste, Do not touch"? All these regulations refer to things
> that perish with use; they are simply human commands
> and teachings. These have indeed an appearance of wis-
> dom in promoting self-imposed piety, humility, and severe
> treatment of the body, but they are of no value in checking
> self-indulgence. (Colossians 2:20-23)

Michael Jackson's "Thriller" provides endlessly useful imagery for describing how we love the law:

> Darkness falls across the land
> The midnight hour is close at hand
> Creatures crawl in search of blood
> To terrorize y'all's neighborhood

We creep toward regulations and lurch toward instruction. Although we
know that the law kills (cf. 2 Cor 3:6), we worship it anyway, functionally
preferring a *Weekend at Bernie's* zombie life. We say things like, "God helps
those who help themselves," or "Jesus is my co-pilot." (*Cue drooling, heavy
mouth-breathing, and limbs occasionally falling off.*)

Our creepshow-selves come out. Paradoxically, that is what happens
when we seek to display proper and lawful behavior intended to ingratiate
ourselves to a God who has already forgiven us in Christ. It turns out that
our desire for rules, as it has always been, is rooted in unbelief; you know,
the dead guy St. Paul tells us we're tied to (v. 20). The law is bloodthirsty
for a life that we don't believe is already ours in Christ! "What a world,
what a world!"

To the Colossian "walking dead," Paul shouts, "get back in the grave!"
That's where the power is; not in the works of your hands but in the hands
that were pierced for all the night-walking, law-loving (but rarely law-abid-
ing) transgressors like you and me.

According to the letter of the law, the Old Kingdom produces only
death. But an upside-down rapture has occurred in Christ. "Love lifted

me"…down into a grave! Shocking zombies everywhere for over 2,000 years, it turns out that it is only the cross of Christ that delivers us real life! Abducted from the kingdom of obligation, we are ushered by King Jesus, who is literally *the* embodiment of love and acceptance, into the New (and forever) Kingdom of His life.

— *Matt Magill*

October 21

> Do not worry about anything, but in everything by prayer and supplication with thanksgiving let your requests be made known to God. (Philippians 4:6)

A couple of years ago, a semi-prominent motivational speaker branded as a Christian argued that anxiety and gratitude cannot coexist. I, along with a lot of commenters, took umbrage at this oversimplification. For many of us, anxiety is a condition, not a choice. And it can't be spirited away by a Bible verse here or a quick prayer there. It remains, uninvited, no matter what we do or take or try.

I feel God knows this. After all, he *made* me. As Psalm 139 says, he "created my inmost being" (v. 13 NIV). And none of it was accidental. So when Paul tells the Philippians not to worry—or, in some translations, not to be anxious—what exactly is God trying to communicate?

Even after parsing through the differences between worry and anxiety, the exhortation to "not worry about anything" is a bit unreasonable. We're human, after all. But Paul is telling us that, at some point, we have a choice. We can actively pray, and we can do so with thanksgiving. Also, we can tell God what's on our mind by giving him our requests. This is an *invitation*. It is a beckoning toward a better way. Because when I'm honest with myself, I know that while my anxiety is its own beast altogether, there are plenty of moments when I could be looking up rather than around. I am constantly like Peter on the water, moving my eyes from Jesus to the waves (Mt 14:29-30).

God doesn't condemn me for this. He just wants me to know that there is a better way. There is *him*.

Not long ago, I absently picked up my phone and felt a voice gently offer me an option—not as a discipline or rule, but an option—to consider praying before picking up my phone. "What if..." the thought began. Then I considered how often my voracious need for information, for *control*, can steer me away from a moment of remembering my belovedness. It won't dry up all my anxiety, but the grace of God is so often like this: a gentle invitation, a "what if..." beckoning us into a better Way—and Truth, and Life.

— *Stephanie Phillips*

October 22

One of the criminals who were hanged there kept deriding him and saying, "Are you not the Messiah? Save yourself and us!" But the other rebuked him, saying, "Do you not fear God, since you are under the same sentence of condemnation? And we indeed have been condemned justly, for we are getting what we deserve for our deeds, but this man has done nothing wrong." Then he said, "Jesus, remember me when you come into your kingdom." He replied, "Truly I tell you, today you will be with me in Paradise." (Luke 23:39-43)

The thief on the cross is the final answer to two questions: What does Jesus require of us for entry into Paradise, and what happens when we die?

Here is a man who, by his own admission, has lived a life worthy of death and has absolutely no time to make up for any of it. There is no good deed he can perform, no kind word he can offer, no baptismal font in which his many sins can be washed away. He is a spiritual paralytic, unable to do much more than squeeze out a phrase or two in between agonizing inhalations on his way to a slow, silent death.

And yet, he asks for deliverance. It is a foolish, almost obscene request. Desperate words from a desperate man. Who does he think he is? Of course, he knows exactly who and what he is, and that his only hope is hanging on the cross beside him. In this unnamed man's words, we find the whole of the gospel—that the only requirement for entry into God's kingdom is daring to believe that Jesus might actually be true—that this penniless, pathetic preacher from Nazareth is God in the flesh, and that he has the power and willingness to take him home.

And what is Jesus' response? "[T]oday you will be with me in Paradise." Not tomorrow, or in a few months, or a few thousand years when Jesus gets around to returning and raising the dead. Today. Right now. Paradise is just on the other side of this agonizing moment.

None of us are far from death, and as we prepare for (or deny) that moment, the thief on the cross reminds us that all we must do to be with God in Paradise is ask.

— *R-J Heijmen*

Not that we are competent of ourselves to claim anything as coming from us; our competence is from God, who has made us competent to be ministers of a new covenant, not of letter but of spirit; for the letter kills, but the Spirit gives life.

Now if the ministry of death, chiseled in letters on stone tablets, came in glory so that the people of Israel could not gaze at Moses' face because of the glory of his face, a glory now set aside, how much more will the ministry of the Spirit come in glory? (2 Corinthians 3:5-8)

Just about everybody, religious or not, has familiarity with the "old" covenant that Paul alludes to in verses 6-7. At the risk of over-simplification, that old covenant works like this: *The law says "don't"; but we did; the law says "now you die."* It's not that the law is bad—those "stone tablets" on which the commandments were etched actually present a beautiful vision of life as it should be. The problem is that *we* are not as we should be.

The law rightly diagnoses what is wrong with us; it is simply incapable of helping us achieve the life it describes. In *Grace in Practice*, Paul Zahl memorably claims that the law "reduces its object, the human person, to despair." In fact, Paul the Apostle goes so far as to say that the letter of the law "kills."

Paul says these things to scare us straight. He wants to spare us the tragic mistake of looking to old religious legalisms for the source of new life. Why not gaze instead at an empty tomb, a life-giving Holy Spirit, and a glorious "ministry of justification" (v. 9)? May the Spirit give you such joy in your forgiveness today that someone might say that you are *positively glowing*.

— *Larry Parsley*

October 24

"I have made your name known to those whom you gave me from the world. They were yours, and you gave them to me, and they have kept your word. Now they know that everything you have given me is from you; for the words that you gave to me I have given to them, and they have received them and know in truth that I came from you; and they have believed that you sent me. I am asking on their behalf; I am not asking on behalf of the world, but on behalf of those whom you gave me, because they are yours." (John 17:6-9)

Franz Kafka, the 20th-century writer, once said, "In German the word *sein* signifies both things: to be and to belong to Him." Of course, this is a grammatical rule, but Kafka chose to capitalize the "H" of "Him." You exist *and* you belong to God. In other words, your belonging to God does not hinge on your successes or failures or *anything* other than the fact that you exist.

There often comes a deep sense of comfort with the realization that your life is not even your own. Everything belongs to God on the grounds that he made it.

As human beings, we are so hardwired to find belonging that we'll sacrifice anything for it. Your sense of belonging, however, is not based on your appearance, your achievements, your failures, or your status. It is based on Jesus Christ, who speaks and prays on your behalf, who lives and dies on your behalf, who is your advocate with the Father and who reminds his Father that you belong to him.

The renowned German pastor Dietrich Bonhoeffer wrestled with his own identity in the cell of a concentration camp in Flossenbürg during World War II. In his poem "Who Am I," he writes this:

> Am I one person today and tomorrow another?
> Am I both at once? A hypocrite before others,
> and before myself a contemptible woebegone weakling? ...
> Who am I? They mock me, these lonely questions of mine.
> Whoever I am, thou knowest, O God, I am thine!

— *Sam Bush*

October 25

> Indeed, the word of God is living and active, sharper than
> any two-edged sword, piercing until it divides soul from
> spirit, joints from marrow; it is able to judge the thoughts
> and intentions of the heart. (Hebrews 4:12)

The double-edged sword shows up several times in the Bible. The Greek adjective used here—*distomos*—literally means two-mouthed. Sharpened on both edges, this sword was known as a "drinker of blood" for the way it sliced through battlefields, imbibing the blood of the men it killed. A vivid adjective, we find it also in the great tragedies of Euripides—*Helen* and *Orestes*—in passages which drip with violence and death. The writer of Hebrews, however, uses *distomos* in relation to the word of God. The word of God is *sharper* than any two-edged sword. The word of God penetrates, divides, judges.

More unsettlingly than the "drinker of blood," the word of God does not just divide life from bodies. The word of God divides our souls, our spirits, our joints, our marrow, our thoughts, our attitudes, our very hearts. The word of God slices deeper than any human sword could ever hope to cut, revealing our failings, exposing our self-justifications, condemning our sinful hearts to death. We can have no earthly defense against the living word of God.

There is only one other book in the New Testament where *distomos* appears:

> In his right hand he held seven stars, and from his mouth
> came a sharp, two-edged sword, and his face was like the
> sun shining with full force.
>
> When I saw him, I fell at his feet as though dead. But
> he placed his right hand on me, saying, "Do not be afraid;
> I am the first and the last, and the living one. I was dead,
> and see, I am alive forever and ever; and I have the keys of
> Death and of Hades." (Rev 1:16-18)

Do not fear. Jesus Christ died on the cross. He gave his own body over to the "drinker of blood" for our failings, for our self-justifications, and for our sinful hearts. He bled so that we would not. He died so that we may live. The word of God uncovers our sin, but the Word of God clothes us in the rich robes of righteousness. The double-edged sword becomes both death and life for the believer, condemning and saving not only our bodies but our souls, spirits, and hearts.

> *Thank you, Lord, for the mercy of your Son's life and death, so that we who live by the sword may no longer die by the sword.*

— *Derrill H. McDavid*

October 26

> Such was the appearance of the likeness of the glory of the
> LORD. And when I saw it, I fell upon my face, and I heard
> the voice of one speaking.
>
> And he said to me, "Son of man, stand upon your feet,
> and I will speak with you." (Ezekiel 1:28-2:1 RSV)

This conversation—it's a word that has become debased by its declension to mean a *one-way* conversation with the prior intent of trying to change someone's mind about something; but hey, whatever!—this conversation between God and Ezekiel is a two-way meeting.

On the one hand, and as the required first step, the man must reverence the superiority of God. The man in fact falls upon his face. The conversation is not between two equals.

On the other hand, God strangely, wonderfully honors the man. God tells him to stand upon his feet. The prophetic word is going to be given to a person who somehow "commands" respect. "R-E-S-P-E-C-T" (Aretha Franklin, 1967). This is extraordinary.

Even though there is between the two entities what Kierkegaard called the "infinite qualitative distinction," God and the man stand on a level plane. It *is* a two-way street! It *will* be a "conversation," in the true sense of the word.

He wants that for us. First, you have to acknowledge His unquantifiable superiority. Falling on your face is probably a good place to start. But then, He'll really talk to you. He wants to know what you think. More importantly, He wants to know how you feel. It's heart to Heart.

Try it.

P.S. God spoke initially to Ezekiel through the means and vehicle of a Flying Saucer. That is so like Him!

— Paul Zahl

October 27

Then Jesus gave a loud cry and breathed his last. And the curtain of the temple was torn in two, from top to bottom. (Mark 15:37-38)

Doors, gates, and curtains all send one basic message: a "NO" to unrestricted access. That denial of access may be as in-your-face as an iron gate or as easily brushed aside as a tent curtain. Nevertheless, the message remains the same: These barriers deny entry to this particular property.

"The earth is the LORD's and all that is in it," the psalmist sings (24:1). But even the one with cosmic real estate holdings put down roots in a particular spot. The Holy of Holies, the cube-shaped inner sanctum of the temple, was God's space in Israel. Here was the epicenter of glory. Here was the heart of holiness. Here, too, was restricted access, for a thick curtain hung as a barrier between God's turf and the rest of the world.

When Jesus cried out and took his last breath, God grabbed the top of the temple curtain with both hands and yanked downward. That rip was him kicking down the front door of his home, taking the front gate off the hinges, and walking away into the big, broad world with his glory in tow. God went international.

The death of Jesus released God's glory and holiness into the world. His ministry had already prepared us for it. In touching lepers, embracing pariahs, and dining with undesirables, Jesus sent a loud and clear signal that business as usual was over. God's glory now hovered over a table full of tax collectors. Holiness hung as halos over untouchables. The "inner sanctum" became that space where the Friend of Sinners summoned the broken.

Christ's death sealed the deal. Just as God's breath exhaled life upon creation at the start, now the Son's exhalation upon the cross breathed new life across the cosmos. The Lord has come to save us, to sanctify us, to make us his own.

— *Chad Bird*

October 28

> Jesus said to him, "If it is my will that he remain until I
> come, what is that to you? Follow me!" (John 21:22)

This little rebuke makes me laugh. Peter and Jesus have just had their pivotal reconciliation moment. Then Peter asks, perhaps with a little competitive spirit, about another disciple, known to us as "the one Jesus loved." Jesus has just laid Peter's future out before him, and I can't blame Peter if the future doesn't exactly have him drooling with excitement (*I will be taken where I "do not wish to go" (v. 18)? Is there at least a bed there?*). He sees this other disciple meandering down the beach—the favorite one, the good-looking one—and has to know: *Surely he has a better outcome awaiting him...what does he get?*

Jesus cuts him short. "What is that to you? You must follow *me.*" It seems that, despite being named the "rock" on which the Lord will build his Church, Peter's still doubting, floundering, and denouncing.

Like Peter, I know I should mind my own business, but it's hard when everyone's business *is* my business. If my friend is struggling with a problem I've had before, it's my job to give him some pointers. And if I've asked my wife if she wouldn't mind running the vacuum upstairs, it's for her own good that I send her a reminder.

Trying to live someone else's life is a form of insanity. It robs them of their dignity and ensures exhaustion and resentment. Whenever you feel exhausted or resentful, it is often a sign that you're living beyond your means.

A friend of mine has a mantra that perfectly paraphrases Jesus' rebuke: *Stay in your hula hoop.* Imagine yourself standing with a hula hoop around your waist. Try as you may to pull big, external problems into your hoop, they just won't fit. These problems aren't for you to handle, but they are all too often the ones wearing you down. Imagine if ultimately, maybe reluctantly, you heeded the invitation to hand those problems over to the One whose business it actually is.

— *Ethan Richardson*

October 29

So all the generations from Abraham to David are fourteen
generations; and from David to the deportation to Babylon,
fourteen generations; and from the deportation to Babylon
to the Messiah, fourteen generations. (Matthew 1:17)

In this genealogy, the list of names goes on and on with little fanfare to
many. It starts off with Abraham, the one to whom God promised the
world, and it all goes downhill from there. Matthew is actually telling a
story worthy of any tabloid, with repeated notes of scandal and disobedience. Solomon is born from David by "the wife of Uriah"—an illegitimate
child born to a murderer. The majority of the kings that follow David "did
what was evil in the sight of the LORD" (1 Kings 11:6, etc.). This evil leads
to the "deportation to Babylon," the cataclysmic destruction of the nation
itself by the sword of an invader. Matthew's genealogy narrates the repeated
tragic failures of Israel, the disturbing shadow side of its history. The coming of the Messiah is not the crowning moment of an illustrious story of
faith and salvation, but the advent of a savior to a violent and sinful people.

Jesus came to redeem sinners, to rescue the "lost sheep" who have wandered away from God. The disastrous history of Israel was not met with
retributive fires of judgment, but with grace. Christ came with merciful
judgment over Israel and the world, preaching forgiveness of sin and the
rescue of the lost. The history of Israel is his own, and he takes it upon
himself in order to expunge its transgressions from the record.

Our sin is nothing new to God. He has seen it all before, time and time
again. We might be people with questionable moral character or checkered
pasts, but we are neither better nor worse than Rahab, Ruth, David, Solomon, or Hezekiah. In the economy of the grace of the Messiah, our sin is
the only currency we have; our righteousness is of no value. His judgment
is both true and gracious. He purchases our death by his death and gives
us his life in return.

— Todd Brewer

October 30

[D]o not fear, for I am with you,
 do not be afraid, for I am your God;
I will strengthen you, I will help you,
 I will uphold you with my victorious right hand. (Isaiah 41:10)

Fear and assurance are major themes in the Bible. It is said that throughout scripture, some version of the phrase "fear not" appears 365 times. Why is that? When you think back to your own childhood and your first memories, it is impossible not to recall moments of fear. Humans, by nature, are fearful.

When you consider the fears of your childhood, most of them were probably found in the imagination, sparked by the darkness of night. My own imagination would run wild as I tried to sleep, surrounded by porcelain dolls looking down at me. I would pray that God would protect me from an imminent attack by Freddy Kreuger in my waterbed. I would cling to my Bible and recite the Lord's Prayer until I fell asleep.

According to psychologist Sally Goddard Blythe, "Sleep brings with it separation from the outside world and from others, enclosing us in the inner world of the mind. It has sometimes been described as the little death." Left on our own in the dark, we convince ourselves that we are detached from the world, others, and ultimately God. Left alone, we can become captive to our fears and doubt God's goodness.

But guess what? God knows that from our birth to our final sleep, we are creatures bound by fear. So what does our Father do? He assures us by speaking to us. In the verse given to us today, God says, "Do not fear, for I am with you, do not be afraid, for I am your God." Just as parents assure their children that there is no boogie-man under the bed and, most importantly, that the parents are with them, our God does the same thing with us, his little children, reminding us that we need not be afraid, for he is always with us.

Lord, thank you for your word that reminds us we have nothing to fear, for we belong to you. Your word directly assures us that no matter how dark life may become, we will never be apart from you, our Father and Redeemer. In your mercy, hear our prayer.

— *Melina Smith*

October 31

For our sake he made him to be sin who knew no sin, so that in him we might become the righteousness of God. (2 Corinthians 5:21)

Today is Halloween. In other words, it is All Hallows' Eve. In still other words, it is the evening before All Hallows' Day, which is in yet still other words—All Saints' Day.

The word "hallow" comes from Old English *halgian*, meaning to honor someone as "holy." That's the basic etymology of the day when we dress up and demand some candy.

A big part of the appeal of Halloween, for people both young and old, is the dressing up part. It is a relief to not be you, especially if you spend most of your days trying to be better (more holy) than you actually are. For a few hours, you can be Darth Vader or a pirate. But no matter what your costume is, pretending to be somebody else gets tiring, and fast.

In Protestant churches, today is also Reformation Day, commemorating the day in 1517 when Martin Luther nailed his 95 Theses to a church door in Wittenberg, Germany. With beautiful symmetry, Reformation Day speaks directly to those of us who try in vain to dress ourselves up to be holier than we actually are. We are reminded that holiness does not come from within, but is imputed (given) to us by Christ himself. That's what the Apostle Paul tells us, in our verse for the day.

We are clothed in Christ's righteousness. And it's not a costume; it's the real you!

We thank you, heavenly Father, that you desire us to come to you as our true selves. We praise you for clothing us in Christ's righteousness, for it is in His name that we pray. Amen.

— Paul Walker

November 1

Peter, an apostle of Jesus Christ, To the exiles of the [diaspora] in: Pontus, Galatia, Cappadocia, Asia, and Bithynia, who have been chosen and destined by God the Father and sanctified by the Spirit to be obedient to Jesus Christ and to be sprinkled with his blood: May grace and peace be yours in abundance. (1 Peter 1:1-2)

Have you ever known someone who was completely unreliable from one day to another? One day they are cheery, the next day they are depressed, and the next day they are short-tempered. They are a different person depending on when you meet them, and you never know what you're going to get. I've met plenty and probably am one myself. Humans are unreliable characters who change with the weather (literally).

It would be easy to think that God is just like every other person we meet, whose approval or disapproval is dependent upon our conformity to certain expectations: Transgressions are met with ostracization, and obedience is met with a pat on the back. But God is always the same no matter what. As the text outlines, each Person of the Trinity is united in the work of salvation. The Father elects and the Spirit sanctifies by the blood of Jesus. Within the life of God, there is no rivalry or double-mindedness, but unity. God isn't subject to the weather, nor does he change his mind from day to day. God is not fickle or moody or wearing a costume.

How do we know that God is love? Or how do we know whether there isn't some other, more powerful God, hidden from view pulling all the strings? What if God changes his mind and pushes the smite button on his cosmic iPad? Since before the foundation of the world God has been and will be exactly the same (Rev 13:8, Eph 1:4). This God is merciful, slow to anger, abounding in love. Father, Son, and Spirit have always inseparably worked together for our redemption. And on that last day when we see this God face-to-face, we will not be surprised or dismayed at who we find.

— *Todd Brewer*

November 2

When [Jesus] saw the crowds, he had compassion for them, because they were harassed and helpless, like sheep without a shepherd. (Matthew 9:36)

Lyle Lovett's song "The Fat Girl" is scarcely more than two minutes long, but its sharp poignancy and pathos can stop you short. It talks about a young girl who always stays inside and plays piano because the other children make her cry, calling her fat. Her well-meaning mother repeats that the other kids don't mean what they say, hoping in vain to create a truth out of nothing but her repetition. "They don't mean it," she says. "They don't mean it." Of course her mother says this. She tries to call evil good in the face of that sort of pain to take some of it away.

But then the fat girl grows up, and "she ain't fat no more." Quite the opposite, she makes it playing the piano, singing loud and low of love and blind compassion. But "she don't mean it. She don't mean it." She sings of love and care and hope for the world, but the fat girl who grew up does not buy any of what she is selling. Of course not. Sticks and stones may break her bones, but words have done their worst. She sings of goodness, while her heart is harassed and helpless to help itself. It is immensely sad.

In the midst of all these facades—mouthing one thing but secretly knowing the other—Jesus sees things as they really are and has done something about it. He sees the fat girl and all of us as part of the crowd of humanity, each of us unique but also like everyone else—"like sheep without a shepherd." We are harassed and helpless and singing about things we don't mean. But even when we "don't mean it," the Word Himself does. He knows the depths of our hearts, all our desires, and all our secrets. To prove his compassion to us, he suffered the Passion that changed the world.

— *Gil Kracke*

November 3

The writer Tim Kreider once estimated that we spend "87 percent of [our] mental life winning imaginary arguments that are never actually going to take place." He was aiming too low. We live in a culture so besieged with anger and grievance that it can be very difficult to imagine life without it. What are the pretend arguments you're rehearsing today?

By way of contrast, in the Sermon on the Mount, Christ equates anger with murder (vv. 21-22) and then elevates interpersonal reconciliation above worship. Stop whatever you're doing, he seems to say, and go apologize to anyone you've wronged. There is no such thing as a "healthy grudge."

The best apologies, by the way, are short and don't include explanations that can undo them. They avoid little add-ons like "but" ("I'm sorry I forget your birthday, *but* I was stressed out with work") or "if" ("I'm sorry *if* that joke I made at the meeting offended you") that can turn our "sorry" into a "not sorry at all."

And yet we don't apologize—or accept apologies—as much as we should. Perhaps this is because some kinds of anger feel good. How else to explain the phenomenon of "hate-watching/-reading"? As one dictum puts it, the only thing better than being right is being wronged. Apologizing, as well as accepting an apology, involves a loss: of power, of pleasure, of pride.

What grudges are you currently holding? Who might be accusing you, and what is keeping you from seeking reconciliation? Say these things out loud and listen to how they sound.

Thankfully, Jesus doesn't just urge us toward reconciliation. He embodies the kind of atoning love which suffers the loss of all things for its sake. He refuses to go on the defensive or indulge our grievances. Instead, he allows his accusers to hand him over to the judge, paying every last penny of the damages we incur with our stubbornness.

So while you may be litigating and re-litigating other people's wrongdoing (and your own), the only argument that truly matters has been settled. You may have built a strong case against God, but He has dropped the charges against you. No "ifs," "ands," or "buts."

— *David Zahl*

November 4

[F]or all have sinned and fall short of the glory of God.
(Romans 3:23 NIV)

"But..." we say. "At least I'm not like *those* people."

The people who vote that way. The people who spend their money that way. The people who raise their children that way. The people who watch that drivel on television. The people who cheer for that sports team. The people who march for that cause. The people who don't march for any causes. The people who worship with that music. The people whose cell phones ring during church services. The people who drive that way. The people who park that way. The people who change the toilet paper the wrong way. The people who don't change the toilet paper at all. The dog people. The cat people. The lawyers. The politicians. The media. The readers of vampire romance novels. The watchers of that news channel. The one percent. The community organizers. At least I'm not like those people.

But, as today's verse tells us, all have sinned and fall short of the glory of God.

We *all* fall short.

The rest of this passage in Romans proclaims that we receive the grace of God anyway. In spite of our voting record. In spite of the large gap on our resume. In spite of our snappishness with our family. In spite of our snappishness with strangers. In spite of our unrealized dreams. In spite of all of our views, voiced and unvoiced, about Those People.

We fall short. So do they.

We receive. So do they.

This is the outrageous truth of the gospel. *Even Those People.* (And we *are* Those People.) We all fall short, and we all receive the unmerited, undeserved, unearned glory of God through grace and forgiveness.

— *Carrie Willard*

November 5

"Now therefore, if you obey my voice and keep my covenant,
you shall be my treasured possession out of all the peoples.
Indeed, the whole earth is mine, but you shall be for me a
priestly kingdom and a holy nation." (Exodus 19:5-6)

Adam's bride was made from a rib, but God made his own bride from a heel.
The Lord's bride was Israel, named after Israel the person, who started out
life with the name *Ya'akov*. We spell it Jacob, and it means "heel."

Now we can probably all agree that eyes can be pretty, legs attractive,
and ears cute. But a heel? That never ranks as an attractive part of the anatomy. It's quite literally the lowest part of the body. It gets dirty. It gets flat.
It gets smelly. No man marries a woman because he's smitten by her heel.

But God's no ordinary kind of lover. In fact, he cares not one iota for
Israel's ranking in a beauty pageant. The Almighty wasn't ogling the nations,
on the lookout for a voluptuous trophy wife. He chose Israel not because
she was more numerous or powerful or swankier than other nations, but
simply because he loved her.

An amazing transformation happens, however, to the object of God's
grace. That which he loves becomes lovely. A beast becomes a beauty, an
ugly heel a gorgeous face. So, at the foot of Sinai, this ragtag band of escaped
slaves, congenitally cantankerous, prone to fits of rebellion, becomes by virtue of God's gracious decree a "treasured possession...a priestly kingdom
and a holy nation."

It's no different with each of us, and with the church. We're all just a
bunch of Jacobs, a human collective of heels. But we have a God who has
been known to get down on his knees to wash feet. To scrub heels clean of
filth. And—by the touch of his hand, by the washing of his word, by the
merciful acceptance of all—to transform us into his prized possession, regal
priests, who make up the resplendent bride of Christ.

— *Chad Bird*

November 6

"Indeed, God did not send the Son into the world to condemn the world, but in order that the world might be saved through him." (John 3:17)

For every aggressive citation of John 3:16 should come an equally aggressive retort of John 3:17. Okay, maybe not too aggressive. But the two verses are intimately connected. They need each other. Together they provide the blueprint for God's saving work in the world—the good news for people desperate for good news and exhausted by condemnation.

We experience so much condemnation in our everyday lives, but interestingly, that word is almost exclusively used in a religious context (at least according to Google searches in the past decade). But today, even in secular settings, you can be banished by your knitting group for not holding the same values, or "canceled" for tweets decades old, or cast out from your book club for allowing your kids to eat fruit snacks with red dye 40. In such a context, the promise of a world without condemnation is a powerful thing.

Condemnation is often capricious. But we also know that there is something in all of us—somewhere, well hidden—that probably deserves condemnation. The last thing any of us want is to brandish a bright red letter associated with our condemnable offense. (This is why Google invented "safe search.")

So when we read that the Son of God—the only person rightly able to condemn any and all of us at the same time—won't be bringing condemnation but salvation, we are dumbstruck. And into this confusion and uncertainty and almost too-good-to-be-true promise, we are confronted with God's plan for us—a plan of love and hope, grace and mercy.

Because God is coming to save. God has come to save. God has saved.

The point isn't boxing out, but drawing in. Today, may you be drawn into the beautiful promise of a God who offers grace to the guilty, forgiveness to sinners, and absolution for the condemned.

— *Ben Maddison*

November 7

All scripture is inspired by God and is useful for teaching,
for reproof, for correction, and for training in righteousness... (2 Timothy 3:16)

In scripture, God makes it known that it is His voice you are hearing. "Listen
to me! Hello? This is God speaking." When other voices in the world and
in your head sound jumbled and contradictory, God speaks a direct word
of hope and comfort into your life.

Of course, because of our tendency to misinterpret things, simply reading the text is not all that's required. As Thornton Wilder writes in the play
Our Town, "Wherever you come near the human race, there's layers and
layers of nonsense." You see, in order to get through to us, God illuminates
the Word through the Holy Spirit. As we read, we depend on the Spirit
to perform surgery on us, to take out a heart of stone and put in a heart of
flesh. The Spirit—God's breath—is what brings any sort of clarity as to
what God is saying.

The Bible is not a book of theory. And it is different from the Qur'an,
dictated directly by God. It is also different from the Book of Mormon,
communicated through the ministration of an angel. Much of the New Testament is made up of people's letters to each other. But God breathed into
these words so that they would reveal His Word. Because of that, these writ-
ings contain the core message of Christianity. Because scripture is inspired
by God Himself, it is authoritative.

Whenever you are confused, you not only can trust that God is true to
His word, but you can count on Him to make sure the message gets delivered—in fact, the message has already been delivered, over 2,000 years ago,
in the life and words of Jesus Christ. And even though we "received Him
not," He receives us always. Take heart, then, that God's Word does not
wait on your own understanding. Instead, it breaks into your life according
to His perfect timing, not on your terms, but on God's.

— *Sam Bush*

November 8

For we do not have a high priest who is unable to sympathize with our weaknesses, but one who in every respect
has been tempted as we are, yet without sin. (Hebrews
4:15 ESV)

What other religion can claim that their God can sympathize with the human
experience "in every respect"? Or that he's far more than a lofty, mysterious
being in the sky, pulling our strings?

Christians claim a Savior who walked this earth with flesh and bone: He
got tired and hungry, bored and angry, and even had sore muscles and ach-
ing feet from walking everywhere. Jesus does not have a merely hypothetical
understanding of life in this dark world. As *The Message* puts it, he's not
"out of touch with our reality." Instead, he walked before us, encountering
all of our temptations head-on and with absolute perfection.

His humanity makes our relationship and union with Him that much
more personal. He didn't come to Earth and skate through life unscathed,
but he suffered—rejection, betrayal, the death of a best friend, and ultimately his own painful death. So although he lived 2,000 years ago, "there
is nothing new under the sun" (Ecc 1:9), and Jesus faced the same trials that
we do. They might take on a slightly different form now, but the same pain
is still there. Jesus understands those feelings on an intimate level, and as
our High Priest, he can bring all of this directly to the Father.

Having lived "without sin," Jesus went to the cross, taking on our sin
and shame. He opened up a way for us to walk in his footsteps, stumbling
though we may be, but nevertheless covered in his righteousness. We now
can approach God's throne with confidence (v. 16), not hiding our faces or
cowering in the corner, but boldly receiving God's grace, mercy, forgiveness, and love.

— *Margaret Pope*

November 9

And they heard the sound of the LORD God walking in the garden in the cool of the day, and the man and his wife hid themselves from the presence of the LORD God among the trees of the garden. (Genesis 3:8 RSV)

Why does the presence of God inspire such fear in people? Why does the *Church* inspire 'fight or flight' feelings in so many people?

The simple answer is that we have an overwhelming allergy to judgment. We are programmed to run in exactly the opposite direction from *any* degree of judgment.

This is a sorry element in the human makeup, because it stonewalls and stymies amendment of life. Something inside us just instantly congeals and hardens in the presence of…let's call it…criticism.

Similarly, adulation, or just plain praise, causes people to flower and grow. Kind, graceful words, especially from a valued 'other,' are the literal difference between growth and stuntedness in human development.

What Adam and Eve can't realize—and they never do—is that God is not a Being of wrath, He is a Being of mercy.

There is a memorable scene in *The Green Pastures*, which is a play from 1930 with an all African-American cast, in which "De Lawd" discovers, within Himself(!), the characteristic of *mercy*. This divine discovery, which occurs towards the end of the play, is the first cause of the gospel, and the plot element by which the play pivots to the New Testament.

Adam and Eve never found out—I think they know now—that they had misconceived their Author. He is not the 'Hunter and Collector' God of the forest, but the 'Finder and Keeper' God of the plain. Where the rain stays! (Lerner & Loewe, 1956)

— *Paul Zahl*

November 10

> Bless the LORD, O my soul,
> and do not forget all his benefits (Psalm 103:2)

"Count your blessings" is not good news to me. I can't *not* focus on the one thing or the several petty things that are wrong with me, wrong with my neighbor, wrong with the world, wrong with the church, etc. I am perpetually doomed to fear missing out, to fear not being in the know, to fear looking stupid, to fear being left out or forgotten.

I know that God has given me many blessings. He's given me life, strength, health, a wonderful family. Most importantly, He's forgiven my sins and made me His child, but still, I want more.

I'm just like the first sinners, Adam and Eve, who, though they had God Himself in their very midst, though they had every material, physical, emotional need provided, they still wanted the fruit of that one tree they couldn't have. Like them, I keep forgetting the "benefits" I already have and remembering the things I still want, the places where life isn't working out the way I expected.

In contrast to the forbidden tree, there's a better tree, a *cursed* tree, that strangely offers blessings forever and "healing for the nations" (Rev 22:2). Along with the gift of the Holy Spirit, grace gives us God's redemptive benefits despite our memories. He breathed into Adam the breath of life; and through our hearing of the gospel (again and again and again), He breathes into us the One who is the resurrection and the life.

The essence of sin is that I can't remember God's goodness. The glory of grace is that He can't remember my sin.

— *Jason Thompson*

November 11

> Then they laid hands on [Jesus] and arrested him. But one
> of those who stood near drew his sword and struck the
> slave of the high priest, cutting off his ear. Then Jesus said
> to them, "Have you come out with swords and clubs to
> arrest me as though I were a bandit?" (Mark 14:46-48)

We live in a world where power and violence are the ironic standards by which peace and justice are achieved; it is a "dog-eat-dog" world. You can see this in partisan politics, foreign policies, familial and relational dynamics, neighborhood violence, the justice system, etc.

Adding to all that, many of us are increasingly depressed, anxious, tired, and cynical. We find ourselves feeling hopeless that anything will ever change. Will our individual acts of forgiveness ever be enough? In a sense, the answer is no; we are not capable of enacting the tit-for-tat restoration of the world. However, it is not a hopeless "no."

After praying in Gethsemane, Jesus and his disciples head to a valley where Judas will betray him. Judas brings soldiers, police, priests, and Pharisees to arrest Jesus. As the arrest takes place, Simon Peter draws his sword and cuts the ear off of the high priest's slave, Malchus (Jn 18:10).

Jesus scolds his disciple for using violence and claims that he is more than capable of calling in legions of angels to his defense (Mt 26:53). Then, he heals Malchus' ear in front of everyone, as if to show that he is indeed capable. But no legions of angels are called upon. Jesus knows that an angel rescue squad will not get the job done.

In an act of seemingly utter foolishness, he hands himself over to be arrested and ultimately crucified for all—for the betrayers and the oppressors, the defenders and protectors, and especially for the oppressed. Later on the cross, Jesus proclaims that his death is enough. And it is in Jesus' "It is finished" that we can find our rest and hope. As we continue striving for peace and justice, we know that, thanks be to Jesus, all manner of things shall ultimately be well.

— *Bryant Trinh*

November 12

I appeal to you therefore, brothers and sisters, by the mercies of God, to present your bodies as a living sacrifice, holy and acceptable to God, which is your spiritual worship. (Romans 12:1)

This appeal from Paul in Romans is sometimes used in devotions or sermons to make the point that we need to take care of our bodies. The emphasis is on being holy and acceptable to God, insinuating that we should exercise, eat healthy, not get tattoos, and generally use our bodies "for good." But this interpretation misses the depth and mystery of the phrase "living sacrifice," which is in itself an oxymoron. How can we be both sacrificed (killed) and alive?

In ancient Israel, when an animal was sacrificed to God, there was no getting it back after it was burned on the altar. It was a substitute which atoned for the sin of the people, the ones who actually deserved that death. In other words, there was no such thing as a "living sacrifice." You were either the sacrifice (the animal) or the living (the people).

However, Jesus Christ changed all of that. He became the first living sacrifice. He died and is now alive. He invites us to follow him in his death and resurrection. Does that mean we have to wait for our own deaths to be living sacrifices? No, Paul is talking to us in the here and now. He explains how we are simultaneously dead and alive when he says, "Do you not know that all of us who have been baptized into Christ Jesus were baptized into his death? Therefore we have been buried with him by baptism into death, so that, just as Christ was raised from the dead by the glory of the Father, so we too might walk in newness of life" (Rm 6:3-4).

We died in the waters of baptism. Dead to sin, alive in Christ. In baptism (not in taking care of our bodies), God sets us apart and makes us holy and acceptable. To live as a sacrifice is really not possible, but in Christ, the impossible is made real.

— *Juliette Alvey*

November 13

> For the lips of a priest should guard knowledge, and people should seek instruction from his mouth, for he is the messenger of the LORD of hosts. But you have turned aside from the way; you have caused many to stumble by your instruction; you have corrupted the covenant of Levi, says the LORD of hosts, and so I make you despised and abased before all the people... (Malachi 2:7-9)

Corrupt clergy is no little thing. It can cause people not only to stumble in their faith, but to resent and loathe the God whom the clergy supposedly represent. C. S. Lewis illustrated the ramifications of clerical abuse in the seventh and final book of his Chronicles of Narnia series, *The Last Battle*. A donkey named Puzzle disguises himself as the Christ figure, the lion named Aslan. Many Narnians are duped, and when the ruse is finally discovered, many Narnians lose interest in the real Aslan, or even begin to hate him.

Malachi contrasts the corrupt clergy of his day with the ideal priest embodied in the father of the Jewish priesthood, Levi. The only problem with this comparison is that Levi, in Genesis 34, vengefully slaughters the people of Shechem. The crime is so brutal that it turns the people of Shechem away from God. And in 1 Kings 12, Shechem is the site where the dastardly King Rehoboam leads astray ten of the twelves tribes of Israel and establishes what became known as Samaria.

For Malachi, the ideal priest is the messenger of the Lord; people should seek instruction from him. Therefore, Malachi's prophecy looks forward to another priest, one whose work would be the foundation of a new covenant of life.

In John 4, this priest would go through the country of Samaria and in the town of Shechem engage a Samaritan woman at a well. Profoundly moved by her encounter with Jesus, this woman would invite him to come to Shechem, and instead of being slaughtered, the whole village would finally proclaim, "[W]e have heard for ourselves, and we know that this is truly the Savior of the world" (Jn 4:42).

— *Jacob Smith*

November 14

Who has believed what we have heard?
   And to whom has the arm of the LORD been revealed?
For he grew up before him like a young plant,
   and like a root out of dry ground;
he had no form or majesty that we should look at him,
   nothing in his appearance that we should desire him.
He was despised and rejected by others;
   a man of suffering and acquainted with infirmity;
and as one from whom others hide their faces
   he was despised, and we held him of no account.
   (Isaiah 53:1-3)

It is a miracle that we have ever heard the name Jesus of Nazareth. Here is a man who never had any money, or held any political office, who never wrote a book or led an army, who never even had children (sorry, Dan Brown). Jesus carried out a relatively unremarkable three-year public ministry in a backwater locale and died a humiliating criminal death, utterly alone and abandoned. As he hung on the cross—naked, mocked and spat upon—Jesus' closest friends and followers were tripping over themselves to deny that they had ever heard of him.

And yet, as H. G. Wells said, "I am an historian, I am not a believer, but I must confess as an historian that this penniless preacher from Nazareth is irrevocably the very center of history. Jesus Christ is easily the most dominant figure in all history."

How did this happen? There is only one possible explanation. As Isaiah 53:11 says, "Out of his anguish he shall see light." Death was not the end for Jesus. If it was, we would never have heard his name. The Resurrection is the only explanation for the worldwide Christian movement.

Jesus lived and died and rose again. It is all true. We are forgiven, accepted, and bound for glory. And someday, we will see Him face-to-face. Praise be to God.

— R-J Heijmen

November 15

I am astonished that you are so quickly deserting the one
who called you in the grace of Christ and are turning to a
different gospel—not that there is another gospel, but there
are some who are confusing you and want to pervert the
gospel of Christ. But even if we or an angel from heaven
should proclaim to you a gospel contrary to what we proclaimed to you, let that one be accursed! (Galatians 1:6-8)

The Letter to the Galatians is proof that deep down, despite what we sing and say on Sundays, we're addicted to bad news. Like a lot of Christians today, the Galatians assumed they had advanced beyond needing to hear the gospel of Christ.

In taking the gospel for granted, they'd reverted back to the law. There is no middle ground at all between "Christ has done everything for you" and "This is what you must do." The easiest way to invalidate the gospel is to add to it. The way to annul the unconditional promise of the gospel is to add obligation to it. A common way we replicate the Galatians' error is by adding modifiers: *progressive* Christian, *conservative* Christian, *social justice* Christian, *family values* Christian, *inclusive* Christian, *traditional* Christian.

The gospel message is not "Be all you can be." You don't need to die to self or do anything, because the promise of the gospel is that you have already died with Christ. You have been crucified with him for all your sins. All of you, warts and all, is in him. You don't need to become anyone else.

If what makes God holy is God's ability to make and keep an uncon-ditional promise, then what makes us holy is how we relate to God's unconditional promise. Holiness is not about behavior. Holiness is about belief—trust—in the promise of God. Holiness is not about being good or doing good. Holiness is about trusting the good work God has done for you in Jesus Christ. The unconditional promise we call the gospel. If holiness is about trust—faith—then the opposite of vice is not virtue, and the opposite of sin is not sinlessness. The opposite of vice, and sin, is *faith*.

— *Jason Micheli*

November 16

Those of steadfast mind you keep in peace—
in peace because they trust in you. (Isaiah 26:3)

As an anxiety sufferer, my struggles have run the gamut from conventional worry to throat-constricting breathlessness, and I have always been confounded by Bible verses about "peace." To me, peace was a promised-yet-unattainable gift, a virtue bequeathed but never fully realized. At some point, I had to accept that this could be a situation like the one voiced by Inigo Montoya to Vizzini in *The Princess Bride*: I kept using that word, but it might not mean what I thought it meant.

Francis Frangipane said that "rescue is the constant pattern of God's activity," and we see this principle at play throughout the life of Jesus, from his calming of the waves, to his death on the cross. We also see this in the Old Testament, when the Israelites cross the Red Sea, and Daniel is rescued from the lions, and Jonah is vomited from the whale. All of these stories are ready-made for Sunday school and victorious retellings, but we are more comfortable with the endpoint—smooth water, dry land—than we are the period just before.

I would argue that "the period before" constitutes the bulk of our lives.

Some translations of this verse from Isaiah call the peace God gives *perfect*, and Jesus himself says in John 14:27, "Peace I leave with you; my peace I give to you. I do not give to you as the world gives," implying a difference between how the Almighty regards peace and how the rest of creation does. If the peace he gives is perfect, then it seems to me that the peace he gives must be *himself*.

So much of what I regard as peace is actually just an *outcome*: a specific form of rescue, a wish granted, a prayer answered with "Sure! What a great idea! I *will* give you that dream house!" And specific outcomes can be all too easily tied to my own efforts in attaining them. But rescue, like being born, takes no input from me—I am lost at sea, in the darkness of the whale, in the fire of the furnace. Rescue is accomplished *for* me.

This is why true peace can only be a gift, and why it ultimately amounts to the presence of Jesus with us in "the period before"—and every one after. True peace transcends feelings like settledness or nervousness. It sits beside us, it carries us, it rescues us by being *with* us. And it never, ever leaves.

— *Stephanie Phillips*

357

November 17

A Samaritan woman came to draw water, and Jesus said to
her, "Give me a drink." (His disciples had gone to the city
to buy food.) The Samaritan woman said to him, "How is
it that you, a Jew, ask a drink of me, a woman of Samaria?"
(Jews do not share things in common with Samaritans.)
(John 4:7-9)

In highfalutin theological conversations, people will often debate the exact
moment when the church began. Was it in Acts? The calling of Paul or
Peter? Maybe even the baptism of Jesus? There's only one answer to this
question for me, but it is not the official answer. So you would do well to
never quote it.

I believe that the beginning of the church was the woman at the well.
Think about it. Jesus reaches across the chasms of gender and ethnic norms.
He knows about her entire horribly hard life and yet listens to her talk about
it. And then he offers her forgiveness and salvation without her even asking
for it. And she runs to her friends and says, "Come and see a man who told
me everything I have ever done!" (v. 29).

If this is not the beginning of the church, then it is certainly a model
for what the church should look like. We should reach out to people who
we would not normally risk relationship with. We often read this text and
immediately think of people who are not as privileged as we are. That's great.
But also, this is the kingdom of heaven. Think a little bigger.

God may be calling us to reach out to people who are poorer *or richer*.
They may not speak our language or they may be a lady at the PTA that
we think talks too much. And then we listen to them. Which is hard and
time-consuming. And then we say, "Yeah, same." Which is even harder and
might take up more time. And then, deep breath, maybe we invite these
people to church. Not because our church needs to grow or because our
pastor told us to. But because we believe that Jesus has done this for all of
us. Against all odds, he has begun the church in all of our hearts. And we
cannot help but share this good news with others.

— *Sarah Condon*

November 18

Rejoice with those who rejoice, weep with those who weep.
(Romans 12:15)

It sounds easy enough, right? A reliable model for Christian ministry if ever there was one. Unfortunately, we almost always do the opposite.

We mourn with those who are wanting to rejoice. "That's great you got a new job... *But does it have benefits?*" Or we rejoice with those who are mourning. "Don't feel bad about the break-up; there are plenty of fish in the sea," is the classic iteration. We believers have our own versions, such as "When God closes a door, he opens a window." Ugh.

When we invert Paul's words, we learn something about the difference between "helping" and just listening.

There's nothing bad about helping. We all need help, pretty much all the time. The problem is that helping is often received as judgment. It doesn't, er, help.

A 2011 survey on grief found that any attempt to "fix" or diminish someone's loss by offering a platitude, giving advice, or even sharing one's own experience counterproductively communicated to the mourning party that their grief is bad and needs to be "gotten through" as effectively and quickly as possible. Which only makes the griever more self-conscious and overwhelmed and sad.

There's a beautiful scene in the television drama *Friday Night Lights*, a show about a football team in a small Texas town. Former quarterback Matt Saracen learns that his strict, distant father has died while serving in Iraq. Later that day, over dinner at his coach's house, he falls apart and confesses, "I hate him. And I don't like hating people. But I just put all my hate on him so I don't have to hate anybody else... I just want to tell him to his face that I hate him. But I'll never have that chance now." He then runs out the door.

Coach Taylor goes after him, and soon catches up. After a few moments of silence, Coach says, "I'm going to walk you home." He doesn't ask permission or equivocate. He makes no attempt to plaster over Matt's grief with his own wisdom. Instead, he puts his arm around the grieving young man and walks with him. Coach Taylor is simply there, in the absolute worst moment, and that's enough.

God isn't here today to blunt your good news with fine print, or to slap a spiritual smiley face on your pain. Whatever you're going through, he's here to walk you home.

— *David Zahl*

"Hey king of Assyria! Your shepherds are asleep
  and your nobles are lying down!
Your people lie scattered on the mountains,
  and there is no one to gather them together.
There is no healing for your injury—
  your wound is fatal.
Everyone who hears about you will applaud,
  because who hasn't escaped your endless evil?"
(Nahum 3:18-19 ISV)

Who doesn't like to see the bad guys get their comeuppance? It's one of the most satisfying parts of a story's conclusion. If you've seen the film *Die Hard*, you know that watching professional thief Hans Gruber fall from the Nakatomi Tower is one of the film's most cathartic moments. Or maybe you felt a deep sense of relief when, in the movie *Gladiator*, the disgraced general Maximus finally kills the wicked emperor Commodus before succumbing to his own wounds. Nothing sells books, movie tickets, or TV ads like just desserts.

The prophet Nahum has a similar word for the Assyrian Empire. God proclaims through the prophet that the end is near for this once-great empire. The ancient Assyrians were known for their use of extreme violence and gratuitous bloodshed. The Bible and other historical sources are in agreement that the Assyrians went beyond R-rated violence, and their subjugating practices were at least brutal, at most wicked. Truly, the Assyrians are among the Old Testament's baddest bad guys.

And yet, the words of Nahum should not be read apart from the prophetic words from two books prior. The prophet Jonah is best known for his brief stint as fish food, but his ministry of repentance was to the same empire that Nahum condemns. It says something about God that Jonah's call to preach repentance to the Assyrian Empire comes before Nahum's declaration of judgment. Calling villains to repent? Hans Gruber surrendering to the police? Commodus resigning as emperor? Forgiveness and repentance just don't sell the same kind of movie tickets.

This is a key difference between humans and God. Humans love when bad guys get what they deserve. God offers bad guys, even the worst of the worst, a chance to repent. At the end of the day, that's good news. When we play the bad guy in our own lives, may we remember that God's love is for everyone, including villains.

— *Bryan Jarrell*

November 20

Only Luke is with me. Get Mark and bring him with you,
for he is useful in my ministry. (2 Timothy 4:11)

On the surface, this seems like such a throwaway verse. But in fact this verse has a great backstory.

Back in Acts 13, when Paul and Barnabas set off from Antioch on Paul's first missionary journey, Barnabas had selected his young cousin Mark to tag along, presumably as an assistant or apprentice. Their mission began on the pagan-dominated island of Cyprus, a visit that culminated in a showdown in the town of Paphos. According to local Cypriot tradition, it was in Paphos that Paul received perhaps his first lashing, likely at the behest of Elymas. My family lived on that storied island when I was in elementary school and I still vividly remember the heavily-worn marble pillar where locals say Paul was strung up and whipped. It's the kind of image you don't forget.

After departing Paphos, Mark mysteriously bolts and returns prematurely to Jerusalem. Was he sick, homesick, exhausted? Or just scared? The text gives no answer, but given the hardships Paul faced throughout his ministry, it's easy to see why young Mark might bail. Later, in Acts 15, Paul is unwilling to forgive Mark for having "deserted them" (v. 38). The dispute over Mark becomes "so sharp" that Paul and Barnabas part company over it, a sad moment of disunion in the early history of the church.

And yet here in 2 Timothy, in spite of everything, we find Paul in need and sending for Mark, even admitting that Mark has been "useful in my ministry." It seems Paul is now ready to forgive and admit he has been wrong about Mark, who the Bible tells us elsewhere, continued to serve with Barnabas and was later like a "son" to Peter (1 Pt 5:13). According to tradition, this is the same Mark that eventually authored the first of the Gospels and is credited as the founder of the Coptic Church in Egypt, where they even believe—despite Mark's early squeamishness—that he died a martyr, being dragged to death by an angry mob.

If I'm being honest, I love this verse most for the *schadenfreude*: It's nice to see the great Apostle Paul have to eat a little crow by requesting help from someone he'd written off. But the story also gives us all a warm reminder not to give up on people, and that even if we do, God never does.

— *Benjamin Self*

"You that are simple, turn in here!"
    To those without sense she says,
"Come, eat of my bread
    and drink of the wine I have mixed." (Proverbs 9:4-5)

Throughout the Gospels, Jesus fasts a lot, but he also feasts, and his meals are often the more important scenes. In Luke, food bookends his whole life: He's born in a feeding trough (as if he were food). Before he dies, he tells us to keep having his last supper, until the world ends. And after he comes back from the dead, he reveals himself "in the breaking of the bread," as proof that he is still a bodily person. Clearly, God likes food. And wine, too! Because God loves creation. A feast agrees with God: "What God has made clean, you must not call profane" (Acts 10:15). In Jesus, everything is clean.

In another scene from Luke, Jesus talks about himself and his cousin, John the Baptist. The critics said John was too ascetic, too puritanical. But when Jesus comes around, they shame him: "Look, a glutton and a drunk-ard, a friend of tax collectors and sinners!" They've set up a catch-22. Jesus replies, in typical perplexing fashion, "wisdom is vindicated by all her chil-dren" (Lk 7:33-35).

Jesus means he is Wisdom, a strange figure who appears in Proverbs. She (Wisdom) wants to save people from the dangers of foolishness. But she's not a self-help guru or a moralist. She's a cosmic builder: "When he"—the LORD—"established the heavens, I was there." She's God's delight, and she wants everyone to feel that joy (Prov 8-9).

One of Wisdom's main aims is to keep us off the streets and out of Fol-ly's house, where "bread eaten in secret" leads to death. Proverbs introduces Wisdom and Folly, a wise, moral woman and a foolish, promiscuous woman, as obvious foils. When Jesus rolls around, he accepts that pairing, but he flips it. No longer are fools and sinners outside God's party. Because Jesus is the friend of everyone who can't earn their way in, his only foils are the Pharisees, the ones who pretend they can earn it with their own wisdom.

When Jesus defends his strange behavior, he tells the crowd, "blessed is anyone who takes no offense at me" (Mt 11:6), because he's a scandal. St. Paul said that the cross was impotence and idiocy to humans, but to God, clearheadedness and might (1 Cor 1:25). Jesus didn't do wrong, but he endured humiliation and incrimination so that he could get on our level, in all our secret selfishness and vagrant desire. He welcomes us where we are, even when we're in Folly's house.

— *Kendall Gunter*

November 22

Sing, O barren one who did not bear;
   burst into song and shout,
   you who have not been in labor!
For the children of the desolate woman will be more
   than the children of her that is married, says the LORD.
Enlarge the site of your tent,
   and let the curtains of your habitations be stretched out;
   do not hold back; lengthen your cords
   and strengthen your stakes.
For you will spread out to the right and to the left,
   and your descendants will possess the nations
   and will settle the desolate towns. (Isaiah 54:1-3)

You've known those people who, like cats, seem to have at least nine lives. They've survived illnesses and accidents and really toxic relationships, and they are, miraculously, still standing. The Israel that Isaiah addresses here is like that cat—possessing, at the very least, four lives.

- She is the barren woman of the exile in Babylon, fearing that Israel's family tree is in danger of being uprooted (v. 1).
- She is the widowed woman of that same exile, feeling at times like God, her husband, has died (v. 4).
- She is the momentarily deserted wife (vv. 6-7), whom God walked out on in anger over her flagrant unfaithfulness.

Yet somehow, in God's plan, Isaiah prophesies that all those past and tragic lives will be swallowed up in a new "covenant of peace" (v. 10). And her new identity will be that of the reunited wife of God and beloved mother of God's growing brood. In fact, verse 2 suggests that she will need to keep patching that tent, keep widening those stakes in all directions, in order to hold all the children God will bring into her home.

I don't know you, so I don't know how many lives you've had nor which life you are currently living. I do pray, however, that God's presence in your life will enlarge your tent to shelter an ever-widening future.

— Larry Parsley

November 23

For if we have been united with him in a death like his, we
will certainly be united with him in a resurrection like his.
We know that our old self was crucified with him so that
the body of sin might be destroyed, and we might no longer
be enslaved to sin. For whoever has died is freed from sin.
But if we have died with Christ, we believe that we will
also live with him. (Romans 6:5-8)

We drown babies.

I've been trying to convince someone to let me say that during a baptism sermon, in all seriousness, since the realization struck me. But my
long-suffering wife, probably rightly, always says I've gone "too hard" when
I bring it up. "Dial it back, man, you're gonna scare people."

But in my tradition, we do baptize infants. And the waters of baptism
and the death of Christ are inseparable. With Christ, we die (are drowned)
and are buried (stay under the water), and are raised to new life (soaking
wet, usually crying, and promptly returned to our parents).

So yes, especially if you're an infant, it might be scary to be baptized
into the death of Christ, but look at what Paul says is the benefit. To die
with Christ is to rise with Christ—a new creation, a child of God, a person
redeemed and saved by Christ himself.

But it's even more than that. When we die with Christ, we die to sin
as Christ died to it—overcoming it on our behalf. This is no mere empty
hope. Contrary to what you might infer from the walking-corpse-filled pantheon of *Living Dead* films, the dead can't sin. That's the reality and release
of the grave. It's a release that comes while submerged in those waters of
baptism—in that dying with Christ.

But in Christ, the dead don't stay dead—we live. Though still sinners,
we live lives free from sin. Forgiven before it even happens. Forgiven and
free from trying to absolve or justify ourselves. What we find instead is
hope in a life that isn't ours and a freedom that is given, not claimed.

So maybe there's a better way to put it—but if you haven't been
drowned yet with Jesus, you might want to be, ASAP.

— *Ben Maddison*

November 24

For the kingdom of God is not food and drink but righteousness and peace and joy in the Holy Spirit. The one
who thus serves Christ is acceptable to God and has human
approval. Let us then pursue what makes for peace and for
mutual upbuilding. (Romans 14:17-19)

Friends have told me that there is a guy who lives in our town who looks
exactly like me. They've even mistakenly said hello to the guy. I've never
met him, but odds are, when I do inevitably meet this mysterious doppel-
gänger, I probably will not like what I see. This is because, in my experience,
the people I judge most are the ones most like me.

Doppelgängers of all kinds—who share our looks, tastes, hometown,
or anything else—are God-given bridges to connection, but we have the
innate capacity to dislike them. Freud called this the "narcissism of small
differences," the tendency to disregard the 148 things you have in common
with someone to highlight instead the one "important" difference that makes
them some kind of "other." This difference may be imperceptible to most,
but it helps you preserve your fragile sense of superiority.

The same thing is going on here with the fine churchgoers in Rome
who, according to St. Paul, have begun quibbling over minor details. The
major details have been settled by Jesus himself, and Paul has the audacity
to tell each of them to leave the rest alone and turn to God. We'd do well
to do the same.

*Lord, help us discern the line between what is important and
what isn't, what is in your hands and what is in ours. Help us to
see that whenever we draw dividing lines between those who stand
righteous and those who don't, you are there, standing on the side
opposite us. Help us to cross the bridge in faith to where you are.*

— Ethan Richardson

November 25

I am about to do a new thing;
>   now it springs forth, do you not perceive it?
I will make a way in the wilderness
>   and rivers in the desert. (Isaiah 43:19)

Have you ever heard of neuroplasticity? Neuroplasticity refers to the brain's capacity to rewire itself. For instance, in the case of childhood trauma, under the right conditions the brain is eventually able to alleviate the behavioral and emotional problems caused by the original damage. The brain literally makes a new pathway, from darkness and pain toward wholeness and healing. I don't know about you, but that sounds a lot like a divine redemptive plan that was written into our biology. Where darkness would reign, God designed our bodies with the ability to change the script. And of course, Jesus is the ultimate New Way, the final Rewiring of a world gone wrong.

The above passage from Isaiah brims with this hope. Here we catch a glimpse of the thread of Jesus that runs all the way from Genesis to Revelation. In the same moment that sin enters the world, God promises that he will one day overcome it (Gen 3:15). *Jesus.* In Genesis 6, after the flood and with a rainbow as his backdrop, God tells Noah that instead of again destroying mankind because of their wicked hearts, he will do a new thing, he will make a new way, he will give them life abundant. *Jesus.* This same living water winds its way—like a fresh neural pathway—through every book of the Bible, through the hearts of every one of its broken and sinful characters, and it springs forth in every chapter of our own stories.

Dear one, whether or not you perceive it, Jesus is redeeming and rewiring the busted and broken and impossible circuits of your life. Can you look back at your most terrible minutes, and imagine Jesus beside you, whispering truth and love into your ear? What would he speak into your condemnation? What would he speak into your loneliness? What would he speak into your abandonment, fear, failure, or shame? Your worst mistake?

For me, it's something like this: "I am right here; I have always been right here; you are safe in me, hidden in me, and I love you completely."

— *Charlotte Getz*

November 26

> "Jerusalem, Jerusalem, you who kill the prophets and stone those sent to you, how often I have longed to gather your children together, as a hen gathers her chicks under her wings, and you were not willing." (Luke 13:34 NIV)

In terms of animal imagery, Jesus tends to find the most hopeless, aimless animals to tell us who we are. Sheep, as any shepherd can tell you, are not particularly bright. They wander off. They get things stuck on their heads. They are vulnerable and dim. Chickens, for all of their yard bird charm, are downright mean to each other. In the 21st century, we think of these animals as bucolic characters in a farmland bedtime story, baking bread and griping that nobody helped them (The Little Red Put-Upon Hen) or leaping across fences to lull us to sleep. We feature them in mattress commercials and decorate baby nurseries with fluffy, clean versions of these barnyard friends, but deep down, we know that if an actual sheep entered our house, there would have to be a steam cleaner involved at some point.

In Jesus' time, though, when at least one baby was *actually* born among farm critters, there weren't likely any illusions about the livestock that lived among them. Jerusalem, whose people were killing prophets and stoning those sent to help them, wasn't quite ready for a self-sufficient life in the wild. And Jesus doesn't tell the people that he wants to straighten them out, or that he expects better of them. He longs to gather them under his wing. He longs to protect us with the instinct of a mother hen.

For all of their less flattering characteristics, mother hens are notable for protecting their young. They have been known to fight off other animals to protect their chicks, and they have even sacrificed their own lives in the face of extreme danger (like fires), keeping the chicks safe even when they could not save themselves. God longs to pull us under his wings, not like a loud and boastful rooster, but like a mother hen. God longs to protect us from danger, and from our own self-destructive baby-bird-ness. And God's desire to protect us from ourselves, of course, extends to the destruction we may cause for others, with literal or virtual stoning. God's love embraces and protects those in destruction's path, even, or more likely especially, when those perpetrating violence are not willing to be gathered under God's wing.

— *Carrie Willard*

November 27

> And you he made alive, when you were dead through the
> trespasses and sins in which you once walked, following
> the course of this world, following the prince of the power
> of the air, the spirit that is now at work in the sons of dis-
> obedience. (Ephesians 2:1-2 RSV)

For a long time I was skeptical of the term "spiritual warfare." The people
who talked about spiritual warfare seemed flakey, and at times hysterical.
Moreover, the people I knew who swore by it didn't seem to get better!
They just—as I saw it—got more hysterical, sometimes delusional.

I no longer think that way. It's not that 'the crazies' have changed. It's
just that *I* have been confronted by some things in myself that are inexplicable without reference to "principalities" and "powers" (6:12 RSV).

Many problems with which you and I wrestle can be 'brought down' by
good therapy or solid medical care. Many problems can be diminished by
the sheer power of love, especially unconditional love. But not all of them.
Some problems with which we contend—well, it's as if they are unassailable
and insuperable. You might be contending with one of those today: your
unconquerable antagonist, your unbearable counterweight.

In *that* case, this verse is for you. "And you he made alive, when you
were dead." God can handle your one insurmountable grievance, your one
unstanchable wound.

— *Paul Zahl*

November 28

But now thus says the LORD,
  he who created you, O Jacob,
  he who formed you, O Israel:
Do not fear, for I have redeemed you;
  I have called you by name, you are mine.
When you pass through the waters, I will be with you;
  and through the rivers, they shall not overwhelm you;
when you walk through fire you shall not be burned,
  and the flame shall not consume you. (Isaiah 43:1-2)

When I read this text, I am transported back to a moment in my life when I was standing in a mall, with snot running down my face, weeping into a telephone. I had just seen the movie *The Firm*, about a lawyer whose wife was so angry with his behavior that she had thrown a wine bottle at his head. This is what made me cry—that the wife could get angry; that it was acceptable for her to get angry.

At the time, I was separated from my husband of 11 years due to his alcoholism. On the other end of the phone was my new pastor, Mary. I couldn't articulate my problem because I didn't know what it was specifically, except that I had unexpressed anger. But she identified the core issue with this scripture from Isaiah. If God cared about what was going on in my life, why was it such a mess? My fear was based on the uncertainty of the moment.

Mary assured me that God had formed me and knew me before I was born. God calls me by name, and I belong to God. I may feel overwhelmed, but feelings are momentary, and God's view is eternal. She assured me that my present troubles would be redeemed in some future yet unknown to me, in a way yet unknown to me. And they have been.

Mary was a voice of grace in my life. She might have said, "You made your bed, now lie in it." Or, "Get your act together and quit crying!" But she didn't minimize my pain or compare it to others, and instead met me in the darkness with light. God says to each of us, "I have called you by name, and you are mine." We belong to the God of the Universe who cared enough to enter our world as a vulnerable baby, to redeem us. Amen to that.

— *Marilu Thomas*

When I came to you, brothers and sisters, I did not come proclaiming the mystery of God to you in lofty words or wisdom. For I decided to know nothing among you except Jesus Christ, and him crucified. And I came to you in weakness and in fear and in much trembling. My speech and my proclamation were not with plausible words of wisdom, but with a demonstration of the Spirit and of power, so that your faith might rest not on human wisdom but on the power of God. (1 Corinthians 2:1-5)

You are not a brand, and you do not need to promote yourself. This statement seems obvious but is becoming more revolutionary as we progress deeper into the social media age. It is refreshing to read that Paul's work and ministry were not about himself. Paul, the poet and articulator of the riches of the gospel, did not speak with "plausible words of wisdom" but instead relied on the power of God.

The life of a Christian is not primarily about self-promotion or even self-fulfillment. We are called, instead, to boast in our weakness in order to demonstrate the Spirit and power of God. This is convenient because life will give us ample opportunities to boast in our weakness, if only we are honest. The Big Book of AA says that alcoholics can only "recover if they have the capacity to be honest." This is true of Christians as well. There is hope, joy, and peace through Jesus Christ as long as we give an honest assessment of our situation.

We have no power apart from the power of God, and the power of God is illustrated most clearly on the cross. At the moment of his greatest weakness, Jesus Christ claimed power over sin. In his dying—the most literal form of self-abandonment—Jesus destroyed the power of death.

You are not a brand to be marketed as you climb the ladder of spiritual success. There are no bootstraps that could pull you out of the hole you find yourself in, no life-hacks to save you from death. You are a fallen human being who has been brought back to life through Christ and him crucified. That is something to boast about!

— *Connor Gwin*

November 30

But this I call to mind,
   and therefore I have hope:
The steadfast love of the LORD never ceases,
   his mercies never come to an end;
they are new every morning;
   great is your faithfulness.
"The LORD is my portion," says my soul,
   "therefore I will hope in him." (Lamentations 3:21-24)

One of my warmest church memories growing up is singing the hymn, "Great Is Thy Faithfulness." We sang it often, especially around Thanks-giving. As far as I knew, it seemed to be one of those front-porch kinds of songs, where you look out over all God has given and thank Him for His abundant blessings.

So imagine how surprised I was to discover that the genesis of this hymn is deeply embedded in a biblical book that is *very* appropriately titled "Lamentations." Recently, I read through that five-chapter book in a single sitting, and I felt like I was in a Jeep riding through a war zone. Jerusalem is pictured as a widow, weeping bitterly over the incalculable losses foisted upon her by the Babylonian army.

Still, while dodging potholes and debris, the author manages to place a dogged hope in the conviction that "The steadfast love of the LORD never ceases, his mercies never come to an end."

I take great comfort that during the worst seasons of *lamentation* in this life, there are still new mercies to discover, as fresh as manna from heaven. As chaotic as life can feel, the Lord's faithfulness stands strong, whether we are basking in blessings on the front porch or dodging wreckage in the Jeep.

— *Larry Parsley*

December 1

> In the beginning was the Word, and the Word was with
> God, and the Word was God. He was in the beginning with
> God. (John 1:1-2)

Our God is a God of words. As human beings, we know the power of words. We are unique among the animal kingdom for our ability to speak, to write, and to enclose as much as we can of the human heart in permutations of rather odd-looking symbols. Being made in God's own image means that there is power and wonder in words.

The Gospel of John begins with an exquisite example of literary parallelism. The three independent clauses—with their repetition of "the Word"—build gloriously as we learn when the Word was, where the Word was, and finally, who the Word was. The Word was God himself.

With verse 2, the structure becomes what English-teachers-who-take-themselves-too-seriously (guilty!) like to call a chiasmus. A chiasmus is a rhetorical structure where the second half of a parallel sentence reverses itself. It is often charted with an X:

In the beginning was the Word, and the Word was with God,

And the Word was God. He was in the beginning with God.

The chiasmus is so named for the Greek letter *chi*, written like an *x*. Chi became a particularly popular letter for decorating medieval Gospel manuscripts because *chi* and *rho* (shaped like *p*) were shorthand for the man who most famously bore those letters at the beginning of his name: *Christos*. The Book of Kells on display at Trinity College Dublin has a stunning example of a medieval Chi-Rho, ornately illustrated and filling the entire manuscript page, top to bottom. At the most basic structural level, within the filament of the sentences themselves, we see God cry out the truth of his Son, the revelation of the glory of Christ. The Word became the name of a man.

The Word became flesh because words were not enough to save us. No matter what stories we tell and what songs we sing, there is only one power in the universe strong enough to bring us back to the beginning. In the end, the x turned on its side to become the wood of the cross. Christ hung on its beams and breathed out his last earthly words for our salvation, from the beginning of time to the end of the ages.

— *Derrill H. McDavid*

December 2

For the grace of God has appeared, bringing salvation to all, training us to renounce impiety and worldly passions, and in the present age to live lives that are self-controlled, upright, and godly, while we wait for the blessed hope and the manifestation of the glory of our great God and Savior, Jesus Christ. He it is who gave himself for us that he might redeem us from all iniquity and purify for himself a people of his own who are zealous for good deeds.

Declare these things; exhort and reprove with all authority. Let no one look down on you. (Titus 2:11-15)

Human beings do not like to wait. Look around the next time you find yourself in line or in a waiting room. Everyone is reading a magazine or looking at their phone or doing anything other than simply waiting. No one can handle it.

The world is caught in the "already but not yet." The grace of God has appeared, but we are still waiting for the blessed hope and glory of our great God and Savior, Jesus Christ.

In all this we must remember our role. We did not bring about the grace of God nor did we bring salvation to all. Jesus Christ gave himself for us, redeemed us from all iniquity, and purified us for himself. Now we are caught in between the actions of God: the "already" of what God has done now, and the "not yet" of what God will bring about. God is the actor. God is the author. God has the power.

The one thing we do under our own power is wait and witness in our present age for the blessed hope of our Lord Jesus Christ. We wait and declare what has been done on our behalf. To borrow a phrase from Alcoholics Anonymous, we tell "what we were like, what happened, and what we are like now"—while singing of what the world will one day be through Christ.

— *Connor Gwin*

December 3

Then God said, "Let us make [*adam*] in our image, according to our likeness; and let them have dominion over the
fish of the sea, and over the birds of the air, and over the
cattle, and over all the wild animals of the earth, and over
every creeping thing that creeps upon the earth."

So God created [*adam*] in his image,
  in the image of God he created [him];
  male and female he created them. (Genesis 1:26-27)

It would be fitting for God to have a representative, a viceroy to stand
on the earth and declare its holiness by sheer weight of presence (which
the Bible calls "the glory of the LORD"). Wherever this one would walk,
it would be as if to say, "The LORD is near, and the whole round world is
his temple," and all would rejoice at the coming. The lights of the heavens
would look down in awe, and the beasts and birds and writhing masses of
the deep would whoop in celebration. Not one thing, no matter how small
or alien, would withhold its peculiar worship. That would be fitting.

It is a wonder, a testimony to the mad plenitude of God, that when we
first encounter the anointed representative *adam*—the name, in Hebrew,
just means "human"—it is not as a singular *him*, but as *them*. One in authority might go wrong, but many risks chaos. Who is this multiple image of
God? You? Me? The king in Jerusalem? A prophet? A Ming dynasty peas-
ant, a Neolithic hunter, a priest of Baal? A whole wide jabbering world
full of people ("images") who snipe and tear and croak at one another—can
this noise be God's creation?

Look a little further—beyond the one in the garden, for he is but a
shadow of the One to come. The man in the garden once stood alone in
the world, and it was not good. There is another who stands always among
the crowd, found with his sinners, and he bears the sins of many. He holds
them together. He is One, when they are anything but. What God begins
in order cannot end in chaos, nor in erasure, a second flood. Because *he* is
One, so shall *they* be—and so shall *we*.

— Adam Morton

December 4

"And remember, I am with you always, to the end of the age." (Matthew 28:20)

The Great Commission ends with an instruction not to *do*, but to *remember*. To remember is to call something to mind. After Jesus has told his apostles to make disciples of all nations, he asks them—us—to "remember." What does he ask them to remember? Not signs and wonders, not wise words, but a promise of his companionship through whatever the future may bring.

There will be times in our lives when God feels near, and you can see him at work in your life in clear and unambiguous ways. But there may be times when you are in that dark valley, you cannot make out the path before you, and you feel alone, uncertain, lost. There will be times when God feels far away. There will be seasons when he seems so silent you may wonder if he has gone away for good. There will be days, or weeks, or months, when you are trying to remember what God's voice sounds like, and God might just be an idea. And there will be times when you are preoccupied with so many people and juggling so many things that you simply don't have time or space to think about anything else.

No matter what it is that you are going through now, these words were said to you as much as they were said to the apostles: *Remember, I am with you always.* He is with you now. He was with you yesterday. He has been with you all your life. And he will be with you, to the end of your days. *Remember.*

— *Bonnie Poon Zahl*

December 5

This is what he showed me: the LORD was standing beside
a wall built with a plumb line, with a plumb line in his
hand. And the LORD said to me, "Amos, what do you see?"
And I said, "A plumb line." Then the LORD said,

> "See, I am setting a plumb line
> in the midst of my people Israel;
> I will never again pass them by…" (Amos 7:7-8)

A plumb line is a simple tool used by contractors. It's a string with a weight
on the bottom. Gravity pulls down the weight, creating a vertical line. Most
builders use plumb lines to make sure their walls are perfectly straight,
but don't let the simple tool fool you. A plumb line and a bit of trigonom-
etry could build massive arches, fantastic coliseums, and ornate temples.
Regardless of the structure, walls that lean, even a little bit, are in danger
of collapsing.

The prophet Amos has a vision, in which God uses a plumb line to
measure the "uprightness" of Israel. God discovers that the spiritual walls
of Israel are about to collapse. "I will never again pass them by," says God,
meaning, he can't ignore the dangerously crooked walls any longer. They
need to be torn down. God isn't wrong—earlier in Amos, we discover that
Israel has been oppressing the poor, ignoring the Ten Commandments, and
embracing religions that practiced child sacrifice. Shaky walls indeed.

God's judgment is scary. Imagine the God of the universe measuring
your spiritual uprightness, dropping a plumb line in your life. We might
not be sacrificing children, but our spiritual walls are nonetheless crooked.
Whether we are selfish, arrogant, or otherwise self-possessed, or whether
we are just "another brick in the wall" (Pink Floyd) of a questionable cultural
practice, the verdict is the same: These walls are destined for destruction.

The good news is that a plumb line is a tool used for both tearing down
and building up. God isn't afraid to get his hands dirty, to rebuild our walls
and lay new foundations with Jesus' death and resurrection as the cornerstone. May God renovate your spirit and repair all that is exposed by his
divine plumb line.

— *Bryan Jarrell*

December 6

> Zechariah said to the angel, "How will I know that this is
> so? For I am an old man, and my wife is getting on in years."
> The angel replied, "I am Gabriel. I stand in the presence
> of God, and I have been sent to speak to you and to bring
> you this good news. But now, because you did not believe
> my words, which will be fulfilled in their time, you will
> become mute, unable to speak, until the day these things
> occur." (Luke 1:18-20)

When the angel Gabriel pays a visit to Old Zechariah to tell him that he and his elderly wife will have a child, Zechariah asks the question we seem to always ask when faith blows the doors off our worldview: "How?" How could this good news ever possibly be true? And Gabriel responds to "How" with "Who"—as if to say, "Do you know *who* I am?" Or perhaps more significantly, do you truly know who God is, the one who sends Gabriel and his care package of "good news"? In other words, Gabriel does not give an explanation but rather flashes an ID badge.

What comes next for Zechariah is two "signs" or miracles, the first negative and the second positive. Negatively, Zechariah is struck dumb. Positively, after he gets back home, old Elizabeth conceives.

The first miracle feels punitive to me, and maybe that is its primary purpose. Still, when Zechariah staggers out of the Holy Place after his unexpected audience with Gabriel, some kind of holiness must shimmer off of him, because the waiting people realize he has seen a vision (v. 22). Perhaps there are worse things in life than to enter into an enforced silence as we reflect on God's power and grace. Such silent shouts of praise can tune our hearts while our lips wait for their turn.

In less extraordinary ways, some of the inexplicable punishments of our lives function that way. We stagger as one struck dumb, unable to do what normally comes easily. But in the waiting, God is giving birth to faith in us, and not just faith but life.

— Larry Parsley

December 7

Then the kings of the earth and the great men and the generals and the rich and the strong, and every one, slave and free, hid in the caves and among the rocks of the mountains, calling to the mountains and rocks, "Fall on us and hide us from the face of him who is seated on the throne and from the wrath of the Lamb; for the great day of their wrath has come, and who can stand before it?" (Revelation 6:15-17 RSV)

I wish we could face God on our own terms. I mean, if we just could talk to him *pares inter pares* and say to Him, "Let him who is without sin cast the first stone." But He *is* without the sin, and He is entitled to "cast the first stone." I can't fight back—His firepower is infinite and also justified. So no, I cannot face God on my own terms.

This is very important, both "now and at the hour of our death." The famous Danish movie *Vampyr* (1932), by Carl Dreyer, has as its opening shot a kind of scythe held by a man who symbolizes the advent of death. (Fun little movie, *Vampyr*. Dreyer later directed *Day of Wrath*, another fun flick. For your own sake, don't see it. In fact, don't see either of them!) But the *scythe*—"King Harvest Has Surely Come" (The Band, 1969). "Don't Fear the Reaper" (Blue Öyster Cult, 1976) ... NOT!

My death is my own private apocalypse. When I come to die, a part of me will be just like "every one, slave and free" in Revelation, saying "hide us from the face of him who is seated on the throne."

When the time comes, fall on your face, hold back nothing, tell the whole truth (to the extent that you know it), and listen to God's verdict. Hear this also, from the Word: "Come unto me, all ye that labor and are heavy laden, and I will give you rest" (Mt 11:28). Oh, and also, "him that cometh to me I will in no wise cast out" (Jn 6:37 KJV).

— *Paul Zahl*

December 8

> "But," he said, "you cannot see my face; for no one shall see me and live." And the LORD continued, "See, there is a place by me where you shall stand on the rock; and while my glory passes by I will put you in a cleft of the rock, and I will cover you with my hand until I have passed by; then I will take away my hand, and you shall see my back; but my face shall not be seen." (Exodus 33:20-23)

Christianity is unique in that one can fully and permissibly read our sacred texts in any language. One does not need to be conversant in ancient Hebrew or Greek in order to receive and understand the gospel—the good news of Jesus Christ—as revealed in the Bible.

Andrew Walls, the prominent Christian missiologist, once noted that the reason it is acceptable to translate the Bible into any language is because the Incarnation itself is an act of translation. That is to say, in Jesus Christ, God translates himself *into human*; this metamorphosis is infinitely more extreme than any linguistic change. The distance between languages pales in comparison to the chasm God crosses to make himself intelligible to humanity.

In Exodus, and throughout the Bible, God the Father cannot be seen. His glory is simply too great for any person to bear. And yet, in Jesus Christ, "all the fullness of God was pleased to dwell" (Col 1:19)." "No one has ever seen God," but Jesus "has made him known"(Jn 1:18). And, "Whoever has seen [Jesus] has seen the Father" (Jn 14:9).

So much talking and thinking about God is speculation, like wondering what aliens might look like, or what the future might hold. We simply have no idea. And yet, in Christianity, if you want to know about God, just look to Jesus. There is no need to guess or imagine. He has come and walked among us. Through Jesus, humanity has looked God full in the face, and lived to tell the tale.

— *R-J Heijmen*

December 9

"Then the righteous will answer him, 'Lord, when was it that we saw you hungry and gave you food, or thirsty and gave you something to drink? And when was it that we saw you a stranger and welcomed you, or naked and gave you clothing? And when was it that we saw you sick or in prison and visited you?' And the king will answer them, 'Truly I tell you, just as you did it to one of the least of these who are members of my family, you did it to me.'"
(Matthew 25:37-40)

Guilt. When I read this text I feel guilty. I feel like I should be doing more. Is this scripture a prescription for how I should be spending my days? How about when I drive past the guy standing at an intersection with a sign that reads, "God bless you"? Have I visited my neighbor in the hospital? Just couldn't get around to it this week. Maybe I should be volunteering with the prison ministry at church? That's on the kids' soccer night. Or maybe I should be working in the local soup kitchen? I can't get off work mid-day.

Jesus, speaking about the kingdom of God, is telling us that we don't know what we're doing. The righteous are just as clueless as the unrighteous when it comes to recognizing the members of Christ's family in the least, the lost, and the little. And if I am not saved by works but by faith, then grace—not my own eyes or good moral judgment—will lead me where I need to go.

Trusting that the Holy Spirit knows, and that I don't, gives me freedom, knowing that grace is leading me each day to where I will be used, in ways I cannot imagine. I don't need to know because God does. This means surrendering ourselves to God's care and providence, completely knowing that Jesus is the Savior of us all.

— *Marilu Thomas*

December 10

As God's chosen ones, holy and beloved, clothe yourselves
with compassion, kindness, humility, meekness, and patience.
(Colossians 3:12)

There's something wonderful about how this verse begins, by reminding us that we are chosen, holy, and beloved by God. We are named as holy and beloved, and we are given a wardrobe of holy clothing to protect our hearts and remind the world of our own, and their own, belovedness.

Some of us have a professional wardrobe that we put on as a signal that we are ready for work. Some clergy wear vestments. Police officers wear badges. Attorneys wear suits to court. There are some judges who keep an extra suit jacket in their chambers for those attorneys who appear in their courtrooms underdressed. These courtesy jackets might not fit like a tailored suit, but they remind the attorney that they are an officer of the court. That reminder might also come with a hint of condescension from an eye-rolling judge, so attorneys usually don't forget their professional garb more than once. When an attorney is seated next to their client in court, they are expected to button the jacket every time they stand, and unbutton it when they sit. This is taught in moot court classrooms across the country, and is stressed almost as much as the rules of evidence and professional ethics.

But there is good news about God's people clothing themselves with compassion, kindness, humility, meekness, and patience. These are not the castoff jackets of the impatient judge. These are gifts tailored for our holy life, made for us by the God who loves us more than we can imagine. There is no buttoning and unbuttoning with each sitting and standing.

And we take rest in the knowledge that God sees us as holy and beloved even if we can't see or feel that holy clothing ourselves. He wraps us in kindness and compassion, dresses us in humility, meekness, and patience, not as the condescending judge in the courtroom, but as the One who loves us and chooses us.

— *Carrie Willard*

385

December 11

> About midnight Paul and Silas were praying and singing hymns to God, and the prisoners were listening to them. Suddenly there was an earthquake, so violent that the foundations of the prison were shaken; and immediately all the doors were opened and everyone's chains were unfastened. (Acts 16:25-26)

God does big things through small acts. So often, God's work goes unnoticed, and it's only through reflection, or a line of "footsteps in the sand," that we recognize God's work in our lives.

In today's passage, we find Paul and Silas imprisoned and awaiting further persecution. Instead of fighting, they surrender. They begin to pray and sing hymns to God. They create a church *in prison*. Even in that grim place, the followers of Jesus are worshipping!

Side note: If you have ever participated in a prison ministry or worshipped in that setting, then you know the power of this experience. It's the Holy Ghost on a booster rocket. The presence of God is palpable, because in reality, the Holy Ghost is always working; many times, we are just distracted.

So there they are, Paul and Silas, singing and dancing and making noise—when God acts. And this time, God acts in a *huge* way—he frees them from their imprisonment with an earthquake. In the same huge way, God has broken our own chains and freed us from the prison of sin and death. Because on the cross, at Golgotha, God acted. While the world sat and watched and carried on about its business, God was breaking the chains of sin and death, once and for all. It may have seemed like a humdrum crucifixion, one of many ancient Roman executions, but it tore the curtain of the temple in half and opened the way to the good news: Christ died for you and me. He died to set us free. Alleluia!

Even while we sleep, God acts. While we sit, God acts. While we are distracted, God acts. God remains the primary actor in your life and the sole place of freedom, love, and forgiveness. Thanks be to God.

That's the message for today—God acts.

— *Willis Logan*

December 12

In days to come
   the mountain of the LORD's house
shall be established as the highest of the mountains,
   and shall be raised above the hills;
all the nations shall stream to it…
He shall judge between the nations,
   and shall arbitrate for many peoples;
they shall beat their swords into plowshares,
   and their spears into pruning hooks… (Isaiah 2:2,4)

Nothing makes me sadder than when I hear someone say, "I hate surprises." People have their reasons, of course, as unexpected events can be traumatizing. But usually the underlying sentiment is some form of "I really like being in control. I want to know what's coming." Experience tells us, however, that grace almost always comes by surprise.

The writer Leslie Jamison puts it this way:

> Grace isn't the thing you planned, it's what you get instead… It's not a product of narrative or moral cause-and-effect. It catches you off guard… I'm both boggled and inspired by the ways the plotlines we write for ourselves are always getting overturned… [T]he comedian Kyle Kinane says in one of his stand-up routines, that a miracle is just the world letting you know it can still surprise you.

Isaiah's words in today's passage contain two big surprises. First, *all* the nations shall stream to the mountain of the Lord, not just the nation of Israel. The scale of redemption is larger than his hearers—then or now—would have had any right to expect.

Secondly, the coming Lord will not be a militaristic king to conquer and crush, but a prince of peace who will redeem instruments of aggression, fashioning swords into plowshares.

Make no mistake: Jesus Christ upsets the applecart of our precious *quid pro quo*. He refuses to repay sin with more sin—which is part of what gets him killed. And yet, he's full of surprises until the very end, rising from his

three-day grave and coming to his disciples with mercy rather than revenge.
Just as he does with you.

Heavenly Father, surprise us today with your grace.

— David Zahl

December 13

When it was evening on that day, the first day of the week, and the doors of the house where the disciples had met were locked for fear of the Jews, Jesus came and stood among them and said, "Peace be with you." After he said this, he showed them his hands and his side. Then the disciples rejoiced when they saw the Lord. (John 20:19-20)

Having completed his epic journey, Odysseus returns to Ithaca in disguise. The only person to recognize him is Eurycleia, his childhood nurse. And how does she know him? By a scar on Odysseus' leg, just above his knee.

In this gospel passage, Jesus returns from His epic journey of the cross, the descent into hell, and the empty tomb, in order to greet His disciples. Apparently, they don't recognize Him at first. Not until He shows them His scars. When they saw His scars, they "rejoiced when they saw the Lord."

Loath as we are to do so, revealing our weaknesses is the only way to be fully known by another. We may admire strength in another, but that does not inspire intimacy. Remember what the prophet Isaiah says—"by his wounds we are healed" (Is 53:5 NIV).

Thank you, Father, that you know us in our weakness and yet you love us. Please remind us that it is in our weakness that we experience your strength. Amen.

— Paul Walker

December 14

> In the sixth month of Elizabeth's pregnancy, God sent the
> angel Gabriel to Nazareth, a town in Galilee, to a virgin
> pledged to be married to a man named Joseph, a descendant
> of David. The virgin's name was Mary. The angel went to
> her and said, "Greetings, you who are highly favored! The
> Lord is with you."
>
> Mary was greatly troubled at his words and wondered
> what kind of greeting this might be. But the angel said to
> her, "Do not be afraid, Mary; you have found favor with
> God. You will conceive and give birth to a son, and you are
> to call him Jesus." (Luke 1:26-31 NIV)

The news of any child's impending arrival in the world can be exciting and
jarring at the same time, and the annunciation of Jesus is no exception. Mary
shows us right away that she's no fool for flattery. The angel Gabriel tells
her that she's highly favored, and she is immediately troubled and wonders
what kind of greeting this might be.

Some of us may find ourselves nodding in agreement with Mary's skepticism. The angel delivers his message and then hustles out pretty quickly
after she agrees to the terms and conditions, and after telling her that, oh,
by the way, old lady cousin Elizabeth is also (even more) pregnant, so you'll
want to catch up with her pronto.

Mary is left, essentially, alone with this unlikely and improbable news.
We know that she went on to rejoice in the news of Jesus—the news that
she received before anyone else did. But we are left to wonder if any of
the trouble and wonder was left in her heart as she contemplated the great
mystery unfolding inside of her. How many of us have felt alone in our trou-
bledness? How many of us have felt abruptly disjointed from our lives, in
a moment that leaves us forever changed?

> *Lord, help us to be like Mary, who pondered the angel's words in*
> *her heart, then rejoiced and brought Jesus into this world.*

— *Carrie Willard*

December 15

Now the birth of Jesus the Messiah took place in this way. When his mother Mary had been engaged to Joseph, but before they lived together, she was found to be with child from the Holy Spirit. Her husband Joseph, being a righteous man and unwilling to expose her to public disgrace, planned to dismiss her quietly. But just when he had resolved to do this, an angel of the Lord appeared to him in a dream and said, "Joseph, son of David, do not be afraid to take Mary as your wife, for the child conceived in her is from the Holy Spirit." (Matthew 1:18-20)

In W. H. Auden's poem, *For The Time Being: A Christmas Oratorio*, the master poet takes a long, intense look at the Christmas season and the biblical account of the birth of Jesus. In the section titled "The Temptation of St. Joseph," Auden depicts the emotional rollercoaster of Joseph as rumors of his pregnant fiancée circulate throughout the town. Ashamed and at the end of his rope, he cries out to the angel Gabriel:

> JOSEPH:
> All I ask is one
> Important and elegant proof
> That what my Love had done
> Was really at your will
> And that your will is Love.
>
> GABRIEL:
> No, you must believe;
> Be silent, and sit still.

In all of Joseph's confusion, the whispers of the crowd's gossip, and his plea to God and the angel, the common thread through Joseph's temptation was his doubt. He was tempted to doubt his wife-to-be's word and to plead for just some "important and elegant proof" that this was God's will. Joseph's doubt is the same that brought a scoff from Sarah when God promised her a child; it's the same doubt that caused Thomas to prod the wounds of the resurrected Jesus.

But the angel Gabriel insists that what combats the choking weeds of doubt is what we are all so reluctant to do. For Joseph and Mary, for Sarah, for Thomas, for the parent whose child is off the rails, the young adult whose faith has shriveled up, the addict who can't kick the urge, the success story who runs towards self-sufficiency in life's sinking sand—we are called to give up, be silent, sit still, and believe God always keeps his promises. His will, forever and always, is rooted in the finished work of Jesus.

— *Sam Guthrie*

December 16

For by grace you have been saved through faith, and this is
not your own doing; it is the gift of God—not the result of
works, so that no one may boast. (Ephesians 2:8-9)

Have you ever noticed that your favorite presents are from those who know
you the best and love you the most? When I was six years old, I took all my
presents from under the Christmas tree and ranked them in order of what
I guessed would be the worst to the best (nothing neurotic about that). I
saved one present for last. I was convinced it was a remote control car or
some other awesome toy. But when I opened it, I was stunned to find myself
holding an Old Spice Soap on a Rope, no joke. An Old Spice Soap on a
Rope for a six-year-old kid. I can also recall the best presents I have ever
received—an iPod, or a Leatherman, or a record player along with several
classic albums on vinyl. These were all given by those who know me the
best and love me the most, my wife and kids.

God knows you the best and loves you the most. God knows you better
than you know yourself. God loves you more than you could ever imagine.
And God gave—and still gives—you the best present ever, Jesus Christ.
Jesus himself told a Pharisee named Nicodemus one night, "God so loved the
world that he *gave* his only Son" (Jn 3:16). And in Jesus Christ, as today's
verse from Ephesians emphasizes, God gave you the gift of salvation—"by
grace you have been saved…it is the gift of God." Your salvation in Jesus
Christ is an entirely free gift from God. It was and is God's decision, not
yours. You cannot add anything to it—none of us can—which means "no
one can boast."

In addition to this salvation, God gives many other gifts—love, grace,
forgiveness, hope, mercy, peace, eternal life—what is described in the Book
of Common Prayer as "the innumerable benefits procured unto us by the
same." And God's offer of this gift of Jesus Christ, this gift of salvation for
you from the One who knows you the best and loves you the most, still
stands, and always will.

— *David Johnson*

December 17

For the yoke of his burden,
   and the staff for his shoulder,
   the rod of his oppressor,
   you have broken as on the day of Midian...
For to us a child is born,
   to us a son is given;
and the government shall be upon his shoulder,
   and his name shall be called
Wonderful Counselor, Mighty God,
   Everlasting Father, Prince of Peace. (Isaiah 9:4,6 ESV)

In the midst of the Israelites' "gloom of anguish" and "thick darkness" (8:22), Isaiah begins to prophesy about their future hope but speaks as if the events have already happened. He demonstrates the certainty of God's promises and the reality of His power to save them from devastation. Isaiah tells of a great light, increased joy, the broken rod of their oppressors, and the end of bloody battles.

Isaiah also makes clear that God will not save the Israelites in a way that stands to reason by human logic. He alludes to Gideon's defeat of the Midianites in Judges: when God led Gideon, a weak, cowardly Israelite, and his army of only 300 men, to defeat the massive Midianite army. God's strategy? Command Gideon's army to surround the Midianite camp and simultaneously smash clay pots, blare their trumpets, and shine torches. In the chaos, the Midianites not only flee but start attacking *each other*, securing victory for Gideon and his people.

As with Gideon's situation, Isaiah's hearers are hopeless on their own. But here, Isaiah offers a glimpse into what, or rather *who*, the rescue plan is. He will be a Wonderful Counselor, a perfect Teacher who shows the way to eternal life. He will be a son born to them whose kingdom will be everlasting and unwavering, full of justice, righteousness, and peace. A Mighty God who is all-powerful, who will protect them and fight on their behalf against the Enemy. An Everlasting Father, who loves and seeks after His children. And a Prince of Peace, ushering in harmony with God so that those who were once His enemies can enjoy a restored relationship with Him.

Though our world often feels shrouded in the same darkness that the Israelites knew, how much more can we share in their hope, living on this side of Jesus' life, death, and resurrection?

— *Margaret Pope*

December 18

> When Elizabeth heard Mary's greeting, the child leaped in her womb. And Elizabeth was filled with the Holy Spirit and exclaimed with a loud cry, "Blessed are you among women, and blessed is the fruit of your womb. And why has this happened to me, that the mother of my Lord comes to me? For as soon as I heard the sound of your greeting, the child in my womb leaped for joy." (Luke 1:41-44)

What did pre-modern writers do without word processors? Today, if you are a little worried that you might have used the word "transform" a few too many times, you can just right-click the word and replace it with one of the options the thesaurus function suggests (*alter, change, evolve…*).

Elizabeth, however, seems unbothered by repetition. When newly-pregnant Mary hurries to greet her very-pregnant relative Elizabeth, no sooner does she say hello than John the Fetus begins to do the wave! Tiny John, filled with the Holy Spirit *from the womb* (v. 15), "leaped for joy" in awareness that his "Lord" had drawn near. Elizabeth, filled with the same Spirit, prophesies by over-using the word "bless." Mary is blessed, her son is blessed, and Elizabeth cannot believe her good fortune to welcome both of them into her home. All of this leads Elizabeth to add a closing benediction, once again to Mary: "Blessed is she who has believed that the Lord would fulfill his promises to her!" (v. 45 NIV).

I'm sure I could never tire of that word. Speak it over me again and again. Tell me repeatedly about the blessing of Jesus, incarnated in Mary, blessing Mary and blessing Elizabeth and her son John, and blessing you, too, and anyone who "has believed that the Lord would fulfill his promises."

— *Larry Parsley*

December 19

Let the same mind be in you that was in Christ Jesus,
who, though he was in the form of God,
did not regard equality with God
as something to be exploited,
but emptied himself,
taking the form of a slave,
being born in human likeness.
And being found in human form,
he humbled himself
and became obedient to the point of death—
even death on a cross. (Philippians 2:5-8)

There's a renowned therapist named Phoebe Caldwell who works with people with autism. To communicate with nonverbal children and adults, and to cultivate their ability to respond, she pays attention to their repetitive actions, like rhythmic fidgeting, and she imitates them. Many of these actions are self-focused, separating her clients from other people. For her patients, the restless repetitions are a means of grounding themselves in their bodies while their perceptions of the world remain chaotic. But as she imitates them, touching the hand they touch or flicking a string as they do, they begin to recognize her. Their attention turns from themselves to a shared interaction as Caldwell creates an external feedback out of their repetition.

In her words, "You are looking for the thing that has meaning for them, and you are using that to get access to their inner world and draw their attention to interaction rather than solitary self-starvation." Caldwell also emphasizes that her interactions must be un-self-conscious:

> When we are doing this with a person, we are emptying ourselves; we are giving our absolute, total attention. When I say emptying myself, I still have to be there for them. I have to respond to them. It's not a question of me being a mirror exactly; it's a case of me being a living, responding person, whose attention is totally focused in that person when I'm working with them.

These words seemed to me the most helpful way to understand today's verses. Letting the mind of Christ be in me is such a weighty moral command that I know I can't do it and don't want to. But what's remarkable about what Paul says here is that *it works in reverse.*

As theologian Susan Eastman has pointed out, Paul is showing that Christ first imitates us, in becoming a human and suffering with us. And as she notes, our imitation of Christ isn't even just an act of our wills: "Both Plato and contemporary neuroscience recognize that, as often as not, imitation bypasses volition; perception triggers a mimetic response...this is what anyone who observes infants knows immediately."

The demand for imitation is still there, and it weighs heavily on me. But if you feel this burden like I do, to live just like Jesus, then take heart. In his affectionate desire to relate to you, Jesus first lived like you.

— *Kendall Gunter*

December 20

> For once you were darkness, but now in the Lord you are
> light. Live as children of light—for the fruit of the light is
> found in all that is good and right and true. (Ephesians 5:8-9)

Today's theme is "light," and we'll address it first from the dark side.

Have you heard of the term "gaslighting"? It originates from a 1938 play called, perhaps unsurprisingly, *Gas Light*. To gaslight someone is to psychologically manipulate them, sowing seeds of doubt to make them question their own memory, perception, or sanity. You use denial, misperception, contradiction, and outright dishonesty to defend yourself (although you are in the wrong) and debunk the other (although they are in the right).

That may sound extreme, but I'm sure I employ—often unconsciously—some form of gaslighting every day to shore up my cause. *Lord, have mercy.*

In contradistinction to that is the childlike and plaintive hymn, "I Want to Walk as a Child of the Light":

> I want to walk as a child of the light.
> I want to follow Jesus.
> God set the stars to give light to the world.
> The star of my life is Jesus.
> In him there is no darkness at all.
> The night and the day are both alike.
> The Lamb is the light of the city of God.
> Shine in my heart, Lord Jesus.

The first-person accessibility of the hymn invites us to simply follow Jesus. We don't claim to be anything other than what we actually are; we just express a childlike desire to be in the light of Christ. Or as Paul says, "For once you were darkness, but now in the Lord you are light. Live as children of light..." The hymn and scripture describe a beautiful picture; and only God has the power to make it so.

Heavenly Father, please draw our hearts to you, guide our minds, fill our imaginations with your light; through our Lord and Savior Jesus Christ. Amen.

— Paul Walker

December 21

And Mary said,

> "My soul magnifies the Lord,
>   and my spirit rejoices in God my Savior,
> for he has looked with favor on the lowliness of his servant.
>   Surely, from now on all generations will call me blessed;
> for the Mighty One has done great things for me,
>   and holy is his name." (Luke 1:46-49)

Mary's song (often called by its Latin name, the "Magnificat") positions Mary as a kind of crossover artist. As the song opens—"My soul magnifies the Lord"—I can almost picture Mary as Fraulein Maria in *The Sound of Music*, twirling and belting out her wonder at God's goodness. But if the song starts off feeling like a show tune, it transitions in the middle stanzas to something more like a 1960s protest song. Depending on where you sit in the social order of things, the song either delights (God has "lifted up the lowly" (v. 52)) or discourages ("he has…sent the rich away empty" (v. 53)). Before the song wraps up, Mary sneaks in an ode to the flawed yet faithful Father Abraham, who first heard God whisper the outrageous promises that are now coming true in her womb (v. 55).

It may be that you need this song to minister to you in a variety of ways today. You need a strong dose of Mary's wonder at God's creative artistry shown toward the humblest of canvases. Or maybe you need to feel God's law protesting your tendency toward "pride" as you revel in this world's toys and do a pretty sorry job of sharing them with your neighbor.

Yet wherever this song might take you, remember that what God promised Abraham and Mary, in Christ God also promises you: "His mercy is for those who fear him from generation to generation" (v. 50). If I'm doing the math right, that includes your generation as well.

— *Larry Parsley*

December 22

But you, O Bethlehem of Ephrathah,
  who are one of the little clans of Judah,
from you shall come forth for me
  one who is to rule in Israel,
whose origin is from of old,
  from ancient days. (Micah 5:2)

The prophet Micah is famous for tipping us off to the location of Jesus' birth. With the benefit of hindsight and a whole host of Christmas songs extolling the "little town of Bethlehem," where Jesus was born is no surprise to modern churchgoers. To the people of ancient Israel, however, a savior from Bethlehem made little sense. As the New Testament will clarify, God chooses what is foolish in the world to shame the wise (1 Cor 1:27). A savior from Jerusalem certainly made a lot of sense, but a savior from Bethlehem? Such things simply don't happen.

The location of your birth and upbringing will have a huge impact on your life's trajectory. It determines the accent of your speech, the sports teams you will root for. Social scientists say that our zip codes are more predictive than our genetics when it comes to health and income, and other studies have suggested that a good algorithm could accurately guess your age at death simply based on where you live. Some people are from "the wrong side of the tracks," or, as in Cold-War Berlin or the present-day West Bank, "the wrong side of the wall." Some communities value their lifelong members—there's cultural cachet in being a "native New Yorker." In twelve-step literature, attempting to solve a problem by relocating is derisively called a "geographical cure." Let us not underestimate the present and future impact that our community of origin imparts.

A Christ born in Bethlehem, however, upends the hold that our hometowns can have on us. Whether we were born on the wrong side of the tracks or born with a silver spoon in our mouths, the place of our birth means nothing in the kingdom of heaven. No heavenly time is spent assessing your accent or sports team fandom, and no heavenly algorithm is processing your zip code to determine whether you will enter through the pearly gates. That was certainly a revolutionary idea in an ancient world where gods had geographical jurisdictions. And in a modern world where your geography is given nearly deterministic power, it's still radical.

— *Bryan Jarrell*

December 23

"'Every valley shall be filled,
    and every mountain and hill shall be made low,
  and the crooked shall be made straight,
    and the rough ways made smooth;
  and all flesh shall see the salvation of God.'" (Luke 3:5-6)

These are the words spoken by John the Baptizer before the baptism of Jesus, remembering out loud the words written in the book of Isaiah. It's difficult to read them now without imagining John as a soloist in a performance of Handel's *Messiah*, out of place among the other tuxedoed musicians with his locust-and-honey hair, but boldly exhorting his congregation to prepare the way for the Lord.

John spoke these words before baptizing Jesus, before Jesus went into the desert and then began performing miracles. Did the prophet's words sound comforting or foreboding coming from the man who lived in the wilderness? Surely the familiarity of the landscape—the mountains and valleys that marked the congregation's place in the word—had to be a comfort, so why would this Baptizer reiterate that they would be flattened and filled? At the same time, the high mountains and low valleys of their leaders must have been confusing at best, as Herod hauled John to prison.

There are plenty of crooked things that we'd probably like to straighten, and rough ways that we'd like to make smooth. The valleys and hills can stay, but please, Lord, straighten our path. My crooked spine. Your rough path to sobriety. Confusing test results. Ugly divorces.

When we long for smoothness and a straight path, we can look to this passage for reassurance that God can and will make those things happen, and a reminder that it might not happen on our timeline. After all, if mountains are moving and valleys being filled, then God's time must take on a different measure than ours. My crooked spine and your rough path to sobriety feel like a forever sentence when we are living with them. But if God can move mountains and valleys in God's time, God can straighten and smooth in God's time, too.

"And all flesh shall see the salvation of God."

— *Carrie Willard*

December 24

When the woman saw that she could not remain hidden, she came trembling; and falling down before him, she declared in the presence of all the people why she had touched him, and how she had been immediately healed. He said to her, "Daughter, your faith has made you well; go in peace." (Luke 8:47-48)

The trauma psychiatrist Bessel van der Kolk remembers getting a call to visit a young boy in jail on Christmas Eve. The boy had been arrested yet again for burglarizing a house. When he asked the boy who would come see him on Christmas, the boy, whose name was Jack, responded, "Nobody... Nobody ever pays attention to me." Van der Kolk describes it further:

> It turned out that he had been caught during break-ins numerous times before. He knew the police, and they knew him. With delight in his voice, he told me that when the cops saw him standing in the middle of the living room, they yelled, "Oh my God, it's Jack again, that little [expletive]." Somebody recognized him; somebody knew his name. A little while later Jack confessed, "You know, that is what makes it worthwhile." Kids will go to almost any length to feel seen and connected.

You could argue that adults aren't much different. Even if adults don't go to such lengths, we do it in other ways—via Instagram, influential friends, accent socks. Even if we would rather "go unnoticed," like this woman in Luke, it doesn't mean that the desire for recognition has gone. In fact, it's usually evidence that, long ago, our hopes to be seen were met with myriad disappointments. Freud was right: Our lives are all too often marked by the love we never got.

Which is why Jesus could never settle for being merely a miracle dispenser. He knew that, beyond the physical and circumstantial ailments that afflict us, the deeper medicine at the heart of the universe, the medicine we wouldn't dare—or couldn't think—to ask for is the medicine of *being known*.

Most of our lives, being seen and known is an ugly affair. Whether we've fallen on the wrong side of the law like Jack, or fallen victim to embarrassing

403

circumstances like the woman in our story, exposure is synonymous with judgment. It is much easier to hide and forego the whole deal.

But where judgment usually punishes, Christ's judgment loves. Jesus calls out the one he has healed, not to chide her on the mess she's made, not to make an example of her, not even to show everyone else the wideness of his mercy. Jesus calls out the one he has healed because *he recognizes her*. He knows who she is—*daughter*.

— *Ethan Richardson*

December 25

And she gave birth to her firstborn son and wrapped him in bands of cloth, and laid him in a manger, because there was no place for them in the inn.

In that region there were shepherds living in the fields, keeping watch over their flock by night. Then an angel of the Lord stood before them, and the glory of the Lord shone around them, and they were terrified. But the angel said to them, "Do not be afraid; for see—I am bringing you good news of great joy for all the people: to you is born this day in the city of David a Savior, who is the Messiah, the Lord. This will be a sign for you: you will find a child wrapped in bands of cloth and lying in a manger." (Luke 2:7-12)

The shepherds were not ready. They were not in church or at a Bible study. They were not members of a Life Group nor did they have accountability partners. They had never been on retreat or walked a labyrinth. They did not cultivate virtue. They were not pillars of the community. They were working the night shift at a low-paying, dangerous, often tedious job.

When we hear about the shepherds in this all-too-familiar story, we picture cherubic kids in bathrobes at the Christmas pageant. Or maybe valiant looking men, clutching shepherd's crooks with holy hands, glowing slightly, as if in a Thomas Kinkade painting. We should picture tattooed truckers at a rest stop off of I-40 at three o'clock in the morning drinking bad coffee.

Which is why the angel's message is "good news of great joy." The message that God is sending a Savior is good news only if you need saving. The shepherds were overlooked and unimportant sinners, yet God came to them. Later that night, they would follow the angel's command to find the divine Child. And afterwards, they went to tell everyone.

And now I'm telling you. Like the shepherds, you are not ready. You are a mixed bag. Hopefully, your life has a measure of joy and purpose. But, like everyone, there's probably also plenty of regret, failure, disappointment, and scandal (whether others know it or not). But the good news of great joy was for all people. And so the angel's message comes to you, one who needs saving: There is a Savior.

— *Aaron Zimmerman*

December 26

Steadfast love and faithfulness will meet;
    righteousness and peace will kiss each other.
Faithfulness will spring up from the ground,
    and righteousness will look down from the sky.
    (Psalm 85:10-11)

We love those "shalom" signs that hang in our homes, but what *is* peace? Peace is the absence of sin and evil. Peace is utter harmony, and it is an experience we are given, not one that we force. It's the experience of a sailor when the motor is cut off, the sails are hoisted, and the water swishes while the wind powers the boat forward. Think about *The Chronicles of Narnia*, when the Sons of Adam or Daughters of Eve hear or see the lion Aslan: They are overcome with a feeling of peace.

We all clamor for this peace. Whether we are stacking rocks after a long hike or hanging those signs in the doorways of homes, we want to "Give Peace a Chance" (Lennon/Ono). But it usually doesn't end that well, does it? We can only balance our lives for a moment before sin and evil creep around the corner.

Here, the psalmist is not describing a single moment of peace or harmony; rather, the words describe a comprehensive peace ("shalom") that comes down from heaven and descends even to hell in order to bring peace everywhere, along with righteousness, faithfulness, and steadfast love. The psalmist is describing *a person* who is a reality in our lives, who offers us total peace, true harmony with God and ourselves. That person is none other than our Lord and Savior, Jesus.

Peace with God, ourselves, and others is the lasting gift from the Prince of Peace. The glimpses we experience today are just a foretaste of the permanent peace that we will all feel when we pass from this life of strife and conflict to the land of everlasting light and peace. That's the good news: Jesus has claimed you and offers you peace through his death and resurrection.

— *Willis Logan*

December 27

Thus says the LORD:
For three transgressions of Israel,
   and for four, I will not revoke the punishment;
because they sell the righteous for silver,
   and the needy for a pair of sandals—
they who trample the head of the poor into the dust of the
     earth,
   and push the afflicted out of the way... (Amos 2:6-7)

I was trapped in a conversation with a Unitarian clergywoman. Her name was Janice and she kept referring to me as a "pre-enlightened" Christian. Like a reporter, Janice fired question after question: Do you still believe in the resurrection? You don't still believe in Jesus' miracles, do you? And the virgin birth...don't tell me you...?

With my every yes, she grew more incredulous. Towards the end of the interrogation, Janice took a cleansing breath and, adopting a good-cop voice, said, "I just don't see how anyone can see the God of the Old Testament as the same as the God of the New."

Prophets are empowered by God to see what God sees—to see the things the rest of us refuse to see. When you read the Book of Amos you don't find a God who is arbitrary, petulant, or vindictive. You instead find a God who is righteously angry about the way his people use violence on one another, angry because they value silver and gold more than their neighbors, enraged that they're more concerned about the propriety of their worship than they are the poor.

Miroslav Volf writes that a God without wrath is one of many "pleasant captivities of the liberal mind." The true God must be as indignant about injustice as we are, for the gospel is neither sentimentality nor is it, despite what you'd think from many presentations of it, bad news. The hard-nosed realism of the gospel is that the wrath to which God has every right has been silenced through the cross of the Son. The hope of the gospel is that he shall come again to make right all that remains broken in the good gift of his creation.

— *Jason Micheli*

December 28

"My grace is sufficient for you, for [my] power is made perfect in weakness." (2 Corinthians 12:9)

Have you noticed how many pop music singers fall off the stage? Lady
Gaga, Ariana Grande, Britney Spears, Harry Styles, and Blake Shelton
have all taken spills. At a moment when they appeared to be in total control, they went bottoms up. All their coolness, poise, and power vanished
in an instant, but was forever captured on thousands of iPhones. Steven
Tyler was singing "Walk This Way" when he almost fell off the stage! They
are not as powerful as we think. They're only human beings, just like us.
Prancing around and posturing does not change the fact that, at any moment,
the illusion of control may be shattered. Life has a way of coldly exposing
our weaknesses. We judge these bottoms-up moments to be the clear low
points of our lives.

The gospel views our weaknesses differently. Human weakness is
how God gets things done. Our normal assumption is that things get done
through the direct application of power, through force of will—violent
force, if required. If you want to get anything done, from changing the
leadership of a foreign country to finding a new job, the way to make it
happen is to *just make it happen*. Impose your will by force. This will result
in victory, says the world. That's just how things get done.

Then along comes God. God operates differently. The Bible records a long
history of how God uses seemingly insignificant circumstances, weak and
overlooked people, and bottoms-up moments to work His will. The Apostle Paul was confident that God was getting things done through the small,
weak and seemingly insignificant congregations to whom he wrote his letters.

None of Paul's churches were impressive from a Roman point of view.
His congregations were full of weaknesses: divisions, lawsuits, sexual immo-
rality, failure to care for the weak, conflicts over worship, drunkenness at
the Lord's Supper, terrible theology, senior wardens going after other gospels. Folks were constantly falling off the stage. Nevertheless, Paul could see
the Lord at work through those weaknesses. In the face of human weakness,
Paul held tightly to the Lord's promise: "My grace is sufficient for you, for
[my] power is made perfect in weakness."

— *Drew Rollins*

December 29

> On entering the house, [the wise men] saw the child with
> Mary his mother; and they knelt down and paid him hom-
> age. Then, opening their treasure chests, they offered him
> gifts of gold, frankincense, and myrrh. (Matthew 2:11)

Sir Rowan Atkinson is a comedic genius. The misadventures of his legendary alter-ego, Mr. Bean, have provided laughs for decades. One of his best
gags occurs in a department store, where Mr. Bean plays childishly with
a nativity scene. What begins innocently enough quickly devolves into a
bizarre episode that culminates with a tank and a robot protecting baby
Jesus from an invading *Tyrannosaurus rex*. But even Mr. Bean's nativity isn't
as unlikely as the one you might have on your mantel right now.

Despite evidence to the contrary, we have decided to include shepherds
and wise men *together* at the birth of Christ. And with the carol "We Three
Kings" as our guide, we're encouraged to believe that there were *three* wise
men, who were, in fact, *kings* from "the Orient." Tradition has even gone so
far as to assign them the surnames Melchior, Caspar, and Balthazar, each
with their own history, backstory, and personality. But this is all conjec-
ture. We don't even know if they were kings, or how many there were. But
to get mired in those details is to miss the point of why the wise men are
included in scripture in the first place.

This scene displays the sovereign initiative of God, even in the cherubic
form of an infant. Not a single moment of the story was out of his control,
despite his human frame. He was the infinite infant God, wrapped in a robe
of swaddling clothes. All the power of divinity resided in the weakness
of a weaning child. The magi, then, confirm for us that the baby bouncing
on Mary's knee was the King of kings. He was the promised and predicted
Christ, the only wise Lord, at whose sight one day every knee will bow
(Phil 2:10-11). The baby adored by foreign stargazers was the sovereign Savior whose mission was to relieve the world of its sin and renew it through
his passion and resurrection. The wise men are, therefore, indicative of the
wideness of the mercy of God, who would establish, through his own death,
a kingdom of all nations, kindreds, and tongues. He is the One who came
to be like us that we might become like him.

— *Brad Gray*

December 30

Now faith is the assurance of things hoped for, the conviction of things not seen. (Hebrews 11:1)

All of us live our lives against the horizon of the future. We are restless in the present, and look to the future to give an answer to the needs and longings of the present. In our hearts we say: One day, the right circumstances will finally come together. One day, I will figure out how to be my real self at last, and I will be free. One day, the mist will clear, and the yearnings I have carried my whole life will find their fulfillment, and I will know what all this has meant.

In this chapter, the author of Hebrews reframes our hopes and longings against their true horizon in God and God's future. Here we find that we are not wrong to look to the future for what is needed. It is there that the missing pieces will be restored, and the riddle of our lives will be answered. It is there, in God's future, that the soul-wound will finally be healed.

But the text is also clear-eyed about the present. In the midst of a great litany of heroes of faith, we find sobering words: "All of these died in faith without having received the promises" (v. 13). Although they were blessed and helped by the Lord, and accompanied by the Lord, and although their lives were given deep purpose by the Lord, our forefathers in faith did not receive what was promised, right up to the moment of their death.

What they were given, however, was enough. "From a distance," with the eyes of faith, they were given to see what lay at the end of their pilgrimage (v. 13). From a distance they were given to see that at the end of all things there is a city that has been promised (vv. 10, 16), whose foundation will not be moved. And from a distance they learned that in that city there is a river (Ps 46:4-5), filled with the water of life, and that beside that river there is a tree whose leaves are for the healing of the nations (Rev 22:1-2).

For now, we travel on. But if we lift our eyes from time to time, we may catch a glimpse even now of that city, where we will find at last what we have spent our whole lives seeking.

— *Simeon Zahl*

December 31

Jesus said to them, "Very truly, I tell you, before Abraham was, I am." (John 8:58)

In this verse, Jesus spars with a skeptical crowd who accuses him of having a demon. Jesus has been preaching about eternal life, so, the crowd decides, he must be crazy or possessed. They point out that even their greatest ancestor, the father of their faith, Abraham, died. Who does Jesus think he is, walking around, promising that his disciples will live forever? One incredulous person even belittles his age: "You are not yet fifty years old!" The above verse is Jesus' response; in other words, "I am older than you realize."

New Year's can be a weird time. It's a time when all you can think about is time. *Another year gone!* we think, either sentimentally or despairingly. We wonder what we will do in the future, and judge what we did in the past. We evaluate whether we are becoming better or worse, while time ticks on—and the Grim Reaper inches closer.

One New Year's, I completely panicked. I felt that in the last twelve months I hadn't developed in any marked way and was filled with grief for my lack of discernible growth. Time was slipping by, and here I was, like a stagnant puddle in some parking lot.

Toward the end of his time on Earth, the great poet W. H. Auden once commented that he knew only two things. "The first is this," he said. "There is no such thing as time." As evidence, he cited the above verse, where Jesus professes that He *is* before Abraham *was*. Eternity is "without a beginning or an end," Auden went on. And in the words of writer Jay Parini, "we must come to terms with what underlies time, or exists around its edges." Put differently, New Year's is a helpful way to mark a calendar, but it is no way to judge oneself or others.

So what was the second thing Auden knew?

"Ah, that," he said. "The second thing is simply advice. Rest in God, dear boy. Rest in God."

— CJ Green

411

INDEX OF THEMES

AUTHOR INDEX

Nov 15, Dec 27

Morton, Adam: Feb 23, Mar 24, Apr 15, Jun 5, Aug 27, Oct 7, Dec 3

Morton, Tasha Genck: Jan 23, Sep 15

Munroe, Jim: Jan 27, Feb 8, Feb 28, Mar 25, Sep 3

Nicholson, Michael: Mar 31, Apr 3, Jun 18

Olson, Ian: Jul 30, Aug 31

Parsley, Larry: Jan 20, Feb 15, Mar 7, May 3, Jun 1, Jun 13, Jun 16, Jul 12, Aug 1, Sep 23, Oct 23, Nov 22, Nov 30, Dec 6, Dec 18, Dec 21

Phillips, Stephanie: Jan 9, Feb 26, Mar 15, May 11, Jun 17, Jul 25, Aug 9, Oct 21, Nov 16

Pope, Margaret: Jan 4, Feb 9, Mar 28, Apr 18, Nov 8, Dec 17

Retterer, Joshua: Feb 13, Apr 7, Jun 28, Aug 30, Sep 20

Richardson, Ethan: Jan 3, Jan 14, Feb 20, Mar 19, Mar 22, May 5, May 14, Jul 10, Jul 27, Aug 8, Sep 2, Sep 12, Oct 10, Oct 28, Nov 24, Dec 24

Rollins, Drew: Jan 25, Feb 22, Jun 30, Oct 6, Dec 28

Sansbury, Michael: Feb 7, May 18

Self, Benjamin: Jun 10, Jul 4, Aug 5, Aug 29, Nov 20

Shelby, Stuart: Feb 21, Jul 22

Smith, August: Oct 5

Smith, Jacob: Jan 12, Apr 19, Jul 18, Oct 18, Nov 13

Smith, Melina: Jan 18, Oct 30

Thomas, Marilu: Mar 20, May 27, Jun 25, Jul 20, Nov 28, Dec 9

Thompson, Jason: Jan 8, Mar 14, Apr 21, Jun 21, Jul 6, Nov 10

Trinh, Bryant: Jun 27, Nov 11

Walker, Paul: Jan 29, Feb 10, Feb 18, Mar 17, May 6, May 10, Jun 22, Jul 16, Jul 21, Aug 22, Sep 11, Oct 31, Dec 13, Dec 20

Willard, Carrie: Feb 12, Feb 25, May 9, May 22, Jun 8, Jul 1, Sep 27, Oct 16, Nov 4, Nov 26, Dec 10, Dec 14, Dec 23

Woodard, Sarah: Apr 11

Zahl, Bonnie Poon: Apr 20, Apr 24, Jul 31, Aug 17, Dec 4

Zahl, David: Jan 2, Jan 19, Mar 6, Apr 10, May 4, Jun 7, Jul 8, Jul 29, Aug 6, Aug 14, Sep 14, Oct 2, Oct 14, Nov 3, Nov 18, Dec 12

Zahl, John: Jan 28, Mar 9, Apr 14

Zahl, Mary: Jan 7, Feb 16, Mar 16, Jul 11, Aug 20, Sep 25

Zahl, Paul: Jan 13, Feb 27, Mar 2, Mar 29, Apr 9, May 16, Jun 24, Jul 15, Aug 2, Aug 26, Oct 13, Oct 26, Nov 9, Nov 27, Dec 7

Zahl, Simeon: Jan 21, Feb 5, Apr 26, Oct 4, Dec 30

Zimmerman, Aaron: Mar 23, May 15, Sep 16, Dec 25

BIBLICAL REFERENCES INDEX

22:41-42 — May 24
23:32-34 — Jan 5
23:39-42 — Oct 22
24:28-31 — Apr 16

JOHN
1:1-2 — Dec 1
1:5 — Jan 22
1:16-17 — Sep 18
3:5-8 — Jun 18
3:13-15 — Feb 17
3:16 — Jul 21
3:17 — Nov 6
4:7-9 — Nov 17
4:7-10 — May 30
5:2-9 — Oct 2
5:13 — Aug 11
8:7-11 — Sep 25
8:58 — Dec 31
9:1-3 — Jun 24
10:14-15 — Mar 17
11:35 — Apr 28
13:34 — Feb 29
14:8-9 — Mar 30
14:27 — Feb 28
15:1-5 — Feb 3
15:11 — Jun 30
15:13 — Aug 5
16:33 — Jun 20
17:6-9 — Oct 24
19:28 — Mar 25
20:17-18 — Apr 4
20:19-20 — Dec 13
21:4, 7 — Apr 13
21:9-12 — Aug 4
21:17 — Apr 23
21:22 — Oct 28

ACTS
1:6-8 — Aug 1
2:1-4 — May 3
2:38 — Jul 24
2:42-45 — Jun 13
4:12 — Sep 10
4:32-35 — Jun 1
11:5-9 — Mar 23
16:25-26 — Dec 11
17:11 — Apr 25
18:9-11 — Jun 29
27:25-26 — Aug 9

ROMANS
1:16-17 — Sep 30
3:23 — Nov 4
5:6-8 — Apr 6
6:1-4 — Aug 25
6:5-8 — Nov 23
7:7-10 — Jul 16
7:15, 24-25 — Apr 18
8:26-27 — Apr 11
8:38-39 — Feb 4
10:14-15 — Aug 28
10:17 — Mar 26
12:1 — Nov 12
12:15 — Nov 18
15:13 — Jul 31
14:17-19 — Nov 24
15:7-9 — Oct 10
15:13 — Jul 31

1 CORINTHIANS
1:11-13 — May 4
1:18-19 — Jun 9
1:22-25 — Apr 1
2:1-5 — Nov 29
8:8 — Mar 6

11:1 — Dec 30
11:13-16 — Sep 26
12:1-2 — Sep 15
12:22-24 — Aug 31

JAMES
1:17 — Mar 14
1:19-20 — Jul 10
5:16 — May 15

1 PETER
1:1-2 — Nov 1
1:13 — Feb 21
4:19 — Jun 26
5:6-9 — Jan 16
5:10-11 — Apr 29

2 PETER
1:12-15 — Sep 1
3:9 — Jun 4

1 JOHN
1:1 — Mar 12
1:9 — Jul 28
3:2 — Jan 8
4:13 — Oct 13

2 JOHN
3 — Jul 26

JUDE
24-25 — May 25

REVELATION
6:15-17 — Dec 7
7:14-17 — Jan 23
22:16-17, 20-21 — Apr 8

ABOUT MOCKINGBIRD

Founded in 2007, Mockingbird is an organization devoted to connecting the Christian faith with the realities of everyday life in fresh and down-to-earth ways. We do this primarily, but not exclusively, through our publications, conferences, and online resources. A full catalog of Mockingbird publications can be found at www.store.mbird.com. To find out more, visit our main page at www.mbird.com.